# Longman
# Italian
# Pocket
# Traveller

L. G. Alexander
Timothy
and Bianca Holme

Longman

**Longman Group Limited**
*Longman House, Burnt Mill, Harlow,*
*Essex CM20 2JE, England*
*and Associated Companies throughout the world.*

First published 1983
ISBN 0 582 79961 9

Set in 7/8pt. Linotron 202 Helvetica light.

Printed in Hong Kong by
Astros Printing Ltd

We wish to express our gratitude to Elena Jeronimidis
and Maria Riddiford for their contributions to this book.

# Contents

# Indice

# Preface

## The Longman Italian Pocket Traveller contains

a bilingual dictionary which gives you all the words you're likely to need to cope with social situations whether you're travelling for pleasure or on business

a section to 'help you get around' with lists of basic words, key sentence patterns and some short conversations to enable you to make the best use of the dictionary

For example, suppose you want to ask for a ticket or a coffee. All you have to do is to look up 'ticket' or 'coffee' in the dictionary and slot the Italian words into the appropriate key sentence pattern:

*Vorrei /un biglietto/, per favore*  I'd like /a ticket/ please
*Vorrei /un caffè/, per favore*  I'd like /a coffee/ please

a reference section to help you find all the essential information you need to cope abroad, everything from choosing a meal to understanding Italian currency

# Prefazione

## Questo libro contiene

un dizionario bilingue che vi dà tutte le parole necessarie se vi trovate in situazioni sociali o in viaggio di piacere o di affari

una sezione 'per aiutarvi a girare' con una lista di parole base, frasi chiave e brevi conversazioni per mettervi in grado di ottenere il più possibile dal dizionario

Per esempio, se desiderate un biglietto o un caffè, cercate la parola che desiderate (per esempio biglietto o caffè) e immediatamente siete pronti a dire:

*I'd like a /ticket/ please*   Vorrei un /biglietto/, per favore
*I'd like a /coffee/ please*   Vorrei un /caffè/, per favore

una sezione di riferimento per aiutarvi a trovare tutte le informazioni essenziali necessarie a trattare valute straniere, guidare all'estero, ordinare pasti al ristorante ecc.

# English – Italian

# Inglese – Italiano

# To help you get around

## Basics

If you learn these by heart,
you'll find it easier to get around

| | |
|---|---|
| Please | Per favore [*per favoreh*] |
| Thank you | Grazie [*gratsee-eh*] |
| Yes | Sì [*see*] |
| No | No [*no*] |
| Yes please | Sì grazie [*see gratsee-eh*] |
| No thank you | No grazie [*no gratsee-eh*] |
| Sorry? | Come? [*komeh*] |
| Excuse me! | Scusi! [*skoozee*] |
| I'm sorry | Mi dispiace [*mee deespyacheh*] |
| That's all right | Va bene [*va behneh*] |
| Good! | Bene! [*behneh*] |
| I don't understand | Non capisco [*non kapeesko*] |
| Hello | Ciao [*chow*] |
| My name's .... | Mi chiamo .... [*mee keeahmo*] |
| Goodbye | Arrivederci [*areevederchee*] |
| Good morning | Buon giorno [*bwon jorno*] |
| Good afternoon | Buon giorno [*bwon jorno*] |
| Good evening | Buona sera [*bwona sera*] |
| Good night | Buona notte [*bwona notteh*] |
| How are you? | Come sta? [*komeh sta*] |
| Fine thanks | Bene grazie [*behneh gratsee-eh*] |
| Cheers! | Salute! [*salooteh*] |
| It was nice to meet you | Piacere di averla conosciuta [*pyachereh dee averla conoshoota*] |
| Could you repeat that please | Per favore ripeta [*per favoreh reepetta*] |
| Slower please | Più adagio per favore [*pyoo adahjo per favoreh*] |

| | |
|---|---|
| How much is it? | Quanto costa? [**kwan**to **kos**ta] |
| How much are they? | Quanto costano? [**kwan**to **kos**tano] |

## Key sentence patterns

Once you've learnt these key sentence patterns by heart, you'll be able to make up your own sentences using words from the dictionary

| | |
|---|---|
| Where's /the (nearest) bank/ please? | Dov'è /la banca (più vicina)/, per favore? [dov**eh** la **ban**ka (pyoo vee**chee**na) per fa**vo**reh] |
| Is there /a car park/ near here? | C'è /un parcheggio/ qui vicino? [cheh oon par**ke**jo kwee vee**chee**no] |
| Are there /any restaurants/ near here? | Ci sono /dei ristoranti/ qui vicino? [chee **so**no day reesto-**ran**tee kwee vee**chee**no] |
| I'd like to /go swimming/ | Vorrei /andare a fare il bagno/ [vor**ray** and**ar**eh a **far**eh eel **ban**yo] |
| Would you like to /go shopping/? | Vorrebbe /fare delle spese/? [vor**reb**eh **far**eh **del**leh **speh**zeh] |
| Have you got /a street map/ please? | Ha /una pianta della città/, per favore? [a oona py**an**tah della chee**tah** per fa**vo**reh] |
| Have you got /any envelopes/ please? | Ha /delle buste/, per favore? [a **del**leh **boos**teh per fa**vo**reh] |
| I haven't got /any change/ | Non ho /spiccioli/ [non o **spee**cholee] |
| I need /a doctor/ | Mi occorre /un medico/ [mee o**kor**reh oon **meh**deeco] |

| | |
|---|---|
| I need /some traveller's cheques/ | Mi occorrono /dei traveller's cheques/ [*mee o**kor**rono day **trav**ellers cheks*] |
| I'd like /a room/ please | Vorrei /una camera/, per favore [*vor**ray** oona **kam**era per fa**vo**reh*] |
| I'd like /some stamps/ please | Vorrei /dei francobolli/, per favore [*vor**ray** day fran**ko**bollee per fa**vo**reh*] |
| Would you like /a coffee/? | Desidera /un caffè/? [*de**see**dera oon ca**feh**] |
| Would you like /some chocolates/? | Desidera /dei cioccolatini/? [*de**see**dera day chokola**tee**nee*] |
| Could you /call/ /a taxi/ for me please? | Mi /chiami/ /un taxi/, per favore [*mee **kyah**mee oon taksi per fa**vo**reh*] |
| When does /the (next) train/ to /Bologna/ leave? | Quando parte /il (prossimo) treno/ per /Bologna/? [*kwando **par**teh eel (**pross**imo) **tren**o per bol**lon**ya*] |
| When do /the banks/ open? (close) | Quando aprono (chiudono) /le banche/? [*kwando **ap**rono (kyoo**do**no) leh **ban**keh*] |
| Do you like /this colour/? (singular) | Le piace /questo colore/? [*leh pyah**cheh** **kwes**to ko**lor**eh*] |
| Do you like /these shoes/? (plural) | Le piacciono /queste scarpe/? [*leh pyah**chon**o **kwes**teh **skar**peh*] |
| I like /this style/ | Mi piace /questa moda/ [*mee pyah**cheh** **kwes**ta **mo**da*] |
| I don't like /this shape/ | Non mi piace /questa forma/ [*non mee pyah**cheh** **kwes**ta **for**ma*] |

## Conversations

Now that you've learnt the basics and the key sentence patterns, here are a few examples of conversations you can take part in.

### Introductions

| | |
|---|---|
| Buon giorno, signor Fratta. Le presento Marian Harwood | Good morning signor Fratta. This is Marian Harwood |
| Piacere | How do you do |
| Piacere | How do you do |

### Meeting someone you know

| | |
|---|---|
| Buona sera | Good evening |
| Buona sera, signor Fermi | Good evening signor Fermi |
| Come sta? | How are you? |
| Bene grazie. E lei? | Fine thanks. And you? |
| Bene grazie | Fine thanks |

### Finding your way

| | |
|---|---|
| Scusi! | Excuse me |
| Sì? | Yes? |
| Dov'è l'albergo Bristol, per favore? | Where's the Hotel Bristol please? |
| Dritto, e a destra | Straight on, then right |
| Grazie | Thank you |
| Prego | Not at all |

### At the station

| | |
|---|---|
| Un biglietto di andata per Bologna, per favore | A single to Bologna please |
| L2000 (duemila lire) | L2000 |
| Quando parte il prossimo treno? | When does the next train leave? |
| Alle diciotto e quindici | At 6.15 p.m. |

| | |
|---|---|
| Quando arriva il treno a Bologna? | When does the train arrive in Bologna? |
| Alle diciannove e trentasei | At 7.36 |
| Grazie | Thank you |

## At a hotel – you want a room

| | |
|---|---|
| Buon giorno. Desidera? | Good afternoon. Can I help you? |
| Buon giorno. Vorrei una camera doppia, per favore | Good afternoon. I'd like a double room please |
| Quante notti? | For how many nights? |
| Per due notti, per favore | For two nights please |
| Desidera una camera con bagno o senza bagno? | Would you like a room with or without bath? |
| Con bagno, per favore | With bath please |
| Sì, va bene | Yes, that's fine |
| Quanto costa, per favore? | How much is it please? |
| Una notte ventimila lire | 20,000 lire |
| La prendo, grazie | I'll take it please |

## Buying something

| | |
|---|---|
| Buon giorno. Desidera? | Good morning. Can I help you? |
| Buon giorno. Ha del caffè? | Good morning. Have you got any coffee? |
| Sì, quanto ne desidera? | Yes. How much would you like? |
| Ne vorrei un mezzo chilo, per favore | I'd like half a kilo please |
| Bene. Nient'altro? | Good. Anything else? |
| Sì. Vorrei delle mele, per favore | Yes. I'd like some apples please |
| Quante? | How many? |
| Quattro, per favore | 4 please |
| Bene. Duemila cinquecento lire, per favore | OK. L2500 please |
| Grazie | Thank you |

## Choosing something

| | |
|---|---|
| Buon giorno. Desidera? | Good afternoon. Can I help you? |
| Vorrei una maglietta, per favore | I'd like a T-shirt please |
| Che misura desidera? | What size would you like? |
| Quaranta, per favore | 40 please |
| Le piace questa? | Do you like this one? |
| No. Non mi piace questo colore. La ha in rosso? | No. I don't like that colour. Have you got a red one? |
| Si, certo | Yes, of course |
| Quanto costa? | How much is it please? |
| Cinquemila lire | L5000 |
| La prendo. Grazie | I'll take it. Thank you |

# A few tips

## 1 You – 'lei/loro' or 'tu/voi'?

There are two ways of addressing people in Italian.
'Lei' (you, singular) and 'loro' (you, plural) are the forms you will
hear and use most. To be on the safe side, always start by using
'lei/loro', unless the person you are talking to has already used the
'tu' form. 'Tu' (you, singular) and 'voi' (you, plural) are used with
people you know well and with children. Young people use these
forms a lot when talking to each other.

## 2 Masculine or feminine?

In Italian all nouns, whether they refer to people or things, are either
masculine or feminine:

    eg *il ragazzo* (the boy)    *il treno* (the train)
       *la ragazza* (the girl)    *la macchina* (the car)

Most masculine nouns end in 'o' and most feminine nouns end in 'a'.
In the dictionary, any words with different endings or which do not
follow this rule are marked (m) – masculine or (f) – feminine.

## 3 Plurals

Masculine nouns ending in 'o': take off the 'o' and add 'i'.
Feminine nouns ending in 'a': take off the 'a' and add 'e'.
Nouns ending in 'e': take off the 'e' and add 'i'.
All other plurals are given eg 'formica -che' (ant)
Some words do not change in the plural eg 'aerosol (m) -' (aerosol)

## 4 The/a/to the

Before masculine nouns 'the' is *il* and 'a' is *un* in Italian:
  eg *il treno* (the train)     Plural: *i treni* (the trains/trains)
  *un treno* (a train)

Before feminine nouns 'the' is *la* and 'a' is *una*:
  eg *la macchina* (the car)     Plural: *le macchine* (the cars/cars)
  *una macchina* (a car)

Before masculine nouns beginning with a *z* or with *s* followed by another consonant, 'the' is *lo* and 'a' is *uno*:
  eg *lo studente* (the student)     Plural: *gli studenti* (the students/students)
  *uno studente* (a student)

Before masculine or feminine nouns beginning with a vowel:
  *l'appartamento* (the flat)          *l'ambulanza* (the ambulance)
  *un appartamento* (a flat)           *un'ambulanza* (an ambulance)
  *gli appartamenti* (the flats/flats)  *le ambulanze* (the ambulances/ambulances)

Use the following table to find out how to say 'to the':
  *'a'* (to) + the

| masculine | feminine | |
|---|---|---|
| il lo l' | la l' | singular (the) |
| al allo all' | alla all' | singular (to the) |
| i gli | le | plural (the) |
| ai agli | alle | plural (to the) |

eg *alla stazione* (to the station) *all' aeroporto* (to the airport) etc.

## 5 A note on quantity

To indicate quantity in a general way (some/any) use *'di'* (of) + 'the'.

The following table will help you:

| masculine | feminine | |
| --- | --- | --- |
| il lo l' | la l' | singular (the) |
| del dello dell' | della dell' | singular (some/any) |
| i gli | le | plural (the) |
| dei degli | delle | plural (some/any) |

    eg *Vorrei del caffè*      I'd like some coffee
      *Ha dello zucchero?*    Have you got any sugar?
However, 'any' is not translated in negative sentences:
    eg *Non ho francobolli*    I haven't got any stamps

NB *'di'* is of course also used to show possession:
    eg *il passaporto dello studente* (the student's passport)

With the help of the dictionary you can also ask for precise amounts. For example, if you look up 'match' (*fiammifero*) you will find 'a box of matches' (*una scatola di fiammiferi*).

Quantity can also be indicated precisely in terms of volume or weight eg 20 litres of petrol, a kilo of tomatoes, etc. See Equivalents p146

Remember these five 'quantity words' and you will be able to ask for almost anything:

| | |
| --- | --- |
| eg *una bottiglia di* /birra/ | a bottle of /beer/ |
| *un bicchiere di* /latte/ | a glass of /milk/ |
| *un pacchetto di* /sigarette/ | a packet of /cigarettes/ |
| *una fetta di* /prosciutto/ | a slice of /ham/ |
| *un barattolo di* /pomodori/ | a tin of /tomatoes/ |

## 6 Feminine and plural forms of adjectives

In Italian adjectives must 'agree' with the nouns to which they belong:

eg  *il prossimo treno*  (the next train)
    *una bella macchina*  (a beautiful car)

In the dictionary adjectives are given in the masculine singular form only. All adjectives ending in '*-e*' have the same masculine and feminine forms.

Use the following table to make the feminine and plural forms:

|  | masculine | feminine | masculine plural | feminine plural |
|---|---|---|---|---|
| blue | *azzurro* | *azzurra* | *azzurri* | *azzure* |
| sad | *triste* | *triste* | *tristi* | *tristi* |

All adjectives which have an irregular feminine or plural form are given:

eg  *bianco -chi (mpl) -che (fpl)*

## 7 Comparisons

In Italian '*più*' (more) can be used with all adjectives to form the comparative.

eg  *Vorrei qualcosa (di) più grande*   I'd like something bigger
    *Vorrei qualcosa (di) più pesante*  I'd like something heavier

'*Meno*' (less) is used in a similar way:

eg  *Vorrei qualcosa meno costoso*   I'd like something less expensive

Note that some adjectives have alternative forms for comparative adjectives:

eg  *buono* (good)      *più buono/migliore* (better)
    *grande* (big)      *più grande/maggiore* (bigger)
    *piccolo* (small)   *più piccolo/minore* (smaller)

## 8 Verbs

In the dictionary verbs are usually given in the infinitive form only eg
*'chiudere'* (close)

Certain verbs always need the Italian equivalent of 'myself',
'yourself' etc. These are the verbs ending in *'-si'* in the dictionary eg
*'lavarsi'* (to have a wash), *'vestirsi'* (to dress oneself). This is the
form of the verb you will be most likely to need:

   *Vorrebbe lavarsi?*    Would you like to have a wash?

If you are talking about yourself remember to change the *'-si'*
(yourself) to *'-mi'* (myself).

   *Vorrei lavarmi*    I'd like to have a wash

## 9 Signore, Signora, Signorina

Literally, these mean 'Sir', 'Madam', 'Miss'. But they are used all
the time in Italian and you should always use them except with very
close friends.

## 10 Buon giorno, buona sera, buona notte

'Good morning', 'good afternoon/evening', 'good night'. These small
formalities are used very commonly in Italian. *'Arrivederci'*
(Goodbye) can be used when speaking to anybody. *'Ciao'* means
both 'hello' and goodbye' and is used with someone to whom you
would say *'tu'*.

## 11 C'è, ci sono

You will often hear Italians saying *'C'è'* (there is/is there?) or *'ci
sono'* (there are/are there?) in conversation.

   *C'è del tè?*                      Is there any tea?
   *Ci sono due alberghi in centro*    There are two hotels in the
                                      centre

Learn to recognise them quickly in order to understand spoken
Italian.

## 12 Prego

This is best translated as 'You're welcome'. It is commonly used in Italian after someone has said *'Grazie'* (thank you). It is also used to mean 'Can I help you?' in a shop, restaurant etc.

# Pronunciation guide

There are five basic vowel sounds in Italian which are all very clearly pronounced:

| | | | |
|---|---|---|---|
| [a] | between ha̲t and hu̲t | ga̲tto | (cat) |
| [e] | between ha̅te and e̲gg | be̅llo | (beautiful) |
| [ee] | he̅ | ita̅liano | (Italian) |
| [o] | between ho̅me and kno̲t | tro̅ppo | (too) |
| [oo] | zo̲o | bru̲tto | (ugly) |

Most Italian consonants are the same as in English.

Sounds which are close to English sounds but which may look different when written in Italian:

| | | | |
|---|---|---|---|
| [ch] | chu̲rch | città (city) |
| [dz] | lo̅a̅ds | mezzo (middle, half) |
| [g] | gu̲n | ga̲tto (cat) ghiaccio (ice) |
| [j] | jo̲b, gi̲n | ge̲lato (ice cream) |
| [k] | ca̲t | ca̲sa (house), chiesa (church), quando (whe̲n) |
| [ly] | milli̲on | agli̲o (garlic) |
| [ny] | oni̲on | gno̲cchi (type of dumplings) |
| [sh] | sho̲e | pesce (fish) |
| [ts] | ca̲ts | raga̅zza (girl) |
| [w] | wo̲rry | quasi̲ (almost), uomo (man) |
| [y] | ye̲s | ita̅liano (Italian) |

NB 'h' is never pronounced in Italian.

'c' before 'i' or 'e' is pronounced 'ch' as in 'chu̲rch', otherwise 'c' as in 'ca̲t'

'g' before 'i' or 'e' is pronounced soft as 'gi̲n', otherwise hard as in 'gu̲n'

In Italian the accent usually falls on the next to last syllable.

# Abbreviations

# Abbreviazioni

| | | |
|---|---|---|
| (adj) | adjective | aggettivo |
| (adv) | adverb | avverbio |
| (n) | noun | nome |
| (prep) | preposition | preposizione |
| (pron) | pronoun | pronome |
| (vb) | verb | verbo |
| (m) | masculine | maschile |
| (f) | feminine | femminile |
| (s) | singular | singolare |
| (pl) | plural | plurale |
| (infml) | informal | familiare |
| (tdmk) | trademark | marca di fabbrica |
| (eg) | for example | per esempio |
| (etc) | et cetera | eccetera |

# Dictionary
# A—Z
# Vocabolario

# A

a (an) *uno, un* (m) *una, un'* (f)
about (=approximately) *circa*
about (=concerning) *circa*
  **about /your problem/** *circa /il suo problema/*
above (adv) *sopra* (adv)
  **above /my head/** *sopra /la testa/*
abroad *all'estero*
  **he's abroad** *è all'estero*
accept *accettare*
accident *incidente* (m)
accommodation *alloggio*
accountant *ragioniere* (m)
ache *mal/male* (m)(n)
  **I've got backache** *ho mal di schiena*
  **I've got earache** *ho mal d'orecchio*
  **I've got stomachache** *ho mal di stomaco*
across *attraverso*
actor *attore* (m)
actress -es *attrice* (f)
adaptor plug *raccordo elettrico*
add *aggiungere*
address -es *indirizzo*
  **temporary address** *indirizzo provvisorio*
adjust *aggiustare (sistemare)*
admission (=cost) *entrata* (=ammissione)
adult *adulto*
  **adults only** *solo per adulti*
advance (advance of money) *anticipo*
  **advance booking** *prenotazione* (f)
  **in advance** *in anticipo*
advantage *vantaggio*
advertise *fare pubblicità*
advertisement *avviso pubblicitario*
advice *consiglio*
  **I'd like some advice** *vorrei un consiglio*
advise a rest *consigliare riposo*
aerial *antenna*
aeroplane *aeroplano*
  **by air** *per via aerea*
aerosol *aerosol* (m) -

afraid
  **be afraid (of / / )** *aver paura (di / / )*
  **I'm afraid of / /** *ho paura di / /*
after *dopo* (prep)
afternoon *pomeriggio*
  **good afternoon** *buon giorno (di pomeriggio)*
  **this afternoon** *oggi pomeriggio*
  **tomorrow afternoon** *domani pomeriggio*
  **yesterday afternoon** *ieri pomeriggio*
aftershave lotion *dopo barba* (m) -
afterwards *dopo* (adv)
again *ancora* (adv)
against *contro*
age *età* -
agency -ies *agenzia*
agenda *ordine* (m) *del giorno*
agent (of company) *rappresentante* (m)
ago *fa*
  **/three years/ ago** */tre anni/ fa*
agree *essere d'accordo*
  **agree to / /** *acconsentire a / /*
  **I agree** *sono d'accordo*
agreement *accordo*
ahead *avanti*
air *aria*
  **air pressure** *pressione* (f) *atmosferica*
  **by air** *per via aerea*
  **some fresh air** *aria fresca*
air conditioning *aria condizionata*
air letter *lettera aerea*
air terminal *terminale* (m) *aereo*
  **air terminal bus** *autobus* (m) *del terminale aereo*
airline *linea aerea*
airmail *posta aerea*
  **by airmail** *per via aerea*
airport *aeroporto*
  **airport bus -es** *autobus* (m) *dell'aeroporto*
alarm clock *sveglia*
alcohol *alcool* (m)
alcoholic (adj) *alcoolico*
alive *vivo*
  **he's alive** *vive*

**all** *tutto (adj)*
  **all /the children/** *tutti /i bambini/*
  **all /the time/** *tutto /il tempo/*
**allergic** *allergico*
  **I'm allergic /to penicillin/** *sono allergico /alla penicillina/*
**allow** *permettere*
  **allow /smoking/** *permettere di /fumare/*
**allowed** *permesso (adj)*
**almost** *quasi*
**alone** *solo (adj)*
**alphabet** *alfabeto*
**already** *già*
**also** *anche*
**alter** *cambiare*
**alternative** (n) *alternativa*
**always** *sempre*
**a.m.** *di mattina*
  **/four/ a.m.** */le quattro/ di mattina*
**ambassador** *ambasciatore (m)*
**ambulance** *ambulanza*
**amenities** (pl) *comodità (fpl)*
**among** *tra*
  **among /my friends/** *tra /i miei amici/*
**amusement arcade** *sala giochi*
**amusing** *divertente*
**anaemic** *anemico*
  **I'm anaemic** *sono anemico*
**anaesthetic** (n) *anestetico*
**anchor** *ancora (n)*
**and** *e*
**angry** *arrabbiato*
  **I'm angry with/ him/** *sono arrabbiato con /lui/*
**animal** *animale (m)*
**ankle** *caviglia*
  **ankle socks** *calzini (mpl) (da uomo)*
**anniversary -ies** *anniversario*
  **wedding anniversary** *anniversario del matrimonio*
**announcement** *dichiarazione (f)*
  **make an announcement** *fare una dichiarazione*
**annoying** *fastidioso*
**annual** *annuo*

**anorak** *giacca -che a vento*
**another** *un altro (m) un'altra (f)*
  **another /glass of wine/** *un altro /bicchiere di vino/*
**answer** (n) *risposta (n)*
**answer** (vb) *rispondere*
**ant** *formica- che*
**antibiotic** *antibiotico*
**antifreeze** *antigelo*
  **a can of antifreeze** *una lattina di antigelo*
**antique** (n) *oggetto di antiquariato*
**antique shop** *negozio di antiquariato*
**antiseptic** *antisettico*
  **antiseptic cream** *crema antisettica*
  **a tube of antiseptic (cream)** *un tubetto di crema antisettica*
**any**
  **have you got /any stamps/?** *ha /dei francobolli/?*
  **I haven't got /any money/** *non ho /soldi/*
**anything** *qualcosa*
  **anything else?** *niente altro?*
**aperitif** *aperitivo*
**apologise** *domandare scusa*
  **I apologise** *domando scusa*
**apology -ies** *scusa (atta dello scusarsi)*
**appendicitis** *appendicite (f)*
**apple** *mela*
**apple juice -es** *succo di mela*
**application form** *modulo di domanda*
**apply** *applicare*
  **apply to / / for /a visa/** *fare domanda a / / per /un visto/*
  **apply for /a job/** *fare domanda per /un impiego/*
**appointment** *appuntamento*
  **I've got an appointment** *ho un appuntamento*
  **make an appointment** *fissare un appuntamento*
**apricot** *albicocca -che*
**April** *aprile (m)*
**aqualung** *autorespiratore (m)*
**architect** *architetto*
**area** (of town) *zona*

**area** (of country) *regione (f)*
**argue** *discutere*
**argument** *discussione (f)*
**arm** *braccio (m) braccia (fpl)*
**army** *esercito*
**around** *intorno*
  **around /the table/** *intorno /alla tavola/*
**arrange** *organizzare (=fissare)*
  **arrange /a meeting/** *organizzare /un incontro/*
**arrangement** *accordo*
  **arrival** *arrivo*
  **time of arrival** *ora di arrivo*
**arrive** *arrivare*
  **arrive at /four-thirty/ p.m.** *arrivare /alle quattro e mezzo/ pomeridiane*
  **arrive in /July/** *arrivare a /luglio/*
  **arrive on /Monday/** *arrivare /lunedì/*
  **arrive in /Milan/** *arrivare a /Milano/*
**arrow** *freccia -ce*
**art gallery -ies** *galleria d'arte*
**artichoke** *carciofo*
**artificial** *artificiale (=non naturale)*
**artificial respiration** *respirazione (f) artificiale*
**artist** *artista (m&f)*
**ashamed**
  **be ashamed (of / )** *vergognarsi (di / )*
  **I'm ashamed of /him/** *mi vergogno di /lui/*
**ashtray** *portacenere (m)*
**ask** *domandare*
  **please ask how much it is** *domandi quanto è, per favore*
**ask** (a favour) *chiedere (un favore)*
**asleep**
  **he's asleep** *dorme*
**asparagus** *asparagi (mpl)*
**aspirin** *aspirina*
  **a bottle of aspirins** *una bottiglia di aspirine*
  **a packet of aspirins** *un pacchetto di aspirine*
**assistant** *assistente (m&f)*
  **shop assistant** *commesso (m)*

*commessa (f)*
**asthma** *asma*
**at**
  **at seven-thirty** *alle sette e mezzo*
  **at /the hotel/** *all'albergo*
  **at /the university/** *all' università*
**atlas -es** *atlante (m)*
**attack** (n) *attacco*
  **an attack of / /** *un attacco di / /*
**attend** *assistere*
  **attend a /Catholic/ service** *assistere ad una funzione /cattolica/*
**attendant** *guardiano (sorvegliante)*
**attractive** *attraente*
**au pair** *ragazza alla pari*
**aubergine** *melanzana*
**auction** (n) *asta*
**auction** (vb) *vendere all'asta*
**audience** *pubblico (n)*
**August** *agosto*
**aunt** *zia*
**author** *autore (m)*
**authorities** (pl) *autorità (fpl)*
**automatic** *automatico*
**autumn** *autunno*
  **in autumn** *in autunno*
**available** *disponibile*
**avalanche** *valanga*
**average** (n) *media*
**avocado** *avocado*
**avoid** *evitare*
**awake** *sveglio*
  **he's awake** *è sveglio*
**away** *via (=non qui)*
**away** (absent) *assente*
**awful** (of peopl) *antipatico*
**awful** (of things) *orribile*

# B

**baby -ies** *bambino (rn) bambina (f)*
**baby-sit** *fare la baby-sitter*
**baby-sitter** *baby-sitter (m&f)*
**back** *schiena*
  **backache** *mal di schiena*
  **back door** *porta posteriore*

**backwards** *in dietro*
**bacon** *pancetta*
**bad** *cattivo*
**badly** *male (adv)*
  **badly hurt** *ferito male*
**badminton** *volano (sport)*
  **a game of badminton** *una partita a volano*
  **play badminton** *giocare a volano*
**bag** *borsa*
  **carrier bag** *sacchetto*
  **string bag** *borsa di rete*
**bake** *cuocere al forno*
**baker's** *panetteria*
**balcony -ies** *balcone (m)*
**bald** *calvo*
  **he's bald** *è calvo*
**ball** *palla*
  **a ball of /string/** *un gomitolo di /filo/*
  **beach ball** *palla di spiaggia*
  **football** *pallone (m)*
  **golf ball** *pallina da golf*
  **squash ball** *pallina da squash*
  **table tennis ball** *pallina da ping-pong*
  **tennis ball** *palla da tennis*
**ball** (=dance) *ballo*
**ballet** *balletto*
  **ballet dancer** *ballerino (m) ballerina (f)*
**balloon** *palloncino*
**ballpoint pen** *penna a sfera*
**ballroom** *sala da ballo*
**banana** *banana*
**band** (=orchestra) *banda*
**bandage** (n) *benda*
**bandage** (vb) *bendare*
**bank** *banca*
  **bank account** *conto (in banca)*
  **current account** *conto corrente*
**bar** (=for drinks) *bar (m)*
**barbecue** *barbecue (m)*
**bare** *nudo*
**bargain** (n) *affare (m)*
  **it's a bargain** *è un affare*
**bargain** (vb) *contrattare*
  **bargain with / /** *contrattare con / /*

**barrel** *barile (m)*

  **a barrel of / /** *un barile di / /*
**barrier** *barriera*
**basement** *seminterrato*
**basket** *cesto*
  **a basket of / /** *un cesto di / /*
  **shopping basket** *cestino per la spesa*
  **waste paper basket** *cestino per la carta straccia*
**basket** (small) *cestino*
**basketball** (=game) *pallacanestro*
  **a game of basketball** *una partita a pallacanestro*
  **play basketball** *giocare a pallacanestro*
**bat** (cricket) *mazza*
**bath** *bagno*
  **have a bath** *fare il bagno (nella vasca)*
  **Turkish bath** *bagno turco*
**bath mat** *tappeto di bagno*
**bath mat** *tappeto di bagno*
**bath salts** (pl) *sali (mpl) da bagno*
**bathe** (eyes etc) *bagnare (=inumidire)*
**bathe** (in the sea etc) *fare il bagno (in mare)*
**bathing costume** (one piece) *costume (m) da bagno*
**bathing trunks** (pl) *pantaloncini (mpl) da bagno*
**bathroom** *(stanza da) bagno*
**battery -ies** (radio) *pila (per la radio)*
**battery -ies** (car) *batteria*
  **I've got a flat battery** *ho la batteria scarica*
**bay** (=part of sea) *baia*
**be** *essere*
**be called** (a name) *chiamarsi*
**beach -es** *spiaggia - gge*
  **beach hut** *cabina per bagnanti*
  **beach umbrella** *ombrellone (m)*
**beads** (pl) *perline (fpl)*
  **string of beads** *filo di perline*
**bean** *fagiolo*
  **broad bean** *fava*
  **French bean** *fagiolino*
**beautiful** *bello*
**beauty salon** *salone (m) di bellezza*
**because** *perchè*

**because of /the weather/** *a causa /del tempo/*
**bed** *letto*
  **bed and breakfast** *letto e colazione*
  **double bed** *letto matrimoniale*
  **go to bed** *andare a letto*
  **in bed** *a letto*
  **make the bed** *fare il letto*
  **single bed** *letto singolo*
**bed clothes** (pl) *biancheria e coperte da letto (fpl)*
**bedpan** *padella da letto*
**bedroom** *camera a letto*
**bee** *ape (f)*
  **bee sting** *puntura d'ape*
**beef** *manzo*
  **beef sandwich** *panino di manzo*
**beer** *birra*
  **a beer** *una birra*
  **a bottle of beer** *una bottiglia di birra*
  **a can of beer** *una lattina di birra*
  **a pint of beer** *un mezzo litro di birra*
**beetroot/beetroot** (pl) *barbabietola*
**before** *prima*
  **before /breakfast/** *prima della colazione*
  **before /leaving/** *prima di /partire/*
**begin** *incominciare*
  **when does it begin?** *quando incomincia?*
**behalf**
  **on behalf of / /** *da parte di / /*
**behaviour** *comportamento*
**behind** (prep) *dietro (a) (prep)*
  **behind /the house/** *dietro /alla casa/*
**beige** *beige*
**believe** *credere*
  **believe /me/** *creder/mi/*
  **I don't believe it** *non ci credo*
**bell** (large) *campana*
**bell** (small) *campanello*
**belongings** (pl) *roba (s)*
**below** *sotto*
  **below /the chair/** *sotto /la sedia/*
**belt** *cintura*
**bend** (vb) *piegare*
**bend** (in a road) *curva*

**bent** (adj) *piegato*
**beret** *berretto*
**berth** *cuccetta (su una nave)*
  **/four/-berth cabin** *cabina da /quattro/ cuccette*
  **lower berth** *cuccetta di sotto*
  **upper berth** *cuccetta di sopra*
**beside** (prep) *accanto (a)*
  **beside /her/** *accanto /a/ lei/*
**best** *migliore*
  **the best /hotel/** *il migliore/albergo/*
**bet** (n) *scommessa*
**bet** (vb) *scommettere*
**better** *meglio*
  **he's better** (health) *sta meglio*
  **it's better** (things) *va meglio*
**betting shop** *allibratore (m) (negozio)*
**between /London /and /Rome/** *tra /Londra/ e /Roma/*
**beyond** (prep) *oltre (a)*
  **beyond /the station/** *oltre /alla stazione/*
**bib** *bavaglino*
**Bible** *Bible*
**bicycle/bike** (infml) *bicicletta/bici (f) - (infml)*
**big** *grande*
**bikini** *bikini (m)*
**bill** (for food, hotel, etc.) *conto (al ristorante, albergo)*
**billiards** *biliardo (s)*
  **a game of billiards** *una partita a biliardo*
  **play billiards** *giocare a biliardo*
**bingo** *tombola*
**binoculars** (pl) *binocolo (s)*
  **a pair of binoculars** *un binocolo*
**bird** *uccello*
**biro** (tdmk) *biro (f) -*
**birth** *nascita*
  **birth certificate** *certificato di nascita*
  **date of birth** *data di nascita*
  **place of birth** *luogo di nascita*
**birthday** *compleanno*
**biscuit** *biscotto*
**bite** (=insect b.) *puntura*
**bitter** (adj) *amaro*

**black** nero
  **black coffee** caffè (m)
**blackberry -ies** mora (n)
**blackcurrant** ribes nero (m) -
**blanket** coperta
**bleach** (n) candeggina
**bleach** (vb) (laundry) imbiancare
**bleed** sanguinare
  **my nose is bleeding** mi sanguina il
  naso
  **stop the bleeding** fermare il sangue
**blind** cieco -chi
**blinds** persiane (fpl)
**blister** vescica -che
**block of flats** condominio
**blocked** (eg drain) bloccato (uno
  scarico)
**blonde** biondo
**blood** sangue (m)
  **blood group** gruppo sanguigno
  **blood pressure** pressione (f) del
  sangue
**blotting paper** carta assorbente
**blouse** camicetta
**blue** azzurro
**blunt** (eg knife) spuntato
**boar** (vb) (eg a plane) salire (su un
  aereo etc)
**board** (n) (=cost of meals) pensione (f)
  (albergo)
  **full board** pensione completa
  **half board** mezza pensione
**boarding card** foglio di imbarco
**boat** nave (f)
  **by boat** per nave
  **lifeboat** scialuppa di salvataggio
  **motor-boat** motoscafo
**body -ies** corpo
**boil** (vb) bollire
**bomb** bomba
**bone** osso -a
**book** libro
  **guide book** guida
**booking** prenotazione (f) (treno, aereo)
  **advance booking** prenotazione
  anticipata
**booking office** biglietteria

**bookmaker** allibratore (m) (persona)
**bookshop** libreria
**boots** (pl) stivali (mpl)
  **a pair of boots** un paio di stivali
  **rubber boots** stivali di gomma
  **ski-boots** scarponi (mpl) da sci
**border** (=frontier) frontiera (=confine)
**bored** (to be bored) annoiarsi
  **I'm bored** mi annoio
**boring** noioso
**borrow** prendere in prestito
  **borrow /a pen/** prendere in prestito
  /una penna/
  **may I borrow /your pen/?** posso
  prendere in prestito /la sua penna/?
**boss** (n) padrone (m), padrona (f) (capo)
**both** ambedue/tutti e due (m) tutte e
  due (f)
**bother** (vb) disturbare
  **don't bother** non si disturbi
  **I'm sorry to bother you** mi dispiace
  disturbarla
**bottle** bottiglia
  **a bottle of /  /** una bottiglia di /  /
  **bottle-opener** cava-tappi (m) -
  **feeding bottle** biberon (m) -
**bottom** (part of body) sedere (m)
  **bottom of /  /** fondo di /  /
**bow tie** cravatta a farfalla
**bowl** zuppiera
**bowling** (=ten pin bowling) bocce (fpl)
  **bowling alley** corsia per bocce
**bows** (pl) (of ship) prua (s)
**box -es** scatola
  **a box of /  /** una scatola di /  /
**box office** biglietteria
**boxer** pugilatore (m)
**boxing** pugilato
  **boxing match** incontro di pugilato
**boy** ragazzo
**boyfriend** ragazzo
**bra** reggipetto
**bracelet** braccialetto
  **silver bracelet** braccialetto d'argento
**braces** (pl) bretelle (fpl)
  **a pair of braces** un paio di bretelle
**brake fluid** fluido freni

**brake linings/pads** (pl) (car) *pasticche (fpl) per freni*
**brakes/braking system** *freni (mpl)*
**branch** (of company) **-es** *filiale (m)*
**brand** (=of make) *marca*
  **brand name** *marca*
**brandy -ies** *cognac (m)* -
  **a bottle of brandy** *una bottiglia di cognac*
  **a brandy** *un cognac*
**bread** *pane (m)*
  **a loaf of bread** *pagnotta*
  **a slice of bread** *una fetta di pane*
  **bread and butter** *pane e burro*
  **brown bread** *pane nero*
  **bread roll** *panino*
  **sliced bread** *pane carrè*
  **white bread** *pane bianco*
**break** (vb) *rompere*
**breakdown** (car) *guasto*
**breakfast** *colazione (f)*
  **bed and breakfast** *letto e colazione*
  **breakfast for /two/** *colazione per /due/*
  **breakfast in my room** *colazione in camera*
  **continental breakfast** *colazione*
  **English breakfast** *colazione inglese*
  **have breakfast** *fare colazione*
  **serve breakfast** *servire la colazione*
**breast** *petto*
**breast-feed** *allattare*
**breath** *respiro*
  **out of breath** *senza fiato*
**breathe** *respirare*
**bride** *sposa*
**bridegroom** *sposo*
**bridge** (=card game) *bridge (m)*
  **a game of bridge** *una partita a bridge*
**bridge** *ponte (m) (su fiume)*
  **toll bridge** *ponte a pedaggio*
**bridle** *briglia*
**briefcase** *cartella*
**bring** *portare*
**broadcast** (n) *trasmissione (f)*
**broadcast** (vb) *trasmettere*
**broccoli** *broccoli (mpl)*

**brochure** *opuscolo*
**broken** *rotto*
**brooch -es** *spilla*
  **cameo brooch** *cammeo*
  **silver brooch** *spilla d'argento*
**brother** *fratello*
**brother-in-law /brothers-in-law** (pl) *cognato*
**brown** *marrone*
  **brown hair** *capelli (mpl) marroni*
**bruise** (n) *livido*
**bruised** *contuso*
**brush -es** *scopa*
  **clothes brush** *spazzola per i vestiti*
  **hair-brush** *spazzola per i capelli*
  **nail-brush** *spazzolino per le unghie*
  **paint-brush** *pennello*
  **shaving brush** *pennello da barba*
  **shoe-brush** *spazzola per le scarpe*
  **tooth-brush** *spazzolino da denti*
**bucket** *secchiello*
  **a bucket and spade** *un secchiello e paletta*
**buckle** *fibbia*
**Buddhist** *Buddista (m&f)*
**buffet car** *vagone (m) ristorante*
**builder** *costruttore (m)*
**building** *edificio -ci*
  **public building** *edificio pubblico*
**bulb** (=light bulb) *lampadina*
  **40/60/100/200 watt** *40/60/100/200/ candele*
**bun** (bread) *focaccia -ce*
**bun** (hair) *crocchia*
  **in a bun** *in crocchia*
**bunch -es** *mazzo*
  **a bunch of /flowers/** *un mazzo di /fiori/*
**bungalow** *bungalow (m)-*
**bunk bed** *letto a castello*
**buoy** *boa*
**burglary -ies** *furto con scasso*
**burn** (n) *scottatura*
**burn** (vb) *bruciare*
**burnt** *bruciato*
**burst** (adj) *scoppiato*
  **a burst pipe** *un tubo scoppiato*

**bury** *seppellire*
**bus driver** *conducente (m)*
**bus -es** *autobus (m) -*
  **bus station** *stazione (f) di autobus*
  **bus stop** *fermata di autobus*
  **by bus** *in autobus*
  **the bus for / /** *l'autobus per / /*
**businessman /businessmen** (pl) *uomo d'affari - mini d'affari*
**busy** *occupato*
**but** *ma*
**butane** *butano*
**butcher's** *macelleria*
**butter** *burro*
**butterfly -ies** *farfalla*
**button** *bottone (m)*
**buy** *comprare*
  **buy /an umbrella/** *comprare /un ombrello/*
  **where can I buy /an umbrella/?** *dove posso comprare /un ombrello/?*
**by**
  **by /bus/** *in /autobus/*
  **by /the station/** *vicino /alla stazione/*
  **by** (time)
  **by /three o'clock/** *per /le tre/*
**bypass** (n) **-es** *circonvallazione (f)*

# C

**cabbage** *cavolo*
**cabin** *cabina*
  **cabin cruiser** *panfilo*
  **/four/ berth cabin** *cabina a /quattro/ cucette*
**cable** (n) *cavo*
**cable car** *teleferica -che*
**café** *caffè (m)/bar (m)*
**caffeine** *caffeina*
**cake** *torta*
  **a piece of cake** *una fetta di torta*
**cake shop** *pasticceria*
**calculate** *calcolare*
  **calculate /the cost/** *calcolare /il prezzo/*
**calculator** *calcolatrice (f)*

**pocket calculator** *calcolatore (m) tascabile*
**calendar** *calendario -ri*
**call** (n) (telephone call) *chiamata*
  **alarm call** *chiamata d'allarme*
  **call box -es** *cabina telefonica*
  **early morning call** *sveglia*
  **international call** *chiamata internazionale*
  **local call** *chiamata urbana*
  **long distance call** *chiamata interurbana*
  **make a long distance call** *fare una chiamata interurbana*
  **make a call** *fare una telefonata*
  **personal call** *chiamata personale*
  **transferred charge call** *conversazione (f) con pagamento a destinazione*
**call** *chiamata*
**call** (vb) (=telephone) *chiamare*
  **call again later** *chiamare più tardi*
  **call /the police/** *chiamare /la polizia/*
**call on / /** (=visit) *andare a trovare / /*
**calm** (of sea) *calmo*
**calor gas** *calor gas (m)*
**calories** (pl) *calorie (fpl)*
**cameo** *cammeo*
**camera** *macchina (fotografica)*
  **cine camera** *cinepresa*
  **35 mm camera** *macchina a 35 millimetri*
**camera shop** *negozio fotografico*
**camp** (n) *campeggio -ggi*
  **holiday camp** *campeggio di vacanze*
**camp bed** *branda*
**campfire** *fuoco -chi all'aperto*
**camping** *campeggio*
  **go camping** *fare il campeggio*
**campsite** *campeggio -ggi*
**can** (n) *barattolo*
  **a can of /beer/** *un barattolo di /birra/*
**can** (vb) *potere*
  **I can /do it/** *posso /farlo/*
  **I can't /do it/** *non posso /farlo/*
**canal** *canale (m)*

**cancel /my flight/** cancellare /il mio volo/
**cancellation** annullamento
**cancelled** annullato
**candle** candela
**canoe** (n) canoa
**canoeing** canotaggio
　**go canoeing** fare il canotaggio
**canteen** (eating place) mensa
**canvas** (=material) tela
　**canvas bag** borsa di tela
**cap** (=hat) berretto
　**shower cap** cuffia
　**swimming cap** cuffia da bagno
**cap** (n) (for tooth) capsula
**cap** (vb) (tooth) incapsulare
**cape** (=cloak) cappa
**cape** (eg Cape of Good Hope) capo
**captain** capitano
**car** macchina
　**by car** in macchina
　**buffet car** vagone (m) ristorante
　**car ferry -ies** traghetto per le macchine
　**car hire** auto noleggio
　**car park** parcheggio -ggi
　**car wash** lavaggio macchine
　**sleeping car** vagone (m) letto
**carafe** caraffa
　**a carafe of /wine/** una caraffa di /vino/
**carat** carato
　**/nine/ carat gold** oro a /nove/ carati
**caravan** roulotte (f)
　**caravan site** campeggio per roulotte
　**/four/ berth caravan** roulotte a /quattro/ cuccette
**card** (business card) biglietto
　**birthday card** cartolina di buon compleanno
**cardigan** golf (m)
**cards** (pl) carte (fpl)
　**a game of cards** una partita a carte
　**a pack of cards** un mazzo de carte
**careful** prudente
**careless** imprudente
**caretaker** custode (m)

**carnation** garofano
**carnival** carnevale (m)
**carpet** tappeto
　**fitted carpet** moquette (f)
**carriage** (in a train) carrozza
**carrier bag** sacchetto
**carrot** carota
**carry** portare
**carrycot** culla portatile
**carton of /cigarettes/** (=200) stecca di /sigarette/
**carton of /milk/** cartone di /latte/
**cartridge** (=film cartridge) rotolo (=rullino)
**cartridge** (for gun) cartuccia -ce
**case** (=suitcase) valigia
　**cigarette case** porta sigarette (m)
**case** caso
**cash** (n) contanti (mpl)
　**cash payment** pagamento in contanti
　**cash price** prezzo all'ingrosso
　**pay cash** pagare in contanti
**cash** (vb) incassare
　**cash /a traveller's cheque/** incassare /un traveller's cheque/
**cash desk** cassa
**cashier** cassiere (m) cassiera (f)
**cashmere** cachemire (m)
　**cashmere sweater** golf (m) di cachemire
**casino** casinò
**casserole** (meal) stufato (n)
**casserole** (container) casseruola
**cassette** cassetta
　**cassette player** mangianastri (m)
　**cassette recorder** registratore (m)
　**pre-recorded cassette** cassetta preregistrata
**castle** castello
**casualty department** (hospital) pronto soccorso (all'ospedale)
**cat** gatto
**catalogue** catalogo -ghi
**catch** prendere
　**catch /an illness/** prendere /una malattia/

**catch** /the train/ *prendere /il treno/*
**cathedral** *cattedrale (m)*
**Catholic** (adj) *cattolico*
**cattle** (pl) *bestiame (ms)*
**cauliflower** *cavolfiore (m)*
**cause** (n) *causa*
**cave** *caverna*
**ceiling** *soffitto*
**celery** *sedano*
**cellar** *cantina*
**cement** (n) *cemento*
**cemetery** *cimitero*
**centimetre** *centimetro*
**centre** *centro*
  **in the centre** *in centro*
  **shopping centre** *centro commerciale*
  **town centre** *centro città*
**century -ies** *secolo*
**ceramic** *ceramico*
**cereal** (=breakfast cereal) *cereale (per colazione) (m)*
  **a bowl of cereal** *una ciatola di cereale*
**ceremony -ies** *cerimonia*
**certain** *sicuro* (adj) (=certo, convinto)
  **I'm certain** *sono sicuro*
**certainly** *certamente*
**certificate** *certificato*
**chain** *catena*
**chain store** *negozio a catena*
**chair** *sedia*
  **chair lift** *sedia ascensore*
  **high chair** *seggiolone (m)*
  **wheelchair** *sedia a rotelle*
**chairman /chairmen** (pl) *presidente (m)*
**chalet** *chalet (m) -*
**chambermaid** *cameriera (in albergo)*
**champagne** *sciampagna*
  **a bottle of champagne** *una bottiglia di sciampagna*
**change** (n) (= alteration) *cambiamento*
**change** (n) (=money) *resto*
  **small change** *spiccioli (mpl)*
**change** (vb) (clothes) *cambiarsi (di vestiti)*
**change** (vb) *cambiare* (=sostituire)
  **change /the tyre/** *cambiare /la gomma/*

**I'd like to change /some traveller's cheques/** *vorrei cambiare /dei traveller's cheques/*
**change at /** / (of train) *cambiare a / /*
  **do I have to change?** *devo cambiare?*
**changing room** *spogliatoio*
**charcoal** *carbonella*
**charge** (n) (=payment) *prezzo (condizioni)*
**charge** (vb) (=payment) *far pagare*
**charming** *incantevole*
**chart** (= sea map) *carta marina*
**charter flight** *volo charter*
**chauffeur** *autista (m) -i (stipendiato)*
**cheap** *economico*
**cheat** (vb) *imbrogliare*
**check** (vb) *controllare*
  **could you check /the oil and water/ please?** *potrebbe controllare /l'olio e l'acqua/ per favore?*
**check in** (vb) (=of hotel/plane) *registrarsi*
**check out** (vb) (=of hotel) *pagare il conto*
**check up** (n) (=of health) *controllo generale*
**cheek** (of face) *guancia -ce*
**cheers!** (toast) *salute!*
**cheese** *formaggio*
  **cheese /omelette/** */omelette/ al formaggio*
**chemist's** *farmacia*
**cheque** *assegno*
  **cheque book** *libretto di assegni*
  **traveller's cheque** *traveller's cheque (m)*
  **cheque card** *carta di credito*
  **crossed cheque** *assegno sbarrato*
  **pay by cheque** *pagare con assegno*
**cherry -ies** *ciliegia -ge*
**chess** (s) *scacchi (mpl)*
  **a game of chess** *una partita a scacchi*
  **play chess** *giocare a scacchi*

**chest** (part of body) *torace (m)*
**chest of drawers** *cassettone (m)*
**chestnut** *castagna*
**chewing gum** *gomma americana*
**chicken** *pollo*
**chicken pox** *varicella*
**chilblain** *gelone (m)*
**child /children** (pl) *bambino (m)
bambina (f) figli (mpl)*
**chill** (vb) *raffreddare*
**chimney -ies** *camino*
**chin** *mento*
**china** *porcellana*
**chips** (pl) (potato) *patate fritte (fpl)*
**chiropodist** *pedicure (m&f)*
**chocolate** *cioccolata*
  **a bar of chocolate** *una stecca di
  cioccolata*
  **a box of chocolates** *una scatola di
  cioccolatini*
**choice** *scelta (n)*
  **choice between / / and / /** *scelta
  tra / / e / /*
**choir** *coro*
**choose** *scegliere*
  **choose between / / and / /**
  *scegliere tra / / e / /*
**chop** (n) *braciola*
  **lamb chop** *costoletta di agnello*
  **pork chop** *braciola di maiale*
**chop** (vb) *tagliare (a pezzi inegualì)*
**chopsticks** (pl) *bacchette (fpl) per
mangiare alla cinese*
**Christ** *Cristo*
**Christian** *cristiano*
**Christmas** *Natale (m)*
  **Christmas card** *cartolina di Natale*
  **Christmas Day** *il giorno di Natale*
**church -es** *chiesa*
  **a /Protestant/ church** *una chiesa
  /prostestante/*
**cider** *sidro*
  **a bottle of cider** *una bottiglia di sidro*
  **a cider** *un sidro*
**cigar** *sigaro*
  **a box of cigars** *una scatola di sigari*
  **a Havana cigar** *un sigaro avana*

**cigarette** *sigaretta (f)*
  **a carton of cigarettes** (=200) *una
  stecca di sigarette*
  **cigarette** (American type) *sigaretta
  americana*
  **cigarette** (French type) *sigaretta
  francese*
  **filter-tipped cigarettes** *sigarette col
  filtro*
  **smoke a cigarette** *fumare una
  sigaretta*
  **a packet of cigarettes** *un pacchetto
  di sigarette*
**cigarette case** *porta sigarette (m)*
**cigarette lighter** *accendino*
  **gas lighter** *accendigas (m) -*
**cigarette paper** *carta da sigarette*
**cinema** *cinema (m)-*
**circus -es** *circo -chi*
**citizen** *cittadino*
**city -ies** *città -*
  **the new part of the city** *la parte
  nuova della città*
  **the old part of the city** *la parte
  vecchia della città*
**civil servant** *impiegato statale (m)
impiegata statale (f)*
**civilisation** *civiltà -*
**claim** (vb) *reclamare*
  **claim /damages/** *reclamare /danni/*
  **claim on the insurance** *reclamare
  dall'assicurazione*
**clarify** *chiarificare*
**class -es** *classe (f)*
  **cabin class** *classe cabina*
  **/first/ class** */prima/ classe*
  **tourist class** *classe turistica*
**classical** (eg music) *classico*
  **classical music** *musica classica*
**clean** (adj) *pulito*
**clean** (vb) *pulire*
**cleaner's** *lavasecco*
**cleansing cream** *crema detergente*
**clear** (=obvious) *evidente*
**clear** (=transparent) *chiaro* (=limpido)
**clear goods through Customs** *passare
per la dogana*

**clever** (of people) *bravo*
**client** *cliente (m&f)*
**cliff** *scogliera*
**climate** *clima*
**climb** (vb) (=c. mountains) *scalare*
**climbing** *scalata*
  **go climbing** *fare una scalata*
**clinic** *clinica*
  **private clinic** *clinica privata*
**cloakroom** *guardaroba - (in un locale pubblico)*
**clock** *orologio -gi (da muro)*
  **alarm clock** *sveglia*
**clogs** (pl) *zoccoli (mpl)*
  **a pair of clogs** *un paio di zoccoli*
**close** (vb) *chiudere*
**closed** (adj) *chiuso*
**cloth** (dishcloth) *strofinaccio -ci*
**clothes** (pl) *vestiti (mpl)*
  **clothes brush** *spazzola per i vestiti*
  **clothes line** *corda per stendere*
  **clothes peg** *molletta*
**cloud** *nuvola*
**cloudy** *nuvoloso*
**club** *circolo*
  **gambling club** *circolo per il gioco d'azzardo*
  **golf club** (institution) *circolo di golf*
  **golf club** (object) *mazza da golf*
**clutch** (n) (car) *frizione (f)*
**coach -es** *pullman (m) -(tdmk)*
  **by coach** *in pullman*
  **coach** (on a train) *carrozza*
**coal** *carbone (m)*
**coarse** (of person) *volgare*
**coast** *costa*
**coastguard** *polizia costiera*
**coastline** *linea costiera*
**coat** *cappotto*
**coat hanger** *attaccapanni (m) -*
**cockroach -es** *scarafaggio -gi*
**cocktail** *cocktail (m)*
**cocoa** *cacao*
  **a cup of cocoa** *una tazza di cacao*
**coconut** *noce (f) di cocco*
**cod** *merluzzo*
**code** *codice (m)*

**dialling code** *prefisso*
**postal code** *codice postale*
**codeine** *codeina*
**coffee** *caffè (m)*
  **a cup of coffee** *una tazza di caffè*
  **a pot of coffee** *un bricco di caffè*
  **black coffee** *caffè espresso*
  **decaffeinated coffee** *caffè decaffeinizzato*
  **ground coffee** *caffè macinato*
  **instant coffee** *caffè solubile*
  **percolated coffee** *caffè filtrato*
  **white coffee** *caffellatte*
  **white coffee** (smaller cup - frothy and with less milk) *cappuccino*
**coffeepot** *caffettiera*
**coffin** *bara*
**coin** *moneta*
**cold** (adj) *freddo*
  **I'm cold** *ho freddo*
  **it's cold** (of things) *è freddo*
  **it's cold** (of weather) *fa freddo*
**cold** (n) *raffreddore (m)*
  **I've got a cold** *sono raffreddato*
**collar** *colletto*
  **collar bone** *clavicola*
  **dog collar** *collare (m)*
**colleague** *collega (m&f) -ghi (mpl) -ghe (fpl)*
**collect** (from) *ritirare (da)*
  **collect my luggage** *ritirare /le mie valigie/*
**collection** (in a church) *colletta*
**collection** (of objects) *raccolta*
  **last collection** (of post) *ultima raccolta*
**college** *collegio -gi*
**cologne** *acqua di colonia*
**colour** *colore (m)*
  **what colour is it?** *di che colore è?*
**comb** (n) *pettine (m)*
**come** (from) *venire (da)*
  **come in** *entrare*
  **come in!** (command) *avanti!*
**comfortable** *comodo (confortevole)*
**comic** (=funny paper) (s) *fumetti (mpl)*
**commerce** *commercio*

**commission** (=payment) *commissione (f)*
**common** (=usual) *normale*
**company** (=firm) **-ies** *ditta*
**compartment** (in train) *scompartimento*
  **non-smoking compartment** *scompartimento per non fumatori*
  **smoking compartment** *scompartimento per fumatori*
**compass -es** *bussola*
**compensation** *compenso*
**competition** *gara*
**complain** *protestare*
  **complain /to the manager/** *protestare /col direttore/*
  **complain /about the noise/** *protestare per /il rumore/*
**complaint** *protesta*
**complete** (adj) *completo*
**compulsory** *obbligatorio -ri*
**computer** *computer (m)*
**concert** *concerto*
**concert hall** *sala concerti*
**condition** *condizione (f)*
  **in bad condition** *in cattive condizioni (fpl)*
  **in good condition** *in buone condizioni (fpl)*
**conditioner** (for hair) *lozione (f) rinforzante*
  **a bottle of hair conditioner** *una bottiglia di lozione rinforzante per i capelli*
**conducted tour** *visita guidata*
  **go on a conducted tour** *fare una visita guidata*
**conference** *congresso*
**confirm /my flight/** *confermare /il mio volo/*
**confused** *confuso*
  **I'm confused** *sono confuso*
**congratulate /you/ on / /** *congratularsi con /lei/ per / /*
**congratulations** (pl) *complimenti (mpl)*
**connect** *collegare*
**connecting flight** *volo in coincidenza*
**constipated** *soffrire di stitichezza*

**consul** *console (m)*
**consulate** *consolato*
  **the /British/ Consulate** *il consolato /britannico/*
**contact lenses** (pl) *lenti (fpl) a contatto*
**contagious** *contagioso*
**contents** (pl) (eg of a parcel) *contenuto (s)*
**continental** *continentale*
**continual** *continuo*
**continue /a journey/** *proseguire /un viaggio/*
**contraceptives** (pl) *anticoncezionali (mpl)*
  **the Pill** *la pillola*
  **a packet of sheaths** (=Durex) *un pacchetto di preservativi (Durex)*
**contract** (n) *contratto (n)*
**convenient** (of time and distance) *comodo* (=conveniente)
**cook** (vb) *cuocere*
**cooked** *cotto*
**cooker** *cucina (macchina)*
  **electric cooker** *cucina elettrica*
  **gas cooker** *cucina a gas*
**cooking** *cucina* (=cucinare)
  **do the cooking** *cucinare*
**cool** (adj) *fresco -chi* (=non caldo)
**cool** (vb) *raffreddare*
**copper** *rame (m)*
**copy** (vb) *copiare*
**copy** (n) **-ies** *copia*
**coral** *corallo*
**cord** *corda*
**corduroy** *velluto (a corte)*
**cork** *tappo (di sughero)*
**corkscrew** *cavatappi (m) -*
**corn** (eg on a toe) *callo*
  **corn pads** (pl) *callifughi (mpl)*
**corn** *granoturco*
  **sweet corn** *granoturco dolce*
**corner** *angolo*
**correct** (adj) *corretto*
**correct** (vb) *correggere*
**correction** *correzione (f)*
**corridor** *corridoio*
**corset** *busto*

**cost** (n) *prezzo (costo)*
**cost** (vb) *costare*
**cot** *lettino*
**cottage** *villino*
**cotton** *cotone (m)*
  **a reel of cotton** *un rocchetto di cotone*
**cotton wool** *cotone (m) idrofilo*
**couchette** *cuccetta (in treno)*
**cough** (n) *tosse (f)*
  **I've got a cough** *ho la tosse*
**cough** (vb) *tossire*
**cough mixture** *sciroppo per la tosse*
  **a bottle of cough mixture** *una bottiglia di sciroppo per la tosse*
**cough pastilles** (pl) *pastiglie (fpl) per la tosse*
**could**
  **could you /change/ /the tyre/ please?** *potrebbe /cambiare/ /la gomma/ per favore?*
**count** (vb) *contare*
**country** ( =nation) **-ies** *paese (m) (=nazione)*
**countryside** *campagna*
**couple** (married c.) *coppia*
**coupon** *buono (n)*
  **/petrol/ coupon** *buono per /la benzina/*
**courrier** *corriere (m)*
**course** (of food) *piatto (cibo)*
  **first course** *primo piatto*
  **main course** *secondo piatto*
  **last course** *ultimo piatto*
**course**
  **of course!** *certo!*
**court** (law) *tribunale (m)*
  **tennis court** *campo da tennis*
**cousin** *cugino (m) cugina (f)*
**cow** *mucca*
**crab** *granchio*
**crack** (n) *fessura*
**cracked** *rotto*
  **it's cracked** *è rotto*
**cramp** (n) *crampo*
**crash** (into) *scontrarsi (con)*
**crash** (car c.) **-es** *incidente (m)*

**crash helmet** *casco da guidatore*
**crayon** *pastello*
**cream** (from milk) *panna*
**cream** ( =lotion) *crema*
**crease** (vb) *sgualcire*
  **does it crease?** *si sgualcisce?*
**credit** *credito*
  **on credit** *a credito*
  **credit terms** *condizioni (fpl) di credito*
**credit card** *carta di credito*
**crew** *equipaggio (m)*
  **air crew** *equipaggio dell'aereo*
  **ground crew** *personale (m) di servizio a terra*
  **ship's crew** *equipaggio della nave*
**cricket** *cricket (m)*
  **a game of cricket** *una partita a cricket*
  **play cricket** *giocare a cricket*
**crime** *delinquenza*
**criminal** *criminale (m)*
**crisps** ( =potato c.) *patatine*
**crocodile** (leather) *di coccodrillo*
**cross /the road/** *attraversare /la strada/*
**crossroads /crossroads** (pl) *incrocio -ci (di strade)*
**crossword puzzle** *parole incrociate (fpl)*
**crowd** *folla*
**crowded** *affollato*
**crown** (vb) (tooth) *mettere una corona*
**cruise** *crociera*
  **go on a cruise** *fare una crociera*
**cry** (vb) *piangere*
  **the baby's crying** *il bambino piange*
**cube** *cubo*
**cucumber** *cetriolo*
**cuff links** (pl) *gemelli (mpl)*
  **a pair of cuff links** *un paio di gemelli*
**cup** *tazza*
  **a cup of /** / *una tazza di /* /
  **/plastic/ cup** *tazza /di plastica/*
**cupboard** *armadio*
**cure** (n) (health) *guarigione (f)*
**cure** (vb) (health) *guarire*
**curl** (vb) *arricciare*
**curlers** (pl) *bigodini (mpl)*

**currant** *uva passa*
**currency - ies** *valuta*
**current** (=electric c.) *corrente (f) (elettrica)*
  **A.C.** *corrente alternata*
  **D.C.** *corrente continua*
  **one hundred and twenty/ two hundred and forty volt** *cento venti/due cento quaranta volt*
**current** (of water) *corrente (f) (di acqua)*
  **strong current** *corrente forte*
**current** (adj) *corrente (m&f) (adj)*
**curry** *curry (m)*
  **curry powder** *polvere (f) di curry*
**curtain** *tenda (alla finestra)*
**cushion** *cuscino*
**custom** *abitudine (f)*
**Customs** (pl) *dogana*
  **customs declaration form** *dichiarazione (f) per la dogana*
**cut** (n) *taglio*
  **a cut and blow dry** *un taglio e asciugare al fon*
**cut** (vb) *tagliare (senso generale)*
**cut off** (eg of telephone) *interrompere*
  **I've been cut off** *sono stato interrotto (m) sono stata interrotta (f)*
**cutlery** *posateria*
**cutlet** *costoletta*
  **lamb cutlet** *costoletta di agnello*
  **veal cutlet** *costoletta di vitello*
**cycling** *ciclismo*
  **go cycling** *andare in bicicletta*

# D

**daily** *giornaliero*
**damage** (n) (s) *danno (a cose)*
**damaged** *danneggiato*
**damages** (pl) (=compensation) *danni (mpl)*
**damn!** *accidenti!*
**damp** (adj) *umido (di oggetto, persona)*
**dance** (n) *ballo*
**dance** (vb) *ballare*
**dance hall** *sala da ballo*
**dancer** *ballerino (m) ballerina (f)*

**dancing** *ballare*
  **go dancing** *andare a ballare*
**dandruff** (s) *forfora (s)*
**danger** *pericolo*
**dangerous** *pericoloso*
**dark** (of colour) *scuro*
  **dark /green/ /verde/ scuro**
**dark** (=time of day) *buio*
  **it's dark** *è buio*
**darn** (vb) *rammendare*
**dartboard** *bersaglio*
**darts** (pl) *freccette (fpl)*
  **a game of darts** *una partita a freccette*
  **play darts** *giocare a freccette*
**date** (calendar) *data*
  **date of birth** *data di nascita*
**date** (=fruit) *dattero*
**daughter** *figlia*
**daughter-in-law/daughters-in-law** (pl) *nuora*
**dawn** (n) *alba*
**day** *giorno*
  **every day** *ogni giorno*
**dead** *morto*
**deaf** *sordo*
**decaffeinated** *decaffeinizzato*
**December** *dicembre (m)*
**decide** *decidere*
  **decide to / /** *decidere di / /*
  **decide on /a plan/** *decidersi /un piano/*
**deck** *ponte (m) (di nave)*
  **lower deck** *ponte inferiore*
  **upper deck** *ponte superiore*
**deckchair** *sedia a sdraio*
**declare /this watch/** *dichiarare /quest'orologio/*
**deduct** *togliere (=dedurre)*
  **deduct /two thousand lire/ from the bill** *togliere /duemila lire/ dal conto*
**deep** *profondo*
**deep freeze** (=machine) *freezer (m)*
**definitely** *definitivamente*
**degree** (=university d.) *laurea*
**degrees** (pl) *gradi (mpl)*
  **Centigrade** *centigrado*

**Fahrenheit** *fahrenheit*
**deicer** *spray (m) antighiaccio*
**delay** (n) *ritardo*
**delayed** *ritardato*
**delicate** (health) *delicato*
**delicatessen** (=food shop) *rosticceria*
**deliver to** *consegnare a*
**delivery** (goods) *consegna*
**denim** (=material) *stoffa da blue jeans*
  **a pair of denim jeans** *jeans (mpl)*
**dentist** *dentista (m&f)*
  **I must go to the dentist's** *devo andare dal dentista*
**dentures** (pl) *dentiera (s)*
**deodorant** *deodorante (m)*
**depart** *partire*
**department** *reparto*
  **children's department** *reparto bambini*
  **men's department** *reparto uomini*
  **women's department** *reparto donne*
**department** (of company) *reparto*
  **accounts department** *reparto contabilità*
**department store** *grande magazzino*
**departure lounge** *sala di partenza*
**departure time** *ora di partenza*
**depend** *dipendere*
  **it depends** *dipende*
  **it depends on /the weather/** *dipende /dal tempo/*
**deposit** (n) *deposito*
**deposit** (vb) (money) *depositare*
  **deposit /some money/** *depositare /del denaro/*
  **deposit /these valuables/** *depositare /questi oggetti di valore/*
**depth** *profondità -*
**derv** *gasolio*
**describe** *descrivere*
**description** *descrizione (f)*
**design** (n) *disegno (su una stoffa)*
**design** (vb) *disegnare (fare dei piani)*
**desk** *scrivania*
**dessert** *dessert (m)*
**dessertspoonful of / /** *cucchiaio di / /*

**destination** *destinazione (f)*
**detail** *particolare (m)*
**detergent** *detergente (m)*
**detour** *deviazione (f) (per evitare qualcosa)*
  **make a detour** *fare una deviazione*
**develop** *sviluppare*
  **develop and print** (a film) *sviluppare e stampare (una pellicola)*
**diabetes** *diabete (m)*
**diabetic** *diabetico*
**dial** *comporre un numero - composto un numero*
**diamond** *diamante (m)*
**diarrhoea** *diarrea*
**diary -ies** *diario*
**dice/dice** (pl) *dado (da gioco)*
**dictionary -ies** *vocabolario*
  **English/Italian dictionary** *vocabolario inglese/italiano*
  **Italian/English dictionary** *vocabolario italiano/inglese*
  **pocket dictionary** *vocabolario tascabile*
**die** (vb) *morire*
**diesel oil** *nafta*
**diet** (=slimming d.) *dieta*
  **be on a diet** *essere a dieta*
**difference** *diverso*
  **different from / /** *diverso da / /*
**difficult** *difficile*
**difficulty -ies** *difficoltà -*
**dig** (vb) *scavare*
**dinghy -ies** *scialuppa*
  **rubber dinghy** *scialuppa di gomma*
  **sailing dinghy** *scialuppa a vela*
**dining room** *sala da pranzo*
**dinner** (=evening meal) *cena*
  **dinner jacket** *smoking (m)*
  **have dinner** *cenare*
**diplomat** *diplomatico*
**dipstick** *asta di livello*
**direct** (adj) *diretto*
  **direct line** *linea diretta*
  **direct route** *percorso diretto*
**direction** *direzione (f)*
**director** *direttore (m)*

**directory -ies** *elenco*
  **telephone directory** *elenco telefónico*
  **Directory Enquiries** *Informazioni (fpl) (telefoniche)*
**dirty** *sporco*
**disagree with** *non essere d'accordo*
  **I disagree with /you/** *non sono d'accordo con /lei/*
  **it disagrees with /me/** (food) */mi/ fa male*
**disappointed** *deluso*
**disc** *disco (parte del corpo)*
  **a slipped disc** *un disco fuori posto*
**disco** *discoteca*
**disconnect** *distaccare*
**discount** (n) *sconto*
**disease** *malattia*
**disembark** *sbarcare*
**disgusting** *schifoso*
**dish -es** *piatto*
**dishcloth** *strofinaccio -ci*
**dishonest** *disonesto*
**dishwasher** *lavastoviglie (f) -gli*
**disinfectant** *disinfettante (m)*
  **a bottle of disinfectant** *una bottiglia di disinfettante*
**disposable** *da buttare*
  **disposable lighter** *accendino da buttare*
  **disposable nappies** *pannolini da buttare*
**distance** *distanza*
**distributor** (car) *distributore (m) (di automobile)*
**dive into** */ /* *tuffarsi dentro / /*
  **dive into /the water/** *tuffarsi dentro /l'acqua/*
**diversion** *deviazione (f) (stradale, obligatoria)*
**divide** (vb) *dividere*
**diving** *tuffarsi*
  **go diving** *andare a tuffarsi*
  **skin-diving** *tuffarsi in apnea*
  **scuba-diving** *nuoto subacqueo a respiratore*
**divorced** *divorziato*
**dizzy** *stordito*

**I feel dizzy** *mi gira la testa*
**do** *fare*
  **do /some shopping/** *fare /delle spese/*
  **do /me/ a favour** *far/mi/ un favore*
  **could you do /me/ a favour?** */mi/ può fare un favore?*
**docks** (pl) *bacini (mpl) portuali*
**doctor** *medico -ci (n)*
  **I must go to the doctor's** *devo andare dal medico*
**doctor** *medico -ci*
**documents** (pl) *documenti (mpl)*
  **car documents** *documenti della macchina*
  **travel documents** *documenti di viaggio*
**dog** *cane (m)*
  **dog collar** *collare (m) per cani*
**doll** *bambola*
**dollar** *dollaro*
**domestic help** *colf (f)*
**dominoes** (pl) *dornino (s)*
  **a game of dominoes** *una partita a domino*
  **play dominoes** *giocare a domino*
**donkey** *asino*
**door** *porta*
  **back door** *porta posteriore*
  **front door** *porta anteriore*
**doorbell** *campanello (sulla porta)*
**doorman /doormen** (pl) *portiere (m) (in un condominio)*
**dose of /medicine/** *dose (f) di /medicina/*
**double** *doppio*
  **double room** *stanza doppia*
  **a double whisky** *un whisky doppio*
  **pay double** *pagare doppio prezzo*
**doubt** (vb) *dubitare*
  **I doubt it** *dubito*
**down** *giù*
  **are you going down?** *va in giù?*
**downstairs** *giù dalle scale*
**dozen** *dozzina*
  **a dozen /eggs/** *una dozzina di /uova/*

**half a dozen** *una mezza dozzina*
**drains** (pl) (=sanitary system) *fogne (fpl)*
  **the drain's blocked** *lo scarico è bloccato*
**draught** (of air) *corrente (f) (di aria)*
  **it's very draughty** *c'è molta corrente*
**draughts** (pl)(game) *dama (fs)*
  **a game of draughts** *una partita a dama*
**draw** (a picture) *disegnare (arte)*
**drawer** *cassetto*
**dreadful** *orribile*
**dress** (n) **-es** *vestito (da donna)*
**dress** (vb) (a wound) *fasciare*
  **dress /oneself/** *vestir/si/*
  **dress /the baby/** *vestire /il bambino/*
**dress shop** *negozio di abbigliamento*
**dressing** (medical) *bendaggio*
**dressing** (salad dressing) *condimento (per insalata)*
**dressing gown** *vestaglia*
**dressmaker** *sarta*
**drink** (n) *bibita*
  **soft drink** *bibita analcolica*
**drink** (vb) *bere*
**drip-dry** *lavare e asciugare*
  **a drip-dry shirt** *una camicia che non si stira*
**drive** (n) (=entrance) *viale (m) (d'accesso)*
**drive** (vb) *guidare (un'automobile)*
  **go for a drive** *fare un giro in macchina*
**driver** *autista (m&f) -i (di taxi)*
**driving licence** *patente (f)*
  **international driving licence** *patente internazionale*
**drop /of water/** *goccia /d'acqua/*
**drug** *droga*
**drunk** (adj) (=not sober) *ubriaco -chi*
  **early train** *treno di mattina presto*
**dry** (adj) (of the weather) *secco -chi*
**dry** (adj) (of things) *asciutto*
**dry** (adj) (of drinks) *secco -chi*
**dry** (vb) *asciugare*
**dry cleaner's** *tintoria a secco*
**dual carriageway** *strada a doppia corsia*
**duck/duckling** *anitra/anatroccolo*
**due** (to arrive)
  **/the train/'s due /at two o'clock/** */il treno/ deve arrivare /alle due /pomeridiane/*
**dull** (of people and entertainments) *noioso*
**dull** (of the weather) *uggioso*
**dummy** (baby's d.) *cuccio*
**during /the night/** *durante /la notte/*
**dusk** *crepuscolo*
**dust** *polvere (f)*
**dustbin** *bidone (m) per i rifiuti*
**dustman/dustmen** (pl) *netturbino*
**duty** (=tax) **-ies** *dazio -zi*
**duty** (=obligation) **-ies** *dovere (m)(n)*
**duty-free goods** (pl) *merce (fs) esente dal dazio*
**duty-free shop** *negozio esente da dogana*
**duvet** *piumino (m)*
  **duvet cover** *fodera per piumino*
**dye** (vb) *tingere*
  **dye /this sweater/ /black/** *tingere di /nero/ /questo golf/*
**dysentry** *dissenteria*

# E

**each** *ciascuno*
  **each /of the children/** *ciascuno /dei bambini/*
**each** (on price-tag) *l'uno (m) l'una (f) (sul prezzo)*
**ear** *orecchio -chi*
  **earache** *mal (m) d'orecchio*
**early** *presto (=di buon'ora)*
  **early train** *treno di mattina presto*
  **leave early** *partire presto*
**earn** *guadagnare*
**earplugs** (pl) *tappi (mpl) per gli orecchi*
**earrings** (pl) *orecchini (mpl)*
  **clip-on earrings** *orecchini con la clip*
  **earrings for pierced ears** *orecchini per orecchi con foro*
**earth** (=the earth) *terra (pianeta)*

easily *facilemente*
east *est (m)*
Easter *Pasqua*
easy *facile*
eat *mangiare*
eau-de-Cologne *acqua di colonia*
  a bottle of eau-de-Cologne *una bottiglia di acqua di colonia*
education *istruzione (f)*
educational *istruttivo*
EEC *CEE*
efficient *efficiente*
egg *uovo -a*
  boiled egg *uovo alla coque*
  fried egg *uovo fritto*
  hardboiled egg *uovo sodo*
  poached egg *uovo in camicia*
  softboiled egg *uovo alla coque*
  scrambled eggs *uova strapazzate*
elaborate (adj) *elaborato*
elastic (n) *elastico (n)*
elastic band *elastico (n)*
Elastoplast (tdmk) *cerotto*
elbow *gomito*
election (s) *elezione (f)*
electric *elettrico*
  electric shock *scossa elettrica*
  electrical appliance shop *negozio di elettricità*
  electrical system (car) *sistema (m) elettrico*
electrician *elettricista (m) -sti*
electricity *elettricità*
elsewhere *altrove*
embark *imbarcarsi*
embarkation *imbarco*
embassy -ies *ambasciata*
  the /British/ Embassy *l'ambasciata /britannica/*
embroidery *ricamo*
emergency exit *uscita di sicurezza*
emergency -ies *emergenza*
emotional *emotivo*
  she's very emotional *è molto nervosa*
employed by / / *impiegato da / /*
empty (adj) *vuoto (=non pieno)*
empty (vb) *vuotare*

enclose *accludere*
  please find enclosed *qui troverete unito*
end (n) *fine (f)*
end (vb) *finire*
endorse *vistare*
  endorse my ticket to / / *vistare il mio biglietto per / /*
  endorse /my passport/ *vistare /il mio passaporto/*
engaged (to be married) *fidanzato (m) fidanzata (f) (adj)*
engaged (telephone) *occupato*
engaged (toilet) *occupato*
engagement ring *anello di fidanzamento*
engine (eg for a car) *motore (m)*
engineer *ingegnere (m)*
engrave (wood) *incidere*
enjoy oneself *divertirsi*
  enjoy yourself! *buon divertimento!*
enjoyable *piacevole*
enlarge *ingrandire*
enough *abbastanza*
  enough money *abbastanza denaro*
  fast enough *abbastanza veloce*
enroll *iscrivere*
enter *entrare*
  enter /a country/ *entrare in /un paese/*
entertaining *divertente*
entitled
  be entitled to /petrol coupons/ *aver diritto ad avere /i buoni per la benzina/*
entrance *entrata (=ingresso)*
  entrance fee *biglietto di entrata*
  main entrance *entrata principale*
  side entrance *entrata laterale*
envelope *busta*
  a packet of envelopes *un pacchetto di buste*
  airmail envelope *busta aerea*
epidemic (n) *epidemia*
epileptic (adj) *epilettico*
equal *uguale*
equip *equipaggiare*
equipment *equipaggiamento*

**office equipment** *arredamento per ufficio*

**photographic equipment** *equipaggiamento fotografico*

**eraser** *gomma per cancellare*

**escape from / / /** *scappare da / / /*

**escort** (n) *scorta*

**escort** (vb) *scortare (=accompagnare)*

**espresso coffee** *espresso (n) (caffè)*

**estate agent** *agente (m) immobiliare*

**estimate** (n) *stima*

**even** (surface) *liscio*

**evening** *sera*
  **good evening** *buona sera*
  **this evening** *questa sera*
  **tomorrow evening** *domani sera*
  **yesterday evening** *ieri sera*

**evening dress** (for men) (s) *smoking (m)*

**evening dress - evening dresses** (for women) *vestito lungo*

**every** *ogni*

**every day** *ogni giorno*

**everyone** *ognuno*

**everything** *tutto (pron)*

**everywhere** *dappertutto*

**exact** *preciso*

**exactly** *precisamente*

**examination** (=school etc.) *esame (m)*
  **medical examination** *visita medica*

**examine** (medically) *visitare (dal medico)*

**example** *esempio*
  **for example** *per esempio*

**excellent** *eccellente*

**except** *eccetto*

**excess** *eccesso*
  **excess baggage** *bagaglio in eccedenza*
  **excess fare** *supplemento*

**exchange** (vb) *scambiare*
  **exchange /this sweater/** *scambiare /questo golf/*

**exchange rate** *tasso di cambio*

**excited** *eccitato*

**exciting** *emozionante*

**excursion** *gita*

**go on an excursion** *fare una gita*

**excuse** (n) *scusa (=pretesto)*
  **make an excuse** *fare una scusa*

**excuse** (vb) *scusare*
  **excuse me!** (to pass in front of someone) *permesso!*
  **excuse me!** (to attract attention) *scusi!*

**exhaust system** (car) *impianto di scappamento*

**exhibition** *mostra*

**exit** *uscita*
  **emergency exit** *uscita di sicurezza*

**expedition** *spedizione (f) (scientifica)*

**expensive** *costoso*

**experienced** *pratico*

**expert** (adj) *esperto (adj)*

**expert** (n) *esperto (n)*

**expire** (=run out) *scadere*
  **/my visa/ has expired** */il mio visto/ è scaduto*

**explain** *spiegare*

**explanation** *spiegazione (f)*

**export** (vb) *esportare*

**export** (n) *esportazione (f)*

**exposure meter** *esposimetro*

**express**
  **express letter** *lettera espressa*
  **express mail** *posta espressa*
  **express service** *servizio espresso*
  **express train** *treno rapido*

**express train** *rapido*

**extension/seven/** (telephone) *interno (f) /sette/*

**extra** *extra*

**extras** (pl) *extra (mpl)*

**eye** *occhio -chi*

**eye make-up** *trucco per gli occhi*

**eyebrow** *sopracciglio -gli*

**eyelid** *palpebra*

# F

**face** *faccia -cce*

**facecloth** *panno per il viso*

**facial** (=face massage) *massaggio -ggi*

**fact** *fatto*

**factory -ies** *fabbrica -che*

**factory worker** operaio (m) operaia (f)
**faded** (colour) sbiadito
**faint** (vb) svenire
  **I feel faint** mi sento svenire
**fair** (adj) (hair) biondo
**fair** (adj) (skin) chiaro (=non scuro)
**fair** (adj) (=just) giusto (=equo)
  **that's not fair** non è giusto
**fair** (=entertainment) luna park (m)
**fall** (n) caduta
**fall** (vb) cadere
  **I fell downstairs** sono caduto giù per
  le scale
**false** falso
  **false teeth** (pl) dentiera (s)
**family -ies** famiglia
**famous** famoso
**fan** (n) (electric) ventilatore (m)
**fan** (n) (sports) tifoso
**fancy dress** (s) costume (m)
**far** lontano
  **how far is it to /Verona?/** quanto
  dista è /Verona/ da qui?
  **is it far?** è lontano?
  **not far from / /** non lontano da / /
**fare** tariffa (mezzi di trasporto)
  **air fare** tariffa aerea
  **bus fare** tariffa dell'autobus
  **full fare** tariffa intera
  **half fare** tariffa ridotta
  **return fare** tariffa di andata e ritorno
  **single fare** tariffa di sola andata
  **train fare** tariffa ferroviaria
**farm** fattoria
**farmer** fattore (m)
**farmhouse** casa della fattoria
**fashionable** di moda
**fast** veloce
  **fast train** rapido
**fasten** chiudere
**fat** (adj) grasso (=non magro)
**father** padre (m)
**father-in-law/fathers-in-law** (pl)
  suocero
**fattening** ingrassante
**fatty** (of food) grasso (=oleoso)
**fault** colpa

**it's my fault** è colpa mia
**faulty** difettoso
**favour** favore (m)
  **do me a favour** farmi un favore
  **could you do me a favour?** mi può
  fare un favore?
**favourite** (adj) preferito (adj)
**feather** piuma
**February** febbraio
**fed up**
  **be fed up** essere stufo
  **I'm fed up** sono stufo
**feeding bottle** biberon (m) -
**feel** sentire (sensazione)
  **I feel ill** mi sento male
  **I feel sick** mi sento nausea
**feel / /** sembrare / / (al tatto)
  **it feels /rough/** sembra /ruvido/
**felt** (material) feltro
**felt-tip pen** pennarello
**female** (adj) femmina
**feminine** femminile (adj)
**ferry -ies** traghetto
  **by ferry** in traghetto
  **car ferry** traghetto per le macchine
**festival** festa (=festaggiamento)
**fetch** andare a prendere
**fever** febbre (f)
**feverish** febbris (pl)
**few** pochi (mpl)
  **a few** qualche
  **few /people/** poca /gente/
**fewer** meno (di numero)
**fiancé** fidanzato (n)
**fiancée** fidanzata (n)
**field** (n) campo
**fig** fico -chi
**fight** (n) lotta
**fight** (vb) lottare
**figure** (=body) figura
**file** (n) (for papers) cartella
**fill** (tooth) otturare (una carie)
**fill** (vessel) riempire
**fill in** (form) riempire
  **fill in /a form/** riempire /un modulo/
**fill up** (with petrol) fare il pieno
  **fill it up please!** il pieno, per favore!

**fillet** (n)  *filetto*
**fillet** (vb)  *tagliare (=disossare)*
**filling** (tooth)  *otturazione (f) (dentista)*
**filling station**  *distributore (m) (di benzina)*
**film** (for camera)  *pellicola*
  **ASA** (tdmk)  *ASA*
  **black and white film**  *rullino in bianco e nero*
  **cartridge film**  *rotolo*
  **colour film**  *rullino a colori*
  **DIN** (tdmk)  *DIN (tdmk)*
  **Polaroid film** (tdmk)  *pellicola polaroid (tdmk)*
  **Super 8**  *Super 8*
  **16mm**  *16mm*
  **35mm 20/36 exposures**  *35mm con 20/36 pose*
  **120/127/620·**  *120/127/620·*
**film** (=entertainment)  *film (m)*
  **horror film**  *film dell'orrore*
  **pornographic film**  *film pornografico*
  **thriller**  *film giallo*
  **Western**  *Western*
**filter-tipped cigarettes**  *sigarette (fpl) col filtro*
**find**  *trovare*
  **find /this address/**  *trovare /quest'indirizzo/*
**fine** (adj) (of weather)  *bello*
  **it's fine**  *fa bello*
**fine** (adj) (=OK)  *bene*
  **fine thanks!**  *bene grazie!*
**fine** (=sum of money)  *multa*
  **pay a fine**  *pagare una multa*
**finger**  *dito -a*
**finish** (vb)  *finire*
  **finish /my breakfast/**  *finire /la /mia colazione/*
**fire** (n)  *incendio -di*
  **it's on fire**  *è incendiato*
**fire alarm**  *allarme (m) d'incendio*
**fire brigade**  *pompieri (mpl)*
**fire engine**  *autopompa*
**fire escape**  *uscita di sicurezza (antincendio)*
**fire extinguisher**  *pompa antincendio*

**fireman /firemen** (pl)  *pompiere (m)*
**fireworks** (pl)  *fuochi (mpl) d'artificio*
  **firework display**  *spettacolo di fuochi d'artificio*
**firm** (n) (=company)  *ditta*
**first**  *primo (adj)*
  **at first**  *dapprima*
  **first of all**  *prima di tutto*
**first aid**  *pronto soccorso (occorrente per)*
  **first aid kit**  *equipaggiamento di pronto soccorso*
**first class** (adj)  *di prima classe*
**first class** (n)  *prima classe*
**first name**  *nome (m)*
**fish**  *pesce (m)*
**fishing**  *pescare*
  **go fishing**  *andare a pescare*
**fishing line**  *lenza*
**fishing rod**  *canna da pesca*
**fishmonger's**  *pescivendolo*
**fit** (adj) (health)  *in forma*
  **he's fit**  *è in forma*
**fit** (n) (=attack)  *convulsione (f)*
**fit** (vb) (eg exhaust)  *cambiare*
**fit** (vb)  *adattare*
  **it doesn't fit me**  *non mi sta bene*
  **it's a good fit**  *mi sta bene*
**fitting room** (in shop)  *stanza per le prove*
**fix** (vb) (=mend)  *fissare*
**fizzy**  *frizzante*
**flag**  *bandiera*
**flame** (n)  *fiamma*
**flannel** (=cloth)  *flanella*
**flash -es**  *lampo*
  **flash bulb**  *lampo di magnesio*
  **flash cube**  *cubo al magnesio*
**flask** (vacuum flask)  *fiasco -chi*
**flat** (adj)  *piatto (adj)*
**flat** (n)  *appartamento (condominio)*
  **furnished flat**  *appartamento ammobiliato*
  **unfurnished flat**  *appartamento non ammobiliato*
**flavour**  *gusto*
  **banana**  *di banana*

**blackcurrant** *di ribes*
**chocolate** *di cioccolata*
**strawberry** *di fragola*
**vanilla** *di vaniglia*
**flea** *pulce (f)*
**flea market** *mercato delle pulci*
**flea powder** *polvere (f) contro le pulci*
**fleabite** *morso di pulce*
**flight** *volo (= viaggio in aereo)*
  **charter flight** *volo charter*
  **connecting flight** *volo in coincidenza*
  **scheduled flight** *volo di linea*
  **student flight** *volo per studenti*
**flippers** (pl) *pinne (fpl)*
  **a pair of flippers** *un paio di pinne*
**float** (vb) *galleggiare*
**flood** (n) *diluvio -vi*
**flooded** *inondato*
**floor** (of room) *pavimento*
**floor** (of building) *piano (n) (di edificio)*
  **basement** (B) *seminterrato*
  **ground floor** (G) *pianterreno*
  **/first/ floor** */primo/ piano*
  **top floor** *ultimo piano*
**florist's** *fioraio -ai*
**flour** *farina*
**flower** *fiore (m)*
  **a bunch of flowers** *un mazzo di fiori*
**flower pot** *vaso da fiori*
**flu** *influenza*
**fly** (= insect) *mosca -che*
**fly spray** *spray (m) contro le mosche*
**fly to / /** *volare verso / /*
**flying** *volo (= il volare)*
  **go flying** *andare a volare*
**flywheel** *volano (meccanica)*
**fog** *nebbia*
**foggy** *nebbioso*
  **it's foggy** *è nebbioso*
**fold** (vb) *piegare*
**folding** *pieghevole*
  **folding /bed/** */letto/ pieghevole*
  **folding /chair/** */sedia/ pieghevole*
**folk** (adj) *folk*
  **folk art** *arte (f) folk*
  **folk dancing** *ballo folk*
  **folk music** *musica folk*

**folklore** *folklore (m)*
**follow** *seguire*
**fond**
  **be fond of** *aver simpatia per*
  **I'm fond of /him/** *ho simpatia per /lui/*
**food** *cibo*
  **where can I buy some food?** *dove posso trovare del cibo?*
  **food poisoning** *avvelenamento da cibo*
  **health food** *cibo dietetico*
**fool** (n) *stupido (n)*
**foolish** *sciocco -chi*
**foot /feet/** (pl) (= part of body) *piede (m)*
  **on foot** *a piedi*
**football** (= game) *calcio (sport)*
  **a game of football** *una partita di calcio*
  **play football** *giocare a calcio*
**football** (= ball) *pallone (m)*
**footpath** (= through fields) *sentiero*
**for** (prep) *per*
  **for /me/** *per /me/*
  **what's it for?** *a che serve?*
**forehead** *fronte (f) (parte del corpo)*
**foreign** *straniero (adj)*
**foreigner** *straniero (m) straniera (f) (n)*
**forest** *foresta*
**forget** *dimenticare*
**forgive** *perdonare*
**fork** (cutlery) *forchetta*
**form** (= document) *modulo*
**fortunately** *fortunatamente*
**forward to** *inoltrare a*
  **please forward** *pregasi inoltrare*
**fountain** *fontana*
**fountain pen** *penna stilografica*
**foyer** (in hotels and theatres) *entrata (= sala d'ingresso)*
**fragile** *fragile*
  **fragile with care** (= on labels) *fragile*
**frame** (n) (= picture frame) *cornice (f)*
**frame** (vb) *incorniciare*
**free** (= unconstrained) *libero (= senza restrizioni)*

**free** (=without payment) *gratis*
**freeze** *gelare*
  **it's freezing** *si gela*
**frequent** (adj) *frequente*
**fresh** *fresco* (m) *freschi* (mpl) *fresca* (f)
  *fresche* (fpl) (=non vecchio)
  **fresh food** (not stale, not tinned) *cibo fresco*
  **fresh water** (ie not salt) *acqua dolce*
**Friday** *venerdì* (m)
  **on Friday** *venerdì*
  **on Fridays** *di venerdì*
**fridge** *frigorifero*
**friend** *amico* (m) *-ci* (mpl) *amica* (f) *-che* (fpl)
**friendly** *amichevole*
**fringe** (hair) *frangia -ge*
**from**
  **from /eight/ to /ten/** *dalle /otto/ alle /dieci/*
  **from /London/ to /Rome/** *da /Londra/ a /Roma/*
  **I come from / /** *vengo da / /*
**front**
  **in front of / /** *di fronte a / /*
**frontier** *frontiera* (=limite)
**frost** *gelo*
**frosty** *gelato* (adj)
**frozen** (=deep frozen) *congelato*
  **frozen food** *surgelati*
**fruit** *frutta -*
  **fresh fruit** *frutta fresca*
  **tinned fruit** *frutta in scatola*
**fruit juice** (see also under *juice*) *succo di frutta*
  **a bottle of fruit juice** *una bottiglia di succo di frutta*
  **a glass of fruit juice** *un bicchiere di succo di frutta*
**fry** *friggere*
**frying pan** *padella*
**full** *pieno*
  **full board** *pensione* (f) *completa*
**fun** *divertimento*
  **have fun** *divertirsi*
**funeral** *funerale* (m)
**funicular** *funicolare* (f)

**funny** (=amusing) *buffo*
**fur** *pelo*
  **fur coat** *pelliccia*
  **lined with fur** *foderato di pelliccia*
**furnish** *ammobiliare*
**furnished** *ammobiliato*
  **furnished /flat/** /*appartamento*/ *ammobiliato*
**furniture** *mobili* (mpl)
**furniture shop** *negozio di mobili*
**further** *più lontano*
**fuse** (n) *fusibile* (m)
  **/three/ amp fuse** *fusibile da /tre/ ampere*
  **fuse wire** *filo della fusibile*
**fuse** (vb) *saltare* (elettricità)
  **the lights have fused** *le luci sono saltate*
**future** (adj) *futuro* (adj)
**future** (n) *futuro* (n)

# G

**gabardine coat** *gabardina*
**gadget** *aggeggio -ggi*
**gale** *burrasca*
**gallery -ies** *galleria* (in un edificio)
  **art gallery** *galleria d'arte*
**gallon** *gallone*
**gallop** (vb) *galoppare*
**gamble** (vb) *giocare d'azzardo*
**gambling** *gioco d'azzardo*
**gambling club** *circolo di gioco*
**game** (animals) *selvaggina*
  **grouse** *tetraone* (m)
  **hare** *lepre* (f)
  **partridge** *pernice* (f)
  **pheasant** *fagiano*
  **pigeon** *piccione* (m)
  **quail** *quaglia*
  **wild boar** *cinghiale* (m)
**game** *partita*
  **a game of /tennis/** *una partita a /tennis/*
  **play /tennis/** *giocare a /tennis/*
**gaol** *prigione* (f)
  **in gaol** *in prigione*

**garage** *garage (m)*
**garden** *giardino*
**garlic** *aglio*
**gas** *gas (m)*
**gate** (=door) *cancello*
**gate** (=airport exit) *uscita (all'aeroporto)*
**gear** *equipaggiamento*
  **climbing gear** *equipaggiamento per scalare*
  **diving gear** *equipaggiamento subacqueo*
**gears** (pl) (car) *marce (fpl)*
  **first gear** *prima marcia*
  **second gear** *seconda marcia*
  **third gear** *terza marcia*
  **fourth gear** *quarta marcia*
  **fifth gear** *quinta marcia*
  **reverse** *retromarcia*
**general** (adj) *generale (adj)*
**generator** *generatore (m)*
**generous** *generoso*
**Gents'** (lavatory) *gabinetto per gli uomini*
**genuine** *genuino*
**German measles** *rosolia*
**get** (to) (= reach) *arrivare*
  **how does I get there?** *come ci arrivo?*
  **when does /the train/ get to /Stresa/?** *quando arriva /il treno/ a /Stresa/?*
**get /a taxi/** *prendere /un taxi/*
  **where can I get /a taxi/?** *dove posso prendere /un taxi/?*
**get off at / /** *scendere a / /*
**get on at / /** *salire a / /*
**gift** *regalo*
**gift shop** *negozio di regali*
**gin** *gin (m)*
  **a bottle of gin** *una bottiglia di gin*
  **a gin** *un gin*
  **a gin and tonic** *un gin e tonico*
**ginger** (flavour) *zenzero*
**girl** *ragazza* (=giovane donna)
**girlfriend** *ragazza*
**give** *dare*
  **give it to /me/ please** */me/ lo dia, per favore*

**glacier** *ghiacciaio -ai*
**glad** *contento (felice)*
  **he's glad** *è contento*
**glass** (=substance) *vetro*
**glass -es** *bicchiere (m)*
  **a glass of /water/** *un bicchiere /d'acqua/*
  **a wine glass** *un bicchiere da vino*
  **a set of glasses** *un servizio di bicchieri*
**glasses** (pl) *occhiali (mpl)*
  **a pair of glasses** *un paio di occhiali*
**glassware shop** *negozio di vetrerie*
**gliding** *volo a vela*
  **go gliding** *fare volo a vela*
**gloves** (pl) *guanti (mpl)*
  **a pair of gloves** *un paio di guanti*
**glue** *colla*
**go** *andare*
  **go /home/** *andare a /casa/*
  **go /on a picnic/** *andare a /fare un picnic/*
  **go out with / /** *stare con / /*
  **go /shopping/** *andare a /fare la spesa/*
  **let's go** *andiamo!*
**go to /a conference/** *andare ad /un congresso/*
**goal** *gol (m)*
**goalkeeper** *portiere (m) (squadra di calcio)*
**goat** *capra*
**godfather** *padrino*
**God/god** *Dio/dio*
**godmother** *madrina*
**goggles** (pl) *occhialoni (mpl)*
  **underwater goggles** *maschera subacquea*
**go-kart** *go-kart -s*
**gold** (adj) *d'oro*
**gold** (n) *oro*
**golf** *golf (m)*
  **a round of golf** *una partita a golf*
  **golf ball** *pallina da golf*
  **golf club** (=institution) *circolo di golf*
  **golf club** (=object) *mazza da golf*
  **golf course** *campo di golf*

**good** buono (adj)
**goodbye** ciao (=lasciandosi)
**good-looking** bello
  **a good-looking man** un bell' uomo
  **a good-looking woman** una bella donna
**goods** (=merchandise) (pl) merce (fs)
  **goods train** treno merci
**goose/geese** (pl) oca -che
  **wild geese** anatre (fpl) selvatiche
**government** governo
**grade** (=level) grado
**gradually** un po' alla volta
**graduate of / /** laureato a / /
**grammar** grammatica
**grams** (pl) grammi
**grandchild/grandchildren** (pl) nipote (m) (rispetto ai nonni)
**granddaughter** nipote (f) (rispetto ai nonni)
**grandfather** nonno
**grandmother** nonna
**grandson** nipote (m) (rispetto ai nonni)
**grant** (for studies) borsa di studio
**grape** uva
  **a bunch of grapes** un grappolo d'uve
**grapefruit** (fresh) pompelmo
  **tinned grapefruit** pompelmo in scatola
**grass** erba (prato)
**grateful** riconoscente
**gravy** sugo
**grease** (vb) ungere
**greasy** (of food) grasso
**great!** magnifico!
**green** verde
**greengrocer's** fruttivendolo
**grey** grigio -gi
**grill** (vb) cuocere ai ferri
**groceries** (pl) generi (mpl) alimentari
**grocer's** drogheire (m)
**ground** (=the ground) terra (suolo)
**group** gruppo
  **group ticket** biglietto collettivo
**grow** (of person) crescere
**grow** (=cultivate) coltivare
**guarantee** (n) garanzia

**guarantee** (vb) garantire
**guardian** guardiano
**guess** (vb) indovinare
**guest** ospite (m&f) (=visitatore)
**guide** (=person) guida (persona)
**guide** (vb) guidare (=conduire)
**guide book** guida (libro)
**guilty** colpevole
**guitar** chitarra
**gum** (of mouth) gengiva
  **chewing gum** gomma americana
**gun** fucile (m)
**gymnasium** palestra

# H

**hair** capelli (mpl)
**hair dryer** fon (m)
**hair oil** brillantina
  **a bottle of hair oil** una bottiglia di brillantina
**hairbrush** spazzola per capelli
**haircut** taglio di capelli
**hairdresser** parrucchiere (m) parrucchiera (f)
**hairgrip** molletta per capelli
**half -ves** mezzo/metà
  **half a /litre/** mezzo /litro/
  **half a /slice/** mezza /fetta/
**ham** prosciutto
  **ham /sandwich/** /panino/ col prosciutto
  **/six/ slices of ham** /sei/ fette di prosciutto
**hammer** martello
**hand** mano (f) -i
**hand luggage** bagaglio a mano
**handbag** borsetta (da donna)
**handcream** crema per le mani
**handkerchief -ves** fazzoletto
**handle** (eg of a case) manico -ci
**handmade** fatto a mano
**hang** appendere
**hang gliding** deltaplano
**happen** succedere
**happy** felice
**harbour** porto

**harbour master** *capitano di porto*
**hard** (=difficult) *difficile*
**hard** (=not soft) *duro*
**hare** *lepre* (f)
**harpoon gun** *fiocina*
**harvest** *raccolto* (n)
**hat** *cappello*
**hate** (vb) *odiare*
**have** *avere*
  **have fun** *divertirsi*
**have got**
  **I've got /an appointment/** *ho /un appuntamento/*
**hay fever** *febbre* (f) *da fieno*
**he** *lui*
**head** (part of body) *testa*
**headache** *mal* (m) *di testa*
**headlamp bulb** *lampadina per faro*
**headphones** (pl) *cuffie* (fpl)
  **a pair of headphones** *un paio di cuffie*
**headwaiter** *capo cameriere* (m)
**health** *salute* (f)
**health certificate** *certificato di salute*
**healthy** *sano*
**hear** *udire*
**hearing aid** *apparecchio acustico-apparecchi acustici*
**heart** *cuore* (m)
  **heart attack** *infarto*
  **heart trouble** *malattia di cuore*
**heat** (n) *caldo*
**heat wave** *ondata di caldo*
**heater** *stufa*
**heating** *riscaldamento*
  **central heating** *riscaldamento centrale*
**heavy** *pesante*
**heel** (=part of body) *tacco -chi*
**heel** (=part of shoe) *tacco -chi*
  **high heeled** *tacchi alti*
  **low heeled** *tacchi bassi*
**height** *altezza*
**helicopter** *elicottero*
**hello** *ciao (incontrodosi)*
**hello** (on telephone) *pronto!*
**help** (n) *aiuto*

**help** (vb) *aiutare*
**helpful** *servizievole*
**henna** *henné* (m)
**her** (adj) *il suo* (m) *la sua* (f) *i suoi* (mpl) *le sue* (fpl)
  **for her** *per lei*
  **her passport** *il suo passaporto* (m)
  **her bag** *la sua borsa* (f)
  **her hotel** *il suo albergo* (m)
  **her tickets** *i suoi biglietti* (mpl)
  **her keys** *le sue chiavi* (fpl)
**herb** *erba (aromatica)*
**here** *qui*
**hero** *eroe* (m)
**heroine** *eroina*
**herring** *aringa*
**hers**
  **it's hers** *è suo* (m) *è sua* (f)
**he's away** *è via*
**hi!** *ciao!*
**high** *alto*
  **high chair** *sedia alta*
  **high water** *alta marea*
**hijack** (n) *dirottamento*
**hill** *collina*
**hilly** *collinoso*
**him**
  **for him** *per lui*
**hip** *anca*
**hire** (vb) *noleggiare*
**his** *il suo* (m) *la sua* (f) *i suoi* (mpl) *le sue* (fpl)
  **his passport** *il suo passaporto* (m)
  **his bag** *la sua borsa* (f)
  **his hotel** *il suo albergo* (m)
  **his tickets** *i suoi biglietti* (mpl)
  **his keys** *le sue chiavi* (fpl)
  **it's his** *è suo* (m) *è sua* (f)
**history -ies** *storia*
**hit** (vb) *colpire*
**hitchhike** *fare l'autostop*
**hobby -ies** *hobby* (m)
**hockey** *hockey* (m)
  **a game of hockey** *una partita a hockey*
  **play hockey** *giocare a hockey*
**hole** *buco -chi*

**holiday** *vacanza (s)*
  **holiday camp** *campeggio -ggi di vacanze*
  **on holiday** *in vacanza*
  **package holiday** *vacanza organizzata*
  **public holiday** *festa (=giorno festivo)*
**hollow** (adj) *vuoto (=cavo)*
**home** *casa (la propria casa)*
  **at home** *a casa*
  **go home** *andare a casa*
**homemade** *fatto in casa*
**honest** *onesto*
**honey** *miele (m)*
  **a jar of honey** *un vaso di miele*
**honeymoon** *luna di miele*
**hood** (of a garment) *cappuccio -ci*
**hook** *gancio -ci*
**hoover** (tdmk) *aspirapolvere (m)*
**hope** (vb) *sperare*
  **I hope not** *spero di no*
  **I hope so** *spero di sì*
**horrific** *orrendo*
**hors d'oeuvres** *antipasti (pl)*
**horse** *cavallo*
  **horse racing** *corse (fpl) di cavalli*
**hose** (=tube) *canna per innaffiare*
**hose** (car) *tubo di gomma*
**hospital** *ospedale (m)*
**hospitality** *ospitalità*
**host** (m) *ospite (m&f) (=anfitrione)*
**hostel** (=youth hostel) *albergo per la gioventù*
**hostess -es** *padrona di casa (=anfitriona)*
**hot** *caldo (eccessivo) (adj)*
  **I'm hot** *ho caldo*
  **it's hot** (of things/food) *è caldo*
  **it's hot** (of the weather) *fa caldo*
**hotel** *albergo -ghi*
  **cheap hotel** *albergo economico*
  **first class hotel** *albergo di prima classe*
  **medium-priced hotel** *albergo non troppo costoso*
**hot-water bottle** *borsa dell'acqua calda*
**hour** *ora*
**house** *casa (=abitazione)*

**housewife -ves** *massaia*
**hovercraft** *hovercraft (m)*
  **by hovercraft** *in hovercraft*
**how?** *come? (adj)*
  **how are you?** *come sta?*
  **how do you do?** *piacere! (durante una presentazione)*
  **how long?** (time) *quanto tempo?*
  **how many?** *quanti? (mpl) quante? (fpl)*
  **how much?** *quanto? (m) quanta? (f)*
**humid** *umido (clima)*
**humour** *umorismo*
  **sense of humour** *senso dell'umorismo*
**hundred** *cento*
  **hundreds of / /** *centinaia di / /*
**hungry**
  **be hungry** *avere fame*
  **I'm hungry** *ho fame*
**hunting** *caccia*
  **go hunting** *andare a caccia*
**hurry** (n) *fretta*
  **I'm in a hurry** *ho fretta*
**hurry** (vb) *fare presto*
  **please hurry !** *faccia presto per, favore!*
**hurt** (adj) *offeso*
**hurt** (vb) (feel pain)
  **my /arm/ hurts** *mi fa male /il braccio/*
**hurt** (vb) (inflict pain) *far male a*
  **I've hurt /my leg/** *mi sono fatto male /alla gamba/*
**hurt** (vb) (feel pain) *farsi male*
  **my /foot/ hurts** *mi fa male /il piede/*
**husband** *marito*
**hut** *capanna*
**hydrofoil** *idrogetto*
  **by hydrofoil** *in idrogetto*

# I

**I** *io*
**ice** *ghiaccio*
**ice hockey** *hockey (m) sul ghiaccio*

**a game of ice hockey** *una partita a hockey sul ghiaccio*
   **play ice-hockey** *giocare a hockey sul ghiaccio*
**ice skating** *pattinaggio sul ghiaccio*
   **go ice-skating** *fare il pattinaggio sul ghiaccio*
**ice cream** *gelato (n)*
**iced** *(drink/water) ghiacciato*
**icy** *gelido*
**idea** *idea*
**ideal** (adj) *ideale*
**identification** *identificazione (f)*
**identify** *identificare*
**identity card** *carta d'identità*
**if** *se*
   **if you can** *se può*
   **if possible** *se possibile*
**ignition system** *impianto d'accensione*
**ill** (not well) *malato*
   **he's ill** *è malato*
**illegal** *illegale*
**illustration** (in book) *illustrazione (f)*
**immediate** *immediato*
**immediately** *subito*
**immigration** *immigrazione (f)*
   **immigration control** *controllo immigrazione*
**immune** *immune*
**immunisation** *immunizzazione (f)*
**immunise** *immunizzare*
**immunity** *immunità*
   **diplomatic immunity** *immunità diplomatica*
**impatient** *impaziente*
**imperfect** (goods) *difettoso*
**import** (n) *importazione (f)*
**import** (vb) *importare (merci)*
**important** *importante*
**impossible** *impossibile*
**improve** *migliorare*
**in**
   **be in** (adv) *essere in casa*
   **in /July/** *in /luglio/*
   **in summer** *d'estate*
   **in the morning** *di mattina*
   **in the park** *nel parco*

**in front of** *di fronte a/davanti a*
**in case of /fire/** *in caso di /incendio/*
**in front of** *davanti a*
**in front of /** *davanti a / /*
**inch -es** *pollice (m) (misura)*
**include** *comprendere (=includere)*
   **is /service/ included?** *è compreso /il servizio/?*
**including** *compreso*
**incredible** *incredibile*
**independent** *indipendente*
**indigestion** *indigestione (f)*
   **indigestion tablet** *pastiglia per indigestione*
**individual** (adj) *individuale*
**indoors** *all'interno*
   **indoor /swimming pool/** */piscina/ al chiuso*
**industry -ies** *industria*
**inefficient** *inefficiente*
**inexperienced** *inesperto*
**infected** *infettato*
**infectious** *contagioso*
**inflatable** *gonfiabile*
**inflate** *gonfiare*
**inform** *informare*
   **inform /the police/ of / /** *informare /la polizia/ di / /*
**informal** *informale*
**information** (s) *informazione (f)*
   **I'd like some information about /hotels/ please** *vorrei delle informazioni sugli /alberghi/ per favore*
   **information desk** *ufficio informazioni*
   **information office** *ufficio informazioni*
**initials** (pl) *iniziali (mpl)*
**injection** *iniezione (f)*
   **I'd like a /tetanus/ injection** *vorrei un'iniezione /antitetanica/*
**injury -ies** *danno (a persone)*
**ink** *inchiostro*
   **a bottle of ink** *una bottiglia di inchiostro*
**inner tube** (tyre) *camera d'aria*
**innocent** (=not guilty) *innocente*
**inoculate** *inoculare*
**inoculation** *inoculazione (f)*

**inquiry -ies** *richiesta di informazione*
  **make an inquiry about / /** *richiedere informazioni su / /*
**insect** *insetto*
  **insect bite** *puntura d'insetto*
  **insect repellent** *insetticida*
**insecticide** *insetticida*
  **a bottle of insecticide** *una bottiglia di insetticida*
**inside** (adv) *dentro*
**inside** (prep) *dentro a*
  **inside /the house/** *dentro /alla casa/*
**insomnia** *insonnia*
**instead** (of) *invece (di)*
  **instead of /coffee/** *invece /del caffè/*
**instructions** (pl) *istruzioni (fpl)*
  **instructions for use** *istruzioni per l'uso*
**instrument** *strumento*
  **musical instrument** *strumento musicale*
**insulin** *insulina*
**insurance** *assicurazione (f)*
  **insurance certificate** *certificato di assicurazione*
  **insurance policy -ies** *polizza di assicurazione*
**insure** *assicurare*
  **are you insured?** *è assicurato (m) assicurata (f)?*
  **insure /one's life/** *fare un'assicurazione sulla propria vita*
**intelligent** *intelligente*
**intensive** *intensivo*
**intercontinental** (flight) *intercontinentale*
**interested in / /** *appassionato di / /*
**interesting** *interessante*
**internal** *interno (adj)*
**international** *internazionale*
**interpret** *interpretare*
**interpreter** *interprete*
**interval** (=break) *pausa*
**interval** (in theatre) *intervallo*
**interview** (n) *intervista*
  **I've got an interview** *ho un'intervista*
**interview** (vb) *intervistare*

**into** (prep) *dentro (de)*
**introduce** *presentare*
**introduction** *presentazione (f)*
  **letter of introduction** *lettera di presentazione*
**invalid** (n) *invalido*
**investment** *investimento*
**invitation** *invito*
**invite** *invitare*
**invoice** (n) *fattura*
**iodine** *iodio*
  **a bottle of iodine** *una bottiglia di iodio*
**iron** (n) (object) *ferro da stiro*
  **travelling iron** *ferro da viaggio*
**iron** (vb) (clothing) *stirare*
**ironmonger's** *negozio di ferramenta*
**irregular** *irregolare*
**irritation** (medical) *irritazione (f)*
**island** *isola*
**itch** (n) *prurito*

# J

**jack** (car) *cricco*
**jacket** *giacca -che*
  **/tweed/ jacket** *giacca /di tweed/*
**jam** *marmellata*
**January** *gennaio*
**jar** *vaso (=barattolo)*
  **a jar of /jam/** *un vaso di /marmellata/*
**jaw** *mascella*
**jazz** *jazz (m)*
**jealous** *geloso*
  **he's jealous of /me/** *è geloso di /me/*
**jeans** (pl) *jeans (mpl)*
  **a pair of jeans** *un paio di jeans*
**jelly** (see under flavour) *gelatina*
**jellyfish/jellyfish** (pl) *medusa*
**Jew** *ebreo*
**jeweller's** *gioielliere (m)*
**jewellery** *gioielli (mpl)*
**jigsaw puzzle** *puzzle (m)*
**job** *impiego*
**jockey** *fantino*
**joke** *barzelletta*

**journey -ies** *viaggio -ggi (in genere)*
**judo** *judo*
  **do some judo** *fare un po' di judo*
**jug** *brocca*
  **a jug of / /** *una brocca di / /*
**juice** *succo*
  **grapefruit juice** *succo di pompelmo*
  **lemon juice** *succo di limone*
  **orange juice** *succo di arancia*
  **pineapple juice** *succo di ananas*
  **tomato juice** *succo di pomodoro*
**juicy** *succoso*
**July** *luglio*
**jump** (vb) *saltare (di persona, animale)*
**junction** *incrocio -ci (nodo stradale)*
**June** *giugno*
**junk shop** *negozio di articoli di seconda mano*

# K

**keep** *tenere*
**kettle** *bricco*
**key** *chiave (f)*
**key ring** *portachiavi (m)*
**khaki** (colour) *cachi (inv)*
**kick** (n) *calcio (col piede)*
**kick** (vb) *dare un calcio*
**kidneys** (pl) *reni (mpl)*
**kill** (vb) *uccidere*
**kilogramme/kilo** *chilogramma (m)/chilo*
**kilometre** *chilometro*
**kind** (adj) (=friendly) *gentile*
  **it's very kind of you** *è molto gentile da parte sua*
**kind** (n) (=type) *tipo*
  **a kind of /beer/** *un tipo di /birra/*
**kindness -es** *gentilezza*
**king** *re (m) -*
**kiss** (vb) *baciare*
**kiss -es** (n) *bacio -ci*
**kit** *equipaggiamento*
  **first aid kit** *equipaggiamento di pronto soccorso*
**kitchen** *cucina (stanza)*
**kite** *aquilone (m)*

**Kleenex** (tissues) (tdmk) *fazzoletti (mpl) di carta*
  **a box of Kleenex** *una scatola di tazzoletti di carta*
**knee** *ginocchio -chia*
**knife -ves** *coltello*
  **carving knife** *coltello per tagliare la carne*
**knit** *lavorare a maglia*
**knitting** *lavoro a maglia*
  **do some knitting** *lavorare a maglia*
  **knitting needles** *ferri (mpl) da maglia*
  **knitting pattern** *modello di lavoro a maglia*
**knitwear** *maglieria*
**knob** (door) *maniglia*
**knob** (radio) *manopola*
**know** (a fact) *sapere*
  **I know** *lo so*
  **I don't know** *non so*
**know** (a person) *conoscere*
  **I know him** *lo conosco*
**Kosher** *Kosher*

# L

**label** (=luggage label) *etichetta*
  **stick-on label** *etichetta da incollare*
**lace** (=material) *pizzo*
**laces** (pl) *lacci (mpl)*
**ladder** *scala (portatile)*
**Ladies'** (=lavatory) *gabinetto per le donne*
**lady -ies** *signora*
**lake** *lago -ghi*
**lamb** *agnello*
  **a leg of lamb** *una coscia di agnello*
  **lamb chop** *costoletta di agnello*
**lamp** *lampada*
  **bicycle lamp** *lampadina di bicicletta*
**lampshade** *paralume (m)*
**land** *terra (di coltivare)*
**landed** (of a plane) *atterrato*
**landlady -ies** *affittuaria*
**landlord** *affittuario*
**lane** (=traffic lane) *corsia (stradale)*

**lane** (=small road) *vicolo*
**language** lingua (=linguaggio)
**large** (size) *grande*
**last** (=final) *ultimo*
  **at last** *finalmente*
**last** (= previous) *scorso*
**last /Tuesday/** *martedì/ scorso*
**late** *in ritardo*
  **he's late** *lui è in ritardo*
  **I'm sorry I'm late** *mi dispiace, sono in ritardo*
  **it's late** (=time of day) *è tardi*
**later** (=at a later time) *più tardi*
**laugh** (vb) *ridere*
**launder** *lavare e stirare*
**launderette** *lavanderia self-service*
**laundry** (washing) *biancheria*
**laundry** (place) **-ies** *lavanderia*
**lavatory -ies** *gabinetto*
  **Gents'** *gabinetto per gli uomini*
  **Ladies'** *gabinetto per le donne*
**law** *legge (f)*
**lawyer** *avvocato*
**laxative** *lassativo*
  **mild laxative** *lassativo debole*
  **strong laxative** *lassativo forte*
  **suppository** *supposta*
**lay-by** *piazzuola*
**lazy** *pigro*
**leaflet** *opuscolo*
**leak** (n) *perdita*
**leak** (vb) *perdere*
  **it's leaking** *perde*
**learn /Italian/** *imparare /l'italiano/*
**learner** (driver) *uno che impara a guidare*
**leather** *pelle (cuoio)*
  **leather goods shop** *pelletteria*
**leave** (=depart) *partire*
  **leave /at four-thirty p.m./** *partire /alle quattro e mezzo pomeridiane/*
  **leave in /July/** *partire in /luglio/*
  **leave on /Monday/** *partire /lunedì/*
**leave** *lasciare*
  **I've left /my suitcase/ behind** *ho dimenticato /la mia valigia/*
  **leave me alone** *mi lasci stare*

**leave /my luggage/** *lasciare /le mie valigie/*
**left** (=not right) *sinistra*
**left** (direction) *a sinistra*
**left-handed** *mancino*
**left-luggage office** *deposito bagagli*
**leg** *gamba*
**legal** *legale (adj)*
**lemon** *limone (m)*
  **a slice of lemon** *una fetta di limone*
  **lemon juice** *succo di limone*
**lemonade** *limonata*
  **a bottle of lemonade** *una bottiglia di limonata*
  **a can of lemonade** *una lattina di limonata*
  **a glass of lemonade** *un bicchiere di limonata*
**lend** *prestare*
  **could you lend me some /money/?** *mi potrebbe prestare un po' di /soldi/?*
**length** *lunghezza*
  **full length** *lungo*
  **knee length** *al ginocchio*
**lengthen** *allungare*
**lens -es** (of camera) *lente (f)*
  **lens cap** *coperchino lente*
  **wide-angle lens** *obiettivo grandangolare*
  **zoom lens** *lente zoom*
**less** *meno (di quantità)*
**lesson** *lezione (f)*
  **driving lesson** *lezione di guida*
  **/Italian/ lesson** *lezione d'italiano/*
**let** (=allow) *lasciare* (=permettere)
  **let /me/ try** /mi/ *lasci provare*
**let's**
  **let's go!** *andiamo!*
  **let's have /a drink/** *prendiamo /una bibita/*
  **let's meet /at nine/** *incontriamoci /alle nove/*
**letter** (=of the alphabet) *lettera*
**letter** (correspondence) *lettera*
  **air-letter** *lettera aerea*
  **express letter** *lettera espresso*
  **letter box -es** *cassetta delle lettere*

**registered letter** *lettera raccomandata*
**lettuce** *lattuga*
**level** (adj) *piano (adj)*
**level** (n) (=grade) *livello*
**level crossing** *passaggio a livello*
**library -ies** *biblioteca -che*
**licence** *permesso* (n) (=licenza)
**lid** (of eye) *palpebra*
**lid** (of pot) *coperchio*
**lie** (n) (=untruth) *bugia*
**lie** (vb) (=tell an untruth) *dire una bugia*
**lie** (vb) (lie down) *sdraiarsi*
**life** *vita*
**life jacket** *salvagente (m)*
**lifebelt** *cintura di sicurezza*
**lifeboat** *scialuppa di salvataggio*
**lifeguard** *guardia di salvataggio*
**lift** (n) (=elevator) *ascensore (m)*
**lift** (vb) *alzare*
**lift** (vb) (=ride)
  **could you give me a lift to / /?** *mi potrebbe dar un passaggio a / /?*
**light** (adj) (=not dark) *luminoso*
**light** (adj) (=not heavy) *leggero* (=non pesante)
**light** (n) (electric light) *luce (f)*
  **have you got a light?** *mi accende la sigaretta?*
**light /a fire/** *accendere /un fuoco/*
**light bulb** *lampadina*
  **/forty/ watt** */quaranta/ watt*
**light switch -es** *interruttore (m)*
**lighter** (=cigarette lighter) *accendino*
  **disposable lighter** *accendino da buttare*
**lighter fuel** *gas per accendini*
**like** (prep) *come (prep)*
  **what's it like?** *com'è?*
**like** (vb) *piacere (vb)*
  **do you like /swimming/?** *le piace /nuotare/?*
  **I like it** *mi piace*
**likely** *probabile*
**lime** *limetta (frutto)*
  **lime juice** *succo di limetta*
**limit** (n) *limite (m)*
  **height limit** *limite di altezza*

**speed limit** *limite di velocità*
**weight limit** *limite di peso*
**line** *linea*
  **outside line** *linea esterna*
  **telephone line** *linea telefonica*
**linen** *biancheria*
**liner** *transatlantico*
**lingerie** *maglieria femminile*
  **lingerie department** *reparto maglieria femminile*
**lining** *fodera*
  **/fur/ lining** *fodera di /pelliccia/*
**lip** *labbro (m) labbra (fpl)*
  **lower lip** *labbro inferiore*
  **upper lip** *labbro superiore*
**lipstick** *rossetto*
**liqueur** *liquore (m)*
**liquid** *liquido*
**list** *elenco -chi*
  **shopping list** *lista della spesa*
  **wine list** *lista di vini*
**listen to /some music/** *ascoltare /un po' di musica/*
**litre** *litro*
**litter** *rifiuti (mpl)*
**little** (adj) *piccolo*
  **a little boy** *un bambino piccolo*
  **smaller** *più piccolo*
  **smallest** *il più piccolo*
**little** (n) *po'*
  **a little money** *un po' di soldi*
**live** (=be alive) *vivere*
**live** (=reside) *abitare*
  **where do you live?** *dove abita?*
**liver** *fegato*
**load** (vb) *caricare (un camion)*
**loaf -ves** (of bread) *pagnotta*
  **a large loaf** *una pagnotta grande*
  **a small loaf** *una pagnotta piccola*
**lobster** *aragosta*
**local** (adj) *locale*
  **local crafts** *artigianato (ms) regionale*
**lock** (n) *serratura*
**lock** (vb) *chiudere a chiave*
**locker** *armadietto*
  **left-luggage locker** *armadietto deposito*

**logbook** (car) *libretto*
**logbook** *giornale di bordo*
**lonely** *solitario -ri*
**long** *lungo*
**look** (vb)
  **look!** *guarda!*
  **look out!** *attenzione!*
  **I'm just looking** *sto solo guardando*
**look after** *badare a*
  **look after /the baby/** *badare /al bambino/*
**look at** *guardare*
  **look at /this/** *guardare /questo/*
**look for** *cercare*
  **look for /my passport/** *cercare /il mio passaporto/*
**look /smart/** *essere /elegante/*
**loose** (of clothes) *largo (di vestiti)*
**lorry driver** *camionista* (m) *-isti*
**lorry -ies** *camion* (m) -
**lose** *perdere*
  **I've lost /my wallet/** *ho perso /il mio portafoglio/*
**lost** *perso*
  **I'm lost** *sono perso*
**lost property office** *ufficio -ci oggetti smarriti*
**lot** *molto*
  **a lot of /money/** *molti /soldi/*
**loud** *forte (di suono)*
**loudly** *fortemente (di suono)*
**lounge** (in hotel) *sala*
  **departure lounge** *sala di partenza*
  **TV lounge** *sala della televisione*
**love** (n) *amore*
  **give /Mary/ my love** *salutami /Mary/*
  **make love** *fare l'amore*
**love** (vb) *amare*
**low** *basso*
  **low water** *bassa marea*
**lower** (vb) *abbassare*
**LP** (= long playing record) *long playing* (m)
**luck** *fortuna*
  **good luck** *buona fortuna*
**lucky** *fortunato*
  **be lucky** *essere fortunato*

**he's lucky** *è fortunato*
**luggage** *bagaglio -gli*
  **cabin luggage** *bagaglio in cabina*
  **hand luggage** *bagaglio a mano*
  **luggage rack** (in train) *portabagagli* (m)
  **luggage van** (on train) *bagagliaio* (m)
**lump** (body) *gonfiore* (m) (= escrescenza)
  **a lump of sugar** *una zolletta di zucchero*
**lunch -es** *colazione* (f)
  **have lunch** *fare colazione*
  **packed lunch** *colazione al sacco*
**luxury -ies** *lusso*

# M

**machine** *macchina*
**mad** *matto*
**made in / /** *fatto in / /*
**magazine** *rivista (rotocalco)*
**magnifying glass -es** *lente* (f) *d'ingrandimento*
**mahogany** *mogano*
**maid** *cameriera (in casa)*
**mail** *posta*
  **by air-mail** *posta aerea*
  **express mail** *posta espressa*
  **surface mail** *posta normale*
**main** *principale*
  **main road** *strada principale*
**make** (n) (eg of a car) *marca -che*
**make** (vb) *fare*
  **make /a complaint/** *protestare*
  **make /money/** *fare /soldi/*
**make-up** (= face make-up) *trucco*
  **eye make-up** *trucco per gli occhi*
**male** (adj) *maschile*
**mallet** *martello di legno*
**man/men** (pl) *uomo -mini*
  **young man** *giovanotto*
**manager** *direttore* (m)
**manicure** *manicure* (f)
  **manicure set** *necessaire per manicure*
**man-made** *artificiale (fatta dall'uomo)*
  **man-made fibre** *fibra artificiale*

**many** molti (mpl) -te (fpl)
 **not many** non molti
 **too many** troppi (mpl) -pe (fpl)
**map** mappa
 **large-scale map** mappa dettagliata
 **map of /Italy/** mappa /d'Italia/
 **road map** mappa/carta stradale
 **street map** pianta della città
**marble** (material) marmo
**March** marzo
**margarine** margarina
**mark** (=spot/stain) macchia
**market** mercato
 **fish market** mercato di pesce
 **fruit and vegetable market** mercato di frutta e verdura
 **market place** piazza del mercato
 **meat market** mercato della carne
**marmalade** marmellata di arancio
 **a jar of marmalade** un vaso di marmellata di arancio
**maroon** (colour) castano
**married** sposato
**mascara** rimmel (m)
**masculine** maschile
**mask** maschera
 **snorkel mask** snorkel (m)
**mass** (=Catholic service) messa
**massage** (n) massaggio -ggi
**mast** albero (di nave)
**mat** stuoia
 **bath mat** stuoia da bagno
 **door mat** zerbino
**match -es** fiammifero
 **a box of matches** una scatola di fiammiferi
 **matches** cerini
**match -es** (=competition) partita
 **football match** partita di calcio
**material** (=cloth) stoffa
 **checked material** stoffa a quadretti
 **heavy material** stoffa pesante
 **lightweight material** stoffa leggera
 **plain material** stoffa a tinta unita
**matter** (vb)
 **it doesn't matter** non importa
 **what's the matter?** che cosa c'è?

**mattress -es** materasso
**mauve** malva (inv)
**maximum** (adj) massimo
**may** potere (vb)
**May** maggio
**mayonnaise** maionese (m)
**me** me
 **for me** per me
**meal** pasto
 **light meal** pasto leggero
**mean** (=not generous) avaro
**mean** (vb) (of a word) voler dire
 **what does it mean?** che cosa vuol dire?
**measles** morbillo (s)
**measure** (vb) misurare
**meat** carne (f)
 **cold meat** carne fredda
 **beef** manzo
 **lamb** agnello
 **mutton** castrato
 **pork** maiale
**mechanic** meccanico
**mechanism** meccanismo
**medical** medico (adj)
**medicine** medicina
 **a bottle of medicine** una bottiglia di medicina
**medium** (size) medio (talla)
 **medium-dry** mezzo secco
 **medium-rare** (eg of steak) poco cotto
 **medium-sweet** amabile
**meet** (= get to know) incontrare
 **meet /your family/** incontrare /la sua famiglia/
**meet** (at a given time) incontrarsi
**meeting** (business) riunione (f)
**melon** melone (m)
 **half a melon** mezzo melone
 **a slice of melon** una fetta di melone
**member** (of a group) membro
**memo** promemoria
**memory -ies** memoria
 **a good/bad memory** una buona/cattiva memoria
 **happy memories** (pl) bel ricordo (ms)
**mend** aggiustare (=accomodare)

**men's outfitter's** *negozio di vestiti da uomo*

**menu** *menu (m)*
  **à la carte menu** *menu alla carta*
  **set menu** *menu fisso*

**mess -es** *confusione (f)*

**message** *messaggio (m)*
  **can I leave a message please?** *posso lasciare un messaggio per favore?*
  **can I take a message?** *posso prendere un messaggio?*

**metal** *metallo*

**meter** *contatore (m)*
  **electricity meter** *contatore dell'elettricità*
  **gas meter** *contatore del gas*

**method** *metodo*

**methylated spirit** *alcool (m) denaturato*
  **a bottle of methylated spirits** *una bottiglia di alcool denaturato*

**metre** (=length) *metro*

**microphone** *microfono*

**midday** *mezzogiorno*

**middle** *mezzo*
  **in the middle of / /** *nel mezzo di / /*

**middle-aged** *di mezz'età*

**midnight** *mezzanotte*

**migraine** *emicrania*

**mild** *leggiero*

**mild** (of weather) *mite*

**mile** (=measure of lunghezza) *miglio*

**milk** *latte (m)*
  **a bottle of milk** *una bottiglia di latte*
  **a glass of milk** *un bicchiere di latte*
  **powdered milk** *latte in polvere*
  **tinned milk** *latte in scatola*

**milk shake** (see under flavour) *frullato di latte*

**million** *milione (m)*
  **millions of / /** *milioni di / /*

**mince** (vb) *macinare*
  **minced meat** *carne macinata*

**mind** (= look after/watch) *badare*
  **could you mind /my bag/ please?** *potrebbe badare /alla mia borsa/ per favore?*

**mine** (n) *miniera*
  **coal mine** *miniera di carbone*

**mine** (= belongs to me)
  **it's mine** *è mio (m) è mia (f)*

**miner** *minatore (m)*

**mineral water** *acqua minerale*
  **a bottle of mineral water** *una bottiglia di acqua minerale*
  **a glass of mineral water** *un bicchiere di acqua minerale*
  **fizzy mineral water** *acqua minerale gassata*
  **plain mineral water** *acqua minerale naturale*

**minibus -es** *minibus (m)*

**minimum** (adj) *minimo*

**mink** *visone (m)*
  **mink coat** *pelliccia di visone*

**minus** *meno (aritmetica)*

**minute** (time) *minuto*
  **just a minute!** *aspetta un minuto!*

**mirror** *specchio -chi*
  **hand-mirror** *specchio a mano*

**Miss / /** *signorina / /*

**miss /the train/** *perdere /il treno/*

**mist** *foschia*

**mistake** (n) *sbaglio -gli*
  **by mistake** *per sbaglio*

**mix** (vb) *mescolare (= mischiare)*

**mixer** (of food) *frullatore (m)*

**mixture** *miscuglio -gli*

**model** (object) *modello*
  **the latest model** *l'ultimo modello*
  **model /aeroplane/** */aeroplano/ modello*

**model** (profession) *modella*

**modern** *moderno*

**moment** *momento*

**Monday** *lunedì (m)*
  **on Monday** *lunedì*
  **on Mondays** *di lunedì*

**money** *soldi (mpl)*
  **make money** *fare soldi*

**mono** (adj) *mono*

**month** *mese (m)*
  **last month** *il mese scorso*

**next month** *il mese prossimo*
**this month** *questo mese*
**monthly** *mensilmente*
**monument** *monumento*
**mood** *umore (m)*
**in a good/bad mood** *di buon/cattivo umore*
**moon** *luna*
**mop** (n) *scopa*
**moped** *ciclomotore (m)*
**more** *più (adv)*
**more /cake/ please** *ancora /del dolce/, per favore*
**morning** *mattina*
**good morning** *buon giorno (di mattina)*
**this morning** *questa mattina*
**tomorrow morning** *domani mattina*
**yesterday morning** *ieri mattina*
**morning paper** *quotidiano*
**mortgage** (n) *ipoteca -che*
**mosque** *moschea*
**mosquito** *zanzara*
**mosquito net** *zanzariera*
**most** *la maggior parte*
**most /money/** *la maggior parte /dei soldi/*
**most /people/** *la maggior parte /della gente/*
**motel** *motel (m)*
**mother** *madre (f)*
**mother-in-law/mothers-in-law** (pl) *suocera*
**motor** *motore (m)*
**outboard motor** *fuoribordo*
**motor racing** *corsa (fpl) di macchina*
**go motor racing** *fare le corsa di macchina*
**motorail** (ie car on a train) *treno-macchine (m)*
**motorbike** *motocicletta*
**motorboat** *motoscafo*
**motorist** *automobilista (m&f) -isti*
**motorway** *autostrada*
**mouldy** *ammuffito*
**mountain** *montagna*
**mountaineer** *alpinista (m) -isti*

**mountaineering** *alpinismo*
**go mountaineering** *fare l'alpinismo*
**mountainous** *montuoso*
**mouse/mice** (pl) *topo*
**mousetrap** *trappola per topi*
**moustache** *baffi (mpl)*
**mouth** *bocca -che*
**mouthwash -es** *sciacquo per la bocca*
**a bottle of mouthwash** *una bottiglia di sciacquo per la bocca*
**move** (vb) *muovere*
**movement** *movimento*
**Mr / /** *signor / /*
**Mrs / /** *signora / /*
**much** *molto*
**mud** *fango*
**muddy** *fangoso*
**mug** *boccale (m)*
**mumps** *orecchioni (mpl)*
**murder** (n) *assassinio*
**murder** (vb) *assassinare*
**muscle** *muscolo*
**museum** *museo*
**mushroom** *fungo -ghi (pl)*
**mushroom /soup/** */zuppa/ di f.*
**music** *musica*
**classical music** *musica classica*
**folk music** *musica folk*
**light music** *musica leggera*
**pop music** *musica pop*
**musical** (=an entertainment) *commedia musicale*
**musician** *musicista (m) -isti*
**Muslim** *mussola (m) mussolina (f)*
**mussel** *cozza*
**must** *dovere*
**I must /go home/ now** *devo /andare a casa/ adesso*
**must I /pay by cash/?** *devo /pagare in contanti/?*
**you mustn't /park/ /here/** *non deve /parcheggiare/ /qui/*
**mustard** *senape (m)*
**my** *il mio (m) la mia (f) i miei (mpl) le mie (fpl)*
**my passport** *il mio passaporto (m)*
**my bag** *la mia borsa (f)*

# N

**my tickets** *i miei biglietti (mpl)*
**my keys** *le mie chiavi (fpl)*

**nail** (finger/toe) *unghia*
**nailbrush -es** *spazzolino per le unghie*
**nail file** *limetta per le unghie*
**nail scissors** *forbicine per le unghie*
**nail varnish** *smalto per le unghie*
**nail** (metal) *chiodo*
**naked** *nudo*
**name** *nome (m)*
  **first name** *nome (di battesimo)*
  **surname** *cognome (m)*
  **my name's /Paul Smith/** *mi chiamo /Paul Smith/*
  **what's your name please?** *come si chiama per favore?*
**napkin** *tovagliolo*
  **napkin ring** *portatovaglioli*
  **paper napkin** *tovagliolo di carta*
**nappy -ies** *pannolino*
  **disposable nappies** *pannolini da buttare*
**narrow** *stretto (=non largo)*
**nasty** *brutto (=sgradevole)*
**nation** *nazione (f)*
**national** *nazionale*
**nationality -ies** *nazionalità*
**natural** *naturale*
**nature** *natura*
**naughty** (usually of young children) *cattivo (monello)*
**nausea** *nausea*
**navigate** *navigare*
**navy -ies** *marina*
**near** (adv) *vicino (=non lontano)*
**near** (prep) **/the station/** *vicino /alla stazione/*
**neat** (of a drink) *liscio -sci (di liquore)*
**necessary** *necessario -ri*
**necessity -ies** *necessità -*
**neck** *collo*
**necklace** *collana*
**née** *nata*
**need** (n) *bisogno*

**need** (vb) *aver bisogno di*
  **I need /more money/** *ho bisogno di /più soldi/*
**needle** *ago -ghi*
  **knitting needles** *ferri (mpl) da maglia*
**negative** (=film n.) *negativo*
**nephew** *nipote (m) (rispetto agli zii)*
**nervous** (=apprehensive) *apprensivo*
**nervous breakdown** *esaurimento nervoso*
**Nescafe** (tdmk) *nescaffè (m) (tdmk)*
**net** (=fishing n.) *rete (f)*
  **hair net** *retina per capelli*
  **net weight** *peso netto*
**never** *mai*
**new** (of things) *nuovo*
**news** (s) *notizie (fpl)*
**newsagent's** *giornalaio*
**newspaper** *giornale (m)*
  **/English/ newspaper** *giornale /inglese/*
  **evening paper** *giornale della sera*
  **local newspaper** *giornale locale*
  **morning paper** *quotidiano*
**newsstand** *edicola*
**next** *prossimo*
  **next door** *vicino (molto vicino)*
    **next door /to the station/** *vicino /alla stazione/*
    **the house next door** *la casa vicina*
  **next of kin** *parente (m) prossimo*
  **next to / /** *vicino a / /*
**nib** *pennino*
**nice** *bello*
**niece** *nipote (f) (rispetto agli zii)*
**night** *notte (f)*
  **good night** *buona notte*
  **last night** *la notte scorsa*
  **tomorrow night** *domani notte*
  **tonight** *stanotte*
**night life** *vita notturna*
**nightclub** *night (m)*
**nightdress -es** *camicia da notte*
**no** (opposite of 'yes') *no*
  **no /money/** *nessun /soldo/*
  **no one** *nessuno (pron)*
**noisy** *rumoroso*

**nonsense** *sciocchezze (fpl)*
**nonstick** *non attacca*
  **nonstick /frying-pan/** */padella/ che
  non attacca*
**nonstop** *senza fermate*
**normal** *normale*
**north** *nord (m)*
**northeast** *nordest (m)*
**northwest** *nordovest (m)*
**nose** *naso*
**nosebleed** *sangue (m) al naso*
**not** *non*
  **not at all** (replying to 'thank you')
  *prego*
  **not yet** *non ancora*
**note** (=money) *banconota*
  **/ten thousand/ lire note** *banconota
  da /diecimila/ lire*
**note** (written) *bigliettino*
**notebook** *agenda*
**nothing** *niente*
**notice** *avviso*
  **notice board** *cartello per gli avvisi*
**November** *novembre (m)*
**now** *adesso*
**nowhere** *da nessuna parte*
**nude** *nudo*
**number** *numero*
  **number /seven/** *numero /sette/*
  **telephone number** *numero telefonico*
  **wrong number** *numero sbagliato*
**number** *numero*
**nurse** *infermiera*
**nursery -ies** (=day n. for children) *asilo*
**nursery -ies** (=school) *giardino
  d'infanzia*
**nut** (metal) *dado (meccanica)*
  **a nut and bolt** *un dado e un bullone*
**nut** *noce (f) (termine generico)*
  **almond** *mandorla*
  **peanut** *arachide (f)*
**nutcrackers** (pl) *schiaccianoci (ms)*
**nylon** *nailon (m)*
  **a pair of nylons** (stockings) *un paio di
  calze di nailon*

# O

**oak** (wood) *quercia*
**oar** (for rowing) *remo*
**o'clock**
  **it's one o'clock** *è l'una*
  **it's three o'clock** *sono le tre*
**October** *ottobre (m)*
**of** *di*
**off** (of light etc) *spento*
**offence** *infrazione (f)*
  **parking offence** *infrazione di
  parcheggio*
**offer** (n) *offerta*
  **make an offer** *fare un'offerta*
**office** *ufficio -ci*
  **office worker** *impiegato in un ufficio
  (m)/impiegata in un ufficio (f)*
**official** (adj) *ufficiale*
**official** (n) *funzionario -ri*
**often** *spesso (adv)*
**oil** (lubricating) *olio (lubrificante)*
  **a can of oil** *una lattina di olio*
  **oil filter** *filtro dell'olio*
  **oil pump** *pompa dell' olio*
**oil** (salad) *olio (condimento)*
  **olive oil** *olio di oliva*
  **vegetable oil** *olio di semi*
**oil painting** *pittura a olio*
**oily** *unto*
**ointment** *pomata*
  **a jar of ointment** *un vaso di pomata*
  **a tube of ointment** *un tubo di pomata*
**OK** *va bene*
**old** (of people and things) *vecchio -chi
  (di persone e cose)*
  **he is /six/ years old** *ha /sei/ anni*
**old-fashioned** *antiquato*
**olive** *oliva*
  **black olive** *oliva nera*
  **green olive** *oliva verde*
**omelette** *frittata*
**on**
  **on /July 6th/** *il /sei luglio/*
  **on Monday** *lunedì*
  **on the bed** *sul letto (m)*
  **on /the table/** *sulla tavola (f)*

**on** (of light etc) *acceso (lampada, radio)*
**on a coach** *in pullman*
**once** (=one time) *una volta*
**one** (adj) (number) *uno (m) una (f)*
*(numero)*
**one-way street** *senso unico*
**onion** *cipolla*
  **spring onion** *cipollina*
**only** (adv) *solo (adv)*
**OPEC** *OPEP*
**open** (adj) *aperto*
**open** (vb) *aprire*
**open-air restaurant** *ristorante (m)*
  *all'aperto*
  **open-air swimming pool** *piscina*
  *all'aperto*
**opening times** (pl) *orario (s) (di*
  *negozio)*
**opera** *opera*
  **opera house** *teatro dell'opera*
**operate** (surgically) *operare*
**operation** (surgical) *operazione (f)*
**opposite** (adv) *di fronte*
  **opposite /the station/** *di fronte /alla*
  *stazione/*
**optician** *ottico*
**or** (=above) *o*
**orange** (colour) *arancione*
**orange** (fruit) *arancia -ce*
  **orangeade** *aranciata*
  **orange juice** *succo d'arancia*
  **a bottle of orange juice** *una bottiglia*
  *d'arancia*
  **a glass of orange juice** *un bicchiere*
  *d'arancia*
**orchestra** *orchestra*
**order /a steak/** *ordinare /una bistecca/*
**ordinary** *normale*
**organisation** *organizzazione (f)*
**organise** *organizzare (=preparare)*
**original** *originale*
**ornament** *decorazione (f)*
**other** *altro*
  **the other /train/** *l'altro /treno/*
**our** *il nostro (m) la nostra (f) i nostri*
  *(mpl)le nostre (fpl)*
  **our passport** *il nostro passaporto (n)*

  **our bag** *la nostra borsa (f)*
  **our tickets** *i nostri biglietti (mpl)*
  **our keys** *le nostre chiavi (fpl)*
**ours**
  **it's ours** *è nostro (m) è nostra (f)*
**out** *fuori*
  **he's out** *è fuori*
**out of date** (eg clothes) *fuori moda*
**out of date** (eg passport) *scaduto*
**out of order** *non funziona*
**outboard motor** *fuoribordo*
**outside** (adv) *fuori*
**outside** (prep) *fuori di*
  **outside /the house/** *fuori di / casa/*
**oven** *forno*
**over** (=above) *sopra*
  **fly over /the mountains/** *volare*
  *sopra /le montagne/*
**overcoat** *cappotto*
**overcooked** *troppo cotto*
**overheated** (of engine) *surriscaldato*
**overland** *via terra*
**overseas** *all'estero*
**overtake** *sorpassare*
**overweight** *grosso*
  **be overweight** (people) *essere troppo*
  *grosso*
  **he's overweight** *è troppo grosso*
  **be overweight** (things) *pesare troppo*
**owe** *dovere (vb)*
  **how much do I owe you?** *quanto le*
  *devo?*
  **you owe me / / ** *mi deve / /*
**owner** *padrone (m) padrona (f)*
  *(=proprietario)*
**oxygen** *ossigeno*
**oyster** *ostrica -che*
  **a dozen oysters** *dodici ostriche*

# P

**pack** (vb) *impacchettare*
  **pack /my suitcase/** *fare la valigia*
**package holiday** *vacanza organizzata*
**packet** *pacchetto*
  **a packet of /cigarettes/**(=20) *un*
  *pacchetto di /sigarette/*

**packing materials** (to prevent breakages) *imballaggio -ggi*
**pad** (of writing paper) *carta da lettere*
  **sketch-pad** *blocco di carta da disegno*
**paddle** (for canoe) *pagaia*
**padlock** (n) *lucchetto*
**page** (of a book) *pagina*
**pain** *dolore (m)*
**painful** *doloroso*
**painkiller** *analgesico*
**paint** *vernice (f) (colorata)*
  **a tin of paint** *un barattolo di vernice*
**paintbrush -es** *pennello*
  **paintbrush** *pennello*
**painting** (n) *quadro*
  **oil painting** *quadro a olio*
  **watercolour** *quadro a acquarello*
**paints** (pl) *colori (mpl)*
  **box of paints** *scatola di colori*
**pair** *paio*
  **a pair of / /** *un paio di / /*
**palace** *palazzo*
**pale** (of people & things) *pallido*
**pants** (pl) *mutande (fpl)*
  **a pair of pants** *un paio di mutande*
**panty-girdle** *busto*
**paper** *carta*
  **a sheet of paper** *un foglio di carta*
  **airmail paper** *carta aerea*
  **carbon paper** *carta carbone*
  **drawing paper** *carta da disegno*
  **lined paper** *carta rigata*
  **typing paper** *carta da macchina da scrivere*
  **unlined paper** *carta bianca*
  **wrapping paper** *carta da imballaggio*
  **writing paper** *carta da scrivere*
**paper bag** *sacchetto di carta*
**paper clip** *fermaglio -gli per carta*
**paperback** *edizione (f) economica*
**parcel** *pacco -chi*
  **by parcel post** *servizio dei pacchi postali*
**parent** *genitore (m&f)*
**park** (n) *parco -chi*
**park** (vb) *parcheggiare*
**parking** *parcheggio*

**no parking** *parcheggio vietato*
**parking meter** *parchimetro*
**parliament** *parlamento*
**part** *parte (f)*
  **a part of / /** *una parte di / /*
**part** (car) *pezzo (di automobile)*
  **spare parts** *pezzi (mpl) di ricambio*
**partner** (business) *socio -ci*
**partridge** *pernice (f)*
**part-time work** *impiego a mezza giornata*
**party -ies** *festa (=ricevimento)*
  **birthday party** *festa di compleanno*
**party -ies of /people/** *gruppo di /persone/*
**pass -es** (n) (=p. to enter building) *lasciapassare (m)*
  **mountain pass** *valico*
**passage** (on a boat) *passaggio -ggi (su una nave)*
**passenger** (in boat) *passeggero*
**passenger** (in train) *viaggiatore (m)*
  **transit passenger** *viaggiatore in transito*
**passport** *passaporto*
**past**
  **go past /the station/** *passare per /la stazione/*
**pastille** *pastiglia*
  **throat pastille** *pastiglia per la gola*
**pastry -ies** (=cake) *pasticcino*
**patch** (n) *toppa*
**patch** (vb) *rattoppare*
**pâté** *paté (m)*
  **liver pâté** *paté di fegato*
**path** *sentiero*
**patient** (adj) *paziente (adj)*
**patient** (n) *paziente (m) (n)*
  **outpatient** *paziente non residente*
**pattern** *modello*
  **dress pattern** *modello per vestiti*
  **knitting pattern** *modello per golf*
**pavement** *marciapiede (m)*
**pay** *pagare*
  **by /credit card/** *con /carta di credito/*
  **in advance** *in anticipo*

**in cash** *in contanti*
**in /pounds/** *in /sterline/*
**the bill** *il conto*
**pea** *pisello*
**peach -es** *pesca -che (frutta)*
**peanut** *arachide (f)*
  **a packet of peanuts** *un pacchetto di arachidi*
**pear** *pera*
**pearl** *perla*
**pedestrian** *pedone (m)*
  **pedestrian crossing** *passaggio pedonale*
**peel** (vb) *sbucciare*
**peg** (=clothes p.) *molletta*
**pen** (=fountain p.) *penna*
  **ballpoint pen** *penna a sfera*
**pen friend** *amico -ci per corrispondenza / amica -che per corrispondenza*
**pencil** *matita*
  **pencil sharpener** *temperino*
**penicillin** *penicillina*
  **I'm allergic to penicillin** *sono allergico alla penicillina*
**penknife -ves** *temperino (coltello tascabile)*
**people** (pl) *gente (fs)*
**pepper** *pepe (m)*
**pepper** (=vegetable) *peperone (m)*
  **green pepper** *peperone verde*
  **red pepper** *peperone rosso*
**peppermint** (=flavour/drink) *menta*
  **peppermint** (sweet) *mentina*
**per annum** *all'anno*
**per cent** *per cento*
**percolator** *macchina per il caffè*
**perfect** (adj) *perfetto*
**performance** *spettacolo*
**perfume** *profumo*
  **a bottle of perfume** *una bottiglia di profumo*
**perhaps** *forse*
**period** (of time) *periodo*
**period** (=menstrual period) *mestruazioni (fpl)*
**perm** (=permanent wave) *permanente*

(f) (n)
**permanent** *permanente (adj)*
**permission** *permesso (n)*
  (=concessione)
  **permission to /enter/** *permesso di /entrare/*
**permit** (n) *permesso (n)*
  (=autorizzazione)
**permit** (vb) *permettere*
**person** *persona*
**personal** *personale (adj)*
**pet** *animale (m) domestico*
**petrol** *benzina*
  **petrol can** *bidone (m) per benzina*
**petrol station** *distributore (m)*
**petticoat** *sottoveste (f)*
**pheasant** *fagiano*
**phone** (n) *telefono*
  **may I use your phone please?** *posso usare il suo telefono per favore?*
  **external phone** *telefono esterno*
  **internal phone** *interno*
**photocopier** *fotocopiatrice (f)*
**photocopy** (vb) *fare la fotocopia*
**photocopy** (n) **-ies** *fotocopia*
**photograph** (photo) *fotografia*
  **black and white photograph** *fotografia in bianco e nero*
  **colour photograph** *fotografia a colori*
  **take a photograph** *fare una fotografia*
**photographer** *fotografo*
  **photographer's studio** *studio fotografico*
**photographic** *fotografico*
**phrase** *frase (f)*
**phrase book** *frasario -ri*
**piano** *pianoforte (m)*
**pick** (=gather flowers etc) *raccogliere*
**picnic** *picnic (m)*
  **go on a picnic** *fare un picnic*
**picture** (drawing or painting) *quadro*
**piece** *pezzo (parte di un intero)*
  **a piece of / /** *un pezzo di / /*
**pig** *maiale (m) (animale)*
**pigeon** *piccione (m)*
**piles** (illness) *emorroidi (fpl)*
**pill** *pillola*

**a bottle of pills** *una bottiglia di pillole*
**sleeping pills** *sonniferi*
**the Pill** *la pillola*
**pillow** *cuscino (guanciale)*
**pillow case** *federa*
**pilot** *pilota (m) -i*
**pin** *spillino*
**drawing pin** *puntina da disegno*
**pine** (wood) *pino*
**pineapple** *ananas (m) -*
**a slice of pineapple** *una fetta di ananas*
**pineapple juice** *succo di ananas*
**pink** *rosa (adj)*
**pint** *pinta*
**pip** (=seed of citrus fruit) *semino*
**pipe** (smoker's) *pipa*
**pipe cleaner** *nettatpipa (m) -*
**place** (exact location) *luogo -ghi*
**place of birth** *luogo di nascita*
**place of work** *posto di lavoro*
**place** (eg on a plane) *posto (=luogo)*
**plaice/plaice** (pl) *passera*
**plain** (adj) (=not coloured) *smorto*
**plain** (adj) (=not flavoured) *insaporo*
**plain** (adj) (=simple) *semplice*
**plan** (n) *piano (n) (=progetto)*
**plan** (vb) *organizzare (=pianificare)*
**planned** (=already decided) *organizzato*
**plane** (n) (=aeroplane) *aereo (n)*
**by plane** *in aereo*
**plant** (n) *pianta (botanica)*
**plant** (vb) *piantare*
**plaster** (for walls) *intonaco*
**sticking plaster** (for cuts) *cerotto*
**plastic** (adj) *plastica*
**plastic bag** *sacchetto di plastica*
**plate** (=dental plate) *dentiera*
**plate** (=dinner plate) *piatto (di portata)*
**platform /eight/** *binario /otto/*
**platinum** *platino*
**play** (n) (at theatre) *commedia*
**play** (vb) *giocare*
**play a game of / /** *giocare a / /*
**play** (vb) (an instrument) *suonare (uno instrumento)*

**play rugby** *giocare a rugby*
**playground** *campo giochi (m)*
**pleasant** *piacevole*
**please** (request) *per favore*
**yes please** (acceptance of offer) *sì, grazie*
**pleased** *contento (soddisfatto)*
**pleased with / /** *contento di / /*
**plenty** *molto*
**plenty of / /** *molto / /*
**pliers** (pl) *pinze (fpl)*
**a pair of pliers** *un paio di pinze*
**plimsolls** (pl) *scarpe (fpl) da ginnastica*
**a pair of plimsolls** *un paio di scarpe da ginnastica*
**plug** (for sink) *tappo (altri materiali)*
**plug** (electric) *spina (f) (elettricità)*
**adaptor plug** *raccordo elettrico*
**plug in** *attacare (una spina)*
**plum** *prugna*
**plumber** *idraulico*
**plus** *più (aritmetica)*
**p.m.** *di pomeriggio*
**pneumonia** *polmonite (f)*
**poach** *cuocere in camicia*
**pocket** *tasca*
**pocket dictionary -ies** *vocabolario tascabile*
**pocket money** *paga settimanale dei ragazzi*
**pocketknife -ves** *temperino*
**point** (=a sharpened point) *punta*
**point** (vb) (=indicate) *indicare*
**pointed** *appuntito*
**poison** *veleno*
**poisoning** *avvelenamento*
**food poisoning** *avvelenamento da cibo*
**poisonous** *velenoso*
**poker** (=game) *poker (m)*
**a game of poker** *una partita a poker*
**play poker** *giocare a póker*
**police** (pl) *polizia*
**police station** *stazione (f) di polizia*
**policeman/policemen** (pl) *poliziotto*
**polish** (n) *lucido (n)*
**shoe polish** *lucido per le scarpe*

**polish** (vb) *lucidare*
**polite** *cortese*
**political** *politico*
**politician** *uomo politico* -*uomini politici*
**politics** (pl) *politica* (s)
**polo neck sweater** *argentina*
**pond** *stagno*
**pony** -**ies** *pony* (m) -
**pool** (=swimming pool) *piscina*
**poor** (=not rich) *povero*
**poor** (poor quality) *scadente*
**pop** (music) *pop* (m)
**popcorn** *pop-corn* (m)
**popular** *in voga*
**population** *popolazione* (f)
**pork** *maiale* (m) (*carni di*)
**pornographic** *pornografico*
**port** (=harbour) *porto*
**portable** *portatile*
  **portable television** *televisione* (f)
    *portatile*
**porter** (hotel) *portiere* (m) (*in albergo*)
**porter** (railway) *facchino*
**portion** *porzione* (f)
  **a portion of /  /** *una porzione di*
    / /
**portrait** *ritratto*
**position** *posizione* (f)
**possible** *possibile*
**post** (vb) *impostare*
  **post this airmail** *impostare questa per*
    *via aerea*
  **as printed matter** *come stampa*
  **express** *espresso*
  **parcel post** *come pacco*
  **registered** *raccomandata*
  **surface mail** *posta normale*
**post office** *ufficio postale*
**postage** *spese* (fpl) *postali*
**postal order** *vaglia*
**postal rate for /England/** *tariffa*
  *postale per /l'Inghilterra/*
**postbox** -**es** *cassetta delle lettere*
**postcard** *cartolina*
**postcode** *codice* (m) *postale*
**poster** *poster* (m)
**pot** *teiera*

**a pot of tea** *una teiera di tè*
**potato** -**es** *patata*
**potato peeler** *sbuccia patate* (m)
**pottery** (substance) *terraglia*
**poultry** *pollame*
  **chicken** *pollo*
  **duck** *anitra*
  **turkey** *tacchino*
**pound** (weight) *libbra*
**pound** (money) *sterlina*
**pour** *versare*
**powder** (face powder) *cipria*
  **baby powder** *talco*
  **talcum powder** *talco*
**practice** (=custom) *abitudine* (f)
**practice** (=training = sport)
  *allenamento*
**practise** (=put into practice) *praticare*
**practise** (=train) *esercitarsi*
**pram** *carrozzina*
**prawn** *gambero*
**precious** *prezioso*
  **precious stone** *pietra preziosa*
**prefer** *preferire*
**pregnant** *incinta*
**prepare** *preparare*
**prescribe** *prescrivere*
**prescription** *ricetta (medica)*
**present** (n) (adj) *presente (adj)*
**present** (n) (=gift) *regalo*
**present** (n) (time) *presente* (n) (n)
  (*tempo*)
**present** (vb) *presentare*
**president** (of company) *presidente* (m)
**press** (vb) (eg button) *premere*
**press** (vb) (ironing) *stirare*
**pressure** *pressione* (f)
  **blood pressure** *pressione del sangue*
**pressure cooker** *pentola a pressione*
**pretty** *grazioso*
**price** (n) *prezzo (da pagare)*
  **price list** *listino prezzi*
**priest** *prete* (m)
**prince** *principe* (m)
**princess** (-es) *principessa*
**print** (n) (photographic) *copia*
  (*fotografia*)

**print** (vb) *stampare*
**printer** *stampatore (m)*
**prison** *prigione (f)*
**private** *privato*
  **private /bath/** /bagno/ *privato*
**prize** *premio -mi (in una gara)*
**probable** *probabile*
**problem** *problema (m) -i*
**procession** *processione (f)*
**produce** (vb) *produrre*
**product** *prodotto*
**programme** (of events) *programma (m) -i (degli avvenimenti)*
**promise** (n) *promessa*
**promise** (vb) *promettere*
**promotion** (of a person) *promozione (f)*
**promotion** (of a product) *lancio promozionale*
**pronounce** *pronunciare*
**proof** *prova (n) (= evidenza)*
**property -ies** (= belongings) *roba*
**prospectus -es** *opuscolo*
**prostitute** *prostituta*
**protect** *proteggere*
  **protect me from / /** *proteggermi da / /*
**protection** *protezione (f)*
**protective** *protettivo*
**Protestant** (adj) *protestante*
**prove** *dimostrare*
**provisions** (pl) *provviste (fpl)*
**prune** *prugna secca*
**public** *pubblico (adj)*
  **public buildings** (pl) *edifici (mpl) pubblici*
  **public convenience** *gabinetto pubblico*
  **public /garden/** /giardini/ (mpl) *pubblici*
**pull** *tirare (= non spingere)*
**pump** *pompa*
  **bicycle pump** *pompa per biciclette*
  **foot pump** *pompa a piede*
  **water pump** *pompa per acqua*
**puncture** *foratura*
**punish** *punire*
**punishment** *castigo -ghi*

**pupil** *alunno*
**pure** *puro*
**purple** *porpora (inv)*
**purse** *borsellino*
**pus** *pus (m)*
**push** (vb) *spingere*
**pushchair** *passeggino*
**put** *mettere*
  **put on my /coat/** *mettermi /il cappotto/*
**put** *mettere*
**puzzle** *puzzle (m)*
  **jigsaw puzzle** *puzzle (m)*
**pyjamas** (pl) *pigiama (ms)*
  **a pair of pyjamas** *un pigiama*

# Q

**quail** (= bird) *quaglia*
**qualifications** (pl) *qualificazioni (fpl)*
**qualified** *qualificato*
**quality -ies** *qualità -*
**quarrel** (n) *litigio -gi*
**quarter** *quarto*
  **a quarter of /an hour/** *un quarto /d'ora/*
**queen** *regina*
**query** (vb) *fare una domanda*
  **I would like to query /the bill/** *vorrei fare una domanda /sul conto/*
**question** (n) *domanda*
**question** (vb) *domandare*
**queue** (n) *coda (= fila)*
**queue** (vb) *fare la coda*
**quick** *veloce*
  **quick!** *presto! (in fretta)*
**quickly** *velocemente*
**quiet** (adj) *silenzioso*
  **quiet please!** *silenzio, per favore!*
**quinine** *chinino*
**quite** *abbastanza*

# R

**rabbi** *rabbino*
**rabbit** *coniglio*
**rabies** *rabbia*

**race** (n) (=contest) *corsa*
  **horse race** *corsa di cavalli*
  **motor race** *corsa di macchine*
**race** (vb) *correre*
**racecourse** *ippodromo*
**racehorse** *cavallo da corsa*
**races** (pl) (=the races) *corse (fpl)*
**racing** *corsa*
  **horse racing** *corsa di cavalli*
  **motor racing** *corsa di macchine*
**racquet** *racchetta*
  **tennis racquet** *racchetta da tennis*
  **squash racquet** *racchetta da squash*
**radiator** (car) *radiatore (m)*
**radio** *radio (f)*
  **car radio** *autoradio (f)*
  **portable radio** *radio (f) portatile*
  **transistor radio** *radio a transistor*
**radish -es** *ravanello*
**raft** *zattera*
  **life raft** *scialuppa di salvataggio*
**rag** (for cleaning) *panno*
**railway** *ferrovia*
  **railway station** *stazione (f) ferroviaria*
  **underground railway** *metropolitano*
**rain** (n) *pioggia*
**rain** (vb) *piovere*
  **it's raining** *piove*
**raincoat** *impermeabile (m)*
**raisin** *uva passa*
**rally -ies** *rally (m) -*
  **motor rally** *rally automobilistico*
**range** (=range of goods) *varietà*
**range** (=mountain range) *catena di montagne*
**rare** (=unusual) *raro*
**rare** (eg of steak) *al sangue*
  **medium-rare** *poco cotto*
**rash -es** *sfogo (malattia)*
**rasher of bacon** *fetta di pancetta*
**raspberry -ies** *lampone (m)*
  **a punnet of raspberries** *un cestino di lamponi*
**rat** *ratto*
**rate** (n) *tariffa (poste, alberghi)*
  **cheap rate** (mail, telephone) *tariffa ridotta*

**exchange rate** *tasso di cambio*
  **postal rate** *tariffa postale*
  **rate per day** *tariffa giornaliera*
  **rates** (charges) *tariffe (fpl)*
**rattle** (baby's rattle) *sonaglino*
**rattle** (noise) *tintinnio*
**raw** *crudo*
**razor** *rasoio*
  **electric razor** *rasoio elettrico*
  **razor blade** *lametta per rasoio*
  **a packet of razor blades** *un pacchetto di lamette*
**reach** (=attain) (vb) *raggiungere*
**read** *leggere*
  **read /a magazine/** *leggere /una rivista/*
**ready** *pronto*
  **are you ready?** *sei pronto? (m) sei pronta? (f) siete pronti? (mpl) siete pronte? (fpl)*
  **when will it be ready?** *quando sarà pronto?*
**real** *vero (=reale)*
**really** *veramente*
**rear /coach/** */carrozza/ di coda*
**reason** (n) *ragione (f)*
**reasonable** *ragionevole*
**receipt** *ricevuta*
**receive** *ricevere*
**recent** *recente*
**Reception** (eg in a hotel) *ufficio -ci ricevimento*
**recharge** (battery) *ricaricare*
**recipe** *ricetta (di cucina)*
**recognise** *riconoscere*
**recommend** *raccomandare*
**record** (n) *disco (musica)*
  **thirty-three r.p.m. record** *disco a trentatré giri*
  **forty-five r.p.m. record/single** *disco a quarantacinque giri*
  **classical record** *disco classico*
  **jazz record** *disco jazz*
  **light music record** *disco di musica leggera*
  **pop record** *disco pop*
**record** (vb) *registrare (col registratore)*

**record player** *giradischi (m) -*

**record shop** *negozio -zi di dischi*

**rectangular** *rettangolare*

**red** *rosso*

**reduce** (price) *ridurre - ridotto*

  **reduce the price** *ridurre il prezzo*

**reduction** *riduzione (f)*

**reel** *rotolo*

**refill** *refill (m) -*

**refrigerator/fridge** (infml) *frigorifero/frigo*

**refund** (n) *rimborso*

**refund** (vb) *rimborsare*

**regards**

  **give /Julie/ my regards** *mi saluti /Julie/*

**register** (at) (eg a club) *iscriversi*

**registered** (mail) *raccomandata*

**registration number** *numero di targa*

**regret** (vb) *rincrescere*

**regular** *normale*

  **regular /service/** */servizio/ normale*

**regulations** (pl) *regolamenti (mpl)*

**reimburse** *rimborsare*

**relations** (pl) *parenti (mpl)*

**relative** (n) *parente (m&f)*

**reliable** *di fiducia*

**religion** *religione (f)*

**religious** *religioso*

**remedy -ies** *rimedio -i*

**remember** *ricordarsi*

  **I don't remember** *non mi ricordo*

  **I remember /the name/** *mi ricordo /il nome/*

**remove** *togliere (=levare)*

**renew** *rinnovare*

**rent** (n) (payment) *affitto*

**rent /a villa/** *affittare /una villa/*

**repair** (n) *riparazione (f)*

**repair** (vb) *aggiustare (=riparare)*

**repairs** (pl) *riparazioni (fpl)*

  **do repairs** *riparare*

  **shoe repairs** (=shop) *riparazioni scarpe*

  **watch repairs** (=shop) *riparazioni orologi*

**repay** *restituire*

**repay me** *restituirmi*

**repay the money** *restituire il denaro*

**repeat** *ripetere*

**replace** *sostituire*

**reply -ies** (n) *risposta*

  **reply-paid** *risposta pagata*

**report** (n) *relazione (f) (=resoconto)*

**report** (vb) *riferire*

  **report /a loss/** *riferire /una perdita/*

**represent** *rappresentare*

**reproduction** (=painting) *riproduzione (f)*

**request** (n) *richiesta*

  **make a request** *fare una richiesta*

**research** (n) *ricerca (scienza)*

  **market research** *ricerca sul mercato*

**reservation** (hotel, restaurant, theatre) *prenotazione (f) (albergo, teatro)*

  **make a reservation** *fare una prenotazione*

**reserve** (vb) *prenotare (=riservare)*

**reserved** *riservato*

  **reserved seat** *posto riservato*

**responsible** *responsabile*

  **responsible for / /** *responsabile di / /*

**rest** (n) *riposo*

  **have a rest** *riposarsi*

**rest** (vb) *riposarsi*

**restaurant** *ristorante (m)*

  **self-service restaurant** *ristorante self-service*

**restrictions** (pl) *restrizioni (fpl)*

**result** *risultato (n)*

**retired** (adj) *andato in pensione*

  **I'm retired** *sono in pensione*

**return** *ritorno*

  **return** (ticket) *biglietto di andata e ritorno*

**return** (=give back) *restituire*

  **return /this sweater/** *restituire /questa maglietta/*

**return** (=go back) *tornare*

  **return at / four-thirty/** *tornare alle /4.30/*

  **return in /July/** *tornare a /luglio/*

  **return on /Monday/** *tornare /lunedì/*

**reverse** (vb) *innestare la retromarcia*
**reverse** (n) (gear) *retromarcia*
**reverse the charges** *trasferire il pagamento a destinazione*
**I'd like to reverse the charges** *vorrei trasferire il pagamento a destinazione*
**reward** (n) *premio -mi (per buona condotta)*
**reward** (vb) *premiare*
**rheumatism** *reumatismo*
**rib** (part of body) *costola*
**ribbon** *nastro*
  **a piece of ribbon** *un pezzo di nastro*
  **typewriter ribbon** *nastro da macchina*
**rice** *riso* (n)
**rich** *ricco*
**ride** (vb) *cavalcare*
  **ride a bicycle** *andare in bicicletta*
  **ride a horse** *cavalcare*
  **go for a ride** (in a car) *fare un giro in macchina*
**riding** (=horse riding) *equitazione* (f)
  **go riding** *andare a cavalcare*
**right** (=correct) *giusto* (=esatto)
**right** (=not left) *destro* (=non sinistro)
**right** (direction) *a destra*
**right-handed** *non mancino*
**ring** *anello*
  **/diamond/ ring** *anello di /diamanti/*
  **engagement ring** *anello di fidanzamento*
  **wedding ring** *fede* (f)
**ring** (vb) **at the door** *suonare il campanello*
**ring road** *circonvallazione* (f)
**rinse** (n) (clothes) *sciacquo*
  **colour rinse** (hair) *shampoo colorante*
**rinse** (vb) *sciacquare*
**ripe** *maturo*
**river** *fiume* (m)
**road** *strada*
  **main road** *strada principale*
  **ring road** *circonvallazione* (f)
  **side road** *strada secondaria*
**roast** (vb) *arrostire*
  **roast beef** *manzo arrosto*
  **roast chicken** *pollo arrosto*

**rock** (n) *roccia -cce*
**rod** (=fishing r.) *canna da pesca*
**roll** (=bread r.) *panino*
**roll of /toilet paper/** *rotolo di /carta igienica/*
**roller skating** *pattinaggio a rotelle*
  **go roller skating** *fare pattinaggio a rotelle*
**roof** *tetto*
**roof rack** *portapacchi* (m) -
**room** *camera*
  **double room** *camera doppia*
  **quiet room** *camera tranquilla*
  **room service** *servizio in camera*
  **room with a view** *camera con vista*
  **single room** *camera singola*
  **twin-bedded room** *camera con due letti*
  **with /shower/** *con /doccia/*
  **without /bath/** *senza /bagno/*
**rope** *corda*
  **tow rope** *corda da traino*
**rose** *rosa* (n)
  **a bunch of roses** *un mazzo di rose*
**rotten** *marcio -ci*
**rough** (=not calm) *mosso*
**rough** (=not smooth) *ruvido*
**roughly** (=approximately) *approssimativamente*
**round** (adj) *rotondo*
**roundabout** (n) *rotonda* (n)
**route** *percorso*
**row** (a boat) *remare*
**row** (of seats) *fila*
  **the /first/ row** *la /prima/ fila*
**rowing boat** *barca a remi*
**rub** *strofinare*
**rubber** (=eraser) *gomma da cancellare*
**rubber** (substance) *gomma (sostanza)*
  **rubber boots** *stivali* (mpl) *di gomma*
**rubber band** *elastico* (n)
**rubbish** (=litter) *rifiuti* (mpl)
**rucksack** *zaino*
**rude** *scortese*
**rug** *tappetino*
**rugby** *rugby* (m)
  **a game of rugby** *una partita di rugby*

**ruler** (for measuring) *regolo*
**rules** (pl) *regole (fpl)*
**rum** *rhum (m)*
**run** (vb) *correre*
**run** (vb) (colour) *stingere*
  **does it run?** *stinge?*
**run over / /** *investire / /*
**run-resistant** (tights etc) *anti smagliatura (inv)*
**rush hour** *ora di punta*

# S

**saccharine** *saccarina*
  **saccharine tablet** *pastiglia di saccarina*
**sad** *triste*
**saddle** *sella*
**safe** (adj) *sicuro (adj)* (=non periculoso)
**safe** (n) *cassaforte (f)*
**safety belt** *cintura di sicurezza*
**safety pin** *spilla di sicurezza*
**sail** (n) *vela*
**sail** (vb) *veleggiare (vb)*
**sailing** *veleggiare (n)*
  **go sailing** *andare in barca a vela*
  **sailing boat** *barca a vela*
**sailor** *marinaio*
**saint** *santo*
**salad** *insalata*
  **green salad** *insalata verde*
  **mixed salad** *insalata mista*
  **salad dressing** *condimento per insalata*
**salary -ies** *stipendio -di*
**sale** *svendita*
**sales** (of a company) *vendite (fpl)*
  **sales representative** *rappresentante (m) delle vendite*
  **sales manager** *direttore (m) delle vendite*
**salmon/salmon** (pl) *salmone (m)*
  **smoked salmon** *salmone affumicato*
**salt** (n) *sale (m)*
**salted** *salato*
**same** *stesso*

  **the same as / /** *lo stesso de / /*
**sand** *sabbia*
**sandals** (pl) *sandali (mpl)*
  **a pair of sandals** *un paio di sandali*
**sandwich -es** *panino imbottito*
  **a /cheese/ sandwich** *un panino con /formaggio/*
**sandy** *sabbioso*
**sanitary towels** (pl) *assorbenti (mpl)*
**sardine** *sardina*
**satin** (adj) *di raso*
**satin** (n) *raso*
**satisfactory** *soddisfacente*
**Saturday** *sabato*
  **on Saturday** *sabato*
  **on Saturdays** *di sabato*
**sauce** *salsa*
**saucepan** *pentolino*
**saucer** *piattino*
  **a cup and saucer** *una tazza e piattino*
**sauna** *sauna*
**sausage** *salsiccia -cce /salame (m)*
**save** (money) *risparmiare*
**save** (=rescue) *salvare*
**savoury** (=not sweet) *salatino*
**say** (something) *dire*
**scale** (on a map) *scala (carta geografica)*
  **large scale** *scala grande*
  **small scale** *scala piccola*
**scales** (pl) (=weighing machine) *bilancia (s)*
**scallop** *conchiglia di pettine*
**scar** *cicatrice (f)*
**scarf -ves** *sciarpa*
  **/silk/ scarf** *sciarpa di /seta/*
**scenery** *panorama (m) -i*
**schedule** *programma (m) -i* (=orario)
**school** *scuola*
  **language school** *scuola di lingue*
**schoolboy** *scolaro*
**schoolgirl** *scolara*
**science** *scienza*
**scissors** (pl) *forbici (fpl)*
  **a pair of scissors** *un paio di forbici*
**scooter** (=child's s.) *scooter (m)*
  **motor scooter** *scooter (m)*

**score /a goal/** segnare /un gol/
**scratch** (vb) graffiare
**scratch -es** (n) graffio -ffi
**scream** (n) grido (=strillo)
**screen** (=film screen) schermo
**screen** (=movable partition) paravento
**screw** vite (f)
**screwdriver** cacciavite (f)
**sculpture** scultura
**sea** mare (m)
  **by sea** per mare
**seafood** frutti (mpl) di mare
**search** (vb) ricercare
**search -es** (n) ricerca (=cerca)
**seasick**
  **be seasick** avere mal di mare
  **I feel seasick** ho mal di mare
**season** stagione (f)
**season ticket** abbonamento (treno, autobus)
**seat at the front** posto (a sedere) davanti
  **at the back** di dietro
  **at the theatre** al teatro
  **by the exit** vicino all'uscita
  **by the window** vicino alla finestra
  **in a non-smoker** (train) scompartimento per non fumatori
  **in the non-smoking section** (aeroplane) nella sezione per non fumatori
  **in a smoker** (train) scompartimento per fumatori
  **in the smoking section** (aeroplane) nella sezione per fumatori
  **in the middle** in mezzo
  **on a coach** in pullman
  **on a train** in treno
**seasoning** condimento (per altri cibi)
**second** (of time) secondo (tempo)
**second-hand** di seconda mano
  **a second-hand car** una macchina usata
**secret** (adj) segreto (adj)
**secret** (n) segreto (n)
**secretary -ies** segretaria
**security** sicurezza

**security check** controllo speciale di sicurezza
**security control** controllo di sicurezza
**sedative** calmante (m)
**see** vedere
  **I see** (= understand) capisco
  **see /the manager/** vedere /il direttore/
  **see /the menu/** vedere /il menù/
  **see you!** arrivederci!
  **see you soon!** arrivederci a presto!
**self-addressed envelope** busta indirizzata a sé
**sell** vendere
**Sellotape** (tdmk) nastroadesivo
**send** spedire
  **send /a message/** spedire /un messaggio/
  **send / / to me** spedire / / a me
  **send it by / / mail** spedirlo per posta / /
**separate** (adj) separato
**September** settembre (m)
**septic** settico
**serve** servire
**service** (church) funzione (f)
**service** servizio -zi (prestato da camerieri)
  **room service** servizio in camera
  **twenty-four hour service** servizio continuo
**service** (n) (car) revisione (f)
**service** (vb)(car) controllare (l'automobile)
**serviette** tovagliolo
**set** (n) servizio -zi (di piatti, posate)
  **dinner set** servizio da pranzo
  **tea service** servizio da tè
**set** (vb)(hair) mettere in piega
  **shampoo and set** (n) messa in piega
**several** parecchi
**sew** cucire
**sewing** cucire
  **do some sewing** cucire un pò
**sex -es** sesso
**shade** (colour) sfumatura
**shade** ombra

**in the shade** *all'ombra*
**shake** (vb) *scuotere*
  **shake hands** *dare la mano*
**shampoo** (n) *shampoo (m)*
  **a bottle of shampoo** *una bottiglia di shampoo*
  **a sachet of shampoo** *una bustina di shampoo*
  **shampoo and blow dry** *shampoo e asciugare col fon*
  **shampoo and set** *messa in piega*
**shampoo** (vb) *fare lo shampoo*
**shape** (n) *forma*
**share** (vb) *condividere*
**sharp** (of things) *affilato*
**sharpen** *affilare*
**shave** (n) *rasatura*
**shave** (vb) *fare la barba*
  **shaving brush -es** *pennello da barba*
  **shaving cream** *crema da barba*
  **a tube of shaving cream** *un tubetto di crema da barba*
  **shaving soap** *sapone (m) da barba*
  **a stick of shaving soap** *un bastoncino di sapone de barba*
**shawl** *scialle (m)*
**she** *lei (fs, terzo persona)*
**sheath** (=Durex) *preservativo (m) (=Durex)*
  **a packet of sheaths** *un pacchetto di preservativi*
**sheep/sheep** (pl) *pecora*
**sheepskin** *pelle (f) di pecora*
  **sheepskin /rug/** */coperta/ di pelle di pecora*
**sheet** (bed linen) *lenzuolo (m) lenzuola (fpl)*
**sheet** (of paper) *foglio di carta*
**shelf -ves** *scaffale (m)*
  **bookshelf** *libreria*
**shell** (sea-s.) *conchiglia*
**shellfish** (s)/**shellfish** (pl) *crostacei (mpl)*
**sheltered** *riparato (=protetto)*
**sherry** *sherry (m)*
  **a bottle of sherry** *una bottiglia di sherry*

  **a sherry** *uno sherry*
**shiny** *lucido (adj)*
**ship** (n) *nave (f)*
**ship** (vb) *spedire (per nave)*
**shirt** *camicia -ce*
  **casual shirt** *camicia sportiva*
  **/cotton/ shirt** *camicia di /cotone/*
  **formal shirt** *camicia formale*
  **short-sleeved shirt** *camicia a maniche corte*
**shock** (n) *scossa*
  **electric shock** *scossa elettrica*
  **state of shock** *stato di collasso*
**shock absorber** (car) *ammortizzatore (m)*
**shockproof** (eg of watch) *resistente all'urto*
**shoebrush -es** *spazzola per le scarpe*
**shoelaces** (pl) *lacci (mpl)*
  **a pair of shoelaces** *un paio di lacci*
**shoepolish** *lucido per le scarpe*
**shoes** (pl) *scarpe (fpl)*
  **a pair of shoes** *un paio di scarpe*
  **boys' shoes** *scarpe da bambino*
  **girls' shoes** *scarpe da bambina*
  **flat-heeled shoes** *scarpe con tacchi bassi*
  **high-heeled shoes** *scarpe con tacchi alti*
  **ladies' shoes** *scarpe da donna*
  **men's shoes** *scarpe da uomo*
  **walking shoes** *scarpe da camminare*
**shoeshop** *negozio -zi di calzature*
**shoot** (vb) *sparare*
**shop** *negozio -zi*
**shop assistant** *commesso (m) commessa (f)*
**shopping** *spesa*
  **go shopping** *fare la spesa*
  **shopping bag** *borsa per la spesa*
  **shopping centre** *centro commerciale*
**shore** *spiaggia -gge*
**short** (people) *basso (di persone)*
**short** (things) *corto*
**short** (time) *breve*
  **short circuit** *corto circuito*
**shorten** *abbreviare*

**shorts** (pl) *pantaloncini (mpl)*
 **a pair of shorts** *un paio di pantaloncini*
**shot** (n) *sparo*
**shoulder** *spalla*
**shout** (n) *grido (=urlo)*
**shout** (vb) *gridare*
**show** (n) *mostra*
 **fashion show** *sfilata di moda*
 **floor show** *cabaret (m)*
 **strip show** *spogliarello*
 **variety show** *spettacolo di varietà*
**show** (vb) *far vedere*
 **show /it/ to me** *farme/lo/ vedere*
**shower** (=s. bath) *doccia -ce*
 **shower cap** *cuffia*
**shrimp** *gamberetto*
**shut** (adj) *chiuso*
**shut** (vb) *chiudere*
**shutters** (pl) *imposte (fpl) (=persiane)*
**shy** *timido*
**sick**
 **I feel sick** *mi sento nausea*
**side** (n) (in game) *squadra*
**side** (n) (of object) *lato*
**sightseeing** *visitare i luoghi interessanti*
 **go sightseeing** *andare a visitare i luoghi interessanti*
 **sights** (pl)(of a town) *luoghi interessanti (mpl)*
**sign** (n) *indicazione (f)*
**sign /a cheque/** *firmare /un assegno/*
 **sign here** *firmi qui*
**signal** (n) *segnale (m)*
**signal** (vb) *segnalare*
**signature** *firma*
**signpost** *controllo stradale (indicatore)*
**silence** *silenzio*
**silent** *silenzioso*
**silk** (adj) *di seta*
**silk** (n) *seta*
**silver** (adj) *d'argento*
**silver** (n) *argento*
**similar** *simile*
**simple** *semplice*
**sincere** *sincero*
**sing** *cantare*

**singer** *cantante (m&f)*
**single** (=not married) *non sposato*
 **single bed** *letto singolo*
 **single ticket** *biglietto di sola andata*
**sink** (n) *lavello*
**sink** (vb) *affondare*
**sister** *sorella*
**sister-in-law/sisters-in-law** (pl) *cognata*
**sit** (see seat) *sedere*
 **please sit down** *si accomodi, prego*
**site** *luogo -ghi*
 **campsite** *campeggio -ggi*
 **caravan site** *campeggio per roulotte*
**size** *misura (=taglia)*
 **large size** *misura grande*
 **medium size** *misura media*
 **small size** *misura piccola*
 **what size?** *che misura?*
**size** (shoes) *numero di scarpe*
**skating** *pattinaggio*
 **go skating** *andare a pattinare*
 **ice-skating** *pattinaggio sul ghiaccio*
 **roller-skating** *pattinare*
**sketch -es** (n) *schizzo (=disegno)*
**sketchpad** *blocco -chi da disegno*
**ski lift** *ski lift (m)*
**ski-boots** (pl) *scarponi (mpl) da sci*
 **a pair of ski-boots** *un paio di scarponi da sci*
**skid** (n) *slittamento*
**skid** (vb) (car) *slittare*
**skiing** *sciare*
 **go skiing** *andare a sciare*
 **water-skiing** *sci d'acqua*
**skin** *pelle (f) (cute)*
**skin diving** *tuffarsi in apnea*
 **go skin diving** *andare a tuffarsi in apnea*
**skirt** *gonna*
 **long skirt** *gonna lunga*
 **short skirt** *gonna corta*
**skis** (pl) *sci (mpl)*
 **a pair of skis** *un paio di sci*
 **water skis** *sci d'acqua*
**sky -ies** *cielo*
**sleep** (n) *sonno*

**sleep** (vb) *dormire*
  **he's asleep** *dorme*
**sleeper** (on a train) *vagone (m) letto*
**sleeping bag** *sacco -chi a pelo*
**sleeping berth** *cuccetta*
**sleeping car** *vagone (m) letto*
**sleeping pill** *sonnifero*
**sleepy**
  **be sleepy** *avere sonno*
  **I'm sleepy** *ho sonno*
**sleeves** (pl) *maniche (fpl)*
  **long sleeves** *maniche lunghe*
  **short sleeves** *maniche corte*
  **sleeveless** *senza maniche*
**slice** (n) *fetta*
  **a slice of /  /** *una fetta di /  /*
**slice** (vb) *affettare (= tagliare)*
**slide viewer** *macchina per diapositive*
**slides** (pl) *diapositive (fpl)*
  **colour slides** *diapositive a colori*
**slippers** (pl) *pantofole (fpl)*
  **a pair of slippers** *un paio di pantofole*
**slippery** *scivoloso*
**slope** *discesa*
**slot machine** *distributore (m) a gettoni*
**slow** *lento*
**slow train** *treno locale*
**slower** *più lento*
**slowly** *lentamente*
**small** (size) *piccolo*
**smart** (appearance) *elegante*
**smell** (n) *odore (m)*
**smell** (vb) (= perceive with nose) *sentire
  l'odore di /  /*
**smell** (vb) (= have a certain smell!) *avere
  l'odore di /  /*
  **it smells /good/** *ha un /buon/ odore*
**smoke** (n) *fumo*
**smoke /a cigarette/** *fumare /una
  sigaretta/*
**smoked** (of fish & meat etc) *affumicato*
  **smoked /ham/** */prosciutto/
  affumicato*
**smoker** *fumatore (m&f)*
  **non-smoker** *non-fumador*
**smooth** *liscio -sci (non ruvido)*
**snack** *spuntino*

**snack-bar** *snack-bar (m)*
**snake** *serpente (m)*
  **snakebite** *morso di serpente*
**sneeze** (vb) *starnutire*
**snorkel** (n) *snorkel (m)*
  **snorkel mask** *maschera snorkel*
  **snorkel tube** *tubo snorkel*
**snorkel** (vb) *fare lo snorkel*
**snow** (n) *neve (f)*
**snow** (vb) *nevicare*
  **it's snowing** *nevica*
**so** (= therefore) *perciò*
**soak** (vb) *bagnare (mettere a bagno)*
**soap** *sapone (m)*
  **a bar of soap** *una saponetta*
  **shaving soap** *sapone da barba*
  **soap flakes** *sapone in scaglie*
**soapy** *insaponato*
**sober** *sobrio -ri*
**socket** *presa*
  **electric razor socket** *presa per
  rasoio*
  **light socket** *presa per la luce*
  **/three/-pin socket** *presa a /tre/
  spinotti*
**socks** (pl) *calze (fpl) (da uomo)*
  **a pair of socks** *un paio di calze*
  **short socks** *calzini (mpl)*
  **long socks** *calze lunghe*
  **/woollen/ socks** *calze /di lana/*
**soda** (water) *seltz*
  **a bottle of soda** (water) *una bottiglia
  di seltz*
  **a glass of soda** (water) *un bicchiere
  di seltz*
**soft** (= not hard) *morbido*
**sold** *venduto*
**sold out** *esaurito*
**soldier** *soldato*
**sole** (= fish) *sogliola*
**sole** (of shoe) *suola*
**solid** *solido*
**somebody** *qualcuno*
**someone** *qualcuno*
**something** *qualcosa*
  **something to drink** *qualcosa da bere*
  **something to eat** *qualcosa da*

*mangiare*
**sometimes** *qualche volta*
**somewhere** *da qualche parte*
**son** *figlio -gli*
**song** *canzone (f)*
  **folk song** *canzone folk*
  **pop song** *canzone pop*
**son-in-law /sons-in-law** (pl) *genero*
**soon** *presto (tra poco)*
**sore** (adj) *irritato*
**sore throat** *mal (m) di gola*
**sorry?** (= pardon?) *scusi?*
**sorry!** (apology) *mi dispiace!*
**sound** (n) *suono*
**soup** (thick) *brodo*
  **/chicken/ soup** *brodo di /pollo/*
**soup** (clear) *minestra*
**sour** *aspro*
**south** *sud (m)*
  **southeast** *sudest (m)*
  **southwest** *sudovest (m)*
**souvenir** *ricordo (oggetto, regalo)*
**souvenir shop** *negozio -zi di ricordi*
**space** (room) *spazio -zi*
**spade** *badile (m)*
**spanner** *chiave (f) inglese*
  **adjustable spanner** *chiave inglese regolabile*
**spare** (adj) *di riserva*
  **spare parts** (pl) *ricambi (mpl)*
  **spare time** *tempo libero*
**sparking plug** (car) *candela (di automobile)*
**speak** *parlare*
  **speak /English/** *parlare /inglese/*
  **do you speak /English/?** *parla /inglese/?*
  **I don't speak /Italian/** *non parlo /italiano/*
  **speak /to the manager/** *parlare /col direttore/*
  **may I speak /to the manager/ please?** (on phone) *posso parlare /col direttore/ per favore?*
**special** *speciale*
**speed** *velocità -*
**speedboat** *motoscafo*

**spell** *compitare*
**spend** (money) *spendere*
**spend** (time) *passare (tempo)*
**spice** *spezia*
**spicy** *saporito*
**spider** *ragno*
**spilt** *rovesciato (liquidi)*
**spinach** (s) *spinaci (mpl)*
**spine** (part of body) *spina dorsale*
**spirits** (pl) (=alcohol) *liquore (m)*
**spit** (vb) *sputare*
**splendid** *meraviglioso*
**spoil** (vb) *rovinare*
**sponge** (bath s.) *spugna*
**spoon** *cucchiaio -ai (posata)*
**spoonful** *cucchiaio -ai (misura)*
  **a spoonful of / /** *un cucchiaio di / /*
**sport** *sport (m)*
  **sports car** *macchina sportiva*
**spot** (=blemish) *macchiolina*
**spot** (=dot) *punto*
**sprain** (n) *storta (n)*
**sprained** *storto*
**spring** (=season) *primavera*
  **in spring** *in primavera*
**spring** (=wire coil) *molla*
**spring onion** *cipollina*
**sprout** (= Brussels s.) *cavolino (m) di Bruxelles*
**square** (=scarf) *foulard (m) (inv)*
  **a /silk/ square** *un foulard di /seta/*
**square** (shape) *quadrato*
**square** (place) *piazza*
  **main square** *piazza principale*
**squash** *squash (m)*
  **a game of squash** *una partita a squash*
  **play squash** *giocare a squash*
**squeeze** (vb) *spremere*
**stable** (for horses) *stalla*
**stadium** *stadio*
**staff** (=employees) *personale (m)*
**stage** (in a theatre) *palcoscenico -ci*
**stain** *macchia*
  **stain remover** *smacchiatore (m)*
**stained** *macchiato*

**stainless steel** *acciaio inossidabile*
  **stainless steel /cutlery/** */posateria/ di acciaio inossidabile*
**staircase** *scala (in un edificio)*
**stairs** (pl) *scale (fpl)*
**stale** (bread, cheese etc) *vecchio -chi (di cibo)*
**stamp** (n) *francobollo*
  **a /two hundred lire/ stamp** *un francobollo da / duecento/ lire*
**stand** (vb) *stare (essere in piedi)*
**standard** (adj) *standard*
**stapler** *cucitrice (f)*
**staples** (n) (pl) *punti metallici (fpl)*
**star** *diva*
  **film star** *diva del cinema*
**starch** (vb) *inamidare*
**starch -es** (n) *amido*
**start** (n) *partenza*
**start** (vb) *incominciare*
  **start /the journey/** *incominciare /il viaggio/*
**start** (vb) (eg a car) *avviare (un motore)*
  **it won't start** *non si avvia*
**starter** (=hors d'oeuvre) *antipasto*
**starter motor** (car) *motore (m) d'avviamento*
**state** (n) *stato*
**station** (=railway s.) *stazione (f)*
  **bus station** *stazione degli autobus*
  **coach station** *stazione dei pullman*
  **underground station** *stazione (f) della metropolitana*
**stationery** *cartoleria*
**statue** *statua*
**stay** (somewhere) *alloggiare*
  **where were you staying?** *dove alloggiate?*
**stay at / /** *stare a / / (=rimanere)*
  **for a night** *per una notte*
  **for /two/ nights** *per /due/ notti*
  **for a week** *per una settimana*
  **for /two/ weeks** *per /due/ settimane*
  **till / /** *fino a / /*
  **from / / till / /** *da / / a / /*
**steak** *bistecca -che*
  **medium** *non troppo cotta*

  **rare** *al sangue*
  **well-done** *cotta bene*
**steal** *rubare*
**steam** (vb) *cuocere a bagno maria*
**steel** *acciaio*
  **stainless steel** *acciaio inossidabile*
**steep** *ripido*
**steer** (vb) (boat) *virare*
**steer** (vb) (car) *guidare (=essere al volante)*
**steering** (n) (car) *guida (di automobile)*
**step** (n) (movement) *passo*
**step** (n) (part of staircase) *gradino*
**stereo** (adj) *stereofonico*
  **stereo equipment** *equipaggiamento stereofonico*
**stereo** (n) *stereo*
**stern** (of boat) *poppa*
**steward** (plane or boat) *steward (m)*
**stewardess -es** (plane or boat) *hostess (f) -*
**stick** (n) *bastone (m)*
**sticking plaster** *cerotto*
**sticky** *appiccicaticcio -cci*
**sticky tape** (eg Sellotape (tdmk)) *nastro adesivo*
**stiff** *rigido*
**sting** (n) *puntura (n)*
  **/bee/ sting** *puntura /d'ape/*
**sting** (vb) *pungere*
**stir** (vb) *mescolare (ingredienti)*
**stock** (n) (of things) *rifornimento*
**stockings** (pl) *calze (fpl) (da donna)*
  **fifteen/thirty denier** *quindici/trenta denier*
  **a pair of stockings** *un paio di calze*
  **/nylon/ stockings** *calze di /nailon/*
**stolen** *rubato*
**stomach** *stomaco -ci*
  **I've got a stomach ache** *ho mal di stomaco*
  **I've got a stomach upset** *ho un disturbo di stomaco*
**stone** (substance) *pietra*
  **precious stone** *pietra preziosa*
**stone** (of fruit) *nocciolo (di ciliegia, pesca)*

**stool** *sgabello*
**stop** (n) *fermata*
  **bus stop** *fermata dell'autobus*
  **tram stop** *fermata del tram*
**stop** (vb) *fermare*
**stop at** / / *fermarsi a / /*
**store** (=department s.) *magazzino*
**storm** *temporale (m)*
**stormy** *tempestoso*
**story -ies** *racconto*
**straight** *dritto*
**stranger** (n) *sconosciuto (n)*
**strap** *cinturino*
  **watch-strap** *cinturino dell'orologio*
**strapless** *senza cinturino*
**straw** (=drinking s.) *cannuccia -ce*
**strawberry -ies** *fragola*
  **a punnet of strawberries** *un cestino di fragole*
**streak** (n) (of hair) *mèche (f)*
**streak** (vb) (of hair)
  **I'd like my hair streaked** *vorrei farmi le mèches*
**stream** (n) *ruscello*
**street** *strada*
  **main street** *strada principale*
**stretcher** *barella*
**strike** (n) *sciopero*
  **be on strike** *essere in sciopero*
**strike** (vb) (of clock) *suonare (di orologio)*
**string** *spago -ghi*
  **a ball of string** *un rotolo di spago*
  **a piece of string** *un pezzo di spago*
**strip show** *spogliarello*
**striped** *a righe*
**strong** (physically) *forte (altre accezioni)*
  **strong /coffee/** */caffè/ forte*
**stuck** (eg a window) *bloccato (una finestra)*
**student** *studente (m) studentessa (f)*
**studio** *studio*
**study** *studiare*
  **study at** / / *studiare a / /*
  **study /Italian/** *studiare /italiano/*
**stuffing** (material) *imbottitura*
**stuffing** (food) *ripieno (n)*

**stupid** *stupido (adj)*
**style** *stile (m)*
**stylus** *stilo*
  **ceramic** (adj) *di ceramica*
  **diamond** (adj) *di diamante*
  **sapphire** *di zaffiro*
**subscribe to** / / *abbonarsi a / /*
**subscription** *abbonamento (rivista, teatro)*
**substance** *sostanza*
**suburb** *periferia*
**subway** *sottopassaggio -ggi*
**suede** *pelle (f) scamosciata*
  **suede /jacket/** */giacca/ di pelle scamosciata*
**suffer** *soffrire*
  **suffer from /headaches/** *soffrire di /mal di testa/*
**sugar** *zucchero*
  **a spoonful of sugar** *un cucchiaio di zucchero*
**sugar lump** *zolletta di zucchero*
**suggest** *suggerire*
**suit** (n) *vestito (da uomo)*
**suit** (vb) *andare bene*
**suitable** *adatto*
**suitcase** *valigia*
**suite** (=hotel suite) *appartamento (albergo)*
**summer** *estate (f)*
  **in summer** *d'estate*
**sun** *sole (m)*
  **in the sun** *al sole*
**sunbathe** *prendere il sole*
**sunburn** *bruciatura*
**sunburnt** *bruciato del sole*
**Sunday** *domenica*
  **on Sunday** *domenica*
  **on Sundays** *di domenica*
**sunglasses** (pl) *occhiali (mpl) da sole*
  **a pair of sunglasses** *un paio di occhiali da sole*
  **polaroid sunglasses** *occhiali polaroid*
**sunny** *soleggiato*
**sunrise** *alba*
**sunset** *tramonto*
**sunshade** *parasole (m)*

**sunstroke** *insolazione (f)*
**suntan** (n) *abbronzatura*
  **suntan oil** *lozione (f) solare*
**suntanned** *abbronzato*
**supermarket** *supermercato*
**supper** *cena*
  **have supper** *cenare*
**supply** (vb) *rifornire*
**supply -ies** (n) *rifornimento*
**suppository -ies** *supposta*
**sure** *sicuro*
  **he's sure** *è sicuro*
**surface** (n) *superficie (f) -ci*
  **surface mail** *posta normale*
**surfboard** *asse (f) per acquaplano*
**surfing** *acquaplano*
  **go surfing** *fare acquaplano*
**surgery -ies** (=place) *ambulatorio -i*
  **doctor's surgery** *ambulatorio medico*
**surname** *cognome (m)*
**surplus -es** *avanzo*
**surprise** (n) *sorpresa*
**surprised** *sorpreso*
  **surprised at /the result/** *sorpreso /del risultato/*
**surveyor** *agrimensore (m)*
**survive** *sopravivere*
**suspect** (vb) *sospettare*
**suspender belt** *reggicalze (m)*
**suspension** (car) *sospensione (f)*
**swallow** (vb) *inghiottire*
**sweat** (n) *sudore (m)*
**sweat** (vb) *sudare*
**sweater** *golf (m)*
  **/cashmere/ sweater** *golf /di cashmere/*
  **long-sleeved sweater** *golf con maniche lunghe*
  **short-sleeved sweater** *golf con maniche corte*
  **sleeveless sweater** *golf senza maniche*
**sweep** (vb) *spazzare*
**sweet** (=not savoury) (adj) *dolce (adj)*
**sweet** (n) (=confectionery) *caramella*
**sweet** (n)(=dessert) *dolce (m)*
**swelling** *gonfiore (m) (=enfiagione)*

**swim** (n) *nuoto (n)(attività)*
  **have a swim** *fare il bagno*
**swim** (vb) *nuotare*
**swimming** *nuoto (n) (sport)*
  **go swimming** *andare a fare il bagno*
  **swimming costume** *costume (m) da bagno*
  **swimming trunks** (pl) *pantaloncini da bagno*
  **swimming cap** *cuffia da bagno*
  **swimming pool** *piscina*
  **heated swimming pool** *piscina riscaldata*
  **indoor swimming pool** *piscina al chiuso*
  **open air swimming pool** *piscina all'aperto*
  **public swimming pool** *piscina pubblica*
**swing** (n) (children's swing) *altalena*
**switch -es** (=light switch) *interruttore (m)*
**switch off** *spegnere*
**switch on** *accendere (lampada, radio)*
**switchboard** (company) *centralino telefonico*
**swollen** *gonfiato*
**symptom** *sintomo*
**synagogue** *sinagoga*
**synthetic** *sintetico*

# T

**table** *tavola*
**table tennis** *ping-pong (m)*
  **a game of table tennis** *una partita a ping-pong*
  **play table tennis** *giocare a ping-pong*
**tablecloth** *tovaglia*
**tablemat** *sottopiatto*
**tablespoonful of / /** *cucchiaio -ai da tavola di / /*
**tailor** *sarto*
**take** *prendere*
  **I'll take it** (in shop) *lo(m)/la(f) prendo*
**take away** (vb) *portare via*
  **take-away meal** *pasto da portar via*

**take off /a coat/** togliere /un cappotto/
**take out** (tooth) levare
**talcum powder** talco
**talk** (n) (discussion, chat) conversazione (f)
**talk** (vb) parlare
  **talk to me about / /** parlarmi di / /
**tall** alto (persona)
**tame** (adj) addomesticato
**tampons** (pl) interni assorbenti (mpl)
  **a box of tampons** (eg Tampax (tdmk)) un pacchetto di interni assorbenti
**tank** serbatoio
  **water tank** serbatoio d'acqua
**tap** rubinetto
  **cold tap** rubinetto di acqua fredda
  **hot tap** rubinetto di acqua calda
**tape** (n) nastro
  **cassette** cassetta
**tape measure** metro a nastro
**tape recorder** registratore (m)
  **cassette recorder** registratore a cassette
  **open reel recorder** registratore a nastri
**tartan** tartan
  **tartan skirt** gonna scozzese
**taste** (n) gusto
**taste** (vb) (=have a certain taste) sapere di
**taste** (vb) (perceive with tongue) assaggiare
**tasty** gustoso
**tax -es** tassa
  **airport tax** tassa dell'aeroporto
  **income tax** imposta sul reddito
**tax free** esente da tasse
**taxi** taxi (m)
  **by taxi** in taxi
  **taxi rank** stazione (f) dei taxis
  **taxi driver** autista (m&f) -i (mpl) -e (fpl) di taxi
**tea** (meal) tè (m)
  **have tea** prendere il tè
**tea** tè (m)

**a cup of tea** una tazza di tè
**a pot of tea** una teiera di tè
**China tea** tè cinese
**Indian tea** tè indiano
**tea towel** asciugapiatti (m) -
**teabag** bustina di tè
**teach** insegnare
  **teach** (me) **/Italian/** insegnar(mi)/ l'italiano/
  **he teaches** (me) **/Italian/** (mi) insegna /l'italiano/
**teacher** insegnante (m&f)
**team** squadra
**teapot** teiera
**tear** (n) (= hole in material) strappo
**tear** (vb) (material) stracciare
**teaspoon** cucchiaino
  **a teaspoonful of / /** un cucchiaino di / /
**teat** tettarella
**teenager** adolescente (m&f)
**teetotal** astemio (m&f)
**telegram** telegramma (m) -mi
  **send a telegram** mandare un telegramma
  **telegram form** modulo per telegramma
**telephone** (vb) telefonare
  **telephone Reception** telefonare all'ufficio recevimento
  **telephone the exchange** telefonare al centralino
  **telephone the operator** telefonare al centralino
  **telephone this number** telefonare a questo numero
**telephone** telefonare
**telephone/phone** (n) telefono
  **telephone directory -ies** elenco telefonico
  **on the phone** al telefono
  **call box -es** cabina telefonica
  **telephone call** telefonata
**television channel** canale (m)
**television programme** programma televisiva
**television/TV** (infml) televisione (f)

**on television/on T.V.** *alla televisione*

**portable television** *televisore portatile (m)*

**television aerial** *antenna della televisione*

**television channel** *canale (m)*

**television programme** *programma televisivo*

**television set** *televisore (m)*

**telex** (vb) *mandare per télex*

**tell me** (something) **about / /** *raccontarmi di / /*

**he told /me/ about it** */me/ ne ha parlato*

**temperature** (atmosphere, body) *temperatura*

**I've got a temperature** *ho la febbre*

**temple** *tempio*

**temporary** *provvisorio -ri*

**tender** (eg of meat) *tenero*

**tennis** *tennis (m)*

**a game of tennis** *una partita a tennis*

**play tennis** *giocare a tennis*

**tent** *tenda (da campeggio)*

**term** (=expression) *termine (m)*

**term** (=period of time) *trimestre (m)*

**terminal** *terminale (m)*

**air terminal** *terminale aereo (m)*

**terminus** *capolinea*

**bus terminus** *capolinea dell'autobus*

**railway terminus** *stazione (f) di testa*

**tram terminus** *capolinea del tram*

**terms** (pl) *condizioni (fpl)* (=trattamento)

**terrace** *terrazzo*

**terrible** *terribile*

**test** (n) *prova (n)* (=esperimento)

**test** (vb) *provare* (=sperimentare)

**textbook** *libro di testo*

**thank you** *grazie*

**no thank you** *no grazie*

**thank you for / /** (vb) *ringraziare di / /*

**thank you for your hospitality** *la ringrazio della sua ospitalità*

**that one** *quello (m) quella (f)*

**the** *il/lo/l' (m) la l' (f) gli (m) le (fpl)*

**theatre** *teatro*

**theatre programme** *programma (m) -mi (a teatro)*

**theft** *furto*

**their** *il loro (m) la loro (f) i loro (mpl) le loro (fpl)*

**their passport** *il loro passaporto (m)*

**their bag** *la loro borsa (f)*

**their tickets** *i loro biglietti (mpl)*

**their keys** *le loro chiavi (fpl)*

**theirs**

**it's theirs** *è loro*

**them**

**for them** *per loro*

**then** *poi*

**there** *là*

**over there** *laggiù*

**there is** (s) **there are** (pl) *c'è (s) ci sono (pl)*

**are there /any restaurants/ near here?** *ci sono /dei ristoranti/ qui vicino?*

**there's /some beer/** *c'è /della birra/*

**there aren't /any hotels/ near here** *non ci sono /alberghi/ qui vicino*

**thermometer** *termometro*

**Centigrade thermometer** *termometro in centigradi*

**Fahrenheit thermometer** *termometro in fahrenheit*

**clinical thermometer** *termometro clinico*

**these** *questi (mpl) queste (fpl)*

**these ones** *questi qui (mpl) queste qui (fpl)*

**they** *loro*

**thick** *spesso (adj)*

**thigh** *coscia -sce*

**thin** (coat etc) *leggero (un cappotto)*

**thin** (of person) *magro*

**thing** *cosa*

**things** (=belongings) *roba*

**think about /something/** *pensare a /qualcosa/*

**thirsty**

**be thirsty** *avere sete*

**I'm thirsty** *ho sete*

**this** *questo (m) questa (f)*
  **this one** *questo qui (m) questa qui (f)*
**those** *quelli (mpl) quelle (fpl)*
  **those ones** *quelli là (m) quelle là (f)*
**thousand** *mille*
  **thousands of /  /** *migliaia di /  /*
**thread** *filo (per cucire)*
  **a reel of thread** *un rocchetto di filo*
**throat** *gola*
  **sore throat** *mal (m) di gola*
  **throat pastille** *pastiglia per la gola*
**through** *(prep)*
  **through /the streets/** *per /le strade/*
  **through /the countryside** *attraverso
  /la campagna/*
**thumb** *pollice (m) (dito)*
**thunderstorm** *temporale (m)*
**Thursday** *giovedì (m)*
  **on Thursday** *giovedì*
  **on Thursdays** *di giovedì*
**ticket** *biglietto*
  **child's ticket** *biglietto ridotto per
  bambini*
  **first class ticket** *biglietto di prima
  classe*
  **group ticket** *biglietto collettivo*
  **return ticket** *biglietto di andata e
  ritorno*
  **season ticket** *abbonamento*
  **second class ticket** *biglietto di
  seconda classe*
  **single** *biglietto di sola andata*
**ticket office** *biglietteria*
**tide** *marea*
  **high tide** *alta marea*
  **low tide** *bassa marea*
**tidy** *(adj) ordinato*
**tidy** *(vb) mettere in ordine*
**tie** *(n) cravatta*
**tie** *(vb) legare*
**tiepin** *ferma cravatta*
**tight** *stretto (attillato)*
**tights** *(pl) collant (m)*
  **a pair of tights** *un collant*
**till** *(=until) fino a*
**time** *tempo (misura)*
  **the time** *(clock) l'ora*

**/six/ times** */sei/ volte*
**have a good time** *divertirsi*
**in time** *in tempo*
**on time** *in orario*
**what time is it?** *che ora è?*
**timetable** *orario (ferroviario, scolastico)*
  **bus timetable** *orario dell'autobus*
  **coach timetable** *orario dei pullman*
  **train timetable** *orario dei treni*
**tin** *barattolo*
  **a tin of /  /** *un barattolo di /  /*
**tin opener** *apriscatole (m) -*
**tint** *(n) (=hair t.) tintura*
**tint** *(vb) tingere*
**tip** *(n) (money) mancia -ce*
**tip** *(vb) (money) dare la mancia*
  **tip /the waiter/** *dare la mancia /al
  cameriere/*
**tired** *stanco (m) -chi (mpl) stanca (f)
  -che (fpl)*
**tiring** *faticoso*
**tissues** *(pl) /Kleenex (tdmk) fazzoletti
  di carta*
  **a box of tissues** *una scatola di
  fazzoletti di carta*
**title** *titolo*
**to** *(direction) a*
  **to the /station/** *alla /stazione/*
**toast** *(vb) tostare*
**toast** *(n) tost (m)*
  **a slice of toast** *una fetta di tost*
**tobacco** *tabacco*
**tobacconist's** *tabacchi*
**today** *oggi*
**toe** *dito del piede*
**toenail** *unghia del dito del piede*
**together** *insieme*
**toilet** *toilette (f)*
**toilet paper** *carta igienica*
  **a roll of toilet paper** *un rotolo di carta
  igienica*
**toilet water** *acqua di colonia*
**tomato** *-es pomodoro*
  **tomato sauce** *salsa di pomodoro*
**tomato juice** *succo -chi di pomodoro*
  **a bottle of tomato juice** *una bottiglia
  di succo di pomodoro*

a **can of tomato juice** *un barattolo di succo di pomodoro*
a **glass of tomato juice** *un bicchiere di succo di pomodoro*
**tomorrow** *domani*
**ton** *tonnellata*
**tongue** *lingua (parte del corpo)*
**tonic** (water) *tonico -ci*
**tonight** *stanotte*
**tonsillitis** *tonsillite (f)*
**too** (=more than can be endured) *troppo*
 **too /big/** *troppo /grande/*
 **too many** *troppi (mpl) troppe (fpl)*
 **too much** *troppo (m) troppa (f)*
**tool** *arnese (m)*
**tooth/teeth** (pl) *dente (m)*
 **wisdom tooth** *dente del giudizio*
**toothache** (s) *mal di denti*
**toothbrush -es** *spazzolino da denti*
**toothpaste** *dentifricio*
 a **tube of toothpaste** *un tubo di dentifricio*
**toothpick** *stuzzicadenti (m) -*
**top** *parte (f) superiore*
 **the top of / /** *la parte superiore di / /*
**torch -es** *pila (=torcia elettrica)*
**tortoiseshell** (adj) *di tartaruga*
**total** (adj) *totale (pl)*
**total** (n) *totale (m) (n)*
**touch** (vb) *toccare*
**tough** (meat etc) *duro*
**tour** *visita*
 **conducted tour** *visita guidata*
**tourist** *turista (m&f) -i (mpl) -e (fpl)*
 **tourist class** *classe (f) turistica*
 **tourist office** *ufficio turistico*
**tow** (vb) *trainare*
**tow rope** *corda da traino*
**towel** (=bath towel) *asciugamano*
**towelling** (material) *tela per asciugamani*
**tower** *torre (f)*
**town** *città -*
 **town centre** *centrocittà*
 **town hall** *municipio*

**town hall** *municipio*
**toxic** *tossico*
**toy** *giocattolo*
 **toy shop** *negozio -zi di giocattoli*
**track** (of animal) *traccia -ce*
**track** (of tape) *pista*
**track** (=race track) *pista*
**traditional** *tradizionale*
**traffic** *traffico*
 **traffic jam** *ingorgo stradale*
 **traffic lights** (pl) *semaforo (ms)*
**trailer** *rimorchio -chi*
**train** *treno*
 **boat train** *treno per nave*
 **express train** *rapido*
 **fast train** *espresso*
 **slow train** *accelerato*
**train driver** *macchinista (m) -i*
**training** (of personnel) *addestramento*
**tram** *tram (m)*
 **by tram** *in tram*
 **the tram for / /** *il tram per / /*
 **tram stop** *fermata del tram*
 **tram terminus** *capolinea del tram*
**tranquilliser** *tranquillante (m)*
**transfer** (vb) *trasferire*
**transformer** *trasformatore (m)*
**transistor** (transistor radio) *transistor (m)*
**transit passenger** *viaggiatore (m&f) in transito*
 **in transit** *in transito*
**translate** *tradurre*
**translation** *traduzione (f)*
**transmission** (car) *trasmissione (f)*
**transparent** *trasparente*
**transport** (n) *trasporto*
 **public transport** *trasporto pubblico*
**trap** (n) *trappola*
**trap** (vb) *prendere in trappola*
**travel** (vb) *viaggiare*
 **by air** *in aereo*
 **by boat, by bus** *in barca, in autobus*
 **by coach, by car** *in pullman, in macchina*
 **by hovercraft** *in hovercraft*
 **by sea** *per mare*

**by train, by tram, by underground** *in treno, in tram, in metropolitana*
**on foot** *a piedi*
**on the ferry** *in traghetto*
**overland** *per terra*
**to** / **/ a /** /
**travel agent's** *agenzia di viaggio*
**traveller's cheque** *traveller's cheque (m)*
**tray** *vassoio*
**treat** (medically) *curare*
**treatment** *cura*
**tree** *albero* (botanica)
**triangular** *triangolare*
**trim** (vb) *tagliare (i capelli)*
**trim** (n)(haircut) *taglio di capelli*
**trip** (n) *gita*
  **coach trip** *gita in pullman*
  **have a good trip!** *buon viaggio!*
**tripod** *treppiede (m)*
**trolley** (=luggage t.) *carrello*
**tropical** *tropicale*
**trot** (vb) *trottare*
**trouble** *guai (mpl)*
  **I'm in trouble** *sono nei guai*
**trousers** (pl) *pantaloni (mpl)*
  **a pair of trousers** *un paio di pantaloni*
**trout/trout** (pl) *trota*
**true** *vero* (=non falso)
**trunk** (of tree) *tronco -chi*
**trunk** (for luggage) *baule (m)*
**trust** (vb) *fidarsi*
  **I trust /her/** *mi fido /di lei/*
**truth** *verità -*
  **tell the truth** *dire la verità*
**try** (vb) *provare* (=fare un tentativo)
  **try on /this sweater/** *provare /questo golf/*
  **try /this ice-cream/** *provare /questo gelato/*
**T-shirt** *maglietta*
**tube** *tubo*
  **a tube of** / **/ un tubo di /** /
**tube** (for a tyre) *camera d'aria*
**tubeless** (tyre) *gomma tubeless*
**Tuesday** *martedì (m)*
  **on Tuesday** *martedì*

**on Tuesdays** *di martedì*
**tulip** *tulipano (m)*
  **a bunch of tulips** *un mazzo di tulipani*
**tunnel** *galleria* (=traforo)
**turkey** *tacchino*
**turn off** (switch) *spegnere*
**turn on** (switch) *accendere*
**turnip** *rapa*
**turntable** (on record player) *piatto (di giradischi)*
**turpentine** *trementina*
**tweed** *tweed (m)*
**tweezers** (pl) *pinzette (fpl)*
  **a pair of tweezers** *un paio di pinzette*
**twice** *due volte*
**twin** *gemello*
  **twin beds** *letti gemelli*
**type** (vb) *battere a macchina*
**typewriter** *macchina da scrivere*
**typhoid** *tifoide (m)*
**typical** *tipico*
**typist** *dattilografa*
**tyre** *gomma (d'automobile)*
  **flat tyre** *gomma sgonfia*
  **tyre pressure** *pressione (f) delle gomme*

# U

**ugly** *brutto* (=non bello)
**ulcer** *ulcera*
**umbrella** *ombrello*
  **beach umbrella** *ombrellone (m)*
**umpire** *arbitro*
**UN** *ONU*
**uncle** *zio*
**uncomfortable** *scomodo*
**unconscious** *privo di sensi*
**under** *sotto* (prep)
**undercooked** *non cotto abbastanza*
**underground** (u. railway train) *metropolitana*
  **by underground** *in metropolitana*
**underpants** (pl) (for men) *mutande (fpl)*
  **a pair of underpants** *un paio di mutande*
**understand** *capire*

**I don't understand** *non capisco*
**underwear** *biancheria intima*
  **children's underwear** *biancheria intima per bambini*
  **men's underwear** *biancheria intima per uomini*
  **women's underwear** *biancheria intima per donne*
**unemployed** (adj) *disoccupato*
**unemployment** *disoccupazione (f)*
**unfashionable** *fuori moda*
**unfortunately** *sfortunatamente*
**unfriendly** *freddo (nel modo di fare)*
**uniform** (n) *divisa*
  **in uniform** *in divisa*
**unique** *unico*
**university -ies** *università -*
**unlocked** *non serrato*
**unlucky**
  **be unlucky** *essere sfortunato*
  **he's unlucky** *è sfortunato*
**unpack** *disfare le valigie*
**unpleasant** *sgradevole*
**unripe** *acerbo*
**untie** *slegare*
**until** *fino a*
  **until /Friday/** *fino a /venerdì/*
**unusual** *insolito*
**up** *su*
  **are you going up?** *va in su?*
  **be up** (=out of bed) *essere alzato*
  **get up** *alzarsi*
**upset** (adj) *disturbato*
**upset** (n)
  **I've got a stomach upset** *ho un disturbo di stomaco*
**upside-down** *rovesciato (alla rovescia)*
**upstairs** *di sopra*
**urgent** *urgente*
**urinate** *orinare*
**urine** *orina*
**us** *noi (complemento oggetto)*
  **for us** *per noi*
**use** (vb) *usare*
  **use /your phone/** *usare /il suo telefono/*

**useful** *utile*
**usually** *di solito*
**utensil** *utensile (m)*

# V

**V -necked sweater** *golf (m) con collo a V*
**vacancy -ies** (job) *posto vacante*
**vacancy -ies** (room) *camera libera*
**vacant** *libero* (=non occupato)
**vaccinate** *vaccinare*
**vaccination** *vaccinazione (f)*
**vaccine** *vaccino*
**vacuum cleaner** *aspirapolvere (m)*
**vacuum flask** *termos (m)*
**valid** *valido*
  **valid /passport/** */passaporto/ valido*
**valley -ies** *valle (f)*
**valuable** *prezioso*
**valuables** (pl) *oggetti preziosi (mpl)*
**value** (n) *valore (m)*
**value** (vb) *valutare*
**van** *furgone (m)*
  **luggage van** *bagagliaio*
**vanilla** *vaniglia*
**variety -ies** *varietà -*
**various** *vario -ri*
**varnish** (vb) (eg boat) *verniciare*
**varnish -es** (n) *vernice (f) (trasparente)*
  **nail varnish** *smalto per le unghie*
**vase** (=flower v.) *vaso (da fiori)*
**vaseline** *vasellina*
  **a tube of vaseline** *un tubo di vasellina*
**VAT** *I.V.A. (f)*
**veal** *vitello*
**vegetables** (pl) *verdura (fs)*
  **fresh vegetables** *verdura fresca*
  **mixed vegetables** *verdura mista*
**vegetarian** *vegetariano*
**vehicle** *veicolo*
**vein** *vena*
**velvet** *velluto (liscio)*
**venereal disease** (VD) *malattia venerea*
**venison** *selvaggina*
**ventilator** *ventilatore (m)*

**watch**

**very** molto
**vest** maglia (indumento)
  **cotton vest** maglia di cotone
  **woollen vest** maglia di lana
**VHF** alta frequenza
**via** via (attraverso)
  **travel via /Rome/** viaggiare via
  /Roma/
**vicar** parroco -ci
**view** (n) panorama (m) -mi
**viewfinder** mirino
**villa** (=holiday villa) villa
**village** paese (m) (=villagio)
**vinegar** aceto
  **a bottle of vinegar** una bottiglia di
  aceto
  **oil and vinegar** olio e aceto
**vineyard** vigneto
**violin** violino
**visa** visto
**visibility** visibilità
**visit /a museum/** visitare /un museo/
**visitor** visitatore (m) visitatrice (f)
**vitamin pills** (pl) pillole (fpl) di vitamina
  **a bottle of vitamin pills** una bottiglia
  di pillole di vitamina
**vodka** vodka
  **a bottle of vodka** una bottiglia di
  vodka
  **a vodka** una vodka
**voice** voce (f)
**volt** volt (m)
  **/ a hundred and ten/ volts** /cento
  dieci/ volt
**voltage** voltaggio
  **high voltage** voltaggio alto
  **low voltage** voltaggio basso
**volume** volume (m)
**vomit** (vb) vomitare
**voucher** buono (n)
  **hotel voucher** buono di albergo
**voyage** (n) viaggio -ggi (per mare)

# W

**waist** vita (anatomia)
**waistcoat** panciotto

**wait /for me/** aspettar/mi/
  **please wait /for me/** per favore /mi/
  aspetti
**waiter** cameriere (m)
**waiting room** sala d'aspetto
**waitress -es** cameriera (al ristorante)
**wake /me/ up** svegliar/mi/
**walk** (n) passeggiata
  **go for a walk** fare una passeggiata
**walk** (vb) camminare
**walk across/the street/** attraversare/la
  strada/
**walking** passeggiare
  **do some walking** fare una
  passeggiare
**walking stick** bastone (m) da passeggio
**wall** (=inside w.) parete (f)
**wall** (=outside w.) muro
**wallet** portafoglio (m) -
**walnut** (nut) noce (f)
**walnut** (wood) noce (m) (legno)
**want** volere
  **want /a room/** volere /una camera/
  **want to /buy/ it** volere /comprar/lo

**war** guerra
**ward** (in hospital) corsia (ospedaliera)
**wardrobe** guardaroba (armadio per
  abiti)
**warm** (adj) caldo (adj)(piacevole)
**warm** (vb) riscaldare
**warn** avvertire
**warning** avvertimento
**wash** (vb) lavare
**wash -es** (n) lavata
  **have a wash** lavarsi
**wash up** lavare i piatti
**washbasin** lavandino
**washing machine** lavatrice (f)
**washing powder** detersivo
**wasp** vespa
  **wasp sting** puntura di vespa
**waste** (vb) sprecare
**wastepaper basket** cestino per la carta
  straccia
**watch** (vb) guardare
**watch -es** (n) orologio -gi (da pulso)

**face** (of w.) *quadrante (m)*
  **hand** (of w.) *lancetta*
  **watch strap** *cinturino d'orologio*
**watch /T.V./** *guardare /la televisione/*
**watchmaker's** *orologiaio*
**water** *acqua*
  **cold water** *acqua fredda*
  **distilled water** *acqua distillata*
  **drinking water** *acqua potabile*
  **hot water** *acqua calda*
  **running water** *acqua corrente*
**water skiing** *sci acquatico*
  **go water skiing** *fare lo sci acquatico*
**watercolour** (=painting) *acquarello*
**waterproof** (adj) *impermeabile (adj)*
**watt** *watt (m)*
  **/a hundred/ watts** */cento/ watt*
**wave** (radio) *onda*
  **long wave** *onda lunga*
  **medium wave** *onda media*
  **short wave** *onda corta*
  **VHF** *alta frequenza*
**wave** (sea) *onda*
**wax** *cera*
**way** (n) (to a place) *strada*
  **that way** *da quella parte*
  **this way** *da questa parte*
  **which way?** *da quale parte?*
**we** *noi (soggetto)*
**weak** (physically) *debole*
**wear** (vb) (clothes) *indossare*
**weather** *tempo (clima)*
  **weather conditions** (pl) *condizioni
  (fpl) atmosferiche*
  **weather forecast** (s) *previsioni (fpl)
  del tempo*
  **what's the weather like?** *che tempo
  fa?*
**wedding** *matrimonio*
**Wednesday** *mercoledì*
  **on Wednesday** *mercoledì*
  **on Wednesdays** *di mercoledì*
**week** *settimana*
  **this week** *questa settimana*
  **last week** *la settimana scorsa*
  **next week** *la settimana prossima*
**weekend** *fine (f) settimana*

**weekly** (adj) *settimanale*
  **twice weekly** *due volte alla settimana*
**weigh** *pesare*
**weight** *peso*
  **weight limit** *limite (m) di peso*
**welcome** (n) *benvenuto*
**welcome** (vb) *dare il benvenuto*
  **welcome to /  /** *benvenuto a /  /*
  **you're welcome** (in reply to 'thank
  you') *prego*
**well** (=all right) *bene*
  **well done!** (congratulation) *bravo!*
  **well-done** (eg of steak) *cotto bene*
**well** (n) *pozzo*
**Wellingtons** (pl) *stivali (mpl) di gomma*
**west** *ovest (m)*
**Western** (=film) *western (m)*
**wet** *bagnato*
  **I'm wet** *sono bagnato*
  **it's wet** (weather) *c'è tempo piovoso*
  **/this towel/ is wet**
  */quest'asciugamano/ è bagnato*
**what?** *cosa?*
  **at what time?** *a che ora?*
  **what about /Mary/?** *e /Mary/?*
  **what's /your address/?** *qual è /il
  suo indirizzo/?*
**wheel** *ruota*
**wheelchair** *sedia a rotelle*
**when?** *quando?*
  **when do /the shops/ open?** *quando
  si aprono /i negozi/?*
**where?** *dove?*
  **where are you from?** *da dove viene?*
**which?** (adj) *quale?*
  **which /plane/?** *quale /aeroplano/?*
  **which one?/which ones?** *quale?
  (m&f) quali? (pl) (pron)*
**whisky -ies** *whisky (m)*
  **a bottle of whisky** *una bottiglia di
  whisky*
  **a whisky** *un whisky*
**whistle** (n) *fischio -chi (pl)*
**white** *bianco (m) -chi (mpl) bianca (f)
  -che (fpl)*
  **white coffee** *cappuccino*
**who?** *chi?*

**whole** *intero*
  **a whole /month/** *un /mese/ intero*
  **the whole /month/** *tutto /il mese/*
**whose?** *di chi?*
  **whose is it?** *di chi è?*
**why?** *perchè?*
**wick** (lamp, lighter) *lucignolo*
**wide** *largo (dimensione)*
**widow** *vedova*
**widower** *vedovo*
**width** *larghezza*
**wife/wives** (pl) *moglie -gli*
**wig** *parrucca*
**wild** (=not tame) *selvatico*
  **wild animal** *animale (m) selvatico*
**win** (vb) *vincere*
**wind** (n) *vento*
**wind** (vb) (clock) *caricare (un orologio)*
**window** *finestra*
  **French window** *porta-finestra*
  **shop window** *vetrina*
**window** (car) *finestrino*
**windy** *ventoso*
  **it's windy** *è ventoso*
**wine** *vino*
  **a bottle of wine** *una bottiglia di vino*
  **a carafe of wine** *una caraffa di vino*
  **a glass of wine** *un bicchiere di vino*
  **a half bottle of wine** *una mezza bottiglia di vino*
  **dry wine** *vino secco*
  **red wine** *vino rosso*
  **rosé** *vino rosé*
  **sparkling wine** *vino frizzante*
  **sweet wine** *vino dolce*
  **white wine** *vino bianco*
**wine glass -es** *bicchiere (m) da vino*
**wine list** *lista dei vini*
**wine merchant's** *negozio -zi di vini*
  **a piece of wire** *un pezzo di filo*
**with** *con*

**without** *senza*
**witness -es** (n) *testimonio -ni*
**woman/women** (pl) *donna*
**wonderful** *meraviglioso*
**wood** (group of trees) *bosco*
**wood** (substance) *legno*
**wooden** *di legno*
**wool** *lana*
**woollen** *di lana*
**word** *parola*
**work** (n) *lavoro*
  **do some work** *fare un po' di lavoro*
**work** (vb) (of machines) *funzionare*
  **it doesn't work** *non funziona*
**work** (vb) (of people) *lavorare*
**world** (the world) *mondo*
**worn-out** *consunto*
**worried** *preoccupato*
**worse** (in health) *peggio*
  **he's worse** *sta peggio*
**worse** (things) *peggio*
  **worse than / /** *peggio di / /*
  **it's worse** *è peggio*
**worst** *il peggiore*
  **the worst /hotel/** */l'albergo/ peggiore*
  **the worst /room/** */la camera/ peggiore*
**worth**
  **be worth** *valere*
  **it's worth /a million/ lire** *vale /un milione/ di lire*
**would like**
  **I'd like to /go swimming/** *mi piacerebbe /andare a nuotare/*
  **would you like /a drink/?** *vorrebbe /una bibita/?*
**wound** (=injury) *ferita*
**wrap** (vb) *incartare*
  **gift-wrap** (vb) *confezionare per regalo*
**wreath -es** (funeral w.) *corona (a un funerale)*
**wreck** (n) *naufragio -gi*
**wrist** *polso*
**write** *scrivere*
**writing paper** *carta da scrivere*
**wrong** *sbagliato*

**be wrong** *avere torto*
**I'm wrong** *ho torto*
**wrong number** *numero sbagliato*

# X

**x-ray** *raggio x*

# Y

**yacht** *panfilo*
**year** *anno*
  **last year** *l'anno scorso*
  **next year** *l'anno prossimo*
  **this year** *quest'anno*
**yearly** *annuale*
**yellow** *giallo*
**yes** *sì*
**yesterday** *ieri*
**yet**
  **not yet** *non ancora*
**yoghurt** *yogurt (m)*
  **a carton of yoghurt** *un vasetto di yogurt*
  **plain yoghurt** *yogurt semplice*
  **fruit yoghurt** *yogurt alla frutta*

**you** *lei (s) loro (pl) (forma de cortesia)*
  **for you** *per lei (s) per loro (pl)*
**young** *giovane*
**young man/young men** (pl) *giovanotto*
**young woman/young women** *giovane donna*
**your** (polite form) *il suo (m) la sua (f) i suoi (mpl) le sue (fpl)*
  **your passport** *il suo passaporto (m)*
  **your bag** *la sua borsa (f)*
  **your tickets** *i suoi biglietti (mpl)*
  **your keys** *le sue chiavi (fpl)*
**yours**
  **it's yours** *è suo (m) è sua (f)*
**youth hostel** *ostello per la gioventù*

# Z

**zero** (nought degrees) *zero*
  **above zero** *sopra zero*
  **below zero** *sotto zero*
**zero** (=nought) *zero*
**zip** (n) *chiusura lampo (f) chiusure lampo (pl)*
**zoo** *zoo (m)*
**zoom lens -es** *lente (f) zoom*

# English foods     Cibo inglese

## Cooking methods          Tipi di cotture

| | |
|---|---|
| baked | (cotto) al forno |
| boiled | lessato |
| braised | brasato |
| creamed | carne o verdura preparate con la panna |
| devilled | cotto alla graticola con spezie |
| dressed | condito |
| fresh | fresco |
| fried | fritto |
| grilled | alla griglia |
| in batter | in pastella |
| in vinegar | con aceto |
| jugged | in salmì |
| mashed | passato o purè |

| | |
|---|---|
| medium | abbastanza cotto |
| meunière | alla mugnaia |
| overcooked | troppo cotto |
| pickled | sottaceto |
| poached | cotto in acqua bollente |
| rare | poco cotto |
| raw | crudo |
| roast | arrosto |
| scrambled | strapazzato |
| smoked | affumicato |
| steamed | cotto al vapore |
| stewed | stufato |
| stuffed | farcito |
| toasted | tostato |
| undercooked | poco cotto |
| well done | ben cotto |

## Food and drink

## Cibi e bevande

Ricordate:
> Vorrei /   /, per favore
> *I'd like /   / please*
> Ha /   /, per favore
> *Have you got /   / please*

| | |
|---|---|
| à la carte | alla carta |
| ale | birra |
|   brown ale |   b. scura |
|   light ale |   b. leggera |
|   pale ale |   b. chiara |
| almonds | mandorle |
| anchovies | acciughe |
| apple | mela |
|   apple crumble |   mele cotte, ricoperte |
| |     di uno strato di briciole |
| |     di burro, farina e |
| |     zucchero e quindi |
| |     passate al forno |

| | |
|---|---|
| apple pie | mele cotte chiuse in pasta frolla e quindi passate al forno |
| apple tart | pasticcio di mele/torta di mele |
| apricot | albicocca |
| artichoke | carciofo |
| asparagus | asparagi |
|   asparagus tips |   punte di a. |
| assortment | assortimento |
| avocado pear | pera avocado |
| | |
| bacon | pancetta |
|   a rasher of bacon |   una fetta di p. |
| baked Alaska | Alasca stufati |
| baked beans | fagiolini stufati |
| banana | banana |
|   banana split |   b. con gelato e panna |
| beans | fagioli |
|   broad beans |   fave |
|   French beans |   fagiolini |
|   haricot beans |   fagioli di Spagna |
|   kidney beans |   borlotti |
|   runner beans |   fagiolini |
| beef | manzo |
| beefburger | polpetta di manzo fritta con cipolla |
| beer | birra |
|   bitter |   b. piuttosto amara |
|   draught beer |   b. alla spina |
| beverages | bevande |
| biscuits | biscotti |
|   biscuits and cheese |   crackers con formaggi assortiti |
| bitter | amara |
| bitter lemon | limone amaro |

| | |
|---|---|
| blue cheese | formaggio simile al gorgonzola |
| brandy | cognac |
| bread | pane |
| breakfast | prima colazione |
| broad beans | fave |
| broccoli | broccoli |
| broth | brodo |
| brown ale | birra scura |
| brussels sprouts | cavolini di bruxelles |
| bun | focaccina |
| butter | burro |
| butterscotch | croccante |
| | |
| cabbage | cavolo |
|   red cabbage |   c. rosso |
| cake | torta |
|   fruit cake |   t. di frutta |
|   sponge cake |   pan di spagna |
| carrots | carote |
| cauliflower | cavolfiore |
| celery | sedano |
| cereal | cereali per la prima colazione |
| Chateaubriand steak | filetto alla chateaubriand (Vedi p106) |
| | |
| cheese | formaggio |
|   blue c. |   f. tipo gorgonzola |
|   Caerphilly |   f. gallese, bianco e cremoso |
|   Cheddar |   f. dolce |
|   Cheshire |   f. della contea di Cheshire |
|   cottage c. |   ricotta |
|   cream c. |   mascarpone |
|   Stilton |   f. piccante e molto pregiato |
|   Wensleydale |   f. bianco e delicato |

| | |
|---|---|
| cheeseboard | piatto di formaggi a scelta |
| cheesecake | torta di formaggio e pasta frolla |
| cherry | ciliegia |
| chestnut | castagna |
| chicken | pollo |
|   chicken soup | brodo di p. |
| chilli con carne | peperoncini con carne e fagioli |
| China tea | tè cinese |
| chips | patatine fritte |
| chives | erbe cipolline |
| chocolate | cioccolato |
|   milk chocolate | c. al latte |
|   plain chocolate | c. amaro |
| chop | braciola |
|   lamb chop | b. di agnello |
|   pork chop | b. di maiale |
| chowder | zuppa di crostacei, verdura e latte |
| Christmas cake | torta di Natale, fatta di frutta secca ricoperta di marzipane e poi glassata |
| Christmas pudding | budino di Natale con molta frutta secca |
| cider | sidro |
| clam | vongola |
| clotted cream | panna molto densa di solito prodotta in Cornovaglia |
| coconut | noce di cocco |
| cod | merluzzo |
| coffee | caffè |
| coleslaw | cavolo tritato finemente con condimento da insalata |

| | |
|---|---|
| consommé | brodo ristretto |
| coq-au-vin | pollo al vino |
| coquilles St. Jacques | antipasto di pesce e formaggio servito in una conchiglia di capa santa |
| cordial | succo di frutta concentrato, con acqua |
| corn on the cob | pannocchia |
| cottage pie | carne tritata ricoperta di purè di patate e cotta al forno |
| coupe | dolce fatto con gelato |
| courgettes | zucchini |
| course | portata |
| three-course meal | pasto a tre portate |
| cover charge | coperto (al ristorante) |
| crab | granchio |
| cray fish | gambero o aragosta |
| cream | panna |
| clotted | molto densa |
| double | doppia |
| fresh | fresca |
| single | normale |
| whipped | montata |
| cream cheese | mascarpone |
| crisps | patatine |
| crumble | crostata fatta di burro, farina e zucchero sopra frutta cotta e quindi passata al forno |
| cucumber | cetriolo |
| currant bread | pane all'uvetta |
| currant bun | focaccina all'uvetta |
| custard | crema |
| cutlet | costoletta |
| lamb cutlet | c. di agnello |
| damson | susina |

| | |
|---|---|
| date | dattero |
| dessert | frutta, dolce (a fine pasto) |
| dinner | cena |
| doughnut | frittella |
| dressing | condimento (per insalata) |
| duck | anitra |
| eclair | bigné |
| eel | anguilla |
|   jellied eel | a. in gelatina |
| egg | uovo |
|   egg mayonnaise | uovo sodo ricoperto di maionese |
| escalope | scaloppina |
|   veal escalope | s. di vitello |
| escargot | lumaca |
| fillet | filetto |
|   cod fillet | f. di merluzzo |
|   fillet of plaice | f. di passerino |
|   fillet steak | bistecca di f. |
| filling | ripieno |
| fish | pesce |
| fish cake | polpetta di pesce |
| flan | torta con frutta o formaggio |
| fool | frullato di frutta alla panna |
| frankfurter | salsiccia (viennese o) di francoforte |
| French beans | fagiolini |
| French dressing | condimento per l'insalata |
| fricassée | fricassea |
| fritter | frittella |
|   apple fritter | frittella di mela |
| fruit | frutta |
|   fruit cake | torta di f. |
|   fruit cocktail | macedonia di f. |
|   fruit salad | macedonia di f. fresca |

| | |
|---|---|
| fudge | dolce caramellato |
| Gaelic coffee | caffè con whisky e panna |
| game | selvaggina |
| gammon | prosciutto affumicato |
| garlic | aglio |
| garnished with | guarnito di |
| gâteau | torta |
| ginger | zenzero |
| goose | oca |
| gooseberry | uva spina |
| grape | uva |
| grapefruit | pompelmo |
|   grapefruit juice |   succo di p. |
|   grapefruit segments |   spicchi di p. |
| gravy | sugo |
| green pepper | peperone verde |
| green salad | insalata verde |
| ground | macinato |
| Guinness | una birra scura |
| haddock | tipo di merluzzo |
| hake | nasello |
| halibut | passera di mare |
| ham | prosciutto |
| hamburger | polpetta di carne di manzo |
| hare | lepre |
| haricot beans | fagioli di Spagna |
| heart | cuore |
| herbs | erbe |
| herring | arringa |
| honey | miele |
| hors d'œuvres | antipasto |
| horseradish sauce | cren |
| hot dog | tramezzino con salsiccia |
| hotpot | spezzatino di castrato, patate e cipolle |

| | |
|---|---|
| ice | ghiaccio |
| ice cream | gelato |
|   i.c. sundae |     g. con frutta, succo |
| |       dolce e noci |
| icing | glassa |
| Indian tea | tè indiano |
| Irish coffee | caffè con whisky e panna |
| Irish stew | spezzatino di carne e patate |
| jacket potatoes | patate cotte con la buccia |
| jam | marmellata |
| jam tart | torta con la marmellata |
| jellied eel | anguilla in gelatina |
| jelly | gelatina |
| juice | succo |
|   grapefruit j. |   s. di pompelmo |
|   orange j. |   s. di arancia |
|   tomato j. |   s. di pomodoro |
| kedgeree | riso e pesce mescolati con uova |
| |   sode e panna |
| ketchup | salsa di pomodoro (Rubra) |
| kidney | rognone |
| king prawn | gambero grosso |
| kipper | arringa affumicata |
| kirsch | grappa di ciliege |
| knickerbocker glory | gelato con succo dolce e noci |
| lager | birra |
| lamb | agnello |
|   l. chop |   braciola di a. |
|   l. cutlet |   costoletta di a. |
|   leg of l. |   coscia di a. |
| Lancashire hotpot | spezzatino di montone con |
| |   patate e cipolle |
| leek | porro |
| lemon | limone |

| | |
|---|---|
| lemon juice | succo di l. |
| lemon meringue pie | pasticcio di meringhe al limone |
| lemon sole | sogliola al limone |
| lentil soup | minestra di lenticchie |
| lettuce | lattuga |
| light ale | birra chiara |
| lime juice | succo di cedro |
| liqueur | liquore |
| liver | fegato |
| liver sausage | salsiccia di f. |
| lobster | aragosta |
| loin | lombata |
| loin of lamb | l. di agnello |
| loin of pork | l. di maiale |
| lunch | pranzo |
| macaroni | maccheroni |
| macaroni cheese | m. con formaggio |
| mackerel | sgombri |
| marmalade | marmellata di arancia |
| marrow | zucca |
| mayonnaise | maionese |
| meal | pasto |
| meat | carne |
| meatball | polpetta |
| melon | melone |
| menu | menu |
| meringue | meringa |
| milk | latte |
| milk shake | l. frappè |
| mince | tritato |
| mincemeat | miscuglio di frutta secca |
| mince pies | pasticcini con frutta secca |
| mint | menta |
| mint jelly | gelatina di m. |

| | |
|---|---|
| mint sauce | salsa di m. che si mangia con agnello arrosto |
| minute steak | fettina di carne |
| mixed grill | grigliata mista |
| mixed salad | insalata mista |
| mock turtle soup | zuppa di tartaruga |
| moussaka | piatto greco di carne tritata melanzane e formaggio |
| mousse | budino di panna e uova |
| muesli | miscuglio di noci e frutta secca, mangiato a colazione con latte freddo |
| muffin | tartina da tè |
| mullet | triglia |
| mushroom | fungo |
| mussel | cozza |
| mustard | senape |
| English m. | s. inglese (piccante) |
| French m. | s. francese (più dolce, con aceto) |
| mutton | montone |
| new potatoes | patate novelle |
| nut | noce |
| oatmeal | farina d'avena |
| oil | olio |
| corn oil | o. di granoturco |
| olive oil | o. d'oliva |
| okra | abelmosco |
| olive | oliva |
| omelette | frittata |
| onion | cipolla |
| orange | arancia |
| orange juice | succo di a. |
| orange squash | spremuta di a. |
| oyster | ostrica |

| | |
|---|---|
| pale ale | birra chiara |
| pancake | frittatina |
| paprika | paprica |
| parsley | prezzemolo |
| parsnip | pastinaca |
| pastries | pasticcini |
| pastry | pasticceria |
| flaky p. } puff p. } | pasta sfoglia |
| shortcrust p. | pasta frolla |
| pâté | paté |
| peas | piselli |
| peach | pesca |
| p. melba | p. con gelato, panna e marmellata |
| pear | pera |
| pepper | pepe |
| green pepper | peperone verde |
| ground pepper | pepe macinato |
| red pepper | peperone rosso |
| peppermint | menta peperita |
| pheasant | fagiano |
| pickles | sottaceti |
| pie | pasticcio |
| pilchard | sarda |
| pineapple | ananas |
| plaice | passerino |
| plum | prugna |
| pomegranate | melagrana |
| popcorn | granoturco soffiato |
| pork | maiale |
| fillet of p. | filetto di m. |
| loin of p. | lombata di m. |
| p. chop | braciola di m. |
| porridge | pappa d'avena |
| potato | patata |

| | |
|---|---|
| croquette potatoes | crocchette di p. |
| jacket potatoes | p. cotta con la buccia |
| mashed potatoes | purè |
| new potatoes | p. novelle |
| p. salad | insalata di p. |
| potted shrimps | gamberetti conservati |
| poultry | pollame |
| prawn | gambero |
| king p. | g. grosso |
| p. cocktail | cocktail di g. |
| profiteroles | bigné |
| prune | prugna secca |
| pudding | budino |
| puff pastry | pasta sfoglia |
| purée | purea |
| | |
| rabbit | coniglio |
| radish | ravanello |
| ragoût | ragù |
| r. of lamb | r. di agnello |
| raspberry | lampone |
| red cabbage | cavolo rosso |
| redcurrant | ribes |
| rhubarb | rabarbaro |
| rib | costola |
| r. of beef | c. di manzo |
| rice | riso |
| brown r. | r. integrale |
| r. pudding | budino di r. |
| roll | panino |
| Roquefort cheese | formaggio di Roquefort |
| rum | rum |
| rum baba | baba al rum |
| rump steak | bistecca di girello |
| runner beans | fagiolini |
| | |
| sage | salvia |

| | |
|---|---|
| s. & onion stuffing | ripieno di s. e cipolla |
| salad | insalata |
| green s. | i. verde |
| mixed s. | i. mista |
| potato s. | i. di patate |
| s. cream | salsa maionese |
| s. dressing | condimento |
| tomato s. | i. di pomodori |
| salami | salame |
| salt | sale |
| salmon | salmone |
| sandwich | panino imbottito |
| sardine | sardina |
| sauce | salsa |
| apple s. | s. di mele (che si mangia col maiale arrosto) |
| béchamel s. | besciamella |
| bread s. | s. di pane (che si mangia col pollame arrosto) |
| horseradish s. | cren |
| mint s. | s. di menta (che si mangia con l'agnello arrosto) |
| soy s. | s. di soia |
| tabasco s. | s. piccante al pepe |
| tartare s. | s. tartara |
| white s. | s. bianca |
| Worcester s. | s. worcester |
| sausage | salsiccia |
| s. roll | pasta sfoglia con ripieno di s. |
| scallop | conchiglia |
| scone | focaccina |
| Scotch broth | zuppa di verdura, carne e orzo |
| Scotch egg | uovo sodo ricoperto di salsiccia, impanato e fritto |

| | |
|---|---|
| sea food | frutti di mare |
| semolina pudding | pappa di semolino |
| service charge | servizio |
| set meal | pasto a prezzo fisso |
| shandy | birra con la limonata |
| shepherds pie | pasticcio di carne macinata e purè di patate e al forno |
| shrimps | gamberetti |
| shrimp cocktail | cocktail di g. |
| snacks | spuntino |
| snails | lumache |
| soda water | seltz |
| sole | sogliola |
| Dover sole | s. di Dover |
| fillet of sole | filetto di s. |
| lemon sole | s. al limone |
| sorbet | sorbetto |
| soup | brodo |
| soup of the day | zuppa del giorno |
| soufflé | sformato |
| sour cream | panna acida |
| soy sauce | salsa di soia |
| spinach | spinaci |
| sponge cake | pan di spagna |
| squash | spremuta |
| starters | antipasti |
| steak | bistecca |
| Chateaubriand | chateaubriand |
| fillet | filetto |
| minute | fettina di manzo |
| rump | girello |
| sirloin | lombo |
| T-bone | Fiorentina |
| steak and kidney pie | spezzatino di manzo e rognone con pasta frolla, cotta al forno |

| | |
|---|---|
| steak and kidney pudding | spezzatino di manzo e rognone con pasta frolla e grasso di rognone bollito |
| stew | stufato |
| Stilton | formaggio piccante a vene blu |
| stout | birra forte e scura |
| strawberry | fragola |
| stuffing | ripieno |
| sugar | zucchero |
| sundae | gelato con frutta, succo dolce, noci |
| supper | cena |
| swede | rapa |
| sweet | dolce |
| sweetbread | animelle |
| swiss roll | rotolo di pan di spagna ripieno di marmellata e panna |
| tabasco sauce | salsa piccante al pepe |
| table d'hôte | pasto a prezzo fisso |
| tangerine | mandarino |
| tart | crostata |
| tartare sauce | salsa tartara |
| tea | tè |
| China t. | t. cinese |
| Indian t. | t. indiano |
| cup of t. | una tazza di t. |
| pot of t. | una teiera di t. |
| toast | pane tostato |
| tomato | pomodoro |
| t. juice | succo di p. |
| t. salad | insalata di p. |
| tongue | lingua |
| tonic water | acqua brillante |
| treacle | melassa |
| t. tart | crostata di m. |

| | |
|---|---|
| trifle | zuppa inglese |
| tripe | trippa |
| trout | trota |
| tuna | tonno |
| turbot | rombo |
| turkey | tacchino |
| turnip | rapa |
| | |
| vanilla | vaniglia |
| veal | vitello |
| vegetables | verdura |
| venison | carne di cervo selvaggina |
| vichyssoise | zuppa di patate e porri |
| vinaigrette | condimento per insalata |
| vinegar | aceto |
| | |
| waffle | cialda ricoperta di sciroppo |
| walnut | noce |
| water | acqua |
| watercress | crescione |
| water melon | cocomero |
| Welsh rarebit | formaggio fuso con birra e senape su pane tostato |
| whitebait | frittura di pesce |
| white sauce | salsa bianca |
| wine list | lista dei vini |
| Worcester sauce | salsa worcester |
| | |
| yam | patata dolce americana |
| yoghurt | yogurt |
| Yorkshire pudding | pastella servita con il roast beef, cotta al forno con sugo di manzo |

# English signs　　Segnali inglesi

| | |
|---|---|
| 'A' FILM | I bambini debbono essere accompagnati da un adulto |
| 'AA' FILM | Film vietato ai minori di 14 anni |
| AA (AUTOMOBILE ASSOCIATION) | Associazione automobilistica |
| ABROAD | Estero |
| AC (ALTERNATING CURRENT) | Corrente alternata |
| ACCESSORIES | Accessori |
| ACCIDENT | Incidente |
| ACCOMMODATION | Alloggio |
| ACCOUNTS | Conti |
| ADDITIONAL CHARGE | Prezzo extra |
| ADMISSION (FREE) | Entrata (libera) |
| ADMISSIONS | Ricovero (ospedale) |
| ADVANCE BOOKING | Prenotazione |
| AFTERNOON TEAS | Tè e pasticcini |

| | |
|---|---|
| AGENCY | Agenzia |
| AIR | Aria (garage) |
| AIRLINE INFORMATION | Informazioni (compagnia aerea) |
| AIRMAIL | Posta aerea |
| AIRPORT BUS | Autobus per l'aeroporto |
| AIR TERMINAL | Terminale |
| ALARM SIGNAL | Segnale di allarme |
| ALL TICKETS TO BE SHOWN | Si deve presentare il biglietto |
| ALLOW TIME FOR COIN TO DROP | Aspettate che la moneta scenda |
| ALTERNATIVE ROUTE | Itinerario alternativo |
| AMBULANCE | Ambulanza |
| ANNEXE | Dipendenza |
| ANTIQUES | Oggetti d'antiquariato |
| ARRIVALS | Arrivi |
| ASSEMBLY POINT | Punto di riunione |
| AT ANY TIME | Ventiquattro ore |
| ATTENDANT | Inserviente |
| AUTOMATIC | Automatico |
| AUTOMATIC BARRIERS | Sportelli automatici |
| | |
| BANK | Banca |
| BAR | Bar |
| BARGAINS | Occasioni |
| BASEMENT (B) | Sotterraneo |
| BED AND BREAKFAST (B & B) | Alloggio e prima colazione |
| BENDS FOR /1/ MILE | Curve per /un/ miglio |
| BEWARE OF THE DOG | Attenti al cane |
| BOARDING NOW | Si sta svolgendo l'imbarco |
| BOATS FOR HIRE | Barchette a noleggio |
| BOOKABLE | Prenotabile |
| BOOK HERE | Prenotare qui |
| BOOKING OFFICE | Ufficio prenotazioni |
| BOX OFFICE | Biglietteria |
| BUFFET | Bar |
| BUREAU DE CHANGE | Ufficio cambio |

| | |
|---|---|
| BUSINESS ADDRESS | Indirizzo di ufficio |
| BUS LANE | Corsia per gli autobus |
| BUS STOP | Fermata autobus |
| BUSES ONLY | Solo autobus |
| CAFETERIA | Caffè |
| CALL | Chiamare |
| CAMERAS AND FILMS | Macchine fotografiche e pellicole |
| CAMPING | Campeggio |
| CAMPING PROHIBITED | Campeggio vietato |
| CANCELLED | Cancellato |
| CAR ACCESSORIES | Accessori auto |
| CAR FERRY BOOKINGS | Prenotazioni traghetto |
| CAR HIRE | Autonoleggio |
| CAR PARK (FULL) | Parcheggio (esaurito) |
| CAR WASH | Lavaggio auto |
| CASH DESK | Cassa |
| CASHIER | Cassiere |
| CASUALTY | Pronto Soccorso |
| CASUAL WEAR | Indumenti sportivi |
| CATALOGUES | Cataloghi |
| CAUTION | Attenzione |
| CENTRE | Centro |
| CHAMBERMAID | Cameriera |
| CHANGE | Moneta (spiccioli-resto) |
| CHANGING ROOM | Spogliatoio |
| CHARGES | Prezzi, spese |
| CHECK-IN (DESK) | Registrare |
| CHECK OUT (HERE) | Pagare il conto e lasciare l'albergo |
| CHEMIST | Farmacia |
| CHILD(REN) | Bambino(i) |
| CHILDREN CROSSING | Bambini attraversano la strada qui |
| CHILDREN'S DEPARTMENT | Reparto bambini |

| | |
|---|---|
| CHILDREN UNDER 3 MUST BE CARRIED | I bambini al di sotto di 3 anni debbono essere portati in braccio |
| CHINA AND GLASS | Porcellana e cristallo |
| CHURCH | Chiesa |
| CIRCUS | Circo |
| CLEARANCE (SALE) | Svendita |
| CLOAKROOM | Guardaroba |
| CLOSED CIRCUIT SECURITY SYSTEM IN OPERATION | Televisione a circuito chiuso |
| CLOSED (FOR LUNCH) | Chiuso (durante l'ora del pranzo) |
| CLOSE DOOR (FIRMLY) | Chiudere (bene) la porta |
| CLOSING DOWN (SALE) | Svendita per cessazione di attività commerciale |
| CLOSING HOURS | Ore di chiusura |
| COACH DEPARTURES | Partenze pullman |
| COACH FARES | Biglietti del pullman |
| COACH STATION | Stazione pullman |
| COCKTAIL LOUNGE | Salone dei cocktail |
| COFFEE BAR | Bar (caffè) |
| COIN CHANGE | Moneta (spiccioli) |
| COINS | Monete |
| COLD (C) | Freddo (F) |
| COLD DRINKS | Bibite fredde |
| COLLECTION TIMES | Raccolta della posta |
| COLOUR PROCESSING | Sviluppo a colori |
| CO. LTD. | S.p.A. |
| CONCEALED ENTRANCE | Entrata nascosta |
| CONDUCTED COACH TOURS | Viaggi in pullman con guida |
| CONTINENTAL DEPARTURES | Partenze per il continente |
| CONTINUOUS PERFORMANCES | Spettacolo continuo |
| CONTROLLED ZONE | Zona sorvegliata |
| CONVENIENCES | Gabinetti |
| CO-ORDINATES | Co-ordinati |

| | |
|---|---|
| COPYING SERVICE | Servizio copiatura |
| COUNTRY | Altre destinazioni (non città) |
| COURTESY SERVICE | Servizio gratis |
| CRÊCHE | Nido d'infanzia |
| CROSS NOW | Attraversare ora |
| CUL-DE-SAC | Vicolo cieco |
| CUSTOMERS MUST TAKE A BASKET | I clienti sono pregati di prendere un cestino |
| CUSTOMS | (Dichiarazione per la) dogana |
| CUTLERY | Posateria |
| CYCLISTS ONLY | Solo ciclisti |
| | |
| DANGER | Pericolo |
| DANGEROUS CORNER | Curva pericolosa |
| DANGEROUS CURRENTS | Correnti pericolose |
| DAY BELL | Campanello diurno |
| DAY TOURS | Gite di un giorno |
| DC (DIRECT CURRENT) | Corrente continua |
| DEAD SLOW | A passo d'uomo (ridurre velocità) |
| DELAYED | In ritardo |
| DELIVERIES | Consegne |
| DENTAL SURGERY | Ambulatorio dentistico |
| DENTIST | Dentista |
| DEPARTMENT | Reparto |
| DEPARTURE LOUNGE | Sala di partenza |
| DEPARTURES | Partenze |
| DEPARTURE TIMES | Orario di partenza |
| DEPOSITS | Depositi (d. bancari) |
| DESTINATION | Destinazione |
| DETAILS AVAILABLE ON REQUEST | Ulteriori particolari a richiesta |
| DETOUR | Deviazione |
| DISCO | Discoteca |
| DISPENSING CHEMISTS | Farmacia autorizzata a preparare le ricette |

| | |
|---|---|
| DISPOSABLE BAG | Sacchetto da buttare |
| DIVERSION | Deviazione |
| DOCKS | Zona portuale |
| DO NOT DISTURB | Non disturbare |
| DO NOT ENTER | Non entrare |
| DO NOT FEED (THE ANIMALS) | Non dare da mangiare (agli animali) |
| DO NOT OBSTRUCT ENTRANCE | Non ostruire l'ingresso |
| DO NOT SMOKE | Non fumare |
| DO NOT SPEAK TO THE DRIVER | Non parlare all'autista |
| DO NOT STAND NEAR THE STAIRS | Non sostare vicino alle scale |
| DO NOT TOUCH | Non toccare |
| DOOR OPEN/SHUT | Porta aperta/chiusa |
| DOORS OPEN /1.00 P.M./ | Si apre alle /13.00/ |
| DOWN | Giù |
| DRINKING WATER | Acqua potabile |
| DRY CLEANING | Pulitura a secco |
| DUAL CARRIAGEWAY (AHEAD) | Doppia corsia (a /.../ m) |
| DUMPING PROHIBITED | Vietato scarico rifiuti |
| DUTY FREE SHOP | Negozio di merce senza dazio |
| EASTBOUND | Direzione est (metropolitana) |
| EAT BY ... | Mangiare prima delle ... |
| ELECTRICAL GOODS | Materiale elettrico |
| EMBARKATION | Imbarco |
| EMERGENCY | Emergenza |
| EMERGENCY DOOR | Porta di emergenza |
| EMERGENCY EXIT | Uscita di sicurezza |
| EMERGENCY SWITCH | Pulsante d'emergenza |
| EMERGENCY TREATMENT | Pronto soccorso |
| EMPTY | Vuoto |
| END | Fine |
| END OF BUS LANE | Fine della corsia per autobus |

| | |
|---|---|
| ENGAGED | Occupato |
| ENQUIRIES | Informazioni |
| ENTRANCE | Entrata |
| ESCALATOR | Scala mobile |
| EVENING(S) ONLY | La sera soltanto |
| EVENING PERFORMANCE | Spettacolo serale |
| EXACT CHANGE | Moneta giusta |
| EXACT FARE | Moneta giusta |
| EXCEPT FOR ACCESS | Ingresso limitato |
| EXCESS BAGGAGE CHARGE | Tassa per eccesso di peso |
| EXCESS FARES | Supplementi |
| EXCESS PERIOD | Tempo supplementare |
| EXIT | Uscita |
| EXIT ONLY | Uscita soltanto |
| EXPORT FACILITIES AVAILABLE | Facilitazioni per l'estero |
| EXPRESS DELIVERY | Servizio postale espresso |
| EXTRA CHARGES/EXTRAS | Supplementi/Gli extra |
| FARE STAGE | Fermata con variazione del prezzo del biglietto |
| FASHIONS | Moda |
| FASTEN SEAT BELTS | Allacciare le cinture di sicurezza |
| FAST FIT EXHAUST SERVICE | Servizio rapido tubo di scappamento |
| FERRY | Traghetto |
| FILLING STATION | Stazione di rifornimento benzina |
| FINE | Multa |
| FIRE ESCAPE | Scale di sicurezza |
| FIRE (EXIT) | Uscita di sicurezza |
| FIRST CLASS | Prima classe |
| FISH AND CHIPS | Pesce fritto con patatine |
| FISH BAR | Friggitoria pesce |
| FLIGHT | Volo |
| FLORIST | Fiorista |
| FOOD HALL | Reparto alimentare |

| | |
|---|---|
| FOOTPATH | Sentiero |
| FOOTWEAR | Calzature |
| FOR HIRE | A noleggio |
| FRAGILE, WITH CARE | Fragile, con attenzione |
| FREE | Gratis |
| FREE SERVICE | Servizio gratis |
| FUEL | Combustibile |
| FULL | Completo |
| FULLY LICENSED | Autorizzato a vendere tutte le bibite alcoliche |
| FURNISHING FABRICS | Tessuti tappezzeria |
| FURNITURE DEPARTMENT | Reparto mobili |
| GARAGE (IN CONSTANT USE) | Passo carraio |
| GARAGE PARKING | Parcheggio in garage |
| GATE | Cancello |
| GATES CLOSE AT ... | I cancelli si chiudono alle ... |
| GENTLEMEN/GENTS | Signori |
| GET IN LANE | Disporsi nella corsia giusta |
| GIFT SHOP | Negozio di regali |
| GIVE WAY | Dare la precedenza |
| GOLF CLUB/COURSE | Circolo di golf/Campo di golf |
| GOODS TO DECLARE | Merce da dichiarare |
| GRILLS | Grigliate |
| GRIT FOR ROADS | Ghiaia |
| GROUND FLOOR (G) | Pianterreno (T) |
| GUARD DOG | Cane da guardia |
| GUEST HOUSE | Pensione |
| GUIDE | Guida |
| HABERDASHERY | Merceria |
| HAIRDRESSING SALON | Parrucchiere |
| HALF-DAY TOURS | Gite di mezza giornata |
| HALF-PRICE | Metà prezzo |
| HALT | Alt |
| HAND BAGGAGE | Bagaglio a mano |
| HARD SHOULDER | Dosso (autostrada) |

| | |
|---|---|
| HARDWARE | Ferramenta |
| HAVE YOU LEFT YOUR KEY? | Ha lasciato la chiave? |
| HEADROOM | Altezza massima |
| HEATER | Riscaldatore (sistema di riscaldamento) |
| HEEL BAR | Calzolaio |
| HEIGHT LIMIT | Limite di altezza |
| HIGHLY INFLAMMABLE | Molto infiammabile |
| HIGH VOLTAGE | Alto voltaggio |
| HILL 10%/1 IN 10 | Pendenza 1 su 10 |
| HOLD | Dispositivo per tenere aperte le porte |
| HOSPITAL | Ospedale |
| HOSTEL ACCOMMODATION | Alloggio in ostello |
| HOT (H) | Caldo (C) |
| HOT DRINKS | Bibite calde |
| HOTEL | Albergo |
| HOTEL ENTRANCE | Entrata dell'albergo |
| HOTEL MANAGEMENT | Direzione dell'albergo |
| HOTEL RESERVATIONS | Prenotazioni albergo |
| HOT MEALS SERVED ALL DAY | Pasti caldi a tutte le ore |
| HOURS OF BUSINESS | Orario |
| 24 HOUR SERVICE | 24 ore |
| HOUSEHOLD DEPARTMENT | Casalinghi |
| HOVERCRAFT | Aliscafo |
| ICES | Gelati |
| IMMIGRATION | Immigrazione |
| IMMUNISATION | Immunizzazione |
| IN | Entrata |
| IN EMERGENCY BREAK GLASS | In caso di emergenza rompere il vetro |
| INFLAMMABLE | Infiammabile |
| INFORMATION | Informazioni |
| INFORMATION DESK | Banco informazioni |
| INN FOOD | Trattoria |

| | |
|---|---|
| IN-PATIENTS | Pazienti ricoverati |
| INQUIRIES | Informazioni |
| INSERT COIN | Inserire moneta |
| INSERT /5P/ HERE | Inserire /5p/ qui |
| INTERMISSION | Intervallo |
| INTERNATIONAL | Internazionale |
| INTERNATIONAL TRAVELLERS' AID | Aiuto internazionale per i viaggiatori |
| INVISIBLE MENDING | Rammendo invisibile |
| JEWELLERY | Gioielleria |
| JUNCTION (JCT) | Raccordo |
| KEEP AWAY FROM CHILDREN | Tenere lontano dai bambini |
| KEEP CLEAR | Non ostruire l'ingresso |
| KEEP DOORS CLOSED | Tenere le porte chiuse |
| KEEP IN LANE | Conservare la propria corsia |
| KEEP LEFT | Tenere la sinistra |
| KEEP OFF THE GRASS | Non camminare sull'erba |
| KEEP OUT | Vietato entrare |
| KEEP RIGHT | Tenere la destra |
| KEEP SHUT | Tenere chiuso |
| KEYS (CUT HERE) | Chiavi (Taglio chiavi) |
| KNITWEAR | Maglieria |
| KOSHER | Cibo lecito per gli ebrei |
| LADIES/LADIES ROOM | Signore |
| LADIES HAIRDRESSING | Parrucchiere per signora |
| LADIES ONLY | Solo per signore |
| LANDED | Atterrato |
| LANE CLOSED | Corsia sbarrata |
| 2-LANE TRAFFIC | Traffico su due corsie |
| LAST NAME | Cognome |
| LAST TRAIN | Ultimo treno |
| LATE PERFORMANCE | Ultima rappresentazione |
| LATE SHOPPING | Chiusura posticipata dei negozi |
| LATE SHOW | Ultimo spettacolo |

| | |
|---|---|
| LAUNDERETTE/LAUNDROMAT | Lavanderia automatica |
| LAUNDRY | Lavanderia |
| LAYBY | Piazzuola |
| LEAVE BY CENTRE DOORS | Uscita porta al centro |
| LEFT LUGGAGE | Deposito bagagli |
| LEFT LUGGAGE LOCKERS | Armadietti per bagagli |
| LETTERS | Lettere |
| LEVEL CROSSING | Passaggio a livello |
| LIBRARY | Biblioteca |
| LICENSED BAR/RESTAURANT | Bar/ristorante autorizzato a servire tutte le bevande alcooliche |
| LICENSING HOURS | Orario dei bar inglesi |
| LIFEBELTS | Cinture di salvataggio |
| LIFT(S) | Ascensore (i) |
| LIGHT REFRESHMENTS | Spuntino |
| LINE | Linea |
| LITTER | Immondizie |
| LOADING AND UNLOADING ONLY | Per carico e scarico |
| LOCAL | Locale |
| LONG VEHICLE | Veicolo lungo |
| LOOK LEFT/RIGHT | Guardare a sinistra/destra |
| LOOSE CHIPPINGS | Ghiaino non fisso |
| LOST PROPERTY OFFICE | Ufficio oggetti smarriti |
| LOUNGE | Salotto |
| LOUNGE BAR | Bar più elegante e costoso |
| LOW BRIDGE | Ponte basso |
| LOWER DECK | Parte inferiore (dell'autobus) |
| LOWER SALES FLOOR | Piano inferiore di vendita |
| LOW FLYING AIRCRAFT | Aeroplani a bassa quota |
| LTD | S.p.A. |
| LUGGAGE | Bagaglio |
| MADE IN ... | Fatto in ... |
| MAGAZINES | Riviste |

| | |
|---|---|
| MAIL | Posta |
| MAIN LINE STATION | Stazione principale |
| MAJOR ROAD AHEAD | Strada con precedenza più avanti |
| MATINEE | Spettacolo pomeridiano |
| MAXIMUM 2 HOURS | Tempo massimo di parcheggio 2 ore |
| MAX. LOAD /20/ PERSONS OR /3000/ LB | Portata massima (20 persone o 15 quintali) |
| MEMBERS ONLY | Solo per soci |
| MEN | Uomini |
| MEN ONLY | Solo per uomini |
| MENSWEAR | Abbigliamento da uomo |
| MEN WORKING | Lavori in corso |
| MESSAGES | Messaggi |
| METER ZONE | Zona con parchimetri |
| MEZZANINE FLOOR | Mezzanino |
| MIND THE GAP | Attenzione al passo |
| MIND THE STEP | Attenzione al gradino |
| MIND YOUR HEAD | Attenzione alla testa |
| MINICABS | Minitaxi |
| MINIMUM CHARGE | Prezzo minimo |
| MONEY ORDERS | Vaglia |
| MON–SAT | Dal lunedì al sabato |
| MOTEL | Motel |
| MOTOR CYCLES ONLY | Solo motociclette |
| MOTOR VEHICLES PROHIBITED | Divieto agli automezzi |
| MOTORWAY | Autostrada |
| MOTORWAYS MERGE | Collegamento di autostrade |
| N (NIGHT) | Notte (per gli autobus) |
| NATIONAL | Nazionale |
| NCP (NATIONAL CAR PARKS) | Parcheggi statali |
| NEW PATIENTS | Nuovi pazienti |
| NEXT COACH DEPARTS AT ... | Il prossimo pullman parte alle ... |

| | |
|---|---|
| NIGHT BELL | Chiamata notturna |
| NIGHT CHARGE | Tariffa notturna |
| NO ACCESS | Vietato l'accesso |
| NO ADMITTANCE/ADMISSION (EXCEPT ON BUSINESS) | Vietato l'ingresso (ai non addetti ai lavori) |
| NO ADVANCE BOOKING | Non si fanno prenotazioni |
| NO BATHING | Vietato fare il bagno |
| NO CAMPING | Campeggio vietato |
| NO CARAVANS | Non si accetta roulotte |
| NO CHANGE AVAILABLE FROM DRIVER | L'autista non può dare il resto |
| NO CHARGE SUNDAYS AND BANK HOLIDAYS | Gratis di domenica e giorni festivi |
| NO COLLECTIONS SUNDAY, CHRISTMAS DAY, BANK AND PUBLIC HOLIDAYS | Non vi sono collette la domenica, il giorno di Natale e nelle altre festività |
| NO CREDIT | Non si dà credito |
| NO CYCLING | Vietato andare in bicicletta |
| NO DIVING | Vietato tuffarsi |
| NO DOGS | Divieto di ingresso ai cani |
| NO ENTRY | Divieto di ingresso |
| NO L DRIVERS | Divieto di guida ai principianti |
| NO LEFT TURN | Divieto di svolta a sinistra |
| NO LITTER | Divieto di scarico |
| NO LOADING (MON–SAT 8 A.M.–6.30 P.M.) | Divieto di carico e scarico (da lunedì a sabato dalle 8.00 alle 18.30) |
| NO OVERTAKING | Divieto di sorpasso |
| NO PARKING | Divieto di sosta |
| NO PARKING BEYOND THIS POINT | Divieto di sosta oltre questo limite |
| NO PASSING | Divieto di passaggio |
| NO PEDESTRIANS | Vietato ai pedoni |
| NO PERSONS UNDER 18 YEARS OF AGE ALLOWED ON THESE PREMISES | Vietato l'ingresso ai minori di 18 anni |

| | |
|---|---|
| NO PRAMS OR PUSHCHAIRS | Non portare carrozzine e passeggini |
| NO RIGHT TURN | Divieto di svolta a destra |
| NORTHBOUND | Diretto a nord |
| NO SERVICE | Niente servizio |
| NO SMOKING | Vietato fumare |
| NO STANDING | Proibito stare in piedi |
| NO STOPPING | Proibito fermarsi |
| NO SWIMMING | Divieto di nuoto |
| NOTHING TO DECLARE | Niente da dichiarare |
| NO THOROUGHFARE | Vicolo chiuso |
| NO THROUGH ROAD | Vicolo cieco |
| NOTICE | Avviso |
| NOT IN USE | Fuori servizio |
| NO TRAILERS | Proibito ai rimorchi |
| NO TRESPASSING | Proprietà privata |
| NOT TO BE TAKEN AWAY | Da non portar via |
| NOT TRANSFERABLE | Non trasferibile |
| NO U TURNS | Divieto di svolta a U |
| NO VACANCIES | Completo |
| NO WAITING | Divieto di sosta |
| NO WAY OUT | Uscita vietata |
| NOW BEING SERVED | ... è servito |
| NURSERY | Asilo |
| NURSERY | Vivaio piante |
| | |
| OCCUPIED | Occupato |
| OFF | Spento |
| OFFENCE | Infrazione |
| OFF LICENCE | Vendita di bibite alcooliche per esportazione |
| OIL | Olio |
| ON | Acceso |
| ONE WAY | Senso unico |
| ON SALE HERE | In vendita qui |
| OPEN (EVERY DAY)/(TILL) | Aperto (ogni giorno)/(fino alle) |

| | |
|---|---|
| OPEN TO NON-RESIDENTS | Aperto ai visitatori |
| OPENING HOURS | Orario |
| (OPTHALMIC) OPTICIAN | Ottico |
| OUT | Fuori/assente |
| OUTPATIENTS | Pazienti diurni |
| OVERSEAS TELEPHONE CALLS | Telefonate all'estero |
| OVERSEAS VISITORS RECEPTION | Ricevimento turisti stranieri |
| PACKETS | Pacchi (su certe cassette per le lettere) |
| PARKING (P) | Parcheggio |
| PARTS | Parti di ricambio |
| PASSENGERS ARE ADVISED/ REQUESTED NOT TO LEAVE LUGGAGE UNATTENDED | I passeggeri sono invitati a non lasciare incustoditi i propri bagagli |
| PASSENGERS ARE ALLOWED ONE ITEM OF LUGGAGE IN THE AIRCRAFT CABIN | I passeggeri possono portare un solo collo in cabina |
| PASSENGERS MUST KEEP THEIR BAGGAGE WITH THEM AT ALL TIMES | I passeggeri devono tenere costantemente i bagagli appresso |
| PASSPORTS | Passaporti |
| PAY AS YOU ENTER | Si paga all'entrata |
| PAY ATTENDANT | Si paga al cassiere |
| PAY HERE | Si paga qui |
| PEDESTRIAN CROSSING | Strisce pedonali |
| PEDESTRIAN PUSH BUTTON | Pulsante per pedoni |
| PEDESTRIANS ONLY | Solo pedoni |
| PENALTY (FOR IMPROPER USE /£5/) | Multa (per uso illecito £5) |
| PERFORMANCE ENDS | Lo spettacolo termina |
| PERFUMERY | Profumeria |
| PERMIT HOLDERS ONLY | Solo per persone munite di permesso |

| | |
|---|---|
| PETROL | Benzina |
| PETROL STATION | Distributore di benzina |
| PHONE | Telefono |
| 3-PIECE | Vestito a tre pezzi |
| PLACE IN BIN PROVIDED | Mettere dentro il recipiente apposito |
| PLATFORM | Binario |
| PLATFORM TICKETS | Biglietto per binari |
| P.L.C. (Public Limited Company) | S.A. (si possono acquistare le azioni in Borsa) |
| PLEASE ... | Per favore ... |
| PLEASE DRIVE CAREFULLY | Si prega di guidare con attenzione |
| PLEASE FORWARD | Si prega di spedire al destinatario |
| PLEASE LIFT HAND BAGGAGE CLEAR OF GATES | Sollevare il bagaglio a mano oltre i cancelli |
| PLEASE RECLAIM YOUR BAGGAGE ON LEAVING THE COACH | Ritirare i bagagli prima di lasciare il pullman |
| PLEASE RING THE BELL | Suonate il campanello per favore |
| PLEASE SHOW YOUR TICKET | Mostrate il biglietto per favore |
| PLEASE STAND ON THE RIGHT | Fermarsi sulla destra |
| PLEASE TAKE A BASKET | Munirsi di cestello |
| POISON | Veleno |
| POLICE | Polizia |
| POLICE NOTICE | Avviso della polizia |
| PORTER | Facchino |
| POSITION CLOSED | Sportello chiuso |
| POSTE RESTANTE | Fermo posta |
| POSTING BOX | Cassetta per lettere |
| POST OFFICE | Ufficio postale |
| POWDER ROOM | Servizi per signore |
| PRESS BUTTON (FOR ASSISTANCE) | Premere il pulsante (per chiedere aiuto) |

| | |
|---|---|
| PRESS BUTTON FIRMLY AND WAIT FOR CROSS SIGNAL | Premere il pulsante e attendere il segnale di attraversamento |
| PRESS RETURN COIN BUTTON HERE | Premere il pulsante per la restituzione della moneta |
| PRESS TO REJECT | Premere per respingere |
| PRICES SLASHED | Prezzi imbattibili |
| PRIVATE | Privato |
| PRIVATE PARKING ONLY | Parcheggio privato |
| PRIVATE ROAD | Strada privata |
| PROHIBITED | Vietato |
| PUBLIC BAR | Bar meno elegante nei 'pub' inglesi |
| PUBLIC CONVENIENCES | Gabinetti pubblici |
| PUBLIC HOLIDAY CHARGE | Tariffa festiva (taxi) |
| PUBLIC LIBRARY | Biblioteca pubblica |
| PULL | Tirare |
| PUSH | Spingere |
| PUSH BAR TO OPEN | Spingere la sbarra per aprire |
| PUSHCHAIRS MUST BE FOLDED | Le sedie a rotelle debbono essere piegate |
| PUSH ONCE | Suonare una sola volta (autobus) |
| PUT IN /THREE/ /10P/ PIECES | Inserire /tre/ monete da /10p/ |
| QUEUE HERE/Q HERE | Fare la coda qui |
| QUEUING | Mettersi in coda |
| QUEUE OTHER SIDE | Fare la coda dall'altra parte |
| QUEUE THIS SIDE | Fare la coda da questa parte |
| QUIET | Silenzio |
| RAC (ROYAL AUTOMOBILE CLUB) | Club reale automobilistico |
| RAILAIR LINK | Treno per l'aeroporto |
| RAIL-DRIVE | Treno (traghetto) per le macchine |
| RAMP AHEAD | Rampa più avanti |
| RATES OF EXCHANGE | Tasso di cambio |

| | |
|---|---|
| RECEPTION | Ricevimento |
| RECORDED DELIVERY | Raccomandata con ricevuta di ritorno |
| RECORDS | Dischi |
| RED CROSS | Croce rossa |
| REDUCED (FOR CLEARANCE) | Ribassi di fine stagione |
| REDUCE SPEED NOW | Ridurre la velocità ora |
| REDUCTIONS | Riduzioni |
| REFRESHMENTS | Rinfreschi |
| REGISTERED LETTERS | Lettere raccomandate |
| REGISTERED LUGGAGE | Bagagli raccomandati |
| REJECT COINS | Monete respinte |
| RENTALS | Noleggio (televisione ecc.) |
| REPAIRS | Riparazione |
| REPLACE IN HOLDER | Riporre nel sostegno |
| REQUEST (R) | Fermata a richiesta |
| RESERVATIONS | Prenotazioni |
| RESERVED | Prenotato |
| RESIDENTS' LOUNGE | Salotto per i residenti |
| RESIDENTS ONLY | Solo residenti |
| RESTAURANT | Ristorante |
| RESTAURANT CAR | Vagone ristorante |
| RETURN CARS ONLY | Riservato alle automobili restituite dopo il noleggio |
| RETURN TO SEAT | Ritornare al proprio posto |
| RING FOR ATTENDANT | Suonare per inserviente |
| RING FOR SERVICE | Suonare per servizio |
| RING ROAD | Circonvallazione |
| ROAD CLEAR | Strada libera |
| ROAD WORKS AHEAD | Lavori in corso più avanti |
| ROOM SERVICE | Servizio in camera |
| ROOMS TO LET | Stanze da affittare |
| ROUNDABOUT | Rotonda |
| ROW | Fila |
| SAFETY CURTAIN | Sipario di sicurezza |

| | |
|---|---|
| SALE | Vendita |
| SALES AND SERVICE | Vendite e servizio |
| SALOON BAR | Bar più elegante nei 'pub' inglesi |
| SANDWICH BAR | Bar dei tramezzini |
| SCHEDULED TIME | Ora prevista |
| SCHOOL | Scuola |
| SEALINK | Servizio per mare fra l'Inghilterra e il continente |
| SEAT | Posto |
| SEAT RESERVATIONS | Prenotazione posti |
| SECOND CLASS | Seconda classe |
| SECURITY CHECKS IN OPERATION | Controllo di sicurezza in azione |
| SELF-DRIVE CAR HIRE | Noleggio di automobili senz'autista |
| SELF-SERVE/SELF-SERVICE | Autoservizio |
| SELL BY ... | Vendere entro ... |
| SEPARATE PERFORMANCES | Spettacoli ad ore fisse |
| SEPARATES | Vestiti a due pezzi |
| SERVICES (S) | Servizi |
| SERVICE AREA | Zona di servizi (autostrada) |
| SERVICE (NOT) INCLUDED | Servizio (non) compreso |
| SHAVERS ONLY | Solo rasoi elettrici |
| SHOE DEPARTMENT | Reparto scarpe |
| SHOE REPAIRS | Riparazione scarpe |
| SHOPLIFTERS WILL BE PROSECUTED | I taccheggiatori saranno denunciati |
| SHOPPING HOURS | Orario di vendita |
| SHOW TICKETS PLEASE | Mostrate i biglietti per favore |
| SHUT (THE DOOR/THE GATE) | Chiudere (la porta/il cancello) |
| SINGLE FILE TRAFFIC | Traffico a corsia unica |
| SINGLE TRACK WITH PASSING PLACES | Corsia unica con piazzuole per incrocio e sorpasso |
| SLOW | Lento |
| SNACKS | Spuntini |

| | |
|---|---|
| SOLD OUT | Esaurito |
| SOUTHBOUND | Diretto a sud |
| SPARE PARTS | Ricambi |
| SPEAK HERE | Parlare qui |
| SPECIAL OFFER | Offerta speciale |
| STAFF ONLY | Riservato al personale |
| STAGE DOOR | Entrata palcoscenico |
| STAIRS | Scala |
| STAMPS | Francobolli |
| STAND CLEAR OF THE DOORS | Tenersi lontani dalle porte |
| STANDING ROOM ONLY | Posto in piedi soltanto |
| STEEP GRADIENT/HILL | Pendenza ripida |
| STOP | Alt |
| STREET LEVEL | Livello stradale |
| SUBURBAN SERVICES | Servizi per la periferia |
| SUBWAY | Sottopassaggio |
| SURGERY | Ambulatorio |
| SURGERY HOURS | Orario di ambulatorio |
| SUSPENDED | Sospeso |
| SWEETS AND CIGARETTES | Caramelle e sigarette |
| SWIMMING POOL | Piscina |
| SWITCH OFF ENGINE | Spegnere il motore |
| TAKE-AWAY | Da portar via |
| TAKE TICKET – KEEP IT PLEASE | Munirsi di biglietto e conservarlo |
| TARIFF | Tariffa |
| TAXI | Taxi |
| TAXI QUEUE | Coda per i taxi |
| TAXI RANK | Stazione dei taxi |
| TAXIS ONLY | Solo taxi |
| TEAS | Tè in vendita |
| TELEGRAMS | Telegrammi |
| TELEPHONE | Telefono |
| TELEPHONE DIRECTORIES | Elenchi telefonici |
| TELEVISION (TV) | Televisione |

| | |
|---|---|
| TELEX SERVICE | Servizio telex |
| TEMPORARY ROAD SURFACE | Superficie stradale provvisoria |
| THEATRE | Teatro |
| THERE ARE NO TICKETS. YOUR COIN RELEASES THE GATE (Red Arrow Buses) | Biglietti non necessari. Una moneta aprirà il cancello (Nelle corriere 'Red Arrow') |
| THESE ARTICLES WILL BE CARRIED FREE | Questi oggetti saranno trasportati gratis |
| THIS PERFORMANCE | Questo spettacolo |
| THIS SIDE (UP/DOWN) | Questo lato (in alto/in basso) |
| THIS WAY | Da questa parte |
| TICKET HOLDERS ONLY | Solo per persone munite di biglietto |
| TICKETS | Biglietti |
| TILL CLOSED | Cassa chiusa |
| TIMETABLE | Orario |
| TOBACCONIST | Tabaccaio |
| TO COACHES | Ai pullman |
| TODAY'S PERFORMANCE(S) | Spettacolo (-i) odierno |
| TO EAT HERE OR TAKE AWAY | Si può mangiare qui o portar via |
| TOILETRIES | Articoli da bagno |
| TOILETS | Gabinetti |
| TO LET | Affittasi |
| TOLL BRIDGE | Ponte a pedaggio |
| TOLL GATE | Pedaggio |
| TO OPEN IN EMERGENCY TURN TAP AND PULL HANDLES | Per aprire in caso di emergenza girare e tirare le maniglie |
| TO STOP THE BUS RING THE BELL ONCE | Per fermare l'autobus suonare una volta |
| TO THE BOATS | Ai traghetti |
| TOURIST TICKETS | Biglietti turistici |
| TOWN CENTRE | Centro città |
| TOY DEPARTMENT | Reparto giocattoli |
| TRAFFIC SIGNALS AHEAD | Segnali più avanti |
| TRANSFER PASSENGERS | Passeggeri da trasferire |

| | |
|---|---|
| TRANSIT PASSENGERS | Passeggeri in transito |
| TRAVEL AGENCY | Agenzia viaggi |
| TRAVEL OFFICE | Ufficio viaggi |
| TRAYS | Vassoi |
| TRESPASSERS WILL BE PROSECUTED | I non autorizzati saranno denunciati |
| TUNNEL | Galleria |
| TURN HANDLE | Girare la maniglia |
| TWIN TOWN | Città gemella |
| TWO-WAY TRAFFIC | Traffico a due sensi |
| | |
| 'U' FILM | Film per tutti |
| UNACCOMPANIED BAGGAGE | Bagagli non accompagnati |
| UNDERGROUND | Metropolitana (sotterranea) |
| UNDERGROUND STATION | Stazione della metropolitana |
| UNDERWEAR | Maglieria intima |
| UNRESERVED | Non prenotato |
| UNSUITABLE FOR LONG VEHICLES | Non adetto per veicoli lunghi |
| UP | Su |
| UPPER DECK | Parte superiore |
| URBAN CLEARWAY | Strada urbana di grande comunicazione |
| USED BLADES | Lamette usate |
| USED TICKETS | Biglietti usati |
| USE OTHER DOOR | Usate l'altra porta |
| | |
| VACANCIES | (Stanze) libere |
| VACANT | Libero |
| VAT (VALUE ADDED TAX) | IVA |
| VIP LOUNGE | Salotto per viaggiatori importanti |
| | |
| WAIT (HERE) | Aspettare (qui) |
| WAITING AREA | Zona di sosta |
| WAITING LIMITED TO 30 MINUTES IN ANY HOUR | Sosta limitata a 30 minuti in ogni ora |
| WAITING ROOM | Sala di attesa |

| | |
|---|---|
| WARD | Corsia |
| WARNING | Avvertimento |
| WASH ROOM | Servizi |
| WASHING CREAM | Sapone liquido |
| WATCH YOUR STEP | Attenzione al passo |
| WAY IN | Entrata |
| WAY OUT | Uscita |
| WC | Gabinetto |
| WEEKEND CHARGE | Tariffa di fine settimana |
| WEIGHT LIMIT | Limite di peso |
| WELCOME TO ... | Benvenuti a ... |
| WESTBOUND | Diretto ad ovest |
| WET PAINT | Vernice fresca |
| WHERE TO STAY | Dove alloggiare |
| WHILE YOU/U WAIT | Consegna immediata |
| ... WILL ARRIVE ... | ... arriverà ... (all'aeroporto) |
| WINE BAR | Bar dove si vende il vino |
| WINES AND SPIRITS | Vini e liquori |
| WOMEN | Donne |
| | |
| 'X' FILM | Film vietato ai minori di 18 anni |
| X RAY | Raggi x |
| | |
| YELLOW TICKETS THROUGH GATE: OTHER TICKETS THROUGH TICKET COLLECTOR'S GATE | Ingresso automatico con biglietti gialli: mostrare gli altri biglietti al controllore |
| | |
| YHA (YOUTH HOSTEL) | Ostello della gioventù |
| YOU MAY TELEPHONE FROM HERE | Si può telefonare qui |
| | |
| Z BEND | Curva a S |
| ZONE ENDS | Termine zona |
| ZOO | Giardino zoologico |

# Motoring key

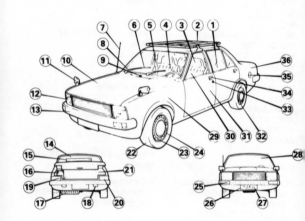

| | | |
|---|---|---|
| 1 | back seat | il sedile posteriore |
| 2 | roof rack | il portapacchi |
| 3 | head restraint | la poggiatesta |
| 4 | passenger's seat | il sedile anteriore destro |
| 5 | seat belt | la cintura di sicurezza |
| 6 | windscreen wiper blade | la spazzola tergicristallo |
| 7 | aerial | l'antenna |
| 8 | windscreen wiper arm | il braccio tergicristallo |
| 9 | windscreen washer | il lavacristallo |
| 10 | bonnet | il cofano |
| 11 | exterior mirror | lo specchietto laterale |
| 12 | headlight | il proiettore |
| 13 | bumper | il paraurti |
| 14 | rear window | il lunotto posteriore |
| 15 | rear window heater | il riscaldamento lunotto posteriore |
| 16 | spare wheel | la ruota di scorta |
| 17 | fuel tank | il serbatoio |
| 18 | hazard warning light | il segnale luminoso di pericolo |
| 19 | brake light | il fanalino dei freni |
| 20 | rear light | il fanalo posteriore |
| 21 | boot | il baule |
| 22 | tyre | la gomma |
| 23 | front wheel | la ruota anteriore |
| 24 | hubcap | la coppa |
| 25 | sidelight | il fanalo laterale |
| 26 | number plate | la targa |
| 27 | registration number | il numero di targa |
| 28 | windscreen | il parabrezza |
| 29 | front wing | l'ala anteriore |
| 30 | driver's seat | il sedile di guida |
| 31 | door | la porta |
| 32 | rear wheel | la ruota posteriore |
| 33 | lock | la serratura |
| 34 | door handle | la maniglia |
| 35 | petrol filler cap | il tappo della benzina |
| 36 | rear wing | l'ala posteriore |

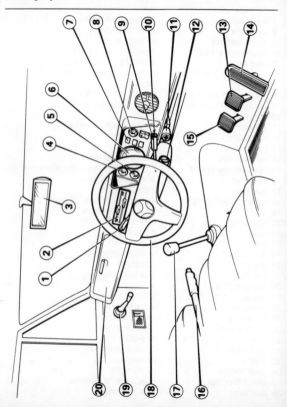

| | | |
|---|---|---|
| 1 | dipswitch | il commutatore luci |
| 2 | heater | l'impianto di riscaldamento |
| 3 | interior mirror | lo specchio retrovisore |
| 4 | water temperature gauge | il termometro acqua |
| 5 | ammeter | l'amperometro |
| 6 | speedometer | il contachilometri |
| 7 | oil pressure warning light | la spia pressione olio |
| 8 | fuel gauge | l'indicatore livello carburante (m) |
| 9 | horn | la tromba |
| 10 | direction indicator | l'indicatore di direzione (m) |
| 11 | choke | la valvola dell'aria |
| 12 | ignition switch | l'interruttore accensione (m) |
| 13 | brake pedal | il pedale freni |
| 14 | accelerator | il pedale acceleratore |
| 15 | clutch pedal | il pedale frizione |
| 16 | handbrake | il freno a mano |
| 17 | gear lever (selector) | la leva cambio |
| 18 | steering wheel | il volante |
| 19 | window winder | la maniglia alzacristallo |
| 20 | glove compartment | il cassetto ripostiglio |

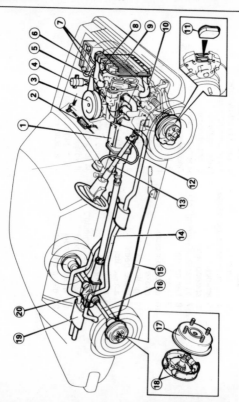

| | | |
|---|---|---|
| 1 | gearbox | la scatola cambio |
| 2 | fuse box | la scatola porta fusibili |
| 3 | air filter | il filtro dell'aria |
| 4 | ignition coil | l'accensione (m) |
| 5 | radiator hose (top) | il tubo radiatore superiore |
| 6 | battery | la batteria |
| 7 | leads (battery) (pl) | i conduttori |
| 8 | filler cap (radiator) | il tappo |
| 9 | radiator | il radiatore |
| 10 | radiator hose (bottom) | il tubo radiatore inferiore |
| 11 | disc brake pad | la pastiglia (del freno) |
| 12 | speedometer cable | il cavetto per contachilometri |
| 13 | steering column | l'albero volante |
| 14 | exhaust pipe | il tubo scarico |
| 15 | handbrake cable | il cavetto freno a mano |
| 16 | rear axle | l'asse posteriore (f) |
| 17 | brake drum | il tamburo di freno |
| 18 | brake shoe | il ceppo del freno |
| 19 | silencer | il silenziatore |
| 20 | differential | il differenziale |

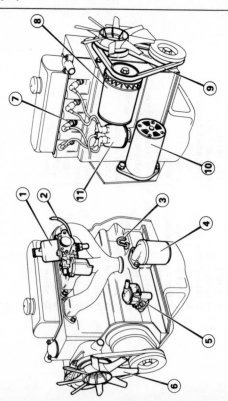

1 carburettor — il carburatore
2 cable — il cavo per traino
3 oil dipstick — l'asticella per controllo livello olio
4 oil filter — il filtro olio
5 fuel pump — la pompa carburante
6 fan — il ventilatore
7 sparking plug — la candela
8 alternator — il dinamo
9 fan belt — la cinghia per ventilatore
10 starter motor — il motorino di avviamento
11 distributor — il distributore

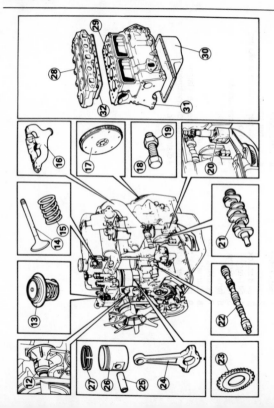

| 12 | water pump | la pompa acqua |
| 13 | thermostat | il termostato |
| 14 | valve | la valvola |
| 15 | spring (n) | la molla |
| 16 | manifold, inlet and exhaust | il collettore d'ammissione e scarico |
| 17 | fly wheel | il volano |
| 18 | bolt | il bullone |
| 19 | nut | il dado |
| 20 | oil pump | la pompa olio |
| 21 | crankshaft | l'albero motore |
| 22 | camshaft | l'albero a camme |
| 23 | sprocket | la ruota dentata |
| 24 | connecting rod | la biella |
| 25 | gudgeon pin | lo spinotto |
| 26 | piston | il pistone |
| 27 | piston rings (pl) | gli anelli del pistone |
| 28 | cylinder head | la testa del cilindro |
| 29 | cylinder | il cilindro |
| 30 | oil sump | la coppa olio |
| 31 | cylinder block | il monoblocco |
| 32 | gasket | la guarnizione |

# Numbers, days and months

## Numbers

| | | | |
|---|---|---|---|
| 0 | zero | 54 | cinquantaquattro |
| 1 | uno | 65 | sessantacinque |
| 2 | due | 76 | settantasei |
| 3 | tre | 87 | ottantasette |
| 4 | quattro | 98 | novantotto |
| 5 | cinque | 100 | cento |
| 6 | sei | 101 | cento uno |
| 7 | sette | 211 | duecento undici |
| 8 | otto | 322 | trecento ventidue |
| 9 | nove | 433 | quattrocento trentatrè |
| 10 | dieci | 544 | cinquecento quarantaquattro |
| 11 | undici | 655 | seicento cinquantacinque |
| 12 | dodici | 766 | settecento sessantasei |
| 13 | tredici | 877 | ottocento settantasette |
| 14 | quattordici | 988 | novecento ottantotto |
| 15 | quindici | 1000 | mille |
| 16 | sedici | 1001 | mille uno |
| 17 | diciassette | 2112 | duemila centododici |
| 18 | diciotto | 3223 | tremila duecento ventitrè |
| 19 | diciannove | | |
| 20 | venti | 4334 | quattromila trecento trentaquattro |
| 21 | ventuno | | |
| 32 | trentadue | 10,000 | diecimila |
| 43 | quarantatrè | | |

0.1 = 0,1 zero virgola uno (literally 'nought comma one')

## The days of the week

| | |
|---|---|
| Monday | Lunedì |
| Tuesday | Martedì |
| Wednesday | Mercoledì |
| Thursday | Giovedì |
| Friday | Venerdì |
| Saturday | Sabato |
| Sunday | Domenica |

## The months of the year

| | |
|---|---|
| January | Gennaio |
| February | Febbraio |
| March | Marzo |
| April | Aprile |
| May | Maggio |
| June | Giugno |
| July | Luglio |
| August | Agosto |
| September | Settembre |
| October | Ottobre |
| November | Novembre |
| December | Dicembre |

# Equivalents

## Italian money

Lira = L

**Coins** (*Monete*)
L 5 cinque lire
L 10 dieci lire
L 20 venti lire
L 50 cinquanta lire
L 100 cento lire
L 200 duecento lire
L 500 cinquecento lire

**Notes** (*Banconote*)
L 500 cinquecento lire
L 1000 mille lire
L 2000 duemila lire
L 5000 cinquemila lire
L 10,000 diecimila lire
L 20,000 ventimila lire
L 50,000 cinquantamila lire
L 100,000 centomila lire

In a bank you can specify how you would like the money:

in ten thousands    in biglietti da diecimila
in twenty thousands    in biglietti da ventimila
in fifty thousands    in biglietti da cinquantamila
in hundred thousands    in biglietti da centomila

## Distances

1 mile = 1.6 kilometres      1.6 chilometri = 1 mile

| Miles | 10 | 20 | 30 | 40 | 50 | 60 | 70 | 80 | 90 | 100 | Miles |
|---|---|---|---|---|---|---|---|---|---|---|---|
| Kilometres | 16 | 32 | 48 | 64 | 80 | 97 | 113 | 128 | 145 | 160 | Chilometri |

## Lengths and sizes

Some approximate equivalents:

| British | | Metric |
|---|---|---|
| 1 inch | | = 2.5 centimetri |
| 6 inches | | = 15 centimetri |
| 1 foot | = 12 inches | = 30 centimetri |
| 2 feet | = 24 inches | = 60 centimetri |
| 1 yard | = 3 feet or 36 inches | = 91 centimetri |
| 1 yard 3 inches | | = 1 metro |

## General clothes sizes (including chest/hip measurements)

| GB | USA | Europe | ins | cms |
|---|---|---|---|---|
| 8 | 6 | 36 | 30/32 | 76/81 |
| 10 | 8 | 38 | 32/34 | 81/86 |
| 12 | 10 | 40 | 34/36 | 86/91 |
| 14 | 12 | 42 | 36/38 | 91/97 |
| 16 | 14 | 44 | 38/40 | 97/102 |
| 18 | 16 | 46 | 40/42 | 102/107 |
| 20 | 18 | 48 | 42/44 | 107/112 |
| 22 | 20 | 50 | 44/46 | 112/117 |
| 24 | 22 | 52 | 46/48 | 117/122 |
| 26 | 24 | 54 | 48/50 | 122/127 |

## Waist measurements

(ins) GB/USA 22 24 26 28 30 32 34 36 38  40  42  44  46  48  50
(cms) Europe 56 61 66 71 76 81 86 91 97 102 107 112 117 122 127

## Collar measurements

(ins) GB/USA 14  14½ 15  15½ 16  16½ 17  17½
(cms) Europe 36  37  38  39  40  41  42  43

### Shoes

| | | | | | | | | | | | | | | | | |
|---|---|---|---|---|---|---|---|---|---|---|---|---|---|---|---|---|
| GB | 3 | 3½ | 4 | 4½ | 5 | 5½ | 6 | 6½ | 7 | 7½ | 8 | 8½ | 9 | 10 | 11 | 12 |
| USA | 4½ | 5 | 5½ | 6 | 6½ | 7 | 7½ | 8 | 8½ | 9 | 9½ | 10 | 10½ | 11½ | 12½ | 13½ |
| Europe | 36 | | 37 | | 38 | | 39 | | 40 | | 41 | | 42 | 43 | 44 | 45 |

### Hats

| | | | | | | | | | |
|---|---|---|---|---|---|---|---|---|---|
| GB | 6⅝ | 6⅜ | 6⅞ | 7 | 7⅛ | 7¼ | 7⅜ | 7½ | 7⅝ |
| USA | 6¾ | 6⅞ | 7 | 7⅛ | 7¼ | 7⅜ | 7½ | 7⅝ | 7¾ |
| Europe | 54 | 55 | 56 | 57 | 58 | 59 | 60 | 61 | 62 |

Glove sizes are the same in every country.

## Weights

Some approximate equivalents:

*Grammi* (g) (grams) and *chilogrammi* (kg) (kilograms)
1000 *grammi* (1000 g) = 1 *chilogrammo* (kilo/kg)

| | | |
|---|---|---|
| 1 oz | = | 25 grammi |
| 4 ozs | = | 100/125 grammi |
| 8 ozs | = | 225 grammi |
| 1 pound (16 ozs) | = | 450 grammi |
| 1 pound 2 ozs | = | 500 grammi (½ chilogrammo) |
| 2 pounds 4 ozs | = | 1 chilogrammo (1 chilo/kg) |
| 1 stone | = | 6 chilogrammi |

### Body weight

Body weight in Italy is measured in kilograms (*chilogrammi*)

Some approximate equivalents:

| Pounds | Stones | Kilogrammes |
|--------|--------|-------------|
| 28 | 2 | 12½ |
| 42 | 3 | 19 |
| 56 | 4 | 25 |
| 70 | 5 | 32 |
| 84 | 6 | 38 |
| 98 | 7 | 45 |
| 112 | 8 | 51 |
| 126 | 9 | 57½ |
| 140 | 10 | 63 |
| 154 | 11 | 70 |
| 168 | 12 | 76 |
| 182 | 13 | 83 |
| 196 | 14 | 90 |

## Liquid measure

In Italy all liquids are measured in litres.
Some approximate equivalents:

1 pint = 0.57 litri (litres)      1 gallon = 4.55 litres

| GB measures | | Litres |
|-------------|---|--------|
| 1 pint | = | 0.5 |
| (20 fluid ounces (fl. ozs.)) | | |
| 1.7 pints | = | 1 |
| 1.1 gallons | = | 5 |
| 2.2 gallons | = | 10 |
| 3.3 gallons | = | 15 |
| 4.4 gallons | = | 20 |
| 5.5 gallons | = | 25 |
| 6.6 gallons | = | 30 |
| 7.7 gallons | = | 35 |
| 8.8 gallons | = | 40 |
| 9.9 gallons | = | 45 |

## Temperature

|                  | **Fahrenheit** (F) | **Centigrade** (C) |
|------------------|--------------------|--------------------|
| Boiling point    | 212°               | 100°               |
|                  | 104°               | 40°                |
| Body temperature | 98.4°              | 36.9°              |
|                  | 86°                | 30°                |
|                  | 68°                | 20°                |
|                  | 59°                | 15°                |
|                  | 50°                | 10°                |
| Freezing point   | 32°                | 0°                 |
|                  | 23°                | −5°                |
|                  | 0°                 | −18°               |

(Convert Fahrenheit to Centigrade by subtracting 32 and multiplying by 5/9. Convert Centigrade to Fahrenheit by multiplying by 9/5 and adding 32.)

## Tyre pressures

| lb/sq in | = kg/cm² | lb/sq in | = kg/cm² | lb/sq in | = kg/cm² |
|----------|----------|----------|----------|----------|----------|
| 20       | = 1.40   | 24       | = 1.68   | 30       | = 2.10   |
| 21       | = 1.47   | 26       | = 1.82   | 34       | = 2.39   |
| 22       | = 1.54   | 28       | = 1.96   | 40       | = 2.81   |

# Countries, currencies, nationalities and languages

| Country, area or continent | Main unit of currency | Description & nationality (feminine form given in brackets) | Main language(s) |
|---|---|---|---|
| Africa | — | Africano (–na) | — |
| Albania | Lek | Albanese (m & f) | Albanese |
| Algeria | Dinar | Algerino (–na) | Arabo/Francese |
| Argentina | Peso | Argentino (–na) | Spagnolo |
| Asia | — | Asiatico (–ca) | — |
| Australia | Dollar | Australiano (–na) | Inglese |
| Austria | Schilling | Austriaco (–ca) | Tedesco |
| Bahrain | Dinar | Bahrainese (m & f) | Arabo |
| Belgium | Franc | Belga (m & f) | Fiammingo/Francese |
| Bolivia | Peso | Boliviano (–na) | Spagnolo |
| Brazil | Cruzeiro | Brasiliano (–na) | Portoghese |
| Bulgaria | Lev | Bulgaro (–ra) | Bulgaro |
| Burma | Kyat | Birmano (–na) | Birmano |
| Canada | Dollar | Canadese (m & f) | Inglese/Francese |
| Chile | Peso | Cileno (–na) | Spagnolo |

| | | | | |
|---|---|---|---|---|
| China | Cina | Yuan | Cinese (m & f) | Cinese |
| Colombia | Colombia | Peso | Colombiano (–na) | Spagnolo |
| Costa Rica | Costarica | Colon | Costaricano (–na) | Spagnolo |
| Cuba | Cuba | Peso | Cubano (–na) | Spagnolo |
| Cyprus | Cipro | Pound | Cipriota (m & f) | Greco/Turco |
| Czechoslovakia | Cecoslovacchia | Koruna | Cecoslovacco (–ca) | Ceco/Slovacco |
| Denmark | Danimarca | Krone | Danese (m & f) | Danese |
| Ecuador | Ecuador | Sucre | Ecuadoriano (–na) | Spagnolo |
| Egypt | Egitto | Pound | Egiziano (–na) | Arabo |
| Eire | Repubblica Irlandese | Punt | Irlandese (m & f) | Inglese/Irlandese |
| England | Inghilterra | Pound | Inglese (m & f) | Inglese |
| Ethiopia | Etiopia | Dollar | Etiopico (–ca) | Amarico |
| Europe | Europa | — | Europeo (–ea) | — |
| Finland | Finlandia | Markka | Finlandese (m & f) | Finlandese |
| France | Francia | Franc | Francese (m & f) | Francese |
| Germany West G. | Germania G. Occidentale | Deutsch-mark | Tedesco (–ca) | Tedesco |
| East G. | G. Orientale | Mark | Tedesco (–ca) | Tedesco |
| Ghana | Gana | New Cedi | Ganese (m & f) | Inglese/Akan |
| Greece | Grecia | Drachma | Greco (–ca) | Greco |
| Guatemala | Guatemala | Quetzal | Guatemalteco (–ca) | Spagnolo |
| Guyana | Guiana | Dollar | Guianese (m & f) | Inglese |
| Holland | Olanda | Guilder | Olandese (m & f) | Olandese |

| Country, area or continent | Main unit of currency | Description & nationality (feminine form given in brackets) | Main language(s) |
|---|---|---|---|
| Hong Kong | Dollar | di Hong Kong (m & f) | Inglese/Cinese |
| Hungary | Forint | Ungherese (m & f) | Ungherese |
| Iceland | Krona | Islandese (m & f) | Islandese |
| India | Rupee | Indiano (–na) | Hindi/Inglese |
| Indonesia | Rupiah | Indonesiano (–na) | Bahasa Indonesiano |
| Iran | Rial | Iranico (–ca) | Farsi |
| Iraq | Dinar | Iracheno (–na) | Arabo |
| Israel | Pound | Israeliano (–na) | Ebreo |
| Italy | Lira | Italiano (–na) | Italiano |
| Jamaica | Dollar | Giamaicano (–na) | Inglese |
| Japan | Yen | Giapponese (m & f) | Giapponese |
| Jordan | Dinar | Giordano (–na) | Arabo |
| Kenya | Shilling | del Kenia (m & f) | Swahili |
| Kuwait | Dinar | del Kuwait (m & f) | Arabo |
| Lebanon | Pound | Libanese (m & f) | Arabo |
| Libya | Dinar | Libico (–ca) | Arabo |
| Luxemburg | Franc | Lussemburghese (m & f) | Francese/Tedesco |

Country, area or continent:
Hong Kong
Ungheria
Islanda
India
Indonesia
Iran
Irak
Israele
Italia
Giamaica
Giappone
Giordania
Kenia
Kuwait
Libano
Libia
Lussemburgo

| Country | | Currency | Language |
|---|---|---|---|
| Malaysia | Malesia | Dollar | Malese (m & f) | Malese/Cinese |
| Malta | Malta | Pound | Maltese (m & f) | Maltese/Inglese |
| Mexico | Messico | Peso | Messicano (–na) | Spagnolo |
| Morocco | Marocco | Dirham | Marocchino (–na) | Arabo/Francese |
| New Zealand | Nuova Zelanda | Dollar | Neozelandese (m & f) | Inglese |
| Nicaragua | Nicaragua | Cordoba | Nicaraguense (m & f) | Spagnolo |
| Nigeria | Nigeria | Naira | Nigeriano (–na) | Hausa/Ibo/ Yorobua/ Inglese |
| Northern Ireland | Irlanda del nord | Pound | Irlandese (m & f) | Inglese |
| Norway | Norvegia | Krona | Norvegese (m & f) | Norvegese |
| Pakistan | Pakistan | Rupee | Pakistano (–na) | Urdu |
| Paraguay | Paraguai | Guarani | Paraguaiano (–na) | Spagnolo |
| Peru | Peru | Sol | Peruviano (–na) | Spagnolo |
| Poland | Polonia | Zloty | Polacco (–ca) | Polacco |
| Portugal | Portogallo | Escudo | Portoghese (m & f) | Portoghese |
| Romania | Rumania | Leu | Rumeno (–na) | Rumeno |
| Saudi Arabia | Arabia Saudita | Riyal | Arabo (–ba) Saudita | Arabo |
| Scotland | Scozia | Pound | Scozzese (m & f) | Inglese/Gaelico |
| Singapore | Singapore | Dollar | di Singapore (m & f) | Malese/Cinese/ Inglese/Tamil |
| South Africa | Sud Africa | Rand | Sudafricano (–na) | Afrikaans/Inglese |
| Spain | Spagna | Peseta | Spagnolo (–la) | Spagnolo |
| Sudan | Sudan | Pound | Sudanese (m & f) | Arabo |

| Country, area or continent | Main unit of currency | Description & nationality (feminine form given in brackets) | Main language(s) |
| --- | --- | --- | --- |
| Sweden | Svezia | Krona | Svedese (m & f) | Svedese |
| Switzerland | Svizzera | Franc | Svizzero (–ra) | Francese/Tedesco/Italiano/Romancio |
| Syria | Siria | Pound | Siriano (–na) | Arabo |
| Tanzania | Tanzania | Shilling | Tanzaniano (–na) | Swahili |
| Thailand | Tailandia | Baht | Tailandese (m & f) | Tai |
| Tunisia | Tunisia | Dinar | Tunisino (–na) | Arabo/Francese |
| Turkey | Turchia | Lira | Turco (–ca) | Turco |
| Union of Soviet Socialist Republics (USSR)/Russia | Unione delle Repubbliche Socialiste Sovietiche (URSS)/Russia | Rouble | Russo (–sa) | Russo |
| United Kingdom (UK) (England, Northern Ireland, Scotland, Wales, | Regno Unito (Inghilterra, Irlanda del nord, Scozia, Galles, | Pound sterling | Britannico (–ca) | Inglese |

| | | | | |
|---|---|---|---|---|
| Channel Islands) | Isole Normanne) | | | |
| United States of America (USA) | Stati Uniti d'America (USA) | Dollar | Americano (-na) | Inglese |
| Uruguay | Uruguay | Peso | Uruguaino (-na) | Spagnolo |
| Venezuela | Venezuela | Bolivar | Venezuelano (-na) | Spagnolo |
| Vietnam | Vietnam | Dong | Vietnamita (m & f) | Vietnamita |
| Wales | Galles | Pound | Gallese (m & f) | Gallese/Inglese |
| Yugoslavia | Iugoslavia | Dinar | Iugoslavo (-va) | Serbo-croato |
| Zaire | Zaire | Zaire | dello Zaire (m & f) | Francese |
| Zimbabwe | Zimbabwe | Dollar | di Zimbabwe (m & f) | Inglese |

# Travel hints

## Useful addresses

Every town has its own 'Ente Turismo' (tourist) office which will supply free leaflets, maps and information. At most stations there is an 'Ufficio Informazioni' (information office) which offers a similar service. Usual opening hours: 9.00 to 12.30, 3.0 p.m. to 7.0 p.m. (Usually closed on Sunday.)

## Social behaviour

Shaking hands is common in Italy, both on meeting and parting. When being introduced, say 'Piacere' and your *surname* as you shake hands. A woman is usually addressed as 'Signora' (when married) or 'Signorina' (when not). 'Signore', for a man, is less common.

To attract attention say 'Scusi.'

Queues are rare in Italy. It's every man for himself, but without being aggressive about it.

Bargaining is getting rarer. Only try it if you feel the atmosphere is right.

Lunch or dinner guests usually take flowers or chocolates for their host.

## Accommodation

Contact any 'Ente Turismo' office. All big stations have a hotel information service. Hotel categories: luxury, I, II, III and IV. 'Pensioni' are roughly British B&B standard, can be excellent and cheap. They are also divided into categories – I, II and III. Student hostels (ostelli della gioventù) can be found in some places.

# Getting around

Allow for big city rush hours which can cause serious hold-ups, particularly in Milan and Rome. Maps can be bought from all stationers and booksellers, and the 'Ente Turismo' office will always give you one of its own city.

**By taxi** You don't usually stop taxis in the street. The normal system is to go to a rank (common in all big cities) or telephone. Most public telephones have taxi numbers prominently displayed. The colour of Italian taxis varies from place to place, but they are always very distinctive. Payment is shown on the meter. Add 10 per cent for the tip.

**By bus** Again things vary from city to city. If there is a conductor you pay him, if not tickets are sold in tobacconists and many newspaper kiosks. Sometimes there are ticket machines in the bus itself. Bus doors open automatically, and you get on at the back and off in the middle or at the front.

**By underground** Underground networks can only be found in Rome and Milan, and they cover very little ground by comparison with London or Paris. There is usually one first class compartment, but for all the difference it makes, you might as well go second. Tickets on sale at the station newspaper kiosk.

**By train** Remember that Italian trains are usually crowded, and it's rarely worth travelling first class in the hope of getting a seat because of the shortage of first class seats. The exception to this rule is provided by the 'rapidi' (express trains) which are excellent and extremely comfortable, but for which you always have to pay a supplement and sometimes are obliged to travel first class as well. 'Rapidi' are perfect for inter-city travel.

NB There are special rates for rail travel on Sundays and public holidays.

**By coach** It's simpler to travel by train, but coaches are the only means of transport to many villages. Coach services are not all that

frequent, and the price corresponds with a second-class rail fare.
Ask for information at any travel agency.

## Changing money

Banks are open from 8.30–1.30 Mon–Fri except on public holidays.
Hotels and bigger shops will usually accept travellers' cheques.
Note that exchange, and most other banking operations, are carried
out in two distinct phases. First you do the necessary form filling etc
with the clerk who will then say 'Alla cassa', sending you to the
cash counter where you are handed the money.

## Shopping

**Shops** Opening hours vary, but can be approximately summed up
as 8.30–1.0 and 4.30–7.30. If you're relying on food shops, it's as
well to ask about the early closing day which differs from town to
town. In the mid to late seventies, there was an acute change
shortage in Italy. This has improved greatly, but you are still liable
to be offered stamps, sweets or, particularly, telephone tokens as
change. Telephone tokens have the status of money.

**Post Offices** Life can be complicated in Italian post offices, but
fortunately stamps are obtainable from tobacconists where you can
also buy express letters – which is advisable if you don't want your
mail to take a couple of weeks.

## Food and drink

Restaurant meals are expensive, and only the bigger cities offer
snack bar or café alternatives. Most young people, and a lot of their
elders as well, opt for the 'rosticceria' or the 'pizzeria', where other
dishes besides 'pizza' are served. Most cafés do snacks and a
toast (pronounced 'tost' and signifying a toasted ham and cheese
sandwich). This makes a very good light meal. You can usually get
food and drink up to midnight in cities and, at the height of the
summer, way into the small hours. In cafés and motorway self-

service bars you are usually expected to go to the cash-desk and pay before you are served.

## Tipping

Ten per cent is a good rule, but needn't be followed slavishly. When you get over the ten thousand lire mark you can start to scale it down slightly according to your own judgement. If the person who serves you is obviously the proprietor you don't tip. Railway porters – a dying race anyway – have fixed rates per piece of baggage, but don't object to a small tip over and above this.

## Entertainments

**To find out what's going on** look at entertainments column of daily or evening paper. Remember that Italian entertainments start late (never before nine and often after the advertised time of starting), and include at least one long interval. You book at the 'biglietteria' (theatre box office). Much sought-after shows like the opera at 'La Scala' in Milan are often sold out for months in advance. The seating in Italian theatres is divided up as follows (with slight variations from theatre to theatre): 'platea' (stalls) consisting of 'poltronissime' (front stalls) and 'poltrone' (back stalls), 'balconate' (dress circle), 'prima galleria numerata' (numbered seats in the upper circle), 'seconda galleria non numerata' or 'loggione' (gallery) and 'palchi' (boxes). In many theatres the boxes are 'rented' by families for an entire season.

Matinées (spettacolo pomeridiano) are extremely rare in Italy. The evening show ('spettacolo' or 'spettacolo serale') usually starts at 9.0 or 9.30.

**Museums and galleries** Closing days vary, but are usually on a Monday. A student card will get you in free or at a reduced rate to many national museums and galleries. Sunday mornings are free.

**1** ✈ **Venezia—Marco Polo** (N of city)
Bus to Piazzale Roma 13km.

**2** ✈ **Milano—Linate** (E of city)
Bus every 20 mins (05.40—20.00) to Viale L. Sturzo (20 mins) 8km.

**3** ✈ **Torino—Caselle** (N of city)
Bus to Via P. Gobetti (30 mins) 16km.

**4** ✈ **Roma—Fiumicino** (SW of city)
Bus every 15 mins to Via G. Giolitti (07.00 —21.00) every 30 mins (21.00—07.00) (45 mins) 30km.

**5** ✈ **Olbia—Costa Smeralda** (S of city)
Bus to Corso Umberto 4km.

**6** ✈ **Napoli—Capodichino** (NW of city)
Bus to Via Pisanelli (40 mins) 8km.

**7** ✈ **Alghero—Fertilia** (N of city)
Bus to Corso V. Emanuele (15 mins) 11km.

**8** ✈ **Palermo—Punta Raisi** (NW of city)
Bus to Via Mazzini 32km.

# Italiano – Inglese

## Italian – English

# Per aiutarvi a girare

## Parole base

Se imparate queste a memoria vi sarà più facile girare

| | |
|---|---|
| Per favore | Please [*pliiz*] |
| Grazie | Thank you [**tsank** *iu*] |
| Sì | Yes [*ies*] |
| No | No [*nou*] |
| Sì grazie | Yes please [*ies pliiz*] |
| No grazie | No thank you [*nou tsank iu*] |
| Come? | Sorry? [*sorri*] |
| Scusi! | Excuse me! [*ekschiuz mi*] |
| Mi dispiace | I'm sorry [*aim **sorri***] |
| Va bene | That's all right [**tsats** *ol* **rait**] |
| Bene! | Good! [*gud*] |
| Non capisco | I don't understand [*ai **dont** ander**stand***] |
| | |
| Ciao | Hello [*hallo*] |
| Mi chiamo | My name's ... [*mai neimz*] |
| Arrivederci | Goodbye [*gud **bai***] |
| Buon giorno | Good morning [*gud **mornin***] |
| Buon giorno (usato nel pomeriggio) | Good afternoon [*gud after**nun***] |
| | |
| Buona sera | Good evening [*gud **iv**inin*] |
| Buona notte | Good night [*gud **nait***] |
| Come sta? | How are you? [*hau **ar** iu?*] |
| Bene grazie | Fine thanks [**fain** *tsanks*] |
| Salute! | Cheers! [*cirs*] |
| Piacere di averla consciuta | (It was) nice to meet you [*(it uas) nais tu **mit** iu*] |
| | |
| Per favore ripeta | Could you repeat that please? [*kud iu ri**pit** tsat **pliiz***] |
| | |
| Più adagio per favore | Slower please [**slouar** *pliiz*] |

| | |
|---|---|
| Quanto costa? | How much is it? [*hau **mac**(e)\* iz it?*] |
| Quanto costano? | How much are they? [*hau **mac**(e)\* ar tsei*] |

## Frasi chiave

Quando avrete imparato questi modelli di frasi chiave potrete formare le vostre frasi usando le parole dal dizionario

| | |
|---|---|
| Dov'è la /banca (più vicina)/, per favore? | Where's the /(nearest) bank/ please? [*huerz tse nirest **bank** pliiz*] |
| C'è /un parcheggio/ qui vicino? | Is there a /car park/ near here? [*iz tser e **kar** park niir hiir*] |
| Ci sono dei /ristoranti/ qui vicino? | Are there any /restaurants/ near here? [*ar tser eni **rest**orants niir hiir*] |
| Vorrei /andare a fare il bagno/ | I'd like to /go **swim**ming/ [*aid laik tu go **suim**min*] |
| Vorrebbe /fare delle spese/? | Would you like to /go shopping/? [*ud iu laik tu go **sciop**pin?*] |
| Ha una /pianta della città/, per favore? | Have you got a /street map/ please? [*hav iu got e **striit** map pliiz*] |
| Ha delle /buste/, per favore? | Have you got any /envelopes/ please? [*hav iu got eni **en**velops pliiz*] |
| Non ho /spiccioli/ | I haven't got any /change/ [*ai havnt got eni **ceng**(e)\**] |
| Mi occorre un /medico/ | I need a /doctor/ [*ai niid e **dok**tar*] |

\* c(e), g(e): la 'e' fra parentesi è muta
NB 'c' è sempre pronunciato soffice

| | |
|---|---|
| Mi occorrono dei /traveller's cheques/ | I need some /traveller's cheques/ [*ai niid som travellez ceks*] |
| Vorrei una /camera/, per favore | I'd like a /room/ please [*aid laik e rum pliiz*] |
| Vorrei dei /francobolli/, per favore | I'd like some /stamps/ please [*aid laik som stamps pliiz*] |
| Desidera un /caffè/? | Would you like a coffee/? [*ud iu laik e koffi*] |
| Desidera dei /cioccolatini/? | Would you like some /chocolates/? [*ud iu laik som ciokolats*] |
| Mi chiami un /taxi/, per favore | Could you call a /taxi/ for me please? [*kud iu koll e taxi for mi pliiz*] |
| Quando parte il /(prossimo) treno/ per /Brighton/? | When does the /(next) train/ to /Brighton/ leave? [*huen daz tse nekst tren tu braiton liiv*] |
| Quando aprono (chiudono) le /banche/? | When do the /banks/ open? (close) [*huen du tse banks open (klos)*] |
| Le piace /questo colore/? | Do you like /this colour/? [*du iu laik tsis kalar*] |
| Le piacciono /queste scarpe/? | Do you like /these shoes/? [*du iu laik tsiiz scius*] |
| Mi piace /questo modello/ | I like /this style/ [*ai laik tsis stail*] |
| Non mi piace /questa forma/ | I don't like /this shape/ [*ai dont laik tsis sceip*] |

\* c(e), g(e): la 'e' fra parentesi è muta
N.B. 'c' è sempre pronunciato soffice

## Conversazioni

Ora che avete imparato le frasi basi e i modelli delle frasi chiave, ecco alcuni esempi di conversazioni in cui potete prendere parte.

### Presentazioni

Good morning Mr Baker. This is Maria Negrente
How do you do
How do you do

Buon giorno, Mr Baker. Le presento Maria Negrente
Piacere
Piacere

### Incontro con qualcuno

Good evening
Good evening Mr Allen
How are you?
Fine thanks. And you?
Fine thanks

Buona sera
Buona sera, Mr Allen
Come sta?
Bene grazie. E lei?
Bene grazie

### Trovare la strada

Excuse me!
Yes?
Where's the Hotel Bristol please?
Straight on, then right
Thank you
Not at all

Scusi!
Sì?
Dov'è l'albergo Bristol, per favore?
Dritto, e a destra
Grazie
Prego

### Alla stazione

A single to Cambridge please

£3.40 (three pounds forty)

When does the next train leave?

Un biglietto di andata per Cambridge, per favore
£3.40 (tre sterline e quaranta pence)
Quando parte il prossimo treno?

| | |
|---|---|
| At four fifteen | Alle 16.15 |
| When does the train arrive in Cambridge? | Quando arriva il treno a Cambridge? |
| At five thirty-six | Alle 17.36 |
| Thank you | Grazie |

## Nell'albergo – desidera una stanza

| | |
|---|---|
| Good afternoon. Can I help you? | Buon giorno. Desidera? |
| Good afternoon. I'd like a double room please | Buon giorno. Vorrei una camera doppia, per favore |
| For how many nights? | Quante notti? |
| For two nights | Per due notti |
| Would you like a room with or without bath? | Desidera una camera con bagno o senza bagno? |
| With bath please | Con bagno, per favore |
| Yes, that's fine | Sì, va bene |
| How much is it please? | Quanto costa, per favore? |
| Twenty pounds a night | Una notte £20 |
| I'll take it please | La prendo, grazie |

## Comperare qualcosa

| | |
|---|---|
| Good morning. Can I help you? | Buon giorno, Desidera? |
| Good morning. Have you got any coffee? | Buon giorno. Ha del caffè? |
| Yes. How much would you like? | Sì. Quanto ne desidera? |
| I'd like a pound please | Ne vorrei un mezzo chilo, per favore |
| Good. Anything else? | Bene. Nient'altro? |
| Yes. I'd like some apples please | Sì. Vorrei delle mele, per favore |
| How many? | Quante? |
| Four please | 4, per favore |
| OK. Two pounds thirty please | OK. £2.30, per favore |
| Thank you | Grazie |

## Scegliere qualcosa

| | |
|---|---|
| Good afternoon. Can I help you? | Buon giorno. Desidera? |
| I'd like a T-shirt please | Vorrei una maglietta, per favore |
| What size would you like? | Che misura desidera? |
| Twelve please | 12, per favore |
| Do you like this one? | Le piace questa? |
| No. I don't like that colour. Have you got a red one? | No. Non mi piace questo colore. La ha in rosso? |
| Yes, of course | Si, certo |
| How much is it please? | Quanto costa? |
| Two pounds fifty | £2.50 |
| I'll take it. Thank you | La prendo. Grazie |

# Alcuni brevi accenni

Sotto molti aspetti l'inglese è molto meno complicato dell'italiano:

## 1 *You* – lei/loro, tu/voi

C'è soltanto un modo di rivolgersi ad una o più persone in inglese, *'you'*. È singolare come plurale, formale e familiare.

## 2 L'articolo

L'articolo definito in inglese è *'the'* ed è invariable. Si usa con tutti i nomi singolari e plurali.
NB *Mr, Mrs,* e *Miss* non hanno mai l'articolo e si usano sempre con il cognome o nome e cognome. *Mr Brown* = Il Signor Brown, *Mrs Brown* = La Signora Brown, *Miss Brown* = La Signorina Brown.
L'articolo indefinito è *'a'* oppure *'an'* davanti alle parole che cominciano con vocale.

## 3 Nomi

I nomi in inglese non hanno genere e cambiano solo al plurale.

## 4 Plurale

Per formare il plurale della maggioranza dei nomi in inglese si aggiunge semplicemente una *'-s'* al singolare. Tutte le forme plurali irregolari sono date nel dizionario. Es:
*address -es* (indirizzo)
*baby -ies* (neonato)
*knife -ves* (coltello)
*sheep/sheep* (pl) (pecora) in questo esempio il singolare ed il
   plurale sono uguali.

## 5 Aggettivi

Gli aggettivi non cambiano mai e stanno davanti ai nomi a cui si riferiscono:

*a red car*    = una macchina rossa
*red gloves*   = guanti rossi

## 6 Comparativi

In inglese per formare il comparativo di un aggettivo con una o due sillabe, aggiungete semplicemente '*-er*':

*I'd like something bigger*    Vorrei qualcosa più grande
*I'd like something heavier*   Vorrei qualcosa più pesante

NB La consonante finale degli aggettivi è spesso raddoppiata, così, per esempio, '*big*' diventa '*bigger*'.
La '*y*' finale diventa '*i*' prima di '*-er*': '*heavy*' diventa '*heavier*'.
Gli aggettivi con più di due sillabe formano il comparativo con '*more*' (più)

*I'd like something more comfortable*    Vorrei qualcosa più comodo

'*Less*' (meno) è usato con tutti gli aggettivi:
*I'd like something less expensive*   Vorrei qualcosa meno caro

*Comparativi irregolari:*

| | |
|---|---|
| good – better | buono – migliore |
| bad – worse | cattivo – peggiore |
| much/many – more | molto/molti – più |
| little – less | poco – meno |
| small – smaller | piccolo – più piccolo |

## 7 Nota sulla quantità

Il dizionario vi metterà in grado d'indicare quantità molto precise. Se cercate 'fiammifero' (*match*), per esempio, troverete anche 'una scatola di fiammiferi' (*a box of matches*) sotto la parola principale, così potete dire:

| | |
|---|---|
| *I'd like some matches please* | Vorrei dei fiammiferi, per favore (quantità generale) |
| *I'd like a box of matches please* | Vorrei una scatola di fiammiferi, per favore (quantità precisa) |

Si può anche indicare la precisa quantità usando termini di volume o di peso.

Per esempio 'quattro galloni di benzina', 'una libbra di pomodori', ecc.

Vedere gli Equivalenti a p284

Ricordate questi sei 'vocaboli di quantità' e potrete chiedere quasi tutto.

| | |
|---|---|
| *a bottle of /beer/* | una bottiglia di /birra/ |
| *a glass of /milk/* | un bicchiere di /latte/ |
| *a packet of /cigarettes/* | un pacchetto di /sigarette/ |
| *a piece of /cake/* | un pezzo di /torta/ |
| *a slice of /ham/* | una fetta di /prosciutto/ |
| *a tin of /tomatoes/* | una barattolo di /pomodori/ |

## 8 Verbi

Di solito in questo dizionario i verbi sono dati soltanto all' infinito. Per esempio *'close'* (chiudere)

## 9 Avere: *'have got'*

Se sentite la parola *'got'* è la forma inglese per rinforzare il verbo avere:

| | |
|---|---|
| *I've got a ticket* | Ho un biglietto |
| *I haven't got any change* | Non ho spiccioli |
| *Have you got the keys?* | Ha le chiavi? |

# Guida per la pronuncia

La pronuncia inglese non è proprio facile, ma con queste regole ognuno può farsi capire

| | |
|---|---|
| [c] | cat (gatto) come casa<br>city (città) come Silvia |
| [ch] | church (chiesa) come cena |
| [g] | girl (ragazza) come gatto<br>gentleman (signore) come gelato |
| [gl] e [gn] | Nei gruppi 'gn' e 'gl' è sempre pronunciata dura<br>Es. g-liding (volo a vela), ig-nore (trascurare)<br>Il gruppo 'ng' è pronunciato insieme.<br>Es. long (lungo), singing (canto). |
| [h] | La consonante 'h' è quasi sempre aspirata.<br>Es. house (casa) |
| [r] | La consonante 'r' suona meno chiara che in italiano ed è spesso muta.<br>Es. right (destra) – meno chiara, father (padre) – muta. |
| [sh] | sheet (lenzuolo) come sci<br>NB In alcune parole come 'sure' (sicuro) e 'sugar' (zucchero) la 's' è pronunciata come sci |
| [th] e [tio] | thin (magro) si pronuncia come la 's' blesa, spingendo la lingua contro i denti, ma il gruppo (tio) si pronuncia come sciolto.<br>Es. station (stazione), action (azione). |

Consonanti che non esistono in italiano.

| | |
|---|---|
| [j] | John (Giovanni) |
| [k] | key (chiave) |
| [x] | taxi (tassi) suona come 'cs' in facsimile |
| [w] | wind (vento) 'u' + suono della vocale che segue. Es. west (ovest) |
| [y] | yellow (giallo) 'i' + suono della vocale che segue. Es. yard (iarda = 1 m.) |

Le vocali inglesi sono molto variabili, ma queste regole molto generali
vi aiuteranno: ASCOLTATE GLI INGLESI

| | |
|---|---|
| [a] | spesso suona come 'a' in 'gatto'. |
| | Es. sad (triste) |
| | Seguìta da una consonante + 'e' ha il suono di 'ei' come in 'dei'. |
| | Es. date (data). |
| [e] | spesso suona come 'e' in 'letto'. Non si pronuncia mai la 'e' finale. |
| [ee] | feet (piedi) come filo. |
| [i] | spesso suona come 'i' in pino. Es. tin (barattolo), ma davanti a una consonante + 'e' suona come 'ai' come in mai. Es. fine (bello). • |
| [o] | spesso suona come 'o' in rotto. Es. hot (caldo), ma davanti a una consonante + 'e' si pronuncia lungo come 'ou'. Es. bone (osso). |
| [oo] | di solito come 'u' in tubo. Es. room (stanza), ma 'oor' si pronuncia come porta. Es. door (porta) come in dormire. |
| (ow) | si pronuncia come 'au' in causa. Es. now (ora) |
| (u) | la 'u' iniziale si pronuncia generalmente 'iu' come in più'. Es. use (usare). |
| | Spesso si pronuncia 'a' come in pacco. Es. butter (burro). |
| | Dopo 'l' e 'r' si pronuncia 'u' come in luna. Es. rule (regola). |

# Abbreviazioni

aggettivo
avverbio
nome
preposizione
pronome
verbo
maschile
femminile
singolare
plurale
familiare
marca di fabbrica
per esempio
eccetera

# Abbreviations

| | |
|---|---|
| (adj) | adjective |
| (adv) | adverb |
| (n) | noun |
| (prep) | preposition |
| (pron) | pronoun |
| (vb) | verb |
| (m) | masculine |
| (f) | feminine |
| (s) | singular |
| (pl) | plural |
| (infml) | informal |
| (tdmk) | trademark |
| (eg) | for example |
| (etc) | et cetera |

# Vocabolario
# A – Z
# Dictionary

# A

a

**all'albergo** at /the hotel/
  **alla stazione** to /the station/
  **alle sette e mezzo** at seven-thirty
  **all'università** at /the university/
**abbassare** lower (vb)
**abbastanza** enough
  **abbastanza denaro** enough money
  **abbastanza veloce** fast enough
**abbonamento** (treno, autobus) season ticket
**abbonamento** (rivista, teatro) subscription
**abbonarsi a / /** subscribe to / /
**abbreviare** shorten
**abbronzato** suntanned
**abbronzatura** suntan (n)
**abitare** live (=reside)
  **dove abita?** where do you live?
**abitudine** (f) custom
**accanto** (a) beside (prep)
  **accanto /lei/** beside /her/
**accendere** (lampada, radio) switch on, turn on
**accendere /un fuoco/** light /a fire/
  **mi accende la sigaretta?** have you got a light?
**accendigas** (m) - gas lighter
**accendino** cigarette lighter
  **accendino da buttare** disposable lighter
  **gas per accendini** lighter fuel
**acceso** (lampada, radio) on (of light etc)
**accettare** accept
**acciaio** steel
  **acciaio inossidabile** stainless steel
  **/posateria/ di acciaio inossidabile** stainless steel /cutlery/
**accidenti!** damn!
**accludere** enclose
**accomodarsi** make oneself comfortable
  **si accomodi, prego** please sit down
**acconsentire a / /** agree to / /
**accordo** agreement
  **essere d'accordo** agree

**non essere d'accordo** disagree with
**sono d'accordo** I agree
**non sono d'accordo con /lei/** I disagree with /you/
**acerbo** unripe
**aceto** vinegar
  **olio e aceto** oil and vinegar
  **una bottiglia di aceto** a bottle of vinegar
**acqua** water
  **acqua calda** hot water
  **acqua corrente** running water
  **acqua distillata** distilled water
  **acqua dolce** fresh water (ie not salt)
  **acqua fredda** cold water
  **acqua potabile** drinking water
**acqua di colonia** eau-de-Cologne
  **una bottiglia di acqua di colonia** a bottle of eau-de-Cologne
**acqua minerale** mineral water
  **acqua minerale gassata** fizzy mineral water
  **acqua minerale naturale** plain mineral water
  **una bottiglia di acqua minerale** a bottle of mineral water
  **un bicchiere di acqua minerale** a glass of mineral water
**acquaplano** surfing
  **fare acquaplano** go surfing
**acquarello** watercolour (=painting)
**adattare** fit (vb)
**adatto** suitable
**addestramento** training (of personnel)
**addomesticato** tame (adj)
**adesso** now
**adolescente** (m&f) teenager
**adulto** adult
  **solo per adulti** adults only
**aereo** (n) plane (n) (=aeroplane)
  **in aereo** by plane
**aereo** (adj)
  **lettera aerea** air letter
  **linea aerea** airline
  **per via aerea** by air
  **posta aerea** airmail
**aeroplano** aeroplane

**aeroporto** *airport*
  **autobus** (m) **dell'aeroporto** *airport bus -es*
**aerosol** (m) – *aerosol*
**affare** (m) *bargain (n)*
  **è un affare** *it's a bargain*
**affettare** (=tagliare) *slice (vb)*
**affilare** *sharpen*
**affilato** *sharp (of things)*
**affittare /una villa/** *rent /a villa/*
**affitto** *rent (n) (payment)*
**affittuaria** *landlady -ies*
**affittuario** *landlord*
**affollato** *crowded*
**affondare** *sink (vb)*
**affumicato** *smoked (of fish & meat etc)*
  **/prosciutto/ affumicato** *smoked /ham/*
**agenda** *notebook*
**agente** (m) **immobiliare** *estate agent*
**agenzia** *agency -ies*
**aggeggio -ggi** *gadget*
**aggiungere** *add*
**aggiustare** (= sistemare) *adjust*
**aggiustare** (=accomodare) *mend*
**aggiustare** *repair (vb)*
**aglio** *garlic*
**agnello** *lamb*
  **costoletta di agnello** *lamb chop*
  **una coscia di agnello** *a leg of lamb*
**ago -ghi** *needle*
**agosto** *August*
**agrimensore** (m) *surveyor*
**aiutare** *help (vb)*
**aiuto** *help (n)*
**ala** *wing (bird or plane)*
**alba** *dawn, sunrise*
**albergo -ghi** *hotel*
  **albergo di prima classe** *first class hotel*
  **albergo economico** *cheap hotel*
  **albergo non troppo costoso** *medium-priced hotel*
  **albergo per la gioventù** *hostel* (= youth hostel)
**albero** (di nave) *mast*
**albero** (botanica) *tree*

**albicocca -che** *apricot*
**alcool** (m) *alcohol*
  **alcool** (m) **denaturato** *methylated spirit*
  **una bottiglia di alcool denaturato** *a bottle of methylated spirits*
**alcoolico** *alcoholic (adj)*
**alfabeto** *alphabet*
**all'anno** *per annum*
**allarme** (m) **d'incendio** *fire alarm*
**allattare** *breast-feed*
**allergico** *allergic*
  **sono allergico /alla penicillina/** *I'm allergic /to penicillin/*
**all'estero** *overseas*
**allibratore** (m) (negozio) *betting shop*
**allibratore** (m) (persona) *bookmaker*
**alloggiare** *stay*
  **dove alloggiate?** *where are you staying?*
**alloggio** *accommodation*
**allungare** *lengthen*
**alpinismo** *mountaineering*
  **fare l'alpinismo** *go mountaineering*
**alpinista** (m) **-isti** *mountaineer*
**alta frequenza** *VHF*
**altalena** *swing (n) (children's swing)*
**alternativa** *alternative (n)*
**altezza** *height*
**alto** *high*
  **alta marea** *high water*
  **sedia alta** *high chair*
**alto** (persona) *tall*
**altro** *other*
  **l'altro /treno/** *the other /train/*
  **un altro** (m) **un'altra** (f) *another*
  **un altro /bicchiere di vino/** *another /glass of wine/*
**altrove** *elsewhere*
**alunno** *pupil*
**alzare** *lift (vb)*
**alzarsi** *get up*
**alzato**
  **essere alzato** *be up* (= out of bed)
**amabile** *medium-sweet*
**amare** *love (vb)*
**amaro** *bitter (adj)*

**ambasciata** *embassy -ies*
  **l'ambasciata /britannica/** *the
  /British/ Embassy*
**ambasciatore** (m) *ambassador*
**ambedue** *both*
**ambulanza** *ambulance*
**ambulatorio -i** *surgery -ies (=place)*
  **ambulatorio medico** *doctor's surgery*
**amichevole** *friendly*
**amico** (m) **-ci** (mpl) **amica** (f) **-che** (fpl)
  *friend*
**amico -ci per corrispondenza / amica
  -che per corrispondenza** *pen friend*
**amido** *starch -es* (n)
**ammobiliare** *furnish*
**ammobiliato** *furnished*
  **/appartamento/ ammobiliato**
  *furnished /flat/*
**ammortizzatore** (m) *shock absorber*
  *(car)*
**ammuffito** *mouldy*
**amore** (m) *love* (n)
  **fare l'amore** *make love*
**analgesico** *painkiller*
**ananas** (m) **-** *pineapple*
  **succo di ananas** *pineapple juice*
  **una fetta di ananas** *a slice of
  pineapple*
**anatre** (fpl) **selvatiche** *wild geese*
**anca** *hip*
**anche** *also*
**ancora** (adv) *again*
  **ancora /del dolce/, per favore** *more
  /cake/ please*
**ancora** (n) *anchor*
**andare** *go*
  **andare a /casa/** *go /home/*
  **andare ad /un congresso/** *go to /a
  conference/*
  **andare a /fare la spesa/** *go
  /shopping/*
  **andare a /fare un picnic/** *go /on a
  picnic/*
  **andiamo!** *let's go*
**andare a pattinare** *go skating*
**andare a prendere** *fetch*
**andare a trovare /   /** *call on /   /*

**(=visit)**
**andare bene** *suit* (vb)
**andare in bicicletta** *ride a bicycle*
**andiamo!** *let's go!*
**anello** *ring*
  **anello di /diamanti/** */diamond/ ring*
  **anello di fidanzamento** *engagement
  ring*
**anemico** *anaemic*
  **sono anemico** *I'm anaemic*
**anestetico** *anaesthetic* (n)
**angolo** *corner*
**animale** (m) *animal*
  **animale /domestico/** *pet*
**anitra/anatroccolo** *duck/duckling*
**anniversario** *anniversary -ies*
  **anniversario del matrimonio**
  *wedding anniversary*
**anno** *year*
  **ha /sei/ anni** *he is /six/ years old*
  **l'anno prossimo** *next year*
  **l'anno scorso** *last year*
  **quest'anno** *this year*
**annoiarsi** *bored (to be bored)*
  **mi annoio** *I'm bored*
**annuale** *yearly*
**annullamento** *cancellation*
**annullato** *cancelled*
**annuo** *annual*
**antenna** *aerial*
**anti smagliatura** (inv) *run-resistant
  (tights etc)*
**antibiotico** *antibiotic*
**anticipo** *advance (advance of money)*
  **in anticipo** *in advance*
**anticoncezionali** (mpl) *contraceptives
  (pl)*
  **la pillola** *the Pill*
  **un pacchetto di preservativi** (Durex
  (tdmk)) *a packet of sheaths (=Durex
  (tdmk))*
**antigelo** *antifreeze*
  **una lattina di antigelo** *a can of
  antifreeze*
**antipasti** (pl) *hors d'oeuvres*
**antipasto** *starter (=hors d'oeuvre)*
**antipatico** *awful (of peopl)*

**antiquariato**
  **negozio di antiquariato** *antique shop*
  **oggetto di antiquariato** *antique (n)*
**antiquato** *old-fashioned*
**antisettico** *antiseptic*
  **crema antisettica** *antiseptic cream*
  **un tubetto di crema antisettica** *a tube of antiseptic (cream)*
**ape** (f) *bee*
  **puntura d'ape** *bee sting*
**aperitivo** *aperitif*
**aperto** *open (adj)*
  **piscina all'aperto** *open-air swimming pool*
  **ristorante** (m) **all'aperto** *open-air restaurant*
**apparecchio acustico- apparecchi acustici** *hearing aid*
**appartamento** (condominio) *flat (n)*
  **appartamento ammobiliato** *furnished flat*
  **appartamento non ammobiliato** *unfurnished flat*
**appartamento** (albergo) *suite (=hotel suite)*
**appassionato di / /** *interested in / /*
**appendere** *hang*
**appendicite** (f) *appendicitis*
**appiccicaticcio -cci** *sticky*
**apprensivo** *nervous (=apprehensive)*
**approssimativamente** *roughly (=approximately)*
**appuntamento** *appointment*
  **fissare un appuntamento** *make an appointment*
  **ho un appuntamento** *I've got an appointment*
**appuntito** *pointed*
**aprile** (m) *April*
**aprire** *open (vb)*
**apriscatole** (m) - *tin opener*
**aquilone** (m) *kite*
**arachide** (f) *peanut*
  **un pacchetto di arachidi** *a packet of peanuts*
**aragosta** *lobster*
**arancia -ce** *orange (fruit)*

**succo d'arancia** *orange juice*
  **una bottiglia d'arancia** *a bottle of orange juice*
  **un bicchiere d'arancia** *a glass of orange juice*
**aranciata** *orangeade*
**arancione** *orange (colour)*
**arbitro** *umpire*
**architetto** *architect*
**argentina** *polo neck sweater*
**argento** *silver (n)*
  **d'argento** *silver (adj)*
**aria** *air*
  **aria condizionata** *air conditioning*
  **aria fresca** *some fresh air*
**aringa** *herring*
**armadietto** *locker*
  **armadietto deposito** *left-luggage locker*
**armadio** *cupboard*
**arnese** (m) *tool*
**arrabbiato** *angry*
  **sono arrabbiato con /lui/** *I'm angry with/ him/*
**arredamento per ufficio** *office equipment*
**arricciare** *curl (vb)*
**arrivare** *arrive*
  **arrivare /alle quattro e mezzo/ pomeridiane** *arrive at /four-thirty/ p.m.*
  **arrivare a /luglio/** *arrive in /July/*
  **arrivare /lunedì/** *arrive on /Monday/*
  **come ci arrivo?** *how do I get there?*
  **quando arriva /il treno/ a /Brighton/?** *when does /the train/ get to /Brighton/?*
  **arrivare a /Brighton/** *arrive in /Brighton/*
**arrivederci!** *see you!*
**arrivo** *arrival*
  **ora di arrivo** *time of arrival*
**arrostire** *roast (vb)*
  **manzo arrosto** *roast beef*
  **pollo arrosto** *roast chicken*
**artificiale** (=non naturale) *artificial*
  **respirazione** (f) **artificiale** *artificial respiration*

**artificiale** (fatta dall'uomo) *man-made*
**fibra artificiale** *man-made fibre*
**artigianato** (ms) **regionale** *local crafts*
**artista** (m&f) *artist*
**ascensore** (m) *lift* (n) (= *elevator*)
**asciugamano** *towel* (= *bath towel*)
**asciugapiatti** (m) - *tea towel*
**asciugare** *dry, wipe*
**asciutto** *dry* (adj) (*of things*)
**ascoltare /un po' di musica/** *listen to /some music/*
**asilo** *nursery -ies* (= *day n. for children*)
**asino** *donkey*
**asma** *asthma*
**asparagi** (mpl) *asparagus*
**aspettar/mi/** *wait /for me/*
  **per favore /mi/ aspetti** *please wait /for me/*
**aspirapolvere** (m) *hoover* (tdmk), *vacuum cleaner*
**aspirina** *aspirin*
  **una bottiglia di aspirine** *a bottle of aspirins*
  **un pacchetto di aspirine** *a packet of aspirins*
**aspro** *sour*
**assaggiare** *taste* (vb) (*perceive with tongue*)
**assassinare** *murder* (vb)
**assassinio** *murder* (n)
**asse** (f) **per acquaplano** *surfboard*
**assegno** *cheque*
  **assegno sbarrato** *crossed cheque*
  **libretto di assegni** *cheque book*
  **pagare con assegno** *pay by cheque*
**assente** *away* (*absent*)
**assicurare** *insure*
  **è assicurato** (m) **assicurata** (f)? *are you insured?*
**assicurazione** (f) *insurance*
  **fare un'assicurazione sulla propria vita** *insure /my life/*
  **certificato di assicurazione** *insurance certificate*
  **polizza di assicurazione** *insurance policy -ies*
**assistente** (m&f) *assistant*

**assistere** *attend*
  **assistere ad una funzione /cattolica/** *attend a /Catholic/ service*
**assorbenti** (mpl) *sanitary towels* (pl)
**asta** *auction* (n)
**asta di livello** *dipstick*
**astemio -mi** *teetotal*
**atlante** (m) *atlas -es*
**atmosferica** *atmospheric*
  **condizioni** (fpl) **atmosferiche** *weather conditions* (pl)
**attaccare** (una spina) *plug in*
**attaccapanni** (m) - *coat hanger*
**attacco** *attack* (n)
  **un attacco di / /** *an attack of / /*
  **attenzione!** *look out!*
**atterrato** *landed* (*of a plane*)
**attore** (m) *actor*
**attraente** *attractive*
**attraversare /la strada/** *cross /the road/*
**attraverso** *across, through*
  **attraverso /la campagna/** *through /the countryside/*
**attrice** (f) *actress -es*
**autista** (m&f) **-i** (*stipendiato*) *chauffeur*
**autista** (m&f) **-i** (*di taxi*) *driver*
  **autista** (m&f) **-i** (mpl) **-e** (fpl) **di taxi** *taxi driver*
**auto noleggio** *car hire*
**autobus** (m) - *bus -es*
  **fermata di autobus** *bus stop*
  **in autobus** *by bus*
  **l'autobus per / /** *the bus for / /*
  **stazione** (f) **di autobus** *bus station*
**automatico** *automatic*
**automobilista** (m&f) **-isti** *motorist*
**autopompa** *fire engine*
**autore** (m) *author*
**autorespiratore** (m) *aqualung*
**autorità** (fpl) *authorities* (pl)
**autostop**
  **fare l'autostop** *hitchhike*
**autostrada** *motorway*
**autunno** *autumn*
  **in autunno** *in autumn*
**avanti** *ahead*

**avanti!** come in! (command)
**avanzo** surplus -es
**avaro** mean (=not generous)
**aver simpatia per** be fond of
  **ho simpatia per /lui/** I'm fond of
  /him/
**avere** have
  **ha /dei francobolli?/** have you got
  /any stamps?/
  **ho fretta** I'm in a hurry
  **ho /un appuntamento/** I've got /an
  appointment/
  **non ho /soldi/** I haven't got /any
  money/
**avocado** avocado
**avvelenamento** poisoning
  **avvelenamento da cibo** food
  poisoning
**avvertimento** warning
**avvertire** warn
**avviare** (un motore) start (vb) (eg a car)
  **non si avvia** it won't start
**avviso** notice
  **avviso pubblicitario** advertisement
  **cartello per gli avvisi** notice board
**avvocato** lawyer
**azzurro** blue

# B

**baby-sitter** (m&f) baby-sitter
  **fare la baby-sitter** baby-sit
**baciare** kiss (vb)
**bacini** (mpl) **portuali** docks (pl)
**bacio** -ci kiss -es (n)
**badare a** mind, look after
  **potrebbe badare /alla mia borsa/
  per favore?** could you mind /my bag/
  please?
  **badare /al bambino/** look after /the
  baby/
**badile** (m) spade
**baffi** (mpl) moustache
**bagagliaio** luggage van
**bagaglio** -gli luggage
  **bagaglio a mano** hand luggage
  **bagaglio in cabina** cabin luggage

**bagaglio in eccedenza** excess
baggage
**bagnare** (=inumidire) bathe (eyes etc)
**bagnare** (mettere a bagno) soak (vb)
**bagnato** wet
  /**quest'asciugamano/ è bagnato**
  /this towel/ is wet
  **sono bagnato** I'm wet
**bagno** bath
  **andare a fare il bagno** go swimming
  **bagno turco** Turkish bath
  **cuffia da bagno** swimming cap
  **fare il bagno** (nella vasca) have a
  bath
  **fare il bagno** (in mare) have a swim
  (stanza da) **bagno** bathroom
  **tappeto di bagno** bath mat
**baia** bay (=part of sea)
**balcone** (m) balcony -ies
**ballare** dance (vb), dancing (n)
  **andare a ballare** go dancing
**ballerino** (m) **ballerina** (f) dancer, ballet
dancer
**balletto** ballet
**ballo** ball, dance
  **sala da ballo** ballroom, dance hall
**bambino** (m) **bambina** (f) (= piccino)
baby -ies
**bambino** (m) **bambina** (f) child
/children (pl)
**bambola** doll
**banana** banana
**banca** bank
**bancanota** note (=money)
  **bancanota da /diecimila/ lire** /ten
  thousand lire note
**banda** band (=orchestra)
**bandiera** flag
**bara** coffin
**barattolo** can, tin
  **un barattolo di /birra/** a can of
  /beer/
**barba**
  **crema da barba** shaving cream
  **fare la barba** shave (vb)
  **pennello da barba** shaving brush -es
  **rasoio da barba** razor

**sapone** (m) **da barba** *shaving soap*
**un bastoncino di sapone de barba** *a stick of shaving soap*
**un tubetto di crema da barba** *a tube of shaving cream*
**barbabietola** *beetroot/beetroot (pl)*
**barbecue** (m) *barbecue*
**barca a remi** *rowing boat*
**barca a vela** *sailing boat*
**andare in barca a vela** *go sailing*
**barella** *stretcher*
**barile** (m) *barrel*
**un barile di / /** *a barrel of / /*
**barriera** *barrier*
**barzelletta** *joke*
**basso** (di cose) *low*
**bassa marea** *low water*
**basso** (di persone) *short (people)*
**bastone** (m) *stick (vb)*
**bastone** (m) **da passeggio** *walking stick*
**battere a macchina** *type (vb)*
**batteria** *battery -ies (car)*
**ho la batteria scarica** *I've got a flat battery*
**baule** (m) *trunk (for luggage)*
**bavaglino** *bib*
**beige** *beige*
**bello** *beautiful, fine*
**fa bello** (tempo) *it's fine (weather)*
**bello** *good-looking*
**un bell' uomo** *a good-looking man*
**una bella donna** *a good-looking woman*
**benda** *bandage (n)*
**bendaggio** *dressing (medical)*
**bendare** *bandage (vb)*
**bene** *well (=all right)*
**bene grazie!** *fine thanks!*
**va bene** *OK*
**benvenuto** *welcome (n)*
**benvenuto a / /** *welcome to / /*
**dare il benvenuto** *welcome (vb)*
**benzina** *petrol*
**bidone** (m) **per benzina** *petrol can*
**bere** *drink (vb)*
**berretto** *cap*

**bersaglio** *dartboard*
**bestiame** (ms) *cattle (pl)*
**biancheria** *linen*
**biancheria e coperte da letto** (fpl) *bed clothes (pl)*
**biancheria intima** *underwear*
**biancheria intima per bambini** *children's underwear*
**biancheria intima per donne** *women's underwear*
**biancheria intima per uomini** *men's underwear*
**bianco** (m) **-chi** (mpl) **bianca** (f) **-che** (fpl) *white*
**biberon** (m) **-** *feeding bottle*
**bibita** *drink (n)*
**bibita analcolica** *soft drink*
**Bible** *Bible*
**biblioteca -che** *library -ies*
**bicchiere** *glass -es*
**un bicchiere /d'acqua/** *a glass of /water/*
**un bicchiere da vino** *a wine glass*
**un servizio di bicchieri** *a set of glasses*
**bicicletta/bici** (f) **-** (infml) *bicycle/bike (infml)*
**andare in bicicleta** *go cycling*
**bidone** (m) **per i rifiuti** *dustbin*
**biglietteria** *box office, ticket office*
**bigliettino** *note (written)*
**biglietto** *ticket*
**abbonamento** *season ticket*
**biglietto collettivo** *group ticket*
**biglietto di andata e ritorno** *return ticket*
**biglietto di prima classe** *first class ticket*
**biglietto di seconda classe** *second class ticket*
**biglietto ridotto per bambini** *child's ticket*
**biglietto di sola andata** *single*
**biglietto** (= cartoncino) *card (business card)*
**bigodini** (mpl) *curlers (pl)*
**bikini** (m) *bikini*

**bilancia** (s) *scales (pl) (=weighing machine)*

**biliardo** (s) *billiards*
  **giocare a biliardo** *play billiards*
  **una partita a biliardo** *a game of billiards*

**biglietteria** *booking office*

**binario /otto/** *platform /eight/*

**binocolo** (s) *binoculars (pl)*
  **un binocolo** *a pair of binoculars*

**biondo** *blonde, fair*

**biro** (f) - *biro (tdmk)*

**birra** *beer*
  **una birra** *a beer*
  **una bottiglia di birra** *a bottle of beer*
  **una lattina di birra** *a can of beer*
  **un mezzo litro di birra** *a pint of beer*

**biscotto** *biscuit*

**bisogno** *need (n)*
  **aver bisogno di** *need (vb)*
  **ho bisogno di /più soldi/** *I need /more money/*

**bistecca -che** *steak*
  **al sangue** *rare*
  **cotta bene** *well-done*
  **non troppo cotta** *medium*

**bloccato** (uno scarico) *blocked (eg drain)*

**bloccato** (una finestra) *stuck (eg a window)*

**blocco -chi da disegno** *sketchpad*

**boa** *buoy*

**bocca -che** *mouth*

**boccale** (m) *mug*

**bocce** (fpl) *bowling (=ten pin bowling)*
  **corsia per bocce** *bowling alley*

**bollire** *boil (vb)*

**bomba** *bomb*

**borsa** *bag*
  **borsa dell'acqua calda** *hot-water bottle*
  **borsa di rete** *string bag*
  **borsa per la spesa** *shopping bag*

**borsa di studio** *grant (for studies)*

**borsellino** *purse*

**borsetta** (da donna) *handbag*

**bosco** *wood (group of trees)*

**bottiglia** *bottle*
  **una bottiglia di / /** *a bottle of / /*

**bottone** (m) *button*

**braccialetto** *bracelet*
  **braccialetto d'argento** *silver bracelet*

**braccio** (m) **braccia** (fpl) *arm*

**braciola** *chop (n)*
  **braciola di maiale** *pork chop*

**branda** *camp bed*

**bravo** *clever (of people)*

**bravo!** *well done! (congratulation)*

**bretelle** (fpl) *braces (pl)*
  **un paio di bretelle** *a pair of braces*

**breve** *short (time)*

**bricco** *kettle*

**bridge** (m) *bridge (=card game)*
  **una partita a bridge** *a game of bridge*

**briglia** *bridle*

**brillantina** *hair oil*
  **una bottiglia di brillantina** *a bottle of hair oil*

**brocca** *jug*
  **una brocca di / /** *a jug of / /*

**broccoli** (mpl) *broccoli*

**brodo** *soup*
  **brodo di /pollo/** */chicken/ soup*

**bruciare** *burn (vb)*

**bruciato** *burnt*
  **bruciato del sole** *sunburnt*

**bruciatura** *sunburn*

**brutto** (=sgradevole) *nasty*

**brutto** (=non bello) *ugly*

**buco -chi** *hole*

**Buddista** (m&f) *Buddhist*

**buffo** *funny (=amusing)*

**bugia** *lie (n) (=untruth)*
  **dire una bugia** *lie (vb) (=tell an untruth)*

**buio** *dark (=time of day)*
  **è buio** *it's dark*

**bungalow** (m) = *bungalow*

**buono** (adj) *good*

**buono** (n) *voucher, coupon*
  **buono di albergo** *hotel voucher*
  **buono per /la benzina/** */petrol/ coupon*

**burrasca** *gale*

**burro** *butter*
**bussola** *compass -es*
**busta** *envelope*
  **busta aerea** *airmail envelope*
  **busta indirizzata a sé** *self-addressed envelope*
  **un pacchetto di buste** *a packet of envelopes*
**bustina di tè** *teabag*
**busto** *corset, panty-girdle*
**butano** *butane*
**buttare** *throw away*
  **da buttare** *disposable*
  **accendino da buttare** *disposable lighter*
  **pannolini da buttare** *disposable nappies*

# C

**cabaret** (m) *floor show*
**cabina** *cabin*
  **cabina a /quattro/ cucette** */four/ berth cabin*
  **cabina per bagnanti** *beach hut*
  **cabina telefonica** *call box -es*
**cacao** *cocoa*
  **una tazza di cacao** *a cup of cocoa*
**caccia** *hunting*
  **andare a caccia** *go hunting*
**cacciavite** (f) *screwdriver*
**cachemire** (m) *cashmere*
  **golf** (m) **di cachemire** *cashmere sweater*
**cachi** (inv) *khaki (colour)*
**cadere** *fall (vb)*
  **sono caduto giù per le scale** *I fell downstairs*
**caduta** *fall (n)*
**caffè** (m) *black coffee*
**caffè** (m) *coffee*
  **caffè decaffeinizzato** *decaffeinated coffee*
  **caffè espresso** *black coffee*
  **caffè filtrato** *percolated coffee*
  **caffellatte /cappuccino** *white coffee*
  **caffè macinato** *ground coffee*

  **caffè solubile** *instant coffee*
  **una tazza di caffè** *a cup of coffee*
  **un bricco di caffè** *a pot of coffee*
**caffè** (m)/**bar** (m) *café*
**caffeina** *caffeine*
**caffettiera** *coffeepot, coffee machine*
**calcio** (sport) *football (=game)*
  **giocare a calcio** *play football*
  **una partita di calcio** *a game of football*
**calcio** (col piede) *kick (n)*
  **dare un calcio** *kick (vb)*
**calcolare** *calculate*
  **calcolare /il prezzo/** *calculate /the cost/*
**calcolatore** (m) **tascabile** *pocket calculator*
**calcolatrice** (f) *calculator*
**caldo** *heat (n)*
  **ondata di caldo** *heat wave*
**caldo** (eccessivo) (adj) *hot*
  **è caldo** *it's hot (of things/food)*
  **fa caldo** *it's hot (of the weather)*
  **ho caldo** *I'm hot*
**caldo** (adj)(piacevole) *warm (adj)*
**calendario -ri** *calendar*
**callifughi** (mpl) *corn pads (pl)*
**callo** *corn (eg on a toe)*
**calmante** (m) *sedative*
**calmo** *calm (of sea)*
**calor gas** (m) *calor gas*
**calorie** (fpl) *calories (pl)*
**calvo** *bald*
  **è calvo** *he's bald*
**calzature** *
  **negozio -zi di calzature** *shoeshop*
**calze** (fpl) (da uomo) *socks (pl)*
  **calze /di lana/** */woollen/ socks*
  **calze lunghe** *long socks*
  **un paio di calze** *a pair of socks*
**calze** (fpl) (da donna) *stockings (pl)*
  **quindici/trenta denier** *fifteen/thirty denier*
  **calze di /nailon/** */nylon/ stockings*
  **un paio di calze** *a pair of stockings*
**calzettoni** *knee-high socks*
**calzini** (mpl) *short socks*

**cambiamento** *change (n) (= alteration)*
**cambiare** (=alterare) *alter (change)*
**cambiare** (=sostituire) *change (vb)*
  **cambiare /la gomma/** *change /the tyre/*
**cambiare** (di valuta) *change*
  **vorrei cambiare /dei traveller's cheques/** *I'd like to change /some traveller's cheques/*
**cambiare a / /** *change at / / (of train)*
  **devo cambiare?** *do I have to change?*
**cambiarsi** (di vestiti) *change (vb) (clothes)*
**camera** *room*
  **camera con due letti** *twin-bedded room*
  **camera con vista** *room with a view*
  **camera da letto** *bedroom*
  **camera doppia** *double room*
  **camera libera** *vacancy -ies*
  **camera singola** *single room*
  **camera tranquilla** *quiet room*
  **con /doccia/** *with /shower/*
  **senza /bagno/** *without /bath/*
**camera d'aria** *inner tube (tyre)*
**cameriera** (in albergo) *chambermaid*
**cameriera** (in casa) *maid*
**cameriera** (al ristorante) *waitress -es*
**cameriere** (m) *waiter*
**camicetta** *blouse*
**camicia -ce** *shirt*
  **camicia a maniche corte** *short-sleeved shirt*
  **camicia da notte** *nightdress -es*
  **camicia di /cotone/** */cotton/ shirt*
  **camicia formale** *formal shirt*
  **camicia sportiva** *casual shirt*
  **una camicia che non si stira** *a drip-dry shirt*
**camino** *chimney -ies*
**camion** (m) - *lorry -ies*
**camionista** (m) -**isti** *lorry driver*
**cammeo** *cameo (brooch)*
**camminare** *walk (vb)*
**campagna** *countryside*
**campana** *bell (large)*

**campanello** *bell (small)*
  **campanello** (sulla porta) *doorbell*
**campeggio** *camp*
  **fare il campeggio** *go camping*
  **campeggio di vacanze** *holiday camp*
**campeggio -ggi** (sito) *campsite*
  **campeggio per roulotte** *caravan site*
**campo** *field (n)*
  **campo da tennis** *tennis court*
  **campo giochi** (m) *playground*
**canale** (m) *canal*
**canale** (televisione) *television channel*
**cancellare /il mio volo/** *cancel /my flight/*
**cancello** *gate (=door)*
**candeggina** *bleach (n)*
**candela** *candle*
**candela** (di automobile) *sparking plug (car)*
**cane** (m) *dog*
  **collare** (m) **per cani** *dog collar*
**canna da pesca** *rod (=fishing r.)*
**canna per innaffiare** *hose (=tube)*
**cannuccia -ce** *straw (=drinking s.)*
**canoa** *canoe (n)*
**canottaggio** *canoeing*
  **fare il canotaggio** *go canoeing*
**cantante** (m&f) *singer*
**cantare** *sing*
**cantina** *cellar*
**canzone** (f) *song*
  **canzone folk** *folk song*
  **canzone pop** *pop song*
**capanna** *hut*
**capelli** (mpl) *hair*
  **molletta per capelli** *hairgrip*
  **spazzola per capelli** *hairbrush*
  **taglio di capelli** *haircut*
**capire** *understand*
  **capisco** *I see (= understand)*
  **non capisco** *I don't understand*
**capitano** *captain*
**capo** *boss*
**capo** (geografia) *cape (eg Cape of Good Hope)*
**capo cameriere** (m) *headwaiter*

**capolinea** *terminus*
  **capolinea dell'autobus** *bus terminus*
  **capolinea del tram** *tram terminus*
**cappa** *cape (=cloak)*
**cappello** *hat*
**cappotto** *coat, overcoat*
**cappuccino** *white coffee (smaller cup - frothy and with less milk)*
**cappuccino** *white coffee*
**cappuccio -ci** *hood (of a garment)*
**capra** *goat*
**capsula** *cap (n) (for tooth)*
**caraffa** *carafe*
  **una caraffa di /vino/** *a carafe of /wine/*
**caramella** *sweet (n) (=confectionery)*
**carato** *carat*
  **oro a /nove/ carati** */nine/ carat gold*
**carbone** (m) *coal*
**carbonella** *charcoal*
**carciofo** *artichoke*
**caricare** (un camion) *load (vb)*
**caricare** (un orologio) *wind (vb) (clock)*
**carne** (f) *meat*
  **carne fredda** *cold meat*
  **agnello** *lamb*
  **castrato** *mutton*
  **maiale** *pork*
  **manzo** *beef*
  **selvaggina** *venison*
**carnevale** (m) *carnival*
**carota** *carrot*
**carrello** *trolley (=luggage t.)*
**carrozza** *carriage (in a train)*
**carrozzina** *pram*
  **blocco di carta da disegno** *sketch-pad*
**carta** *paper*
  **carta aerea** *airmail paper*
  **carta assorbente** *blotting paper*
  **carta bianca** *unlined paper*
  **carta carbone** *carbon paper*
  **carta da disegno** *drawing paper*
  **carta da imballaggio** *wrapping paper*
  **carta da lettere** *pad*
  **carta da macchina da scrivere** *typing paper*

**carta da scrivere** *writing paper*
**carta di credito** *credit card*
**carta d'identità** *identity card*
**carta igienica** *toilet paper*
  **un rotolo di carta igienica** *a roll of toilet paper*
**carta marina** *chart (=sea map)*
**carta rigata** *lined paper*
**un foglio di carta** *a sheet of paper*
**carte** (fpl) *cards (pl)*
  **una partita a carte** *a game of cards*
  **un mazzo de carte** *a pack of cards*
**cartella** *briefcase*
**cartella** (= raccolta di documenti) *file (n) (for papers)*
**cartoleria** *stationery*
**cartolina** *postcard*
  **cartolina di buon compleanno** *birthday card*
**cartone** (=contenitore) *carton*
  **un cartone di /latte/** *a carton of /milk/*
**cartone** (= sostanza) *cardboard*
**cartuccia -ce** *cartridge (for gun)*
**casa** (la propria casa) *home*
  **a casa** *at home*
  **andare a casa** *go home*
**casa** (=abitazione) *house*
  **casa della fattoria** *farmhouse*
**casco da guidatore** *crash helmet*
**casinò** *casino*
**caso** *case*
  **in caso di /incendio/** *in case of /fire/*
**cassa** *cash desk*
**cassaforte** (f) *safe (n)*
**casseruola** *casserole (container)*
**cassetta** *cassette*
  **cassetta preregistrata** *pre-recorded cassette*
**cassetta delle lettere** *postbox -es*
**cassetto** *drawer*
**cassettone** (m) *chest of drawers*
**cassiere** (m) **cassiera** (f) *cashier*
**castagna** *chestnut*
**castano** *maroon (colour)*
**castello** *castle*
**castigo -ghi** *punishment*

**catalogo -ghi** *catalogue*
**catena** *chain*
  **catena di montagne** *range*
  *(=mountain range)*
**cattedrale** (m) *cathedral*
**cattivo** *bad*
**cattivo** *(= monello) naughty (usually of*
  *young children)*
**cattolico** *Catholic (adj)*
**causa** *cause (n)*
  **a causa /del tempo/** *because of /the*
  *weather/*
**cavalcare** *ride (a horse) (vb)*
  **andare a cavalcare** *go riding*
**cavallo** *horse*
  **cavallo da corsa** *racehorse*
  **corse** (fpl) **di cavalli** *horse racing*
**cavatappi** (m) - *corkscrew*
**caverna** *cave*
**caviglia** *ankle*
**cavo** *cable (n)*
**cavolfiore** (m) *cauliflower*
**cavolino** (m) **di Bruxelles** *sprout*
  *(=Brussels s.)*
**cavolo** *cabbage*
**c'è** (s) **ci sono** (pl) *there is (s) there are*
  *(pl)*
  **c'è /della birra/** *there's /some beer/*
  **ci sono /dei ristoranti/ qui vicino/**
  *are there /any restaurants/ near here?*
  **non ci sono /alberghi/ qui vicino**
  *there aren't /any hotels/ near here*
**CEE** *EEC*
**cemento** *cement (n)*
**cena** *dinner (=evening meal), supper*
**cenare** *have dinner, have supper*
**centigrado** *Centigrade*
**centimetro** *centimetre*
**centinaia di / /** *hundreds of / /*
**cento** *hundred*
**centralino telefonico** *switchboard*
  *(company)*
**centro** *centre*
  **centro città** *town centre*
  **centro commerciale** *shopping centre*
  **in centro** *in the centre*
**cera** *wax*

**ceramico** *ceramic*
**cercare** *look for*
  **cercare /il mio passaporto/** *look for*
  */my passport/*
**cereale** (per colazione) (m) *cereal*
  *(=breakfast cereal)*
  **una ciatolo di cereale** *a bowl of*
  *cereal*
**cerimonia** *ceremony -ies*
**cerini** *matches*
**cerotto** *Elastoplast (tdmk), sticking*
  *plaster*
**certamente** *certainly*
**certificato** *certificate*
  **certificato di salute** *health certificate*
**certo!** *of course!*
**cestino** *basket (small)*
  **cestino per la carta straccia** *waste*
  *paper basket*
  **cestino per la spesa** *shopping basket*
**cesto** *basket*
  **un cesto di / /** *a basket of / /*
**cetriolo** *cucumber*
**chalet** (m) - *chalet*
**chi?** *who?*
  **di chi?** *whose?*
  **di chi è?** *whose is it?*
**chiamare** *call (vb) (=telephone)*
  **chiamare /la polizia/** *call /the police/*
  **chiamare più tardi** *call again later*
**chiamarsi** *be called (a name)*
  **mi chiamo /Paul Smith/** *my name's*
  */Paul Smith/*
  **come si chiama, per favore?** *what's*
  *your name please?*
**chiamata** (n) *(telephone call)*
  **chiamata d'allarme** *alarm call*
  **chiamata internazionale** *international*
  *call*
  **chiamata interurbana** *long distance*
  *call*
  **chiamata personale** *personal call*
  **chiamata urbana** *local call*
  **fare una chiamata interurbana** *make*
  *a long distance call*
**chiarificare** *clarify*
**chiaro** *(=limpido) clear (=transparent)*

**chiaro** (=non scuro) *fair (adj) (skin)*
**chiave** (f) *key*
  **chiudere a chiave** *lock*
**chiave** (f) *spanner*
  **chiave inglese** *spanner*
  **chiave inglese regolabile** *adjustable spanner*
**chiedere** (un favore) *ask (a favour)*
**chiesa** *church -es*
  **una chiesa /prostestante/** *a /Protestant/ church*
**chilogramma** (m)/**chilo** *kilogramme/kilo*
**chilometro** *kilometre*
**chinino** *quinine*
**chiodo** *nail (metal)*
**chitarra** *guitar*
**chiudere** *shut, close*
  **chiudere a chiave** *lock (vb)*
**chiuso** *closed, shut*
  **/piscina/ al chiuso** *indoor /swimming pool/*
**chiusura lampo** (f) **chiusure lampo** (pl) *zip (n)*
**ciao** (lasciandosi) *goodbye*
  **ciao** *goodbye (on phone)*
**ciao** (incontradosi) *hello*
**ciao!** *hi!*
**ciascuno** *each*
  **ciascuno /dei bambini/** *each /of the children/*
**cibo** *food*
  **avvelenamento da cibo** *food poisoning*
  **cibo dietetico** *health food*
  **dove posso trovare del cibo?** *where can I buy some food?*
**cicatrice** (f) *scar*
**ciclismo** *cycling*
**ciclomotore** (m) *moped*
**cieco -chi** *blind (adj)*
**cielo** *sky -ies*
**ciliegia -ge** *cherry -ies*
**cimitero** *cemetery*
**cinema** (m)- *cinema*
**cinepresa** *cine camera*
**cintura** *belt*
  **cintura di sicurezza** *safety belt*

**cinturino** *strap*
  **cinturino dell'orologio** *watch-strap*
  **senza cinturino** *strapless*
**cioccolata** *chocolate*
  **una stecca di cioccolata** *a bar of chocolate*
  **una scatola di cioccolatini** *a box of chocolates*
**cipolla** *onion*
**cipollina** *spring onion*
**cipria** *powder (face powder)*
**circa** *about*
  **circa /il suo problema/** *about /your problem/*
**circo -chi** *circus -es*
**circolo** *club*
  **circolo di golf** *golf club (institution)*
  **circolo per il gioco d'azzardo** *gambling club*
  **circolo di gioco** *gaming club*
**circonvallazione** (f) *bypass (n) -es*
**città** - (grande) *city -ies*
  **la parte nuova della città** *the new part of the city*
  **la parte vecchia della città** *the old part of the city*
**città** - (piccola e media) *town*
  **centrocittà** *town centre*
**cittadino** *citizen*
**civiltà** - *civilisation*
**classe** (f) *class -es*
  **classe cabina** *cabin class*
  **classe turistica** *tourist class*
  **/prima/ classe** */first/ class*
**classico** *classical (eg music)*
  **musica classica** *classical music*
**clavicola** *collar bone*
**cliente** (m&f) *client*
**clima** *climate*
**clinica** *clinic*
  **clinica privata** *private clinic*
**cocco**
  **noce** (f) **di cocco** *coconut*
**coccodrillo**
  **di coccodrillo** *crocodile (leather)*
**cocktail** (m) *cocktail*
**coda** (=fila) *queue (n)*

**fare la coda** queue (vb)
**coda** (parte posteriore) rear
**/carrozza/ di coda** rear /coach/
**codeina** codeine
**codice** (m) code
   **codice postale** postal code, postcode
**cognac** (m) - brandy -ies
   **una bottiglia di cognac** a bottle of
   brandy
   **un cognac** a brandy
**cognata** sister-in-law/sisters-in-law (pl)
**cognato** brother-in-law /brothers-in-law
   (pl)
**cognome** (m) surname
**colazione** (f) (= prima colazione)
   breakfast
   **colazione in camera** breakfast in my
   room
   **colazione inglese** English breakfast
   **colazione per / due/** breakfast for
   /two/
   **fare colazione** have breakfast
   **letto e colazione** bed and breakfast
   **servire la colazione** serve breakfast
**colazione** (f) (= seconda colazione)
   lunch
   **colazione al sacco** packed lunch
   **fare colazione** have lunch
**colf** (f) domestic help
**colla** glue
**collana** necklace
**collant** (m) tights (pl)
   **un collant** a pair of tights
**collare** (m) dog collar
**collega** (m&f) **-ghi** (mpl) **-ghe** (fpl)
   colleague
**collegare** connect
**collegio** **-gi** college
**colletta** collection (in a church)
**colletto** collar
**collina** hill
**collinoso** hilly
**collo** neck
**colore** (m) colour
   **di che colore è?** what colour is it?
**colori** (mpl) paints (pl)
   **scatola di colori** box of paints

**colpa** fault
   **è colpa mia** it's my fault
**colpevole** guilty
**colpire** hit (vb)
**coltello** knife -ves
   **coltello per tagliare la carne** carving
   knife
**coltivare** grow (=cultivate)
**come?** (adj) how?
   **come sta?** how are you?
**come** (prep) like (prep)
   **com'è?** what's it like?
**commedia** play (n) (at theatre)
   **commedia musicale** musical
**commercio** commerce
**commesso** (m) **commessa** (f) shop
   assistant
**commissione** (f) commission
   (=payment)
**comodità** (fpl) amenities (pl)
**comodo** (= confortevole) comfortable
**comodo** (=conveniente) convenient (of
   time and distance)
**compenso** compensation
**compitare** spell
**compleanno** birthday
**completo** complete (adj)
**complimenti** (mpl) congratulations (pl)
**comporre un numero** dial
**comportamento** behaviour
**comprare** buy
   **comprare /un ombrello/** buy /an
   umbrella/
   **dove posso comprare**
   **/un ombrello/?** where can I buy /an
   umbrella/?
**comprendere** (= capire) understand
**comprendere** (=includere) include
**compreso** including
   **è compreso /il servizio/?** is
   /service/ included?
**computer** (m) computer
**con** with
**concerto** concert
**conchiglia** shell (sea-s.)
   **conchiglia di pettine** scallop
**condimento** (per insalata) dressing
   (salad dressing)

**condimento** (per altri cibi) *seasoning*
**condividere** *share* (vb)
**condizione** (f) *condition*
  **in buone condizioni** (fpl) *in good condition*
  **in cattive condizioni** (fpl) *in bad condition*
**condizioni** (fpl) (=trattamento) *terms (pl)*
**condominio** *block of flats*
**conducente** (m) *bus driver*
**confermare** /il mio volo/ *confirm /my flight/*
**confezionare per regalo** *gift-wrap* (vb)
**confusione** (f) *mess -es*
**confuso** *confused*
  **sono confuso** *I'm confused*
**congelato** *frozen* (=deep frozen)
**congratularsi con** /lei/ per / / *congratulate /you/ on / /*
**congresso** *conference*
**coniglio** *rabbit*
**conoscere** *know* (a person)
  **lo conosco** *I know him*
**consegna** *delivery* (goods)
**consegnare a** *deliver to*
**consigliare riposo** *advise a rest*
**consiglio** *advice*
  **vorrei un consiglio** *I'd like some advice*
**consolato** *consulate*
  **il consolato** /britannico/ *the /British/ Consulate*
**console** (m) *consul*
**consunto** *worn-out*
**contagioso** *contagious, infectious*
**contanti** (mpl) *cash* (n)
  **pagamento in contanti** *cash payment*
  **pagare in contanti** *pay cash*
**contare** *count* (vb)
**contatore** (m) *meter*
  **contatore del gas** *gas meter*
  **contatore dell'eletricittà** *electricity meter*
**contento** (felice) *glad*
  **è contento** *he's glad*
**contento** (soddisfatto) *pleased*

**contento di / /** *pleased with / /*
**contenuto** (s) *contents* (pl) (eg of a parcel)
**continentale** *continental*
**continuo** *continual*
**conto** (in banca) *bank account*
  **conto corrente** *current account*
**conto** (al ristorante, albergo) *bill (for food, hotel, etc.)*
**contrattare** *bargain* (vb)
  **contrattare con / /** *bargain with / /*
**contratto** (n) *contract* (n)
**contro** *against*
**controllare** *check* (vb)
  **potrebbe controllare** /l'olio e l'acqua/ per favore? *could you check /the oil and water/ please?*
**controllare** (l'automobile) *service* (vb)(car)
**controllo generale** (medico) *check up* (n) (=of health)
**controllo stradale** (indicatore) *signpost*
**contuso** *bruised*
**conversazione** (f) *talk* (n) (discussion, chat)
  **conversazione** (f) con pagamento a destinazione *transferred charge call*
**convulsione** (f) *fit* (n) (=attack)
**coperchio** *lid* (of pot)
**coperta** *blanket*
**copia** *copy* (n) -ies
**copia** (fotografia) *print* (n) (photographic)
**copiare** *copy* (vb)
**coppia** *couple* (married c.)
**corallo** *coral*
**corda** *rope*
  **corda per stendere** *clothes line*
  **corda da traino** *tow rope*
**cornice** (f) *frame* (n) (=picture frame)
**coro** *choir*
**corona** (a un funerale) *wreath -es(funeral w.)*
**corpo** *body -ies*
**correggere** *correct* (vb)
**corrente** (f) (elettrica) *current* (=electric c.)

**corrente alternata** A.C.
**corrente continua** D.C.
**cento venti/due cento quaranta volt**
one hundred and twenty/ two hundred
and forty volt
**corrente** (f) (di acqua) current (of water)
  **corrente forte** strong current
**corrente** (f) (di aria) draught (of air)
  **c'è molta corrente** it's very draughty
**corrente** (m&f) (adj) current (adj)
**correre** race (vb), run (vb)
**corretto** correct (adj)
**correzione** (f) correction
**corridoio** corridor
**corriere** (m) courrier
**corsa** race, racing
  **cavallo da corsa** racehorse
  **corsa di cavalli** horse race
  **corsa di macchine** motor race
  **fare le corsa di macchina** go motor
  racing
**corse** (fpl) races (pl) (=the races)
**corsia** (stradale) lane (=traffic lane)
**corsia** (ospedaliera) ward (in hospital)
**cortese** polite
**corto** short (things)
  **corto circuito** short circuit
**cosa** thing
  **che cosa c'è?** what's the matter?
**cosa?** what?
**coscia -sce** thigh
**costa** coast (n)
**costare** cost (vb)
**costola** rib (part of body)
**costoletta** cutlet
  **costoletta di agnello** lamb cutlet
  **costoletta di vitello** veal cutlet
**costoso** expensive
**costruttore** (m) builder
**costume** (m) fancy dress (s)
  **costume** (m) **da bagno** swimming
  costume
**cotone** (m) cotton
  **un rocchetto di cotone** a reel of
  cotton
  **cotone** (m) **idrofilo** cotton wool
**cotto** cooked

**cotto bene** well-done
**poco cotto** (eg bistecca) medium-rare
(eg of steak)
**non cotto abbastanza** undercooked
**troppo cotto** overcooked
**cozza** mussel
**crampo** cramp (n)
**cravatta** tie (n)
  **cravatta a farfalla** bow tie
  **ferma cravatta** tiepin
**credere** believe
  **creder/mi/** believe /me/
  **non ci credo** I don't believe it
**credito** credit
  **a credito** on credit
  **condizioni** (fpl) **di credito** credit terms
**crema** cream (=lotion)
  **crema da barba** shaving cream
  **crema detergente** cleansing cream
  **crema per le mani** handcream
**crepuscolo** dusk
**crescere** grow
**cricco** jack (car)
**cricket** (m) cricket
  **giocare a cricket** play cricket
  **una partita a cricket** a game of
  cricket
**criminale** (m) criminal
**cristiano** Christian
**Cristo** Christ
**crocchia** bun (hair)
  **in crocchia** in a bun
**crociera** cruise
  **fare una crociera** go on a cruise
**crostacei** (mpl) shellfish (s)/shellfish (pl)
**crudo** raw
**cubo** cube
  **cubo al magnesio** flash cube
**cuccetta** (su una nave) berth
  **cabina da /quattro/ cuccette**
  /four/-berth cabin
  **cuccetta di sopra** upper berth
  **cuccetta di sotto** lower berth
**cuccetta** (in treno) couchette
**cucchiaino** teaspoon
  **un cucchiaino di / /** a teaspoonful
  of / /

**cucchiaio -ai** (posata) *spoon*
**cucchiaio -ai** (misura) *spoonful*
  **un cucchiaio di / /** *a spoonful of*
  */ /*
  **cucchiaio -ai da tavola di / /**
  *tablespoonful of / /*
**cucina** (macchina) *cooker*
  **cucina a gas** *gas cooker*
  **cucina elettrica** *electric cooker*
**cucina** (=cucinare) *cooking*
**cucina** (stanza) *kitchen*
**cucinare** *do the cooking*
**cucire** *sew*
  **cucire un pò** *do some sewing*
**cucitrice** (f) *stapler*
**cuffia** *shower cap*
  **cuffia da bagno** *swimming cap*
**cuffie** (fpl) *headphones (pl)*
  **un paio di cuffie** *a pair of*
  *headphones*
**cugino** (m) **cugina** (f) *cousin*
**cuiccio** *dummy (baby's d.)*
**culla portatile** *carrycot*
**cuocere** *cook (vb)*
  **cuocere a bagno maria** *steam (vb)*
  **cuocere ai ferri** *grill (vb)*
  **cuocere al forno** *bake*
  **cuocere in camicia** *poach*
**cuore** (m) *heart*
  **malattia di cuore** *heart trouble*
**cura** *treatment*
**curare** *treat (medically)*
**curry** (m) *curry -ies*
**curva** *bend (in a road)*
**cuscino** (termine generico) *cushion*
**cuscino** (guanciale) *pillow*
**custode** (m) *caretaker*

# D

**da**
  **dalle /otto/ alle /dieci/** *from /eight/*
  *to /ten/*
  **da /Londra/ a /Roma/** *from*
  */London/ to /Rome/*
  **vengo da / /** *I come from / /*
**dado** (da gioco) *dice/dice (pl)*

**dado** (meccanica) *nut (metal)*
  **un dado e un bullone** *a nut and bolt*
**dama** (fs) *draughts (pl)(game)*
  **una partita a dama** *a game of*
  *draughts*
**danneggiato** *damaged*
**danni** (mpl) *damages (pl)*
  *(=compensation)*
**danno** (a cose) *damage (n) (s)*
**danno** (a persone) *injury -ies*
**dappertutto** *everywhere*
**dapprima** *at first*
**dare** *give*
  **dare la mano** *shake hands*
  **/me/ lo dia, per favore** *give it to*
  */me/ please*
**data** *date (calendar)*
  **data di nascita** *date of birth*
**dattero** *date (=fruit)*
**dattilografa** *typist*
**davanti a** *in front of*
**dazio -zi** *duty (=tax) -ies*
**debole** *weak*
**decaffeinizzato** *decaffeinated*
**decidere** *decide*
  **decidersi /un piano/** *decide on /a*
  *plan/*
  **decidere di / /** *decide to / /*
**decorazione** (f) *ornament*
**definitivamente** *definitely*
**delicato** *delicate (health)*
**delinquenza** *crime*
**deltaplano** *hang glider*
**deluso** *disappointed*
**dente** (m) *tooth/teeth (pl)*
  **dente del giudizio** *wisdom tooth*
  **mal di denti** *toothache*
  **spazzolino da denti** *toothbrush -es*
**dentiera** (s) *dentures (pl), false teeth*
  *(pl)*
**dentifricio** *toothpaste*
  **un tubo di dentifricio** *a tube of*
  *toothpaste*
**dentista** (m&f) **-i** *dentist*
  **devo andare dal dentista** *I must go*
  *to the dentist's*
**dentro** *inside (adv)*

**dentro a** *into, inside (prep)*
  **dentro /alla casa/** *inside /the house/*
**deodorante** (m) *deodorant*
**depositare** *deposit (vb) (money)*
  **depositare /del denaro/** *deposit /some money/*
  **depositare /questi oggetti di valore/** *deposit /these valuables/*
**deposito** *deposit (n)*
  **deposito bagagli** *left-luggage office*
**descrivere** *describe*
**descrizione** (f) *description*
**dessert** (m) *dessert*
**destinazione** (f) *destination*
**destro** (=non sinistro) *right (=not left)*
  **a destra** *right (direction)*
**detergente** (m) *detergent*
**detersivo** *washing powder*
**deviazione** (f) (per evitare qualcosa) *detour*
  **fare una deviazione** *make a detour*
**deviazione** (f) (stradale, obligatoria) *diversion*
**di** *of*
**di**
  **d'estate** *in /summer/*
  **di fronte a** *in front of*
  **di mattina** *in the morning*
**diabete** (m) *diabetes*
**diabetico** *diabetic*
**diamante** (m) *diamond*
**diapositive** (fpl) *slides (pl)*
  **diapositive a colori** *colour slides*
  **macchina per diapositive** *slide viewer*
**diario** *diary -ies*
**diarrea** *diarrhoea*
**dicembre** (m) *December*
**dichiarare /quest'orologio/** *declare /this watch/*
**dichiarazione** (f) *announcement*
  **fare una dichiarazione** *make an announcement*
**dieta** *diet (=slimming d.)*
  **essere a dieta** *be on a diet*
**dietro** (a) (prep) *behind (prep)*
  **dietro /alla casa/** *behind /the house/*

**in dietro** *backwards*
**difettoso** *faulty, imperfect (goods)*
**difficile** *difficult, hard*
**difficoltà -** *difficulty -ies*
**diluvio -vi** *flood (n)*
**dimenticare** *forget*
  **ho dimenticato /la mia valigia/** *I've left /my suitcase/ behind*
**dimostrare** *prove*
**Dio/dio** *God/god*
**dipendere** *depend*
  **dipende** *it depends*
  **dipende /dal tempo/** *it depends on /the weather/*
**diplomatico** *diplomat*
**dire** *say (something)*
**diretto** *direct (adj)*
  **linea diretta** *direct line*
  **percorso diretto** *direct route*
**direttore** (m) *manager*
**direttore** (m) **delle vendite** *sales manager*
**direzione** (f) *direction*
**diritto** *right (= privilege)*
  **aver diritto ad avere /i buoni per la benzina/** *be entitled to /petrol coupons/*
**dirottamento** *hijack (n)*
**discesa** *slope*
**disco** (parte del corpo) *disc*
  **un disco fuori posto** *a slipped disc*
**disco** (musica) *record (n)*
  **disco a trentatré giri** *thirty-three r.p.m. record*
  **disco a quarantacinque giri** *forty-five r.p.m. record/single*
  **disco classico** *classical record*
  **disco di musica leggera** *light music record*
  **disco jazz** *jazz record*
  **disco pop** *pop record*
  **negozio -zi di dischi** *record shop*
**discoteca** *disco*
**discussione** (f) *argument*
**discutere** *argue*
**disegnare** (fare dei piani) *design (vb)*
**disegnare** (arte) *draw (a picture)*

**disegno** (su una stoffa) *design* (n)
**disfare le valigie** *unpack*
**disinfettante** (m) *disinfectant*
  **una bottiglia di disinfettante** *a bottle of disinfectant*
**disoccupato** *unemployed* (adj)
**disoccupazione** (f) *unemployment*
**disonesto** *dishonest*
**disponibile** *available*
**dissenteria** *dysentery*
**distaccare** *disconnect*
**distanza** *distance*
  **tuffarsi dentro /l'acqua/** *dive into /the water/*
**distributore** (m) (di benzina) *filling station, petrol station*
**distributore** (m) (di automobile) *distributor (car)*
**distributore** (m) **a gettoni** *slot machine*
**disturbare** *bother* (vb)
  **mi dispiace disturbarla** *I'm sorry to bother you*
  **non si disturbi** *don't bother*
**disturbato** *upset* (adj)
**dito -a** *finger*
  **dito del piede** *toe*
  **unghia del dito del piede** *toenail*
**ditta** *company -ies, firm*
**diva** *star*
  **diva del cinema** *film star*
**diverso** *difference*
  **diverso da / /** *different from / /*
**divertente** *amusing, entertaining*
**divertimento** *fun*
  **buon divertimento!** *enjoy yourself!*
**divertirsi** *enjoy oneself, have fun, have a good time*
**dividere** *divide* (vb)
**divisa** *uniform* (n)
  **in divisa** *in uniform*
**divorziato** *divorced*
**doccia -ce** *shower* (=s. bath)
**documenti** (mpl) *documents* (pl)
  **documenti della macchina** *car documents*
  **documenti di viaggio** *travel documents*

**dogana** *Customs* (pl)
  **dichiarazione** (f) **per la dogana** *customs declaration form*
  **passare per la dogana** *clear goods through Customs*
**dolce** (adj) *sweet* (=not savoury) (adj)
**dolce** (m) *sweet* (n)(=dessert)
**dollaro** *dollar*
**dolore** (m) *pain*
**doloroso** *painful*
**domanda** *question, application*
  **fare domanda a / / per /un visto/** *apply to / / for /a visa/*
  **fare domanda per /un impiego/** *apply for /a job/*
  **fare una domanda** *query* (vb)
  **modulo di domanda** *application form*
  **vorrei fare una domanda /sul conto/** *I would like to query /the bill/*
**domandare** *ask*
  **domandi quanto è, per favore** *please ask how much it is*
**domani** *tomorrow*
**domenica** *Sunday*
  **arriverò domenica** *I'll arrive on Sunday*
  **di domenica** *on Sundays*
**domino** (s) *dominoes* (pl)
  **giocare a domino** *play dominoes*
  **una partita a domino** *a game of dominoes*
**donna** *woman/women* (pl)
**dopo** (prep) *after*
**dopo** (adv) *afterwards*
**dopo barba** (m) - *aftershave lotion*
**doppio** *double*
  **stanza doppia** *double room*
  **un whisky doppio** *a double whisky*
  **pagare doppio prezzo** *pay double*
**dorme** *he's asleep*
**dormire** *sleep* (vb)
  **dormi** *he's asleep*
**dose** (f) **di /medicina/** *dose of /medicine/*
**dove?** *where?*
  **da dove viene?** *where are you from?*
**dovere** (vb) *must*

**devo /andare a casa/ adesso** I must /go home/ now

**/il treno/ deve arrivare /alle due /pomeridiane/** /the train/'s due /at two o'clock/

**devo /pagare in contanti/?** must I /pay by cash/?

**non deve /parcheggiare/ /qui/** you mustn't /park/ /here/

**dovere** (vb) owe

**mi deve /  /** you owe me /  /

**quanto le devo?** how much do I owe you?

**dovere** (m)(n) duty (=obligation) -ies

**dozzina** dozen

**una dozzina di /uova/** a dozen /eggs/

**una mezza dozzina** half a dozen

**dritto** straight

**droga** drug

**droghiere** (m) grocer's

**dubitare** doubt (vb)

**dubito** I doubt it

**due**

**tutti e due** both

**durante /la notte/** during /the night/

**duro** hard, tough

# E

**e** and

**e /Mary/?** what about /Mary/?

**ebreo** Jew

**eccellente** excellent

**eccesso** excess

**eccetto** except

**eccitato** excited

**economico** cheap

**edicola** newsstand

**edificio -ci** building

   **edificio pubblico** public building

**edizione** (f) **economica** paperback

**efficiente** efficient

**elaborato** elaborate (adj)

**elastico** (n) elastic, rubber band

**elegante** smart (appearance)

**elenco -chi** list

**elenco telefónico** telephone directory

**elettricista** (m) **-sti** electrician

**elettricità** electricity

**elettrico** electric

   **scossa elettrica** electric shock

**elezione** (f) election (s)

**elicottero** helicopter

**emergenza** emergency -ies

**emicrania** migraine

**emorroidi** (fpl) piles (illness)

**emotivo** emotional

**emozionante** exciting

**entrare** enter, come in

   **entrare in /un paese/** enter /a country/

   **entrata** (=ammissione) admission (=cost)

**entrata** (=ingresso) entrance

   **biglietto di entrata** entrance fee

   **entrata laterale** side entrance

   **entrata principale** main entrance

   **entrata** (=sala d'ingresso) foyer (in hotels and theatres)

**epidemia** epidemic (n)

**epilettico** epileptic (adj)

**equipaggiamento** equipment, gear, kit

   **equipaggiamento di pronto soccorso** first aid kit

   **equipaggiamento fotografico** photographic equipment

   **equipaggiamento per scalare** climbing gear

   **equipaggiamento subacqueo** diving gear

**equipaggiare** equip

**equipaggio -ggi** crew

   **equipaggio dell'aereo** air crew

   **equipaggio della nave** ship's crew

**equitazione** (f) riding (=horse riding)

**erba** (prato) grass

**erba** (aromatica) herb

**eroe** (m) hero

**eroina** heroine

**esame** (m) examination (=school etc.)

**esaurimento nervoso** nervous breakdown

**esaurito** sold out

**esempio** *example*
  **per esempio** *for example*
**esercitarsi** *practise (=train)*
**esercito** *army*
**esperto** (adj) *expert (adj)*
**esperto** (n) *expert (n)*
**esportare** *export (vb)*
**esportazione** (f) *export (n)*
**esposimetro** *exposure meter*
**espresso** (n) (caffè) *espresso coffee*
**espresso** (treno) *fast train*
**espresso** (adj)
  **lettera espressa** *express letter*
  **posta espressa** *express mail*
  **servizio espresso** *express service*
**essere** *be*
  **essere /elegante/** *look /smart/*
  **essere in casa** *be in*
  **sono le tre** *it's three o'clock*
**est** (m) *east*
**estate** (f) *summer*
  **d'estate** *in summer*
**estero** *foreign*
  **all'estero** *abroad*
  **è all'estero** *he's abroad*
**età** - *age*
  **di mezz'età** *middle-aged*
**etichetta** *label (=luggage label)*
  **etichetta da incollare** *stick-on label*
**evidente** *clear (=obvious)*
**evitare** *avoid*
**extra** *extra*
  **extra** (mpl) *extras (pl)*

# F

**fa** *ago*
  **/tre anni/ fa** */three years/ ago*
**fabbrica -che** *factory -ies*
**facchino** *porter (railway)*
**faccia -cce** *face*
**facile** *easy*
**facilmente** *easily*
**fagiano** *pheasant*
**fagiolino** *French bean*
**fagiolo** *bean*
**fahrenheit** *Fahrenheit*

**falso** *false*
**fame**
  **avere fame** *be hungry*
  **ho fame** *I'm hungry*
**famiglia** *family -ies*
**famoso** *famous*
**fango** *mud*
**fangoso** *muddy*
**fantino** *jockey*
**far male a** *hurt (vb) (inflict pain)*
  **farsi male** *hurt (vb) (feel pain)*
  **mi fa male /il piede/** *my /foot/ hurts*
  **mi sono fatto male /alla gamba/** *I've hurt my /leg/*
**fare** *do, make*
  **fare /delle spese/** *do /some shopping/*
  **far/mi/ un favore** *do /me/ a favour*
  **/mi/ può fare un favore?** *could you do /me/ a favour?*
  **fare /soldi/** *make /money/*
  **fatto a mano** *handmade*
  **fatto in /  /** *made in /  /*
  **fatto in casa** *homemade*
**fare il bagno** *have a swim*
**farfalla** *butterfly -ies*
**farina** *flour*
**farmacia** *chemist's*
**fasciare** *dress (vb) (a wound)*
**fastidioso** *annoying*
**faticoso** *tiring*
**fatto** *fact*
**fattore** (m) *farmer*
**fattoria** *farm*
**fattura** *invoice (n)*
**fava** *broad bean*
**favore** (m) *favour*
  **farmi un favore** *do me a favour*
  **mi può fare un favore?** *could you do me a favour?*
  **per favore** *please (request)*
**fazzoletti di carta** *tissues (pl) /Kleenex (tdmk)*
  **una scatola di fazzoletti di carta** *a box of tissues*
**fazzoletto** *handkerchief -ves*
**febbraio** *February*

**febbre** (f) *fever*
**ho la febbre** *I've got a temperature*
**febbre** (f) **da fieno** *hay fever*
**febris** (pl) *feverish*
**fede** (f) *wedding ring*
**federa** *pillow case*
**fegato** *liver*
**felice** *happy*
**feltro** *felt (material)*
**femmina** (n) *female*
**femminile** (adj) *feminine, female*
**ferita** *wound (=injury)*
**fermaglio -gli per carta** *paper clip*
**fermare** *stop (vb)*
**fermarsi a / /** *stop at / /*
**fermata** *stop (n)*
**fermata dell'autobus** *bus stop*
**fermata del tram** *tram stop*
**ferri** (mpl) **da maglia** *knitting needles*
**ferro da stiro** *iron (n) (object)*
**ferro da viaggio** *travelling iron*
**ferrovia** *railway*
**fessura** *crack (n)*
**festa** (=festaggiamento) *festival*
**festa** (=giorno festivo) *public holiday*
**festa** (=ricevimento) *party -ies*
**festa di compleanno** *birthday party*
**fetta** *slice (n)*
**una fetta di / /** *a slice of / /*
**fetta di pancetta** *rasher of bacon*
**fiamma** *flame (n)*
**fiammifero** *match -es*
**una scatola di fiammiferi** *a box of matches*
**fiato** *breath*
**senza fiato** *out of breath*
**fibbia** *buckle*
**fico -chi** *fig*
**fidanzata** (n) *fiancée*
**fidanzato** (n) *fiancé*
**fidanzato** (m) **fidanzata** (f) (adj) *engaged (to be married)*
**fidarsi** *trust (vb)*
**mi fido /di lei/** *I trust /her/*
**fiducia** *confidence*
**di fiducia** *reliable*
**figlia** *daughter*
**figlio -gli** *son*
**figura** *figure (=body)*
**fila** *row (of seats)*
**la /prima/ fila** *the /first/ row*
**filetto** *fillet (n)*
**filiale** (m) *branch (of company) -es*
**film** (m) *film (=entertainment)*
**film dell'orrore** *horror film*
**film giallo** *thriller*
**film pornografico** *pornographic film*
**Western** *Western*
**filo** (per cucire) *thread*
**un rocchetto di filo** *a reel of thread*
**filo** (di metallo) *wire*
**un pezzo di filo** *a piece of wire*
**finalmente** *at last*
**fine** (f) *end (n)*
**finestra** *window*
**finestrino** *window (car)*
**finire** *finish (vb), end (vb)*
**finire /la mia colazione/** *finish /my breakfast/*
**fino a** *until*
**fino a /venerdì/** *until /Friday/*
**fiocina** *harpoon gun*
**fioraio -ai** *florist's*
**fiore** (m) *flower*
**un mazzo di fiori** *a bunch of flowers*
**vaso da fiori** *flower pot*
**firma** *signature*
**firmare /un assegno/** *sign /a cheque/*
**firmi qui** *sign here*
**fischio -chi** (pl) *whistle (n)*
**fissare** *fix (vb) (=mend)*
**fiume** (m) *river*
**flanella** *flannel (=cloth)*
**fluido freni** *brake fluid*
**focaccia -ce** *bun (bread)*
**fodera** *lining*
**fodera di /pelliccia/** */fur/ lining*
**foglio di carta** *sheet (of paper)*
**fogne** (fpl) *drains (pl) (=sanitary system)*
**folk** *folk (adj)*
**arte** (f) **folk** *folk art*
**ballo folk** *folk dancing*
**musica folk** *folk music*

**folklore** (m) *folklore*
**folla** *crowd*
**fon** (m) *hair dryer*
**fondo**
  **fondo di / /** *bottom of / /*
**fontana** *fountain*
**foratura** *puncture*
**forbici** (fpl) *scissors (pl)*
  **un paio di forbici** *a pair of scissors*
**forchetta** *fork (cutlery)*
**foresta** *forest*
**forfora** (s) *dandruff (s)*
**forma** *shape (n), form (n)*
  **in forma** *fit (adj) (health)*
  **è in forma** *he's fit*
**formaggio** *cheese*
  **/omelette/ al formaggio** *cheese /omelette/*
**formica- che** *ant*
**forno** *oven*
**forse** *perhaps*
**forte** (di suono) *loud*
**forte** (altre accezioni) *strong (physically)*
  **/caffè/ forte** *strong /coffee/*
**fortemente** (di suono) *loudly*
**fortuna** *luck*
  **buona fortuna** *good luck*
**fortunato** *lucky*
  **essere fortunato** *be lucky*
  **è fortunato** *he's lucky*
**fortunatamente** *fortunately*
**foschia** *mist*
**fotocopia** *photocopy (n) -ies*
  **fare la fotocopia** *photocopy (vb)*
**fotocopiatrice** (f) *photocopier*
**fotografia** *photograph (photo)*
  **fare una fotografia** *take a photograph*
  **fotografia a colori** *colour photograph*
  **fotografia in bianco e nero** *black and white photograph*
**fotografico** *photographic*
  **negozio fotografico** *camera shop*
  **studio fotografico** *photographer's studio*
**fotografo** *photographer*
**foulard** (m) (inv) *square (= scarf)*

  **un foulard di /seta/** *a /silk/ square*
**fragile** *fragile*
**fragola** *strawberry -ies*
  **un cestino di fragole** *a punnet of strawberries*
**francobollo** *stamp (n)*
  **un francobollo da / duecento/ lire** *a /two hundred/ lire stamp*
**frangia -ge** *fringe (hair)*
**frasario -ri** *phrase book*
**frase** (f) *phrase*
**fratello** *brother*
**freccia -ce** *arrow*
**freddo** *cold (adj)*
  **è freddo** *it's cold (of things)*
  **fa freddo** *it's cold (of weather)*
  **ho freddo** *I'm cold*
**freddo** (nel modo di fare) *unfriendly*
**freezer** (m) *deep freeze (= machine)*
**freni** (mpl) *brakes/braking system*
**frequente** *frequent (adj)*
**fresco -chi** (= non caldo) *cool (adj)*
**fresco** (m) **freschi** (mpl) **fresca** (f)
  **fresche** (fpl) (= non vecchio) *fresh*
  **cibo fresco** *fresh food*
**fretta** *hurry (n)*
  **ho fretta** *I'm in a hurry*
**friggere** *fry*
**frigorifero/frigo** *refrigerator/fridge (infml)*
**frittata** *omelette*
**frizione** (f) *clutch (n) (car)*
**frizzante** *fizzy*
**fronte** (f) (parte del corpo) *forehead*
**fronte**
  **di fronte** *opposite (adv)*
  **di fronte a / /** *in front of / /*
  **di fronte /alla stazione/** *opposite /the station/*
**frontiera** (= confine) *border*
**frontiera** (= limite) *frontier*
**frullatore** (m) *mixer (of food)*
**frutta -** *fruit*
  **frutta fresca** *fresh fruit*
  **frutta in scatola** *tinned fruit*
  **succo di frutta** *fruit juice*
  **una bottiglia di succo di frutta** *a*

*bottle of fruit juice*
  **un bicchiere di succo di frutta** *a glass of fruit juice*
**frutti (mpl) di mare** *seafood*
**fruttivendolo** *greengrocer's*
**fucile (m)** *gun*
**fumare /una sigaretta/** *smoke /a cigarette/*
**fumatore (m&f)** *smoker*
  **non-fumador** *non-smoker*
**fumetti (mpl)** *comic (= funny paper) (s)*
**fumo** *smoke (n)*
**funerale (m)** *funeral*
**fungo -ghi (pl)** *mushroom*
  **/zuppa/ di fungo** *mushroom /soup/*
**funicolare (f)** *funicular*
**funzionare** *work (vb) (òf machines)*
  **non funziona** *it doesn't work*
**funzionario -ri** *official (n)*
**funzione (f)** *service (church)*
**fuochi (mpl) d'artificio** *fireworks (pl)*
  **spettacolo di fuochi d'artificio** *firework display*
**fuoco - chi all'aperto** *campfire*
**fuori** *out, outside*
  **è fuori** *he's out*
  **fuori di / casa/** *outside /the house/*
**fuori moda** *unfashionable*
**fuoribordo** *outboard motor*
**furgone (m)** *van*
**furto** *theft*
**furto con scasso** *burglary -ies*
**fusibile (m)** *fuse*
  **fusibile da /tre/ ampere** */three/ amp fuse*
**futuro (adj)** *future (adj)*
**futuro (n)** *future (n)*

# G

**gabardina** *gabardine coat*
**gabinetto** *lavatory -ies*
  **gabinetto per gli uomini** *Gents'*
  **gabinetto per le donne** *Ladies'*
**galleggiare** *float (vb)*
**galleria (in un edificio)** *gallery -ies*
  **galleria d'arte** *art gallery*

**galleria** (=traforo) *tunnel (n)*
**gallone** *gallon*
**galoppare** *gallop (vb)*
**gamba** *leg*
**gamberetto** *shrimp*
**gambero** *prawn*
**gàncio -ci** *hook*
**gara** *competition*
**garage (m)** *garage*
**garantire** *guarantee (vb)*
**garanzia** *guarantee (n)*
**garofano** *carnation*
**gas (m)** *gas*
**gasolio** *diesel oil*
**gatto** *cat*
**gelare** *freeze*
  **si gela** *it's freezing*
**gelatina** *jelly*
**gelato (adj)** *frosty*
**gelato (n)** *ice cream*
**gelido** *icy*
**gelo** *frost*
**gelone (m)** *chilblain*
**geloso** *jealous*
  **è geloso di /me/** *he's jealous of /me/*
**gemelli (mpl)** *cuff links (pl)*
  **un paio di gemelli** *a pair of cuff links*
**gemello** *twin*
  **letti gemelli** *twin beds*
**generale (adj)** *general (adj)*
**generatore (m)** *generator*
**generi (mpl) alimentari** *groceries (pl)*
**genero** *son-in-law /sons-in-law (pl)*
**generoso** *generous*
**gengiva** *gum (of mouth)*
**genitore (m&f)** *parent*
**gennaio** *January*
**gente (fs)** *people (pl)*
**gentile (adj)** *kind (adj)*
  **è molto gentile da parte sua** *it's very kind of you*
**gentilezza** *kindness -es*
**genuino** *genuine*
**ghiacciaio -ai** *glacier*
**ghiacciato** *iced (drink/water)*
**ghiaccio** *ice*

**già** *already*
**giacca -che** *jacket*
  **giacca a vento** *anorak*
  **giacca /di tweed/** */tweed/ jacket*
**giallo** *yellow*
**giardino** *garden*
**giardino d'infanzia** *nursery -ies*
  *(=school)*
**gin** (m) *gin*
  **una bottiglia di gin** *a bottle of gin*
  **un gin** *a gin*
  **un gin e tonico** *a gin and tonic*
**ginocchio -chia** *knee*
**giocare** *play (vb)*
  **giocare a / /** *play (a game of) / /*
  **giocare d'azzardo** *gamble (vb)*
**giocattolo** *toy*
  **negozio -zi di giocattoli** *toy shop*
**gioco** *gambling*
  **gioco d'azzardo** *gambling*
**gioielli** (mpl) *jewellery*
**gioielliere** (m) *jeweller's*
**giornalaio** *newsagent's*
**giornale** (m) *newspaper*
  **giornale della sera** *evening paper*
  **giornale /italiano/** */Italian/*
  *newspaper*
  **giornale locale** *local newspaper*
  **giornale di bordo** *logbook*
**giornaliero** *daily*
**giorno** *day*
  **buon giorno** (di mattina) *good*
  *morning*
  **buon giorno** (di pomeriggio) *good*
  *afternoon*
  **ogni giorno** *every day*
**giovane** *young*
  **giovane donna** *young woman/young*
  *women*
**giovanotto** *young man/young men* (pl)
**giovedì** (m) *Thursday*
  **arriverò giovedì** *I'll arrive on*
  *Thursday*
  **di giovedì** *on Thursdays*
**giradischi** (m) - *record player*
**giro**
  **fare un giro in macchina** *go for a*

*drive, go for a ride (in a car)*
**gita** *trip, excursion*
  **fare una gita** *go on an excursion*
  **gita in pullman** *coach trip*
**giù** *down*
  **va in giù?** *are you going down?*
  **giù dalle scale** *downstairs*
**giugno** *June*
**giusto** *(=equo) fair (adj) (=just)*
  **non è giusto** *that's not fair*
  **giusto** *(=esatto) right (=correct)*
**goccia /d'acqua/** *drop /of water/*
**go-kart -s** *go-kart*
**gol** (m) *goal*
**gola** *throat*
  **mal di gola** *sore throat*
  **pastiglia per la gola** *throat pastille*
**golf** (m) *(partita) golf*
  **campo da golf** *golf course*
  **circolo di golf** *golf club (=institution)*
  **mazza da golf** *golf club (=object)*
  **pallina da golf** *golf ball*
  **una partita a golf** *a round of golf*
**golf** (m) *(=maglione) sweater*
  **golf** (m) **con collo a V** *V -necked*
  *sweater*
  **golf con maniche corte** *short-sleeved*
  *sweater*
  **golf con maniche lunghe**
  *long-sleeved sweater*
  **golf /di cashmere/** */cashmere/*
  *sweater*
  **golf senza maniche** *sleeveless*
  *sweater*
**gomito** *elbow*
**gomitolo**
  **un gomitolo di /filo/** *a ball of /string/*
**gomma** *(sostanza) rubber (substance)*
  **gomma da cancellare** *rubber*
  *(=eraser)*
  **stivali** (mpl) **di gomma** *rubber boots*
**gomma** *(d'automobile) tyre*
  **gomma sgonfia** *flat tyre*
  **gomma tubeless** *tubeless (tyre)*
**gomma americana** *chewing gum*
**gonfiabile** *inflatable*
**gonfiare** *inflate*

**gonfiato** *swollen*
**gonfiore** (m) (=escrescenza) *lump (body)*
**gonfiore** (m) (=enfiagione) *swelling*
**gonna** *skirt*
  **gonna corta** *short skirt*
  **gonna lunga** *long skirt*
**governo** *government*
**gradi** (mpl) *degrees* (pl)
**gradino** *step* (n) (part of staircase)
**grado** *grade* (=level)
**graffiare** *scratch* (vb)
**graffio -ffi** *scratch -es* (n)
**grammatica** *grammar*
**grammi** (pl) *grams* (pl)
**granchio** *crab*
**grande** *big, large*
**grano** *corn, wheat*
**granoturco** *corn*
  **granoturco dolce** *sweet corn*
**grasso** (=non magro) *fat* (adj)
**grasso** (=oleoso) *fatty, greasy*
**gratis** *free* (=without payment)
**grazie** *thank you*
  **no grazie** *no thank you*
  **si, grazie** *yes please* (acceptance of offer)
**grazioso** *pretty*
**gridare** *shout* (vb)
**grido** (=strillo) *scream* (n)
**grido** (=urlo) *shout* (n)
**grigio** *grey* (=grey-haired)
**grigio -gi** *grey*
**grosso** *big, overweight* (people)
  **essere troppo grosso** *be overweight*
  **è troppo grosso** *he's overweight*
**gruppo** *group*
  **gruppo di /persone/** *party -ies of /people/*
**guadagnare** *earn*
**guai** (mpl) *trouble*
  **sono nei guai** *I'm in trouble*
**guancia -ce** *cheek* (of face)
**guanti** (mpl) *gloves* (pl)
  **un paio di guanti** *a pair of gloves*
**guardare** *look at, watch*
  **sto solo guardando** *I'm just looking*

  **guarda!** *look!*
**guardare /la televisione/** *watch /T.V./*
  **guardare /questo/** *look at /this/*
**guardaroba** (armadio per abiti) *wardrobe*
**guardaroba -** (in un locale pubblico) *cloakroom*
**guardia di salvataggio** *lifeguard*
**guardiano** (sorvegliante) *attendant*
**guardiano** *guardian*
**guarigione** (f) *cure* (n) (health)
**guarire** *cure* (vb) (health)
**guasto** *breakdown* (car)
**guerra** *war*
**guida** (persona) *guide* (=person)
**guida** (libro) *guide book*
**guida** (di automobile) *steering* (n) (car)
**guidare** (un'automobile) *drive* (vb)
  **uno che impara a guidare** *learner (driver)*
**guidare** (=condurre) *guide* (vb)
**guidare** (=essere al volante) *steer* (vb) (car)
**gusto** *flavour, taste*
  **di banana** *banana*
  **di cioccolata** *chocolate*
  **di fragola** *strawberry*
  **di ribes** *blackcurrant*
  **di vaniglia** *vanilla*
**gustoso** *tasty*

## H

**henné** (m) *henna*
**ho un disturbo di stomaco** *I've got a stomach upset*
**hobby** (m) - *hobby -ies*
**hockey** (m) *hockey*
  **giocare a hockey** *play hockey*
  **una partita a hockey** *a game of hockey*
**hockey** (m) **sul ghiaccio** *ice hockey*
  **giocare a hockey sul ghiaccio** *play ice-hockey*
  **una partita a hockey sul ghiaccio** *a game of ice hockey*

**hostess** (f) - *stewardess -es*
**hovercraft** (m) *hovercraft*
  **in hovercraft** *by hovercraft*

# I

**idea** *idea*
**ideale** *ideal (adj)*
**identificare** *identify*
**identificazione** (f) *identification*
**idraulico** *plumber*
**idrogetto** *hydrofoil*
  **in idrogetto** *by hydrofoil*
**ieri** *yesterday*
**il/lo/l'** (m) **la l'** (f) **gli** (mpl) **le** (fpl) *the*
**il /sei luglio/** *on /July 6th/*
**illegale** *illegal*
**illustrazione** (f) *illustration (in book)*
**imballaggio -ggi** *packing materials (to prevent breakages)*
**imbarcarsi** *embark*
**imbarcazione** (f) *boat*
**imbarco** *embarkation*
  **foglio di imbarco** *boarding card*
**imbiancare** *bleach (vb) (laundry)*
**imbottitura** *stuffing (material)*
**imbrogliare** *cheat (vb)*
**immediato** *immediate*
**immigrazione** (f) *immigration*
  **controllo immigrazione** *immigration control*
**immune** *immune*
**immunità** *immunity*
  **immunità diplomatica** *diplomatic immunity*
**immunizzare** *immunise*
**immunizzazione** (f) *immunisation*
**impacchettare** *pack (vb)*
**imparare /l'inglese/** *learn /English/*
**impaziente** *impatient*
**impermeabile** (m) *raincoat*
**impermeabile** (adj) *waterproof (adj)*
**impianto d'accensione** *ignition system*
**impianto di scappamento** *exhaust system (car)*
**impiego** *job*
  **impiegato da / /** *employed by / /*

**impiegato in un ufficio** (m)/**Impiegata in un ufficio** (f) *office worker*
**impiegato statale** (m) **impiegata statale** (f) *civil servant*
**impiego a mezza giornata** *part-time work*
**importante** *important*
**importare** (merci) *import (vb)*
**importare** (=avere importanza)
  **non importa** *it doesn't matter*
**importazione** (f) *import (n)*
**impossibile** *impossible*
**imposta sul reddito** *income tax*
**impostare** *post (vb)*
  **come pacco** *parcel post*
  **come stampa** *as printed matter*
  **espresso**
  **impostare questa per via aerea** *post this airmail*
  **posta normale** *surface mail*
  **raccomandato** *registered*
**imposte** (fpl) (=persiane) *shutters (pl)*
**imprudente** *careless*
**in**
  **in /luglio/** *in /July/*
  **nel parco** *in /the park/*
  **in /autobus/** *by /bus/*
**in ritardo** *late*
**inamidare** *starch (vb)*
**incantevole** *charming*
**incapsulare** *cap (vb) (tooth)*
**incartare** *wrap (vb)*
**incassare** *cash (vb)*
  **incassare /un traveller's cheque/** *cash /a traveller's cheque/*
**incendiato**
  **è incendiato** *it's on fire*
**incendio -di** *fire (n)*
**inchiostro** *ink*
  **una bottiglia di inchiostro** *a bottle of ink*
**incidente** (m) *accident*
**incidere** *engrave*
**incinta** *pregnant*
**incominciare** *start (vb)*
  **incominciare /il viaggio/** *start /the*

journey/
**quando incomincia?** when does it
start?
**incontrare** meet (= get to know)
**incontrare /la sua famiglia/** meet
/your family/
**incontrarsi** meet (at a given time)
**incontriamoci /alle nove/** let's meet
/at nine/
**incorniciare** frame (vb)
**incredibile** incredible
**incrocio -ci** (di strade) crossroads
/crossroads (pl)
**incrocio -ci** (nodo stradale) junction
**indicare** point (vb) (=indicate)
**indicazione** (f) sign (n)
**indigestione** (f) indigestion
**pastiglia per indigestione** indigestion
tablet
**indipendente** independent
**indirizzo** address -es
**indirizzo provvisorio** temporary
address
**individuale** individual (adj)
**indossare** wear (vb) (clothes)
**indovinare** guess (vb)
**industria** industry -ies
**inefficiente** inefficient
**inesperto** inexperienced
**infarto** heart attack
**infermiera** nurse
**infettato** infected
**influenza** flu
**informale** informal
**informare** inform
**informare /la polizia/ di / /** inform
/the police/ of / /
**informazione** (f) information (s)
**richiedere informazioni su / /**
make an inquiry about / /
**ufficio informazioni** information office
**richiesta di informazione** inquiry -ies
**vorrei delle informazioni sugli
/alberghi/ per favore** I'd like some
information about /hotels/ please
**Informazioni** (fpl) (telefoniche) Directory
Enquiries

**infrazione** (f) offence
**infrazione di parcheggio** parking
offence
**ingegnere** (m) engineer
**inghiottire** swallow (vb)
**ingorgo stradale** traffic jam
**ingrandire** enlarge
**ingrassare** (= aumentare di peso) put
on weight
**ingrassante** fattening
**iniezione** (f) injection
**vorrei un'iniezione /antitetanica/** I'd
like a /tetanus/ injection
**iniziali** (mpl) initials (pl)
**innestare la retromarcia** reverse (vb)
**innocente** innocent (= not guilty)
**inoculare** inoculate
**inoculazione** (f) inoculation
**inoltrare a** forward to
**pregasi inoltrare** please forward
**inondato** flooded
**insalata** salad
**condimento per insalata** salad
dressing
**insalata mista** mixed salad
**insalata verde** green salad
**insaponato** soapy
**insaporo** tasteless
**insegnante** (m&f) teacher
**insegnare** teach
**insegnar(mi) /l'inglese/** teach (me)
/English/
(mi) **insegna /l'inglese/** he teaches
(me) /English/
**insetticida** insecticide
**una bottiglia di insetticida** a bottle of
insecticide
**insetto** insect
**puntura d'insetto** insect bite
**insetticida** insect repellent
**insieme** together
**insolazione** (f) sunstroke
**insolito** unusual
**insonnia** insomnia
**insulina** insulin
**intelligente** intelligent
**intensivo** intensive

**intercontinentale** *intercontinental (flight)*
**interessante** *interesting*
**internazionale** *international*
**interni assorbenti** (mpl) *tampons (pl)*
  **un pacchetto di interni assorbenti** *a box of tampons (eg Tampax (tdmk))*
**interno** (adj) *internal*
  **all'interno** *indoors*
**interno** (f) **/sette/** *extension /seven/ (telephone)*
**intero** *whole*
  **un /mese/ intero** *a whole /month/*
**interpretare** *interpret*
**interprete** *interpreter*
**interrompere** *cut off (eg of telephone)*
  **sono stato interrotto** (m) **sono stata interrotta** (f) *I've been cut off*
**interruttore** (m) *switch -es (= light switch)*
**intervallo** *interval (in theatre)*
**intervista** *interview (n)*
  **ho un'intervista** *I've got an interview*
**intervistare** *interview (vb)*
**intonaco** *plaster (for walls)*
**intorno** *around*
  **intorno /alla tavola/** *around /the table/*
**invalido** *invalid (n)*
**invece** (di) *instead (of)*
  **invece /del caffè/** *instead of /coffee/*
**inverno** *winter*
  **d'inverno** *in winter*
**investimento** *investment*
**investire / /** *run over / /*
**invitare** *invite*
**invito** *invitation*
**io** /
**iodio** *iodine*
  **una bottiglia di iodio** *a bottle of iodine*
**ipoteca -che** *mortgage (n)*
**ippodromo** *racecourse*
**irregolare** *irregular*
**irritato** *sore (adj)*
**irritazione** (f) *irritation (medical)*
**iscrivere** *enroll*
**iscriversi** *register (at) (eg a club)*

**isola** *island*
**istruttivo** *educational*
**istruzione** (f) *education*
**istruzioni** (fpl) *instructions (pl)*
  **istruzioni per l'uso** *instructions for use*
**I.V.A.** (f) *VAT*

## J

**jazz** (m) *jazz*
**jeans** (mpl) *jeans (pl)*
  **stoffa da blue jeans** *denim (= material)*
  **un paio di jeans** *a pair of jeans*
**judo** *judo*
  **fare un po' di judo** *do some judo*

## K

**Kosher** *Kosher*

## L

**là** *there*
**labbro** (m) **labbra** (fpl) *lip*
  **labbro inferiore** *lower lip*
  **labbro superiore** *upper lip*
**lacci** (mpl) *laces (pl)*
  **un paio di lacci** *a pair of laces*
**laggiù** *over there*
**lago -ghi** *lake*
**lampada** *lamp*
**lampadina** *bulb (= light bulb)*
  **40/60/100/200/ candele** *40/60/100/200 watt*
**lampadina** *light bulb*
  **lampadina di bicicletta** *bicycle lamp*
  **lampadina per faro** *headlamp bulb*
  **/quaranta/ watt** */forty/ watt*
**lampo** *flash -es*
  **lampo di magnesio** *flash bulb*
**lampone** (m) *raspberry -ies*
  **un cestino di lamponi** *a punnet of raspberries*
**lana** *wool*
  **di lana** *woollen*

**lancetta** hand (of w.)
**lancio promozionale** promotion (of a product)
**larghezza** width
**largo** (dimensione) wide
**largo** (di vestiti) loose (of clothes)
**lasciapassare** (m) pass -es (n) (=p. to enter building)
**lasciare** leave
  **lasciare /le mie valigie/** leave /my luggage/
  **mi lasci stare** leave me alone
**lasciare** (=permettere) let (=allow)
  **/mi/ lasci provare** let /me/ try
**lassativo** laxative
  **lassativo debole** mild laxative
  **lassativo forte** strong laxative
**lato** side (n) (of object)
**latte** (m) milk
  **frullato di latte** milk shake
  **latte in polvere** powdered milk
  **latte in scatola** tinned milk
  **una bottiglia di latte** a bottle of milk
  **un bicchiere di latte** a glass of milk
**lattuga** lettuce
**laurea** degree (=university d.)
**laureato /  /** graduate of /  /
**lavaggio macchine** car wash
**lavanderia** laundry (place) -ies
  **lavanderia self-service** launderette
**lavandino** washbasin
**lavare** wash (vb)
  **lavare e stirare** launder
  **lavare i piatti** wash up
**lavarsi** have a wash
**lavastoviglie** (f) -gli dishwasher
**lavata** wash -es (n)
**lavatrice** (f) washing machine
**lavello** sink (n)
**lavorare** work (vb) (of people)
**lavoro** work (n)
  **fare un po' di lavoro** do some work
**legale** (adj) legal
**legale** (n) lawyer
**legare** tie (vb)
**legge** (f) law
**leggere** read

**leggere /una rivista/** read /a magazine/
**leggero** (=non pesante) light (adj) (=not heavy)
**leggero** (un cappotto) thin (coat etc)
**leggiero** (tobacco) mild
**legno** wood (substance)
  **di legno** wooden
**lei** (fs,terzo persona) she
  **per lei** for her
**lei** (s) **loro** (pl) (forma di cortesia) you
  **per lei** (s) **per loro** (pl) for you
**lentamente** slowly
**lente** (f) lens -es (of camera)
  **coperchino lente** lens cap
  **lente d'ingrandimento** magnifying glass -es
  **lente zoom** zoom lens
  **lenti** (fpl) **a contatto** contact lenses (pl)
**lento** slow
  **più lento** slower
**lenza** fishing line
**lenzuolo** (m) **lenzuola** (fpl) sheet (bed linen)
**lepre** (f) hare
**lettera** letter
  **cassetta delle lettere** letter box -es
  **lettera aerea** air-letter
  **lettera espresso** express letter
  **lettera raccomandata** registered letter
**lettino** cot
**letto** bed
  **a letto** in bed
  **andare a letto** go to bed
  **fare il letto** make the bed
  **letto a castello** bunk bed
  **letto e colazione** bed and breakfast
  **letto matrimoniale** double bed
  **letto singolo** single bed
**levare** take out
**lezione** lesson
  **lezione di guida** driving lesson
  **lezione /d'inglese/** /English/ lesson
**libbra** pound (weight)
**libero** (=senza restrizioni) free (=unconstrained)

**libero** (=non occupato) *vacant*

**libreria** *bookshop*

**libretto** *logbook (car)*

**libro** *book*
  **libro di testo** *textbook*

**limetta** (frutto) *lime*
  **succo di limetta** *lime juice*

**limite** (m) *limit (n)*
  **limite di altezza** *height limit*
  **limite di peso** *weight limit*
  **limite di velocità** *speed limit*

**limonata** *lemonade*
  **una bottiglia di limonata** *a bottle of lemonade*
  **un bicchiere di limonata** *a glass of lemonade*
  **una lattina di limonata** *a can of lemonade*

**limone** (m) *lemon*
  **succo di limone** *lemon juice*
  **una fetta di limone** *a slice of lemon*

**linea** *line*
  **linea esterna** *outside line*
  **linea telefonica** *telephone line*

**linea costiera** *coastline*

**lingua** (=linguaggio) *language*

**lingua** (=parte del corpo) *tongue*

**liquido** *liquid*

**liquore** (m) *spirits (pl) (=alcohol)*

**liscio -sci** *even (surface)*

**liscio -sci** (di liquore) *neat (of a drink)*

**liscio -sci** (non ruvido) *smooth*

**lista** *list*
  **lista di vini** *wine list*
  **lista della spesa** *shopping list*

**litigio -gi** *quarrel (n)*

**litro** *litre*

**livello** *level (n) (=grade)*

**livido** *bruise (n)*

**locale** *local (adj)*

**long playing** (m) *LP (=long playing record)*

**lontano** *far*
  **è lontano?** *is it far?*
  **non lontano da / /** *not far from / /*
  **più lontano** *further*

**loro** *they (pron)*

**per loro** *for them*

**è loro** *it's theirs*

**il loro** (m) **la loro** (f) **i loro** (mpl) **le loro** (fpl) *their*
  **il loro passaporto** (m) *their passport*
  **la loro borsa** (f) *their bag*
  **i loro biglietti** (mpl) *their tickets*
  **le loro chiavi** (fpl) *their keys*

**lotta** *fight (n)*

**lottare** *fight (vb)*

**lozione** (f) **rinforzante** *conditioner (for hair)*
  **una bottiglia di lozione rinforzante per i capelli** *a bottle of hair conditioner*

**lozione** (f) **solare** *suntan oil*

**lucchetto** *padlock (n)*

**luce** (f) *light (n) (electric light)*

**lucidare** *polish (vb)*

**lucido** (n) *polish (n)*
  **lucido per le scarpe** *shoe polish*

**lucido** (adj) *shiny*

**lucignolo** *wick (lamp, lighter)*

**luglio** *July*

**lui** *he*
  **per lui** *for him*

**luminoso** *light (adj) (=not dark)*

**luna** *moon*

**luna di miele** *honeymoon*

**luna park** (m) *fair (=entertainment)*

**lunedì** (m) *Monday*
  **arriverò lunedì** *I'll arrive on Monday*
  **di lunedì** *on Mondays*

**lunghezza** *length*
  **al ginocchio** *knee length*
  **lungo** *full length*

**lungo** *long*

**luoghi interessanti** (mpl) *sights (pl) (of a town)*
  **andare a visitare i luoghi interessanti** *go sightseeing*

**luogo -ghi** *place, site*
  **luogo di nascita** *place of birth*

**lusso** *luxury -ies*

# M

**ma** *but*
**macchia** *mark, spot, stain*
**macchiato** *stained*
**macchina** (fotografica) *camera*
  **macchina a 35 millimetri** *35 mm camera*
**macchina** (= automobile) *car*
  **in macchina** *by car*
**macchina** (= apparecchio) *machine*
  **macchina da scrivere** *typewriter*
  **macchina per il caffè** *percolator*
  **macchina sportiva** *sports car*
  **una macchina usata** *a second-hand car*
**macchinista** (m) **-i** *train driver*
**macchiolina** *spot (= blemish)*
**macelleria** *butcher's*
**macinare** *mince (vb)*
  **carne macinata** *minced meat*
**madre** (f) *mother*
**madrina** *godmother*
**magazzino** *store*
  **grande magazzino** *department store*
**maggio** *May*
**maggior parte**
  **la maggior parte** *most*
  **la maggior parte /dei soldi/** *most /money/*
  **la maggior parte /della gente/** *most /people/*
**maglia**
  **ferri** (mpl) **da maglia** *knitting needles*
  **modello di lavoro a maglia** *knitting pattern*
  **lavorare a maglia** *knit, do some knitting*
**maglia** (indumento) *vest*
  **maglia di cotone** *cotton vest*
  **maglia di lana** *woollen vest*
**maglieria** *knitwear*
  **maglieria femminile** *lingerie*
  **reparto maglieria femminile** *lingerie department*
**maglietta** *T-shirt*
**magnifico!** *great!*

**magro** *thin (of person)*
**mai** *never*
**maiale** (m) (animale) *pig*
**maiale** (m) (carni di) *pork*
**maionese** (m) *mayonnaise*
**mal/male** (m)(n) *ache, sickness*
  **avere mal di mare** *be seasick*
  **ho mal di mare** *I feel seasick*
  **ho mal di schiena** *I've got backache*
  **ho mal di stomaco** *I've got stomachache*
  **ho mal d'orecchio** *I've got earache*
  **mal di denti** *toothache (s)*
  **mi fa male il /braccio/** *my /arm/ hurts*
**malato** *ill (not well)*
  **è malato** *he's ill*
**malattia** *disease*
  **malattia venerea** *venereal disease (VD)*
**male** (adv) *badly*
  **ferito male** *badly hurt*
  **/mi/ fa male** *it disagrees with /me/ (food)*
**malva** (inv) *mauve*
**mancia -ce** *tip (n) (money)*
  **dare la mancia** *tip (vb) (money)*
  **dare la mancia /al cameriere/** *tip /the waiter/*
**mancino** *left-handed*
  **non mancino** *right-handed*
**mangianastri** (m) *cassette player*
**mangiare** *eat*
**maniche** (fpl) *sleeves (pl)*
  **maniche corte** *short sleeves*
  **maniche lunghe** *long sleeves*
  **senza maniche** *sleeveless*
**manico -ci** *handle (eg of a case)*
**manicure** (f) *manicure*
  **necessaire per manicure** *manicure set*
**maniglia** *knob (door)*
**mano** (f) **-i** *hand*
**manopola** *knob (radio)*
**manzo** *beef*
  **panino di manzo** *beef sandwich*
**mappa** *map*

**mappa dettagliata** *large-scale map*
**mappa /d'Inghilterra/** *map of /England/*
**mappa/carta stradale** *road map*
**marca** *brand (=of make)*
**marca** *brand name*
**marca -che** *make (n) (eg of a car)*
**marciapiede** (m) *pavement*
**marce** (fpl) *gears (pl) (car)*
  **prima marcia** *first gear*
  **seconda marcia** *second gear*
  **terza marcia** *third gear*
  **quarta marcia** *fourth gear*
  **quinta marcia** *fifth gear*
  **retromarcia** *reverse*
**marcio -ci** *rotten*
**mare** (m) *sea*
  **per mare** *by sea*
**marea** *tide*
  **alta marea** *high tide*
  **bassa marea** *low tide*
**margarina** *margarine*
**marina** *navy -ies*
**marinaio** *sailor*
**marito** *husband*
**marmellata** *jam*
  **marmellata di arancio** *marmalade*
  **un vaso di marmellata di arancio** *a jar of marmalade*
**marmo** *marble (material)*
**marrone** *brown*
  **capelli** (mpl) **marroni** *brown hair*
**martedì** (m) *Tuesday*
  **arriverò martedì** *I'll arrive on Tuesday*
  **di martedì** *on Tuesdays*
**martello** *hammer*
  **martello di legno** *mallet*
**marzo** *March*
**mascella** *jaw*
**maschera** *mask*
  **maschera subacquea** *underwater goggles*
**maschile** *male, masculine*
**massaggio -ggi** *massage (n)*
**massaia** *housewife -ves*
**massimo** *maximum (adj)*
**materasso** *mattress -es*

**matita** *pencil*
**matrimonio** *wedding*
**mattina** *morning*
  **di mattina** *in the morning, a.m.*
  **domani mattina** *tomorrow morning*
  **ieri mattina** *yesterday morning*
  **/le quattro/ di mattina** */four/ a.m.*
  **questa mattina** *this morning*
**matto** *mad*
**maturo** *ripe*
**mazza** *bat*
  **mazza da golf** *golf club*
**mazzo -es** *bunch -es*
  **un mazzo di /fiori/** *a bunch of /flowers/*
**me** *me*
  **per me** *for me*
  **è mio** (m) **è mia** (f) *it's mine*
**meccanico** *mechanic*
**meccanismo** *mechanism*
**mèche** (f) *streak (n) (of hair)*
  **vorrei farmi le mèches** *I'd like my hair streaked*
**media** *average (n)*
**medicina** *medicine*
  **una bottiglia di medicina** *a bottle of medicine*
**medico** (adj) *medical*
**medico -ci** (n) *doctor*
  **devo andare dal medico** *I must go to the doctor's*
**medio** (talla) *medium (size)*
**medusa** *jellyfish/jellyfish (pl)*
**meglio** *better*
  **sta meglio** *he's better (health)*
  **va meglio** *it's better (things)*
**mela** *apple*
  **succo di mela** *apple juice -es*
**melanzana** *aubergine*
**melone** (m) *melon*
  **mezzo melone** *half a melon*
  **una fetta di melone** *a slice of melon*
**membro** *member (of a group)*
**memoria** *memory -ies*
  **una buona/cattiva memoria** *a good/bad memory*
**meno** (di numero) *fewer*

**meno** (di quantità) *less*
**meno** (aritmetica) *minus*
**mensa** *canteen (eating place)*
**mensilmente** *monthly*
**menta** *peppermint* (=flavour/drink)
**mentina** *peppermint (sweet)*
**mento** *chin*
**menu** (m) *menu*
  **menu alla carta** *à la carte menu*
  **menu fisso** *set menu*
**meraviglioso** *wonderful*
**mercato** *market*
  **mercato della carne** *meat market*
  **mercato delle pulci** *flea market*
  **mercato di frutta e verdura** *fruit and vegetable market*
  **mercato di pesce** *fish market*
  **piazza del mercato** *market place*
**merce** (fs) *goods* (=merchandise) (pl)
  **merce** (fs) **esente dal dazio** *duty-free goods (pl)*
  **treno merci** *goods train*
**mercoledì** *Wednesday*
  **arriverò mercoledì** *I'll arrive on Wednesday*
  **di mercoledì** *on Wednesdays*
**merluzzo** *cod*
**mescolare** (=mischiare) *mix (vb)*
**mescolare** (ingredienti) *stir (vb)*
**mese** (m) *month*
  **il mese prossimo** *next month*
  **il mese scorso** *last month*
  **questo mese** *this month*
**messa** *mass* (=Catholic service)
**messa in piega** *shampoo and set (n)*
**messaggio -ggi** *message*
  **posso lasciare un messaggio per favore?** *can I leave a message please?*
  **posso prendere un messaggio?** *can I take a message?*
**mestruazioni** (fpl) *period* (=menstrual period)
**metallo** *metal*
**metà** *half -ves*
**metodo** *method*
**metro** *metre* (=length)

**metro a nastro** *tape measure*
**metropolitana** *underground* (u. railway)
  **in metropolitana** *by underground*
**mettere** *put*
  **mettermi /il cappotto/** *put on /my coat/*
  **mettere una corona** *crown (vb) (tooth)*
  **mettere in piega** *set (vb)(hair)*
**mettere** *put*
**mezzanotte** *midnight*
**mezzo** *middle*
  **nel mezzo di / /** *in the middle of / /*
**mezzo** *half -ves*
  **mezza /fetta/** *half a /slice/*
  **mezzo /litro/** *half a /litre/*
**mezzogiorno** *midday*
**microfono** *microphone*
**miele** (m) *honey*
  **un vaso di miele** *a jar of honey*
**miglio** (misura di lunghezza) *mile*
**migliorare** *improve*
**migliore** *best*
  **il migliore/albergo/** *the best /hotel/*
**milione** (m) *million*
  **milioni di / /** *millions of / /*
**mille** *thousand*
  **migliaia di / /** *thousands of / /*
**minatore** (m) *miner*
**minibus** (m) *minibus -es*
**miniera** *mine* (n)
  **miniera di carbone** *coal mine*
**minimo** *minimum (adj)*
**minuto** *minute (time)*
  **aspetta un minuto!** *just a minute!*
**mio**
  **il mio** (m) **la mia** (f) **i miei** (mpl) **le mie** (fpl) *my*
  **il mio passaporto** (m) *my passport*
  **la mia borsa** (f) *my bag*
  **i miei biglietti** (mpl) *my tickets*
  **le mie chiavi** (fpl) *my keys*
**mirino** *viewfinder*
**miscuglio -gli** *mixture*
**misura** (=taglia) *size*
  **che misura?** *what size?*

**misura grande** *large size*
**misura media** *medium size*
**misura piccola** *small size*
**misurare** *measure (vb)*
**mite** *mild (of weather)*
**mobili** (mpl) *furniture*
  **negozio di mobili** *furniture shop*
**moda**
  **di moda** *fashionable*
**modella** *model (profession)*
**modello** *model (object)*
  **/aeroplano/ modello** *model*
  */aeroplane/*
  **l' ultimo modello** *the latest model*
**modello** *pattern*
  **modello per golf** *knitting pattern*
  **modello per vestiti** *dress pattern*
**moderno** *modern*
**modulo** *form (=document)*
**mogano** *mahogany*
**moglie -gli** *wife/wives (pl)*
**molla** *spring (=wire coil)*
**molletta** *clothes peg*
**molti** (mpl) **-te** (fpl) *many, a lot of*
  **non molti** *not many*
  **molti /soldi/** *a lot of /money/*
**molto** *plenty*
  **molto /pane/** *plenty of /bread/*
**molto** *very*
  **molto /bello/** *very /beautiful/*
**momento** *moment*
**mondo** *world (the world)*
**moneta** *coin*
**mono** *mono (adj)*
**montagna** *mountain*
**montuoso** *mountainous*
**monumento** *monument*
**moquette** (f) *fitted carpet*
**mora** (n) *blackberry -ies*
**morbido** *soft (=not hard)*
**morbillo** (s) *measles*
**morire** *die (vb)*
**morto** *dead*
**mosca -che** *fly (=insect)*
**moschea** *mosque*
**mosso** *rough (=not calm)*
**mostra** *exhibition, show*

**motel** (m) *motel*
**motocicletta** *motorbike*
**motore** (m) *engine, motor*
  **motore** (m) **d'avviamento** *starter*
  *motor (car)*
**motoscafo** *motorboat, speedboat*
**movimento** *movement*
**mucca** *cow*
**multa** *fine* (n) *(=sum of money)*
  **pagare una multa** *pay a fine*
**municipio** *town hall*
**muovere** *move (vb)*
**muro** *wall (=outside wall)*
**muscolo** *muscle*
**museo** *museum*
**musica** *music*
  **musica classica** *classical music*
  **musica folk** *folk music*
  **musica leggera** *light music*
  **musica pop** *pop music*
**musicista** (m) **-isti** *musician*
**mussola** (m) **mussolina** (f) *Muslim*
**mutande** (fpl) *pants (pl)*
  **un paio di mutande** *a pair of pants*

# N

**nafta** *diesel oil*
**nailon** (m) *nylon*
  **un paio di calze di nailon** *a pair of*
  *nylons (stockings)*
**nascita** *birth*
  **certificato di nascita** *birth certificate*
  **data di nascita** *date of birth*
  **luogo di nascita** *place of birth*
**naso** *nose*
  **fermare il sangue** *stop the bleeding*
**nastro** *ribbon, tape*
  **nastro adesivo** *sticky tape (eg*
  *Sellotape (tdmk))*
  **nastro da macchina** *typewriter ribbon*
  **un pezzo di nastro** *a piece of ribbon*
**nata** *née*
**Natale** (m) *Christmas*
  **cartolina di Natale** *Christmas card*
  **il giorno di Natale** *Christmas Day*
**natura** *nature*

**naturale** *natural*
**naufragio -gi** *wreck (n)*
**nausea** *nausea*
  **mi sento nausea** *I feel sick*
**nave** (f) *boat, ship*
  **per nave** *by boat*
**navigare** *navigate*
**nazionale** *national*
**nazionalità** *nationality -ies*
**nazione** (f) *nation*
**nebbia** *fog*
**nebbioso** *foggy*
  **è nebbioso** *it's foggy*
**necessario -ri** *necessary*
**necessità -** *necessity -ies*
**negativo** *negative* (=*film n.*)
**negozio -zi** *shop*
  **negozio a catena** *chain store*
  **negozio di abbigliamento** *dress shop*
  **negozio di articoli di seconda mano**
  *junk shop*
  **negozio di elettricità** *electrical*
  *appliance shop*
  **negozio di ferramenta** *ironmonger's*
  **negozio di vestiti da uomo** *men's*
  *outfitter's*
  **negozio di vini** *wine merchant's*
  **negozio esente da dogana** *duty-free*
  *shop*
**nero** *black*
**nervoso** *emotional*
  **è molto nervosa** *she's very emotional*
**nescaffè** (m) (tdmk) *Nescafe (tdmk)*
**nessuno** (pron) *no one*
**nessuno** (adj) *no (adj)*
  **da nessuna parte** *nowhere*
  **nessun /soldo/** *no /money/*
**nettapipa** (m) **-** *pipe cleaner*
**netturbino** *dustman/dustmen (pl)*
**neve** (f) *snow (n)*
**nevicare** *snow (vb)*
  **nevica** *it's snowing*
**niente** *nothing*
  **niente altro?** *anything else?*
**night** (m) *nightclub*
**nipote** (m&f) (rispetto ai nonni)
  *grandchild/grandchildren (pl)*

**nipote** (f) (rispetto ai nonni)
  *granddaughter*
**nipote** (m) (rispetto agli zii) *grandson*
**nipote** (m) (rispetto agli zii) *nephew*
**nipote** (f) (rispetto agli zii) *niece*
**no** *no (opposite of 'yes')*
**nocciolo** (di ciliegia, pesca) *stone (of*
  *fruit)*
**noce** (f) (termine generico) *nut*
  **arachide** (f) *peanut*
  **mandorla** *almond*
  **noce** *walnut (nut)*
**noce** (m) (legno) *walnut (wood)*
**noi** (complemento oggetto) *us*
  **per noi** *for us*
**noi** (soggetto) *we*
**noioso** *boring, dull*
**noleggiare** *hire (vb)*
**nome** (m) *name*
  **nome** (di battesimo) *first name*
**non** *not*
  **non ancora** *not yet*
  **non attacca** *nonstick*
  **/padella/ che non attacca** *nonstick*
  */frying-pan/*
  **non funziona** *out of order*
  **non serrato** *unlocked*
  **non sposato** *single* (=*not married*)
**nonna** *grandmother*
**nonno** *grandfather*
**nord** (m) *north*
**nordest** (m) *northeast*
**nordovest** (m) *northwest*
**normale** *normal, ordinary*
  **/servizio/ normale** *regular /service/*
**nostro**
  **il nostro** (m) **la nostra** (f) **i nostri**
  (mpl) **le nostre** (fpl) *our*
  **il nostro passaporto** (n) *our passport*
  **la nostra borsa** (f) *our bag*
  **i nostri biglietti** (mpl) *our tickets*
  **le nostre chiavi** (fpl) *our keys*
  **è nostra** (f) **è nostra** *it's ours*
**notizie** (fpl) *news (s)*
**notte** (f) *night*
  **buona notte** *good night*
  **domani notte** *tomorrow night*

**la notte scorsa** *last night*
**novembre** (m) *November*
**nudo** *bare*
**numero** *number*
  **numero di scarpe** *size (shoes)*
  **numero sbagliato** *wrong number*
  **numero /sette/** *number /seven/*
  **numero telefonico** *telephone number*
**nuora** *daughter-in-law/daughters-in-law (pl)*
**nuotare** *swim (vb)*
**nuoto** (n) (sport) *swimming*
**nuoto** (n) (attività) *swim (n)*
  **nuoto subacqueo a respiratore** *scuba-diving*
**nuovo** *new (of things)*
**nuvola** *cloud*
**nuvoloso** *cloudy*

# O

**o** *or*
**obbligatorio -ri** *compulsory*
**obiettivo** (n) *lens*
  **obiettivo grandangolare** *wide-angle lens*
**oca -che** *goose/geese (pl)*
**occhiali** (mpl) *glasses (pl)*
  **occhiali** (mpl) **da sole** *sunglasses (pl)*
  **occhiali polaroid** *polaroid sunglasses*
  **un paio di occhiali** *a pair of glasses*
  **un paio di occhiali da sole** *a pair of sunglasses*
**occhialoni** (mpl) *goggles (pl)*
**occhio -chi** *eye*
**occupato** *busy*
**occupato** (telefono) *engaged (telephone)*
**odiare** *hate (vb)*
**odore** (m) *smell (n)*
  **avere l'odore di / /** *smell (vb) (= have a certain smell)*
  **ha un /buon/ odore** *it smells /good/*
  **sentire l'odore di / /** *smell (vb) (= perceive with nose)*
**offerta** (n) *offer (n)*
  **fare un'offerta** *make an offer*

**offeso** *hurt (adj)*
**oggi** *today*
**ogni** *every*
  **ogni giorno** *every day*
**ognuno** *everyone*
**olio** (lubrificante) *oil (lubricating)*
  **filtro dell'olio** *oil filter*
  **una lattina di olio** *a can of oil*
  **pompa dell' olio** *oil pump*
**olio** (condimento) *oil (salad)*
  **olio di oliva** *olive oil*
  **olio di semi** *vegetable oil*
**oliva** *olive*
  **oliva nera** *black olive*
  **oliva verde** *green olive*
**oltre** (a) *beyond (prep)*
  **oltre /alla stazione/** *beyond /the station/*
**ombra** *shade*
  **all'ombra** *in the shade*
**ombrello** *umbrella*
**ombrellone** (m) *beach umbrella*
**onda** (radio) *wave (radio)*
  **alta frequenza** *VHF*
  **onda corta** *short wave*
  **onda lunga** *long wave*
  **onda media** *medium wave*
**onda** (mare) *wave (sea)*
**onesto** *honest*
**ONU** *UN*
**OPEP** *OPEC*
**opera** *opera*
  **teatro dell'opera** *opera house*
**operaio** (m) **operaia** (f) *factory worker*
**operare** *operate (surgically)*
**operazione** (f) *operation (surgical)*
**opuscolo** *brochure, leaflet*
**ora** *hour*
  **a che ora?** *at what time?*
  **che ora è?** *what time is it?*
  **in orario** *on time*
  **l'ora** *the time (clock)*
  **ora di punta** *rush hour*
**orario** (s) (di negozio) *opening times (pl)*
**orario** (ferroviario, scolastico) *timetable*
  **orario dell'autobus** *bus timetable*

**orario dei pullman** *coach timetable*
**orario dei treni** *train timetable*
**orchestra** *orchestra*
**ordinare /una bistecca/** *order /a steak/*
**ordinato** *tidy (adj)*
**ordine** (=non disordine) *tidiness*
  **mettere in ordine** *tidy (vb)*
  **ordine** (m) **del giorno** *agenda*
**orecchini** (mpl) *earrings (pl)*
  **orecchini con la clip** *clip-on earrings*
  **orecchini per orecchi con foro** *earrings for pierced ears*
**orecchio -chi** *ear*
  **mal** (m) **d'orecchio** *earache*
**orecchioni** (mpl) *mumps*
**organizzare** (=fissare) *arrange*
  **organizzare /un incontro/** *arrange /a meeting/*
**organizzare** (=preparare) *organise*
**organizzare** (=pianificare) *plan (vb)*
  **organizzato** *planned (=already decided)*
**organizzazione** (f) *organisation*
**originale** *original*
**orina** *urine*
**orinare** *urinate*
**oro** *gold (n)*
  **d'oro** *gold (adj)*
**orologiaio** *watchmaker's*
**orologio -gi** (da muro) *clock*
**orologio -gi** (da pulso) *watch -es (n)*
  **cinturino d'orologio** *watch strap*
**orrendo** *horrific*
**orribile** *awful (of things)*
**ospedale** (m) *hospital*
**ospitalità** *hospitality*
**ospite** (m&f) (=visitatore) *guest*
**ospite** (m&f) (=anfitrione) *host (m) hostess (f)*
**ossigeno** *oxygen*
**osso -a** *bone*
**ostello per la gioventù** *youth hostel*
**ostrica** (f) *oyster*
  **dodici ostriche** *a dozen oysters*
**ottico** *optician*
**ottobre** (m) *October*

**otturare** (una carie) *fill (tooth)*
**otturazione** (f) (dentista) *filling (tooth)*
**ovest** (m) *west*

# P

**pacchetto** *packet*
  **un pacchetto di /sigarette/** *a packet of /cigarettes/(=20)*
**pacco -chi** *parcel*
  **servizio dei pacchi postali** *by parcel post*
**padella** *frying pan*
  **padella da letto** *bedpan*
**padre** (m) *father*
**padrino** *godfather*
**padrona di casa** (=anfitriona) *hostess -es*
**padrone** (m) **padrona** (f) (=proprietario) *owner*
**padrone** (m) **padrona** (f) (capo) *boss (n)*
**paese** (m) (=nazione) *country (=nation) -ies*
**paese** (m) (=villagio) *village*
**paga settimanale dei ragazzi** *pocket money*
**pagaia** *paddle (for canoe)*
**pagare** *pay*
  **con /carta di credito/** *by /credit card/*
  **in anticipo** *in advance*
  **in contanti** *in cash*
  **il conto** *the bill*
  **in /sterline/** *in /pounds/*
  **far pagare** *charge (vb) (=payment)*
  **pagare il conto** (dell'albergo) *check out (vb) (=of hotel)*
**pagina** *page (of a book)*
**pagnotta** *loaf -ves (of bread)*
  **una pagnotta grande** *a large loaf*
  **una pagnotta piccola** *a small loaf*
**paio** *pair*
  **un paio di /  /** *a pair of /  /*
**palazzo** *palace*
**palcoscenico -ci** *stage (in a theatre)*
**palestra** *gymnasium*

**palla** *ball*
  **palla da spiaggia** *beach ball*
  **palla da tennis** *tennis ball*
**pallacanestro** *basketball (=game)*
  **giocare a pallacanestro** *play basketball*
  **una partita a pallacanestro** *a game of basketball*
**pallido** *pale (of people & things)*
**pallina** *ball (small)*
  **pallina da golf** *golf ball*
  **pallina da ping-pong** *table tennis ball*
  **pallina da squash** *squash ball*
**palloncino** *balloon*
**pallone** (m) *football (=ball)*
**palpebra** *eyelid*
**pancetta** *bacon*
**panciotto** *waistcoat*
**pane** (m) *bread*
  **una fetta di pane** *a slice of bread*
  **pane carrè** *sliced bread*
  **pane bianco** *white bread*
  **pane e burro** *bread and butter*
  **pane nero** *brown bread*
  **panino** *bread roll*
**panetteria** *baker's*
**panfilo** *yacht*
**panino** *roll (=bread r.)*
  **un panino con /formaggio/** *a /cheese/ sandwich*
  **panino imbottito** *sandwich -es*
**panna** *cream (from milk)*
**panno** *rag (for cleaning)*
**pannolino** *nappy -ies*
  **pannolini da buttare** *disposable nappies*
**panorama** (m) **-i** *scenery, view*
**pantaloncini** (mpl) *shorts (pl)*
  **un paio di pantaloncini** *a pair of shorts*
  **pantaloncini da bagno** *swimming trunks (pl)*
**pantaloni** (mpl) *trousers (pl)*
  **un paio di pantaloni** *a pair of trousers*
**pantofole** (fpl) *slippers (pl)*
  **un paio di pantofole** *a pair of slippers*
**parafango** *wing (car)*

**paralume** (m) *lampshade*
**parasole** (m) *sunshade*
**paravento** (m) *screen (=movable partition)*
**parcheggiare** *park (vb)*
**parcheggio** *parking*
  **parcheggio vietato** *no parking*
**parcheggio -ggi** (sito) *car park*
**parchimetro** *parking meter*
**parco -chi** *park (n)*
**parecchi** *several*
**parente** (m&f) *relative (n)*
  **parente** (m) **prossimo** *next of kin*
**parete** (f) *wall (=inside w.)*
**parlamento** *parliament*
**parlare** *talk, tell, speak*
  **/me/ ne ha parlato** *he told /me/ about it*
  **non parlo /inglese/** *I don't speak /English/*
  **parlare /inglese/** *speak /English/*
  **parla /inglese/?** *do you speak /English/?*
  **parlare /col direttore/** *speak /to the manager/*
  **posso parlare /col direttore/ per favore?** *may I speak /to the manager/ please? (on phone)*
  **parlarmi di / /** *talk to me about / /*
**parola** *word*
**parole incrociate** (fpl) *crossword puzzle*
**parroco -ci** *vicar*
**parrucca -che** *wig*
**parrucchiere** (m) **parrucchiera** (f) *hairdresser*
**parte** (f) *part*
  **una parte di / /** *a part of / /*
  **la parte superiore di / /** *the top of / /*
  **da parte di / /** *on behalf of / /*
  **da qualche parte** *somewhere*
  **da quale parte?** *which way?*
  **da quella parte** *that way*
  **da questa parte** *this way*
  **parte** (f) **superiore** *top*
**partenza** *start, departure*
  **ora di partenza** *departure time*

**sala di partenza** *departure lounge*
**particolare** (m) *detail*
**partire** *leave (=depart)*
  **partire /alle quattro e mezzo pomeridiane/** *leave /at four-thirty p.m./*
  **partire in /luglio/** *leave in /July/*
  **partire /lunedì/** *leave on /Monday/*
**partita** *game, match -es*
  **una partita a /tennis/** *a game of /tennis/*
  **una partita di calcio** *a football match*
**Pasqua** *Easter*
**passaggio** (in automobile)
  **mi potrebbe dar un passaggio a / /?** *could you give me a lift to / /?*
**passaggio -ggi** (su una nave) *passage (on a boat)*
**passaggio a livello** *level crossing*
**passaggio pedonale** *pedestrian crossing*
**passaporto** *passport*
**passare** (=sortasseare) *pass, go past*
  **passare per /la stazione/** *go past /the station/*
  **passare** (tempo) *spend (time)*
**passeggero** *passenger (in boat)*
**passeggiare** *walking*
**passeggiata** *walk (n)*
  **fare una passeggiata** *go for a walk*
**passeggino** *pushchair*
**passera** *plaice/plaice (pl)*
**passo** *step (n) (movement)*
**pastello** *crayon*
**pasticceria** *cake shop*
**pasticche** (fpl) **per freni** *brake linings/pads (pl) (car)*
**pasticcino** *pastry -ies (=cake)*
**pastiglia** *pastille*
  **pastiglia per la gola** *throat pastille*
**pasto** *meal*
  **pasto leggero** *light meal*
**patata** *potato -es*
  **patate fritte** (fpl) *chips (pl) (potato)*
**patatinas** *crisps (=potato c.)*
**paté** (m) *pâté*
  **paté di fegato** *liver pâté*

**patente** (f) *driving licence*
  **patente internazionale** *international driving licence*
**pattinaggio** *skating*
  **pattinaggio a rotelle** *roller skating*
  **fare pattinaggio a rotelle** *go roller skating*
  **pattinaggio sul ghiaccio** *ice-skating*
  **fare pattinaggio sul ghiaccio** *go ice-skating*
**pattinare** *go skating*
**paura** *aver paura* (di / /) *be afraid (of / /)*
  **ho paura di / /** *I'm afraid of / /*
**pausa** *interval (=break)*
**pavimento** *floor (of room)*
**paziente** (adj) *patient (adj)*
**paziente** (m) (n) *patient (n)*
  **paziente non residente** *outpatient*
**pecora** *sheep/sheep (pl)*
**pedicure** (m&f) *chiropodist*
**pedone** (m) *pedestrian*
**peggio** *worse (things)*
  **peggio di / /** *worse than / /*
  **è peggio** *it's worse*
**peggiore**
  **il peggiore** *worst*
  **/la camera/ peggiore** *the worst /room/*
  **/l'albergo/ peggiore** *the worst /hotel/*
**pelle** (f) (cuoio) *leather*
**pelletteria** *leather goods shop*
**pelle** (f) **di pecora** *sheepskin*
  **/coperta/ di pelle di pecora** *sheepskin /rug/*
**pelle** (f) **scamosciata** *suede (n)*
  **/giacca/ di pelle scamosciata** *suede /jacket/*
**pelle** (f) (cute) *skin*
**pelliccia** *fur coat*
  **foderato di pelliccia** *lined with fur*
**pellicola** *film (for camera)*
  **ASA** *ASA (tdmk)*
  **DIN** (tdmk) *DIN (tdmk)*
  **35mm con 20/36 pose** *35mm 20/36 exposures*

**16mm** *16mm*
**pellicola polaroid** (tdmk) *Polaroid film (tdmk)*
**Super 8** *Super 8*
**rotolo** *cartridge film*
**rullino a colori** *colour film*
**rullino in bianco e nero** *black and white film*
**120/127/620** *120/127/620*
**pelo** *fur*
**penicillina** *penicillin*
  **sono allergico alla penicillina** *I'm allergic to penicillin*
**penna** *pen*
  **penna a sfera** *ballpoint pen*
  **penna stilografica** *fountain pen*
**pennarello** *felt-tip pen*
**pennello** *paintbrush*
  **pennello da barba** *shaving brush*
**pennino** *nib*
**pensare a /qualcosa/** *think about /something/*
**pensione** (f) (albergo) *board (n) (=cost of meals)*
  **mezza pensione** *half board*
  **pensione completa** *full board*
**pensione** (=assegno vitalizio)
  **andato in pensione** *retired (adj)*
  **sono in pensione** *I'm retired*
**pentola a pressione** *pressure cooker*
**pentolino** *saucepan*
**pepe** (m) *pepper*
**peperone** (m) *pepper (=vegetable)*
  **peperone rosso** *red pepper*
  **peperone verde** *green pepper*
**per**
  **per /le strade/** *through /the streets/*
  **per /le tre/** *by /three o'clock/*
  **per /me/** *for /me/*
  **per cento** *per cent*
**per via aerea** (lettera) *by airmail*
**pera** *pear*
**perché** *because*
  **perché?** *why?*
**perciò** *so (=therefore)*
**percorso** *route*
**perdere** (eg. tubo) *leak (vb)*

**perde** *it's leaking*
**perdere** *lose, miss*
  **ho perso /il mio portafoglio/** *I've lost /my wallet/*
  **perdere /il treno/** *miss /the train/*
**perdita** *loss*
**perdonare** *forgive*
**perfetto** *perfect (adj)*
**pericolo** *danger*
**pericoloso** *dangerous*
**periferia** *suburb*
**periodo** *period (of time)*
**perla** *pearl*
**perline** (fpl) *beads (pl)*
  **filo di perline** *string of beads*
**permanente** (f) (n) *perm (=permanent wave)*
**permanente** (adj) *permanent*
**permesso** (adj) *allowed*
**permesso** (n) (=licenza) *licence*
**permesso** (n) (=concessione) *permission*
  **permesso di /entrare/** *permission to /enter/*
**permesso** (n) (=autorizzazione) *permit (n)*
**permettere** *allow, permit*
  **permesso!** *excuse me! (to pass in front of someone)*
  **permettere di /fumare/** *allow /smoking/*
**pernice** (f) *partridge*
**persiane** (fpl) *blinds, shutters*
**perso** *lost*
  **sono perso** *I'm lost*
**persona** *person*
**personale** (adj) *personal*
**personale** (m) *staff (=employees)*
  **personale** (m) **di servizio a terra** *ground crew*
**pesante** *heavy*
**pesare** *weigh*
  **pesare troppo** *be overweight (things)*
**pesca** (attività) *fishing (n)*
  **canna da pesca** *fishing rod*
**pesca -che** (frutta) *peach -es*
**pescare** *fish (vb)*

**andare a pescare** go fishing
**pesce** (m) fish (n)
**pescivendolo** fishmonger's
**peso** weight
  **limite** (m) **di peso** weight limit
  **peso netto** net weight
**pettine** (m) comb (n)
**petto** breast
**pezzo** (parte di un intero) piece
  **un pezzo di / /** a piece of / /
  **pezzo** (di automobile) part (car)
  **pezzi** (mpl) **di ricambio** spare parts
**piacere** (vb) like (vb)
  **mi displace!** sorry! (apology)
  **le piace /nuotare/?** do you like
  /swimming/?
  **mi piace** I like it
  **mi piacerebbe /andare a nuotare/**
  I'd like to /go swimming/
  **piacere!** (durante una presentazione)
  how do you do?
**piacevole** enjoyable, pleasant
**piangere** cry (vb)
  **il bambino piange** the baby's crying
**piano** (adj) level (adj)
**piano** (n) (di edificio) floor (of building)
  **pianterreno** ground floor (G)
  **/primo/ piano** /first/ floor
  **seminterrato** basement (B)
  **ultimo piano** top floor
**piano** (n) (=progetto) plan (n)
**pianoforte** (m) piano
**pianta** (= mappa) map
  **pianta della città** street map
  **pianta** (botanica) plant (n)
**piantare** plant (vb)
**piattino** saucer
  **una tazza e piattino** a cup and
  saucer
**piatto** (adj) flat (adj)
**piatto** (cibo) course (of food)
  **secondo piatto** main course
  **primo piatto** first course
  **ultimo piatto** last course
**piatto** (contenitore per cibo) dish
  (container for food) -es
**piatto** (di portata) plate (= dinner plate)

**piatto** (di giradischi) turntable (on record
  player)
**piazza** square (place)
  **piazza principale** main square
**piazzuola** lay-by
**piccione** (m) pigeon
**piccolo** little, small
  **il più piccolo** smallest
  **più piccolo** smaller
  **un bambino piccolo** a little boy
**picnic** (m) picnic
  **fare un picnic** go on a picnic
**piede** (m) foot /feet (pl) (= part of body)
  **a piedi** on foot
**piegare** (metalli) bend (vb)
**piegare** (carta, abiti) fold (vb)
**piegato** bent (adj)
**pieghevole** folding
  **/letto/ pieghevole** folding /bed/
  **/sedia/ pieghevole** folding /chair/
**pieno** full
  **fare il pieno** fill up (with petrol)
  **il pieno, per favore!** fill it up please!
**pietra** stone (substance)
  **pietra preziosa** precious stone
**pigiama** (ms) pyjamas (pl)
  **un pigiama** a pair of pyjamas
**pigro** lazy
**pila** (per la radio) battery -ies (radio)
**pila** (= torcia elettrica) torch -es
**pillola** pill
  **la pillola** the Pill
  **una bottiglia di pillole** a bottle of pills
  **pillole** (fpl) **di vitamina** vitamin pills
  (pl)
  **una bottiglia di pillole** (fpl) **di
  vitamina** a bottle of vitamin pills
**pilota** (m) **-i** pilot
**ping-pong** (m) table tennis
  **giocare a ping-pong** play table tennis
  **una partita a ping-pong** a game of
  table tennis
**pinne** (fpl) flippers (pl)
  **un paio di pinne** a pair of flippers
**pino** (pine (wood)
**pinta** pint
**pinze** (fpl) pliers (pl)

**un paio di pinze** *a pair of pliers*
**pinzette** (fpl) *tweezers* (pl)
  **un paio di pinzette** *a pair of tweezers*
**pioggia** *rain* (n)
**piovere** *rain* (vb)
  **piove** *it's raining*
**piovoso** *rainy*
  **c'è tempo piovoso** *it's wet (weather)*
**pipa** *pipe (smoker's)*
  **nettapipa** (m) - *pipe cleaner*
**piscina** *swimming pool*
  **piscina al chiuso** *indoor swimming pool*
  **piscina all'aperto** *open air swimming pool*
  **piscina pubblica** *public swimming pool*
  **piscina riscaldata** *heated swimming pool*
**pisello** *pea*
**pista** *track*
**pittura a olio** *oil painting*
**più** (adv) *more*
**più** (aritmetica) *plus*
**piuma** *feather*
**plumine** (m) *duvet*
  **fodera per plumine** *duvet cover*
**pizzo** *lace (=material)*
**plastica** *plastic (adj)*
**platino** *platinum*
**po'** *little* (n)
  **un po' alla volta** *gradually*
  **un po' di soldi** *a little money*
**pochi** (mpl) *few*
  **poca /gente/** *few /people/*
**poi** *then*
**poker** (m) *poker (=game)*
  **giocare a póker** *play poker*
  **una partita a poker** *a game of poker*
**politica** (s) *politics* (pl)
**politico** *political*
  **uomo politico -uomini politici** *politician*
**polizia** *police* (pl)
  **polizia costiera** *coastguard*
**poliziotto** *policeman/policemen* (pl)
**pollame** *poultry*

**anitra** *duck*
**pollo** *chicken*
**tacchino** *turkey*
**pollice** (m) (misura) *inch -es*
**pollice** (m) (dito) *thumb*
**pollo** *chicken*
**polmonite** (f) *pneumonia*
**polso** *wrist*
**polvere** (f) *dust*
  **polvere contro le pulci** *flea powder*
  **polvere di curry** *curry powder*
**pomata** *ointment*
  **un tubo di pomata** *a tube of ointment*
  **un vaso di pomata** *a jar of ointment*
**pomeriggio** *afternoon*
  **di pomeriggio** *p.m.*
  **domani pomeriggio** *tomorrow afternoon*
  **ieri pomeriggio** *yesterday afternoon*
  **oggi pomeriggio** *this afternoon*
**pomodoro** *tomato -es*
  **salsa di pomodoro** *tomato sauce*
  **succo -chi di pomodoro** *tomato juice*
  **un barattolo di succo di pomodoro** *a can of tomato juice*
  **un bicchiere di succo di pomodoro** *a glass of tomato juice*
  **una bottiglia di succo di pomodoro** *a bottle of tomato juice*
**pompa** *pump*
  **pompa antincendio** *fire extinguisher*
  **pompe a piede** *foot pump*
  **pompa per acqua** *water pump*
  **pompa per bicicletta** *bicycle pump*
**pompelmo** *grapefruit (fresh)*
  **pompelmo in scatola** *tinned grapefruit*
**pompiere** (m) *fireman /firemen* (pl)
  **pompieri** (mpl) *fire brigade*
**ponte** (m) (su fiume) *bridge*
  **ponte a pedaggio** *toll bridge*
**ponte** (m) (di nave) *deck*
  **ponte inferiore** *lower deck*
  **ponte superiore** *upper deck*
**pony** (m) - *pony -ies*
**pop** (m) *pop (music)*
**pop-corn** (m) *popcorn*

**popolazione** (f) *population*

**poppa** *stern (of boat)*

**porcellana** *china*

**pornografico** *pornographic*

**porpora** (inv) *purple*

**porta** *door*
  **porta anteriore** *front door*
  **porta posteriore** *back door*

**porta sigarette** (m) *cigarette case*

**portabagagli** (m) *luggage rack (in train)*

**portacenere** (m) *ashtray*

**portachiavi** (m) *key ring*

**porta-finestra** *French window*

**portafoglio** (m) - *wallet*

**portapacchi** (m) - *roof rack*

**portare** (riportare) *bring*

**portare** *carry*

**portare via** *take away (vb)*
  **pasto da portar via** *take-away meal*

**portatile** *portable*

**portiere** (m) (in un condominio) *doorman /doormen (pl)*

**portiere** (m) (squadra di calcio) *goalkeeper*

**portiere** (m) (in albergo) *porter (hotel)*

**porto** *harbour, port*
  **capitano di porto** *harbour master*

**porzione** (f) *portion*
  **una porzione di / /** *a portion of / /*

**posateria** *cutlery*

**posizione** (f) *position*

**possibile** *possible*

**posta** *mail*
  **posta aerea** *by air-mail*
  **posta espressa** *express mail*
  **posta normale** *surface mail*

**poster** (m) *poster*

**posto** (a sedere) *seat*
  **al teatro** *at the theatre*
  **davanti al front** *at the front*
  **di dietro** *at the back*
  **in mezzo** *in the middle*
  **in pullman** *on a coach*
  **in treno** *on a train*
  **nella sezione per fumatori** *in the smoking section (aeroplane)*

**nella sezione per non fumatori** *in the non-smoking section (aeroplane)*

**scompartimento per fumatori** *in a smoker (train)*

**scompartimento per non fumatori** *in a non-smoker (train)*

**vicino alla finestra** *by the window*

**vicino all'uscita** *by the exit*

**posto** (=luogo) *place*
  **posto di lavoro** *place of work*
  **posto vacante** *vacancy -ies(job)*

**potere** (vb)
  **posso /farlo/** *I can /do it/*
  **non posso /farlo/** *I can't /do it/*
  **potrebbe /cambiare/ /la gomma/ per favore?** *could you /change/ /the tyre/ please?*

**povero** (=not rich) *poor*

**pozzo** *well (n)*

**pratica** *practice (=training)*

**praticare** *practise (=put into practice)*

**pratico** *experienced*

**precisamente** *exactly*

**preciso** *exact*

**preferire** *prefer*

**preferito** (adj) *favourite (adj)*

**prefisso** *dialling code*

**prego** *not at all, you're welcome*

**premere** *press (vb) (eg button)*

**premiare** *reward (vb)*

**premio -mi** (in una gara) *prize*

**premio -mi** (per buona condotta) *reward (n)*

**prendere** *take*
  **io**(m)/**la**(f) **prendo** *I'll take it (in shop)*
  **prendere /il treno/** *catch /the train/*
  **prendere in prestito** *borrow*
  **prendere in prestito /una penna/** *borrow /a pen/*
  **posso prendere in prestito /la sua penna/?** *may I borrow /your pen/?*
  **prendere /un taxi/** *get /a taxi/*
  **prendere /una malattia/** *catch /an illness/*
  **prendiamo /una bibita/** *let's /have a drink/*

**prendere** (tempo) *take (time)*

**prendere** (trasporto) *catch (transport)*
**prendere** (malattia) *catch (illness)*
**prenotare** (=riservare) *reserve (vb)*
**prenotazione** (f) (treno, aereo) *booking*
  **prenotazione anticipata** *advance booking*
**prenotazione** (f) (albergo, teatro) *reservation (hotel, restaurant, theatre)*
  **fare una prenotazione** *make a reservation*
**preoccupato** *worried*
**preparare** *prepare*
**presa** *socket*
  **presa per la luce** *light socket*
  **presa per rasoio** *electric razor socket*
  **presa a /tre/ spinotti** */three/-pin socket*
**prescrivere** *prescribe*
**presentare** *introduce, present*
**presentazione** (f) *introduction*
  **lettera di presentazione** *letter of introduction*
**presente** (adj) *present (adj)*
**presente** (m) (n) (tempo) *present (n) (time)*
**preservativo** (m) (=Durex) *sheath (=Durex)*
  **un pacchetto di preservativi** *a packet of sheaths*
**presidente** (m) *chairman /chairmen (pl), president (of company)*
**pressione** (f) *pressure*
  **pressione atmosferica** *air pressure*
  **pressione delle gomme** *tyre pressure*
  **pressione del sangue** *blood pressure*
**prestare** *lend*
  **mi potrebbe prestare un po' di /soldi/?** *could you lend me some /money/?*
**presto** (=di buon'ora) *early*
  **partire presto** *leave early*
  **treno di mattina presto** *early train*
**presto** (tra poco) *soon*
  **arrivederci a presto!** *see you soon!*
  **fare presto** *hurry (vb)*
  **faccia presto, per favore!** *please hurry !*

**presto!** (in fretta) *quick!*
**prete** (m) *priest*
**prezioso** *precious, valuable*
  **oggetti preziosi** (mpl) *valuables (pl)*
  **pietra preziosa** *precious stone*
**prezzo** (condizioni) *charge (n) (=payment)*
**prezzo** (costo) *cost (n)*
**prezzo** (da pagare) *price (n)*
  **listino prezzi** *price list*
  **prezzo all'ingrosso** *cash price*
**prigione** (f) *gaol, prison*
  **in prigione** *in prison*
**prima** (adv) *before (adv)*
  **prima della colazione** *before /breakfast/*
  **prima di /partire/** *before /leaving/*
  **prima di tutto** *first of all*
**primavera** *spring (=season)*
  **in primavera** *in spring*
**primo** (adj) *first*
  **di prima classe** *first class (adj)*
  **prima classe** *first class (n)*
**principale** *main*
  **strada principale** *main road*
**principe** (m) *prince*
**principessa** (f) *princess (-es)*
**privato** *private*
  **/bagno/ privato** *private /bath/*
**probabile** *likely, probable*
**problema** (m) -**i** *problem*
**processione** (f) *procession*
**prodotto** *product*
**produrre** *produce (vb)*
**profondità** - *depth*
**profondo** *deep*
**profumo** *perfume*
  **una bottiglia di profumo** *a bottle of perfume*
**programma** (m) -**i** (degli avvenimenti) *programme (of events)*
**programma** (m) -**i** (=orario) *schedule*
**programma** (m) -**mi** (a teatro) *theatre programme*
**programma televisiva** *television programme*
**promemoria** *memo*

**promessa** *promise (n)*

**promettere** *promise (vb)*

**promozione** (f) *promotion (of a person)*

**pronto** *ready*
  **quando sarà pronto?** *when will it be ready?*
  **sei pronto?** (m) **sei pronta?** (f) **siete pronti?** (mpl) **siete pronte?** (fpl) *are you ready?*

**pronto!** *hello (on telephone)*

**pronto soccorso** (occorrente per) *first aid*
  **equipaggiamento di pronto soccorso** *first aid kit*

**pronto soccorso** (all'ospedale) *casualty department (hospital)*

**pronunciare** *pronounce*

**prosciutto** *ham*
  **/panino/ col prosciutto** *ham /sandwich/*
  **/sei/ fette di prosciutto** */six/ slices of ham*

**proseguire /un viaggio/** *continue /a journey/*

**prossimo** *next*

**prostituta** *prostitute*

**proteggere** *protect*
  **proteggermi da / /** *protect me from / /*

**protesta** *complaint*

**protestante** *Protestant (adj)*

**protestare** *complain*
  **protestare /col direttore/** *complain /to the manager/*
  **protestare /per il rumore/** *complain /about the noise/*

**protettivo** *protective*

**protezione** (f) *protection*

**prova** (n) (=evidenza) *proof*

**prova** (n) (=esperimento) *test (n)*
  **stanza per le prove** *fitting room in shop*

**provare** (=sperimentare) *test (vb)*

**provare** (=fare un tentativo) *try (vb)*
  **provare /questo gelato/** *try /this ice-cream/*
  **provare /questo golf/** *try on /this sweater/*

**provvisorio -ri** *temporary*

**provviste** (fpl) *provisions (pl)*

**prua** (s) *bows (pl) (of ship)*

**prudente** *careful*

**prugna** *plum*
  **prugna secca** *prune*

**prurito** *itch*

**pubblicità** *publicity*
  **fare pubblicità** *advertise*

**pubblico** (n) *audience*

**pubblico** (adj) *public*
  **edifici** (mpl) **pubblici** *public buildings (pl)*
  **gabinetto pubblico** *public convenience*
  **/giardini/** (mpl) **pubblici** *public /garden/*

**pugilato** *boxing*
  **incontro di pugilato** *boxing match*

**pugilatore** (m) *boxer*

**pulce** (f) *flea*
  **morso di pulce** *fleabite*

**pulire** *clean (vb)*

**pulito** *clean (adj)*

**pullman** (f) -(tdmk) *coach -es*
  **in pullman** *by coach*

**pungere** *sting (vb)*

**punire** *punish*

**punta** *point (n) (=a sharpened point)*

**punti metallici** (fpl) *staples (n) (pl)*

**puntina da disegno** *drawing pin*

**punto** *spot (=dot)*

**puntura** (n) *sting (n), bite (n)*
  **puntura /d'ape/** */bee/ sting*

**puro** *pure*

**pus** (m) *pus*

**puzzle** (m) *puzzle*

# Q

**quadrante** (m) *face (of w.)*

**quadrato** *square (shape)*

**quadro** *painting, picture*
  **quadro a acquarello** *watercolour*
  **quadro a olio** *oil painting*

**quaglia** *quail (=bird)*

**qualche** a few
**qualcosa** something
  **qualcosa da bere** something to drink
  **qualcosa da mangiare** something to eat
**qualcosa** anything
**qualcuno** someone
**quale?** (adj) which?
  **quale /aeroplano/?** which /plane/?
  **qual è /il suo indirizzo/?** what's /your address/?
**quale?** (m&f) **quali?** (pl) (pron) which one?/which ones?
**qualificato** qualified
**qualificazioni** (fpl) qualifications (pl)
**qualità** - quality -ies
**quando?** when?
  **quando si aprono /i negozi/?** when do /the shops/ open?
**quanto?** (m) **quanta?** (f) how much?
  **quanto dista è /Brighton/ da qui?** how far is it to /Brighton/?
  **quanto tempo?** how long? (time)
  **quanti** (mpl) **quante** (fpl) how many?
**quarto** quarter
  **un quarto /d'ora/** a quarter of /an hour/
**quasi** almost
**quelli** (mpl) **quelle** (fpl) (adj) those
  **quelli là** (mpl) **quelle là** (fpl) (pron) those ones
**quello** (m) **quella** (f) that
**quercia** oak (wood)
**questi** (mpl) **queste** (fpl) (adj) these
  **questi qui** (mpl) **queste qui** (fpl) (pron) these ones
**questo** (m) **questa** (f) (adj) this
  **questo qui** (m) **questa qui** (f) (pron) this one
**qui** here
**quotidiano** morning paper

# R

**rabbia** rabies
**rabbino** rabbi
**racchetta** racquet

**racchetta da squash** squash racquet
**racchetta da tennis** tennis racquet
**raccogliere** pick (=gather flowers etc)
**raccolta** collection (of objects)
  **ultima raccolta** last collection (of post)
**raccolto** (n) harvest
**raccomandare** recommend
**raccomandata** registered (mail)
**raccontare** tell
  **raccontarmi di / /** tell me (something) about / /
**racconto** story -ies
**raccordo elettrico** adaptor plug
**radiatore** (m) radiator (car)
**radio** (f) radio
  **autoradio** (f) car radio
  **radio portatile** portable radio
  **radio a transistor** transistor radio
**raffreddare** chill, cool
  **sono raffreddato** I've got a cold
**raffreddore** (m) cold (n)
**ragazza** (=giovane donna) girl
  **ragazza alla pari** au pair
**ragazzo** boy
**raggio x** x-ray
**raggiungere** reach (=attain) (vb)
**ragione** (f) reason (n)
**ragionevole** reasonable
**ragioniere** (m) accountant
**ragno** spider
**rally** (m) - rally -ies
  **rally automobilistico** motor rally
**rame** (m) copper
**rammendare** darn (vb)
**rapa** turnip
**rapido** fast train, express train
**rappresentante** (m) agent (of company)
  **rappresentante** (m) **delle vendite** sales representative
**rappresentare** represent
**raro** rare (=unusual)
**rasatura** shave (n)
**raso** satin (n)
  **di raso** satin (adj)
**rasoio** razor
  **lametta per rasoio** razor blade
  **un pacchetto di lamette** a packet of

*razor blades*
**rasoio elettrico** *electric razor*
**ratto** *rat*
**rattoppare** *patch (vb)*
**ravanello** *radish -es*
**re** (m) - *king*
**recente** *recent*
**reclamare** *claim (vb)*
  **reclamare dall'assicurazione** *claim on /the insurance/*
  **reclamare /danni/** *claim /damages.*
**refill** (m) - *refill*
**regalo** *gift, present*
  **negozio di regali** *gift shop*
**reggicalze** (m) *suspender belt*
**reggipetto** *bra*
**regina** *queen*
**regione** (f) *area (of country)*
**registrare** (col registratore) *record (vb)*
**registrarsi** *check in (vb) (=of hotel/plane)*
**registratore** (m) *tape recorder*
  **registratore a cassette** *cassette recorder*
  **registratore a nastri** *open reel recorder*
**regolamenti** (mpl) *regulations (pl)*
**regole** (fpl) *rules (pl)*
**regolo** *ruler (for measuring)*
**relazione** (f) (=resoconto) *report (n)*
**religione** (f) *religion*
**religioso** *religious*
**remare** *row (a boat)*
**remo** *oar (for rowing)*
**reni** (mpl) *kidneys (pl)*
**reparto** *department*
  **reparto bambini** *children's department*
  **reparto contabilità** *accounts department*
  **reparto donne** *women's department*
  **reparto uomini** *men's department*
**resistente all'urto** *shockproof (eg of watch)*
**respirare** *breathe*
**respiro** *breath*
**responsabile** *responsible*

**responsabile di /  /** *responsible for /  /*
**restituire** (=rimborsare) *repay*
  **restituirmi** *repay me*
  **restituire il denaro** *repay the money*
**restituire** (=give back)
  **restituire /questa maglietta/** *return /this sweater/*
**resto** *change (n) (=money)*
**restrizioni** (fpl) *restrictions (pl)*
**rete** (f) *net (=fishing n.)*
**retina per capelli** *hair net*
**retromarcia** *reverse (n) (gear)*
**rettangolare** *rectangular*
**reumatismo** *rheumatism*
**revisione** (f) *service (n) (car)*
**rhum** (m) *rum*
**ribes nero** (m) - *blackcurrant*
**ricambi** (mpl) *spare parts (pl)*
**ricamo** *embroidery*
**ricaricare** *recharge (battery)*
**ricco** *rich*
**ricerca** (=cerca) *search -es (n)*
**ricerca** (scienza) *research (n)*
  **ricerca sul mercato** *market research*
**ricercare** *search (vb)*
**ricetta** (medica) *prescription*
**ricetta** (di cucina) *recipe*
**ricevere** *receive*
**ricevuta** *receipt*
**richiesta** *request (n)*
  **fare una richiesta** *make a request*
**riconoscente** *grateful*
**riconoscere** *recognise*
**ricordarsi** *remember*
  **mi ricordo /il nome/** *I remember /the name/*
  **non mi ricordo** *I don't remember*
**ricordo** (=memoria) *memory*
  **bel ricordo** (ms) *happy memories (pl)*
**ricordo** (oggetto, regalo) *souvenir*
  **negozio -zi di ricordi** *souvenir shop*
**ridere** *laugh (vb)*
**ridurre** *reduce (price)*
  **ridurre il prezzo** *reduce the price*
**riduzione** (f) *reduction*
**riempire** *fill*

**riempire** /un modulo/ fill in /a form/
**riferire** report (vb)
  **riferire** /una perdita/ report /a loss/
**rifiuti** (mpl) rubbish, litter
**rifornimento** supply -ies (n), stock
**rifornire** supply (vb)
**riga**
  **a righe** striped
**rigido** stiff
**rimborsare** refund, reimburse
**rimborso** refund (n)
**rimedio -i** remedy -ies
**rimmel** (m) mascara
**rimorchio -chi** trailer
**rincrescere** regret (vb)
**ringraziare di / /** thank you for
/ /(vb)
  **la ringrazio della sua ospitalità** thank
you for your hospitality
**rinnovare** renew
**riparare** do repairs. repair
**riparato** (=protetto) sheltered
**riparazioni** (fpl) repairs (pl)
  **riparazioni orologi** watch repairs
(=shop)
  **riparazioni scarpe** shoe repairs
(=shop)
**ripetere** repeat
**ripido** steep
**ripieno** (n) stuffing (food)
**riposarsi** have a rest, rest
**riposo** rest (n)
**riproduzione** (f) reproduction
(=painting)
**riscaldamento** heating
  **riscaldamento centrale** central
heating
**riscaldare** warm (vb)
**riserva** reserve
  **di riserva** spare (adj)
**riservato** reserved
  **posto riservato** reserved seat
**riso** (n) rice
**risparmiare** save (money)
**rispondere** answer (vb)
**risposta** (n) answer (n), reply -ies (n)
  **risposta pagata** reply-paid

**ristorante** (m) restaurant
  **ristorante self-service** self-service
restaurant
**risultato** (n) result
**ritardato** delayed
**ritardo** delay (n)
  **in ritardo** late
  **lui è in ritardo** he's late
  **mi dispiace, sono in ritardo** I'm sorry
I'm late
**ritirare** (da) collect (from)
  **ritirare /le mie valigie/** collect /my
luggage/
**ritorno** return
  **biglietto di andata e ritorno** return
(ticket)
**ritratto** portrait
**riunione** (f) meeting (business)
**rivista** (rotocalco) magazine
**roba** (s) belongings (pl), property
**roccia -cce** rock (n)
**rompere** break (vb)
**rosa** (adj) pink
**rosa** (n) rose
  **un mazzo di rose** a bunch of roses
**rosolia** German measles
**rossetto** lipstick
**rosso** red
**rosticceria** delicatessen (=food shop)
**rotolo** (=rullino) cartridge (=film
cartridge)
**rotolo** (=rocchetto) reel (of cotton)
**rotolo** (=rullo) roll
  **rotolo di /carta igienica/** roll of /toilet
paper/
**rotonda** (n) roundabout (n)
**rotondo** round (adj)
**rotto** broken
  **è rotto** it's broken
**roulotte** (f) caravan
  **campeggio per roulotte** caravan site
  **roulotte a /quattro/ cuccette** /four/
berth caravan
**rovesciato** (liquidi) spilt
**rovesciato** (alla rovescia) upside-down
**rovinare** spoil (vb)
**rubare** steal

**rubato** *stolen*

**rubinetto** *tap*
  **rubinetto di acqua calda** *hot tap*
  **rubinetto di acqua fredda** *cold tap*

**rugby** (m) *rugby*
  **giocare a rugby** *play rugby*
  **una partita di rugby** *a game of rugby*

**rumoroso** *noisy*

**ruota** *wheel*

**ruscello** *stream (n)*

**ruvido** *rough (= not smooth)*

# S

**sabato** *Saturday*
  **arriverò sabato** *I'll arrive on Saturday*
  **di sabato** *on Saturdays*

**sabbia** *sand*

**sabbioso** *sandy*

**saccarina** *saccharine*
  **pastiglia di saccarina** *saccharine tablet*

**sacchetto** *bag, carrier bag*
  **sacchetto di carta** *paper bag*
  **sacchetto di plastica** *plastic bag*

**sacco -chi a pelo** *sleeping bag*

**sala** *room, hall*
  **sala concerti** *concert hall*
  **sala da pranzo** *dining room*
  **sala d'aspetto** *waiting room*
  **sala della televisione** *TV lounge*
  **sala di partenza** *departure lounge*
  **sala giochi** *amusement arcade*

**salame** *sausage, salami*

**salatino** *savoury (hors d'oeuvres)*

**salato** *salted*

**sale** (m) *salt (n)*
  **sali** (mpl) **da bagno** *bath salts (pl)*

**salire** (su un aereo etc) *boar (vb) (eg a plane)*
  **salire a /  /** *get on at /  /*

**salmone** (m) *salmon/salmon (pl)*
  **salmone affumicato** *smoked salmon*

**salone** (m) **di bellezza** *beauty salon*

**salsa** *sauce*

**salsiccia -cce /salame** (m) *sausage*

**saltare** (elettricità) *fuse (vb)*

  **le luci sono saltate** *the lights have fused*

**saltare** (di persona, animale) *jump (vb)*

**salutami /Mary/** *give /Mary/ my love*

**salute** (f) *health*

**salute!** *cheers! (toast)*

**saluti**
  **mi saluti /Julie/** *give /Julie/ my regards*

**salvagente** (m) *life jacket*
  **cintura di salvagente** *lifebelt*

**salvare** *save (= rescue)*

**salvataggio**
  **cintura di salvataggio** *lifebelt*
  **guardia di salvataggio** *lifeguard*
  **scialuppa di salvataggio** *lifeboat*

**sandali** (mpl) *sandals (pl)*
  **un paio di sandali** *a pair of sandals*

**sangue** (m) *blood*
  **al sangue** (eg bistecca) *rare (eg of steak)*
  **pressione** (f) **del sangue** *blood pressure*
  **sangue al naso** *nosebleed*

**sanguigno**
  **gruppo sanguigno** *blood group*

**sanguinare** *bleed*
  **mi sanguina il naso** *my nose is bleeding*

**sano** *healthy*

**santo** *saint*

**sapere** *know (a fact)*
  **lo so** *I know*
  **non so** *I don't know*
  **sapere di** *taste (vb) (= have a certain taste)*

**sapone** (m) *soap*
  **sapone da barba** *shaving soap*
  **sapone in scaglie** *soap flakes*
  **una saponetta** *a bar of soap*

**saporito** *well-seasoned*

**sardina** *sardine*

**sarta** *dressmaker*

**sarto** *tailor*

**sauna** *sauna*

**sbagliato** *wrong*
  **numero sbagliato** *wrong number*

**sbaglio -gli** *mistake (n)*
  **per sbaglio** *by mistake*
**sbarcare** *disembark*
**sbiadito** *faded (colour)*
**sbucciare** *peel (vb)*
  **sbuccia patate** (m) *potato peeler*
**scacchi** (mpl) *chess (s)*
  **giocare a scacchi** *play chess*
  **una partita a scacchi** *a game of chess*
**scadente** *poor (poor quality)*
**scadere** *expire (=run out)*
  **scaduto** *out of date (eg passport)*
  **/il mio visto/ è scaduto** */my visa/ has expired*
**scaffale** (m) *shelf -ves*
**scala** (portatile) *ladder*
**scala** (carta geografica) *scale (on a map)*
  **scala grande** *large scale*
  **scala piccola** *small scale*
**scala** (in un edificio) *staircase*
  **scale** (fpl) *stairs (pl)*
**scalare** *climb (vb) (=c. mountains)*
**scalata** *climbing*
  **fare una scalata** *go climbing*
**scambiare** *exchange*
  **scambiare /questo golf/** *exchange /this sweater/*
**scappare da / /** *escape from / /*
**scarafaggio -gi** *cockroach -es*
**scarico** *drain (n)*
  **lo scarico è bloccato** *the drain's blocked*
**scarpe** (fpl) *shoes (pl)*
  **un paio di scarpe** *a pair of shoes*
  **scarpe con tacchi alti** *high-heeled shoes*
  **scarpe con tacchi bassi** *flat-heeled shoes*
  **scarpe da bambina** *girls' shoes*
  **scarpe da bambino** *boys' shoes*
  **scarpe da camminare** *walking shoes*
  **scarpe da donna** *ladies' shoes*
  **scarpe da uomo** *men's shoes*
  **scarpe da ginnastica** *plimsolls (pl)*
  **un paio di scarpe da ginnastica** *a pair of plimsolls*

**scarponi** (mpl) **da sci** *ski-boots (pl)*
  **un paio di scarponi da sci** *a pair of ski-boots*
**scatola** *box -es*
  **una scatola di / /** *a box of / /*
**scavare** *dig (vb)*
**scegliere** *choose*
  **scegliere tra / / e / /** *choose between / / and / /*
**scelta** *choice*
  **scelta tra / / e / /** *choice between / / and / /*
**scendere a / /** *get off at / /*
**schermo** *screen (=film screen)*
**schiaccianoci** (ms) *nutcrackers (pl)*
**schiena** *back*
  **mal di schiena** *backache*
**schifoso** *disgusting*
**schizzo** (=disegno) *sketch -es (n)*
**sci** (mpl) *skis (pl)*
  **un paio di sci** *a pair of skis*
  **sci acquatico** *water skiing*
  **fare lo sci acquatico** *go water skiing*
  **sci d'acqua** *water skis*
**sciacquare** *rinse (vb)*
**sciacquo** *rinse (n) (clothes)*
  **sciacquo per la bocca** *mouthwash -es*
  **una bottiglia di sciacquo per la bocca** *a bottle of mouthwash*
**scialle** (m) *shawl*
**scialuppa** *dinghy -ies, boat*
  **scialuppa a vela** *sailing dinghy*
  **scialuppa di gomma** *rubber dinghy*
  **scialuppa di salvataggio** *lifeboat*
**sciampagna** *champagne*
  **una bottiglia di sciampagna** *a bottle of champagne*
**sciare** *skiing*
  **andare a sciare** *go skiing*
**sciarpa** *scarf -ves*
  **sciarpa /di seta/** */silk/ scarf*
**scienza** *science*
**sciocchezze** (fpl) *nonsense*
**sciocco -chi** *foolish*
**sciopero** *strike (n)*

**essere in sciopero** *be on strike*
**scivoloso** *slippery*
**scogliera** *cliff*
**scolara** *schoolgirl*
**scolaro** *schoolboy*
**scommessa** *bet (n)*
**scommettere** *bet (vb)*
**scomodo** *uncomfortable*
**scompartimento** *compartment (in train)*
  **scompartimento per fumatori**
  *smoking compartment*
  **scompartimento per non fumatori**
  *non-smoking compartment*
**sconosciuto** (n) *stranger (n)*
**sconto** *discount (n)*
**scontrarsi** (con) *crash (into)*
**scooter** (m) *scooter*
**scopa** *brush, mop, broom*
**scoppiato** *burst (adj)*
  **un tubo scoppiato** *a burst pipe*
**scorso** *last (= previous)*
  **/martedi/ scorso** *last /Tuesday/*
**scorta** *escort (n)*
**scortare** (=accompagnare) *escort (vb)*
**scortese** *rude*
**scossa** *shock (n)*
  **scossa elettrica** *electric shock*
**scottatura** *burn (n)*
**scozzese**
  **gonna scozzese** *tartan skirt*
**scrivania** *desk*
**scrivere** *write*
**scultura** *sculpture*
**scuola** *school*
  **scuola di lingue** *language school*
**scuotere** *shake (vb)*
**scuro** *dark (of colour)*
  **/verde/ scuro** *dark /green/*
**scusa** (atta dello scusarsi) *apology -ies*
  **domandare scusa** *apologise*
  **domando scusa** *I apologise*
**scusa** (=pretesto) *excuse (n)*
  **fare una scusa** *make an excuse*
**scusare** *excuse (vb)*
  **scusi!** *excuse me! (to attract attention)*
  **scusi?** *sorry? (= pardon?)*
**sdraiarsi** *lie (vb) (=lie down)*

**se** *if*
  **se possibile** *if possible*
  **se può** *if you can*
**secchiello** *bucket*
  **un secchiello e paletta** *a bucket and spade*
**secco -chi** *dry (adj)*
  **mezzo secco** *medium-dry*
**secolo** *century -ies*
**secondo** (adj) *second (number)*
**secondo** (tempo) *second (of time)*
  **di seconda mano** *second-hand*
**sedano** *celery*
**sedere** (m) *bottom (part of body)*
**sedere** (vb) *sit*
**sedia** *chair*
  **sedia a rotelle** *wheelchair*
  **sedia ascensore** *chair lift*
  **sedia a sdraio** *deckchair*
**seggiolone** (m) *high chair*
**segnalare** *signal (vb)*
**segnale** (m) *signal (n)*
**segnare /un gol/** *score /a goal/*
**segretaria** *secretary -ies*
**segreto** (adj) *secret (adj)*
**segreto** (n) *secret (n)*
**seguire** *follow*
**sella** *saddle*
**seltz** *soda (water)*
  **una bottiglia di seltz** *a bottle of soda (water)*
  **un bicchiere di seltz** *a glass of soda (water)*
**selvaggina** *game (animals)*
  **cinghiale** (m) *wild boar*
  **fagiano** *pheasant*
  **lepre** (f) *hare*
  **quaglia** *quail*
  **pernice** (f) *partridge*
  **piccione** (m) *pigeon*
  **tetraone** (m) *grouse*
**selvatico** *wild (=not tame)*
  **animale** (m) **selvatico** *wild animal*
**semaforo** (ms) *traffic lights (pl)*
**sembrare / /** (al tatto) *feel / /*
  **sembra /ruvido/** *it feels /rough/*
**semino** *pip (= seed of citrus fruit)*

**seminterrato** *basement*
**semplice** *simple, plain*
**sempre** *always*
**senape** (m) *mustard*
**sensi**
  **privo di sensi** *unconscious*
**senso unico** *one-way street*
**sentiero** *path*
**sentire** (audito) *hear*
**sentire** (sensazione) *feel*
  **mi sento male** *I feel ill*
  **mi sento nausea** *I feel sick*
**senza** *without*
  **senza fermate** *nonstop*
**separato** *separate (adj)*
**seppellire** *bury*
**sera** *evening*
  **buona sera** *good evening*
  **domani sera** *tomorrow evening*
  **ieri sera** *yesterday evening*
  **questa sera** *this evening*
**serbatoio** *tank*
  **serbatoio d'acqua** *water tank*
**serpente** (m) *snake*
  **morso di serpente** *snakebite*
**serratura** *lock (n)*
**servire** *serve*
  **a che serve?** *what's it for?*
**servizievole** *helpful*
**servizio -zi** (prestato da camerieri)
  *service*
  **servizio continuo** *twenty-four hour
  service*
  **servizio in camera** *room service*
**servizio -zi** (di piatti, posate) *set (n)*
  **servizio da pranzo** *dinner set*
  **servizio da tè** *tea service*
**sesso -es** *sex -es*
**seta** *silk (n)*
  **di seta** *silk (adj)*
**sete**
  **avere sete** *be thirsty*
  **ho sete** *I'm thirsty*
**settembre** (m) *September*
**settico** *septic*
**settimana** *week*
  **fine** (f) **settimana** *weekend*

**la settimana prossima** *next week*
**la settimana scorsa** *last week*
**questa settimana** *this week*
**settimanale** *weekly (adj)*
**sfilata di moda** *fashion show*
**sfogo** (malattia) *rash -es*
**sfortunatamente** *unfortunately*
**sfortunato**
  **essere sfortunato** *be unlucky*
  **è sfortunato** *he's unlucky*
**sfumatura** *shade (colour)*
**sgabello** *stool*
**sgradevole** *unpleasant*
**sgualcire** *crease (vb)*
  **si squalcisce?** *does it crease?*
**shampoo** (m) *shampoo (n)*
  **fare lo shampoo** *shampoo (vb)*
  **shampoo colorante** *colour rinse (hair)*
  **shampoo e asciugare col fon**
  *shampoo and blow dry*
  **una bottiglia di shampoo** *a bottle of
  shampoo*
  **una bustina di shampoo** *a sachet of
  shampoo*
**sherry** (m) *sherry*
  **una bottiglia di sherry** *a bottle of
  sherry*
  **uno sherry** *a sherry*
**sì** *yes*
**sicurezza** *safety*
  **cintura di sicurezza** *lifebelt, safety
  belt*
  **spilla di sicurezza** *safety pin*
  **uscita di sicurezza** *emergency exit*
  **controllo di sicurezza** *security control*
  **controllo speciale di sicurezza**
  *security check*
**sicuro** (adj) (=certo, convinto) *certain,
  sure*
  **è sicuro** *he's sure*
  **sono sicuro** *I'm certain*
**sicuro** (adj) (=non pericoloso) *safe
  (adj)*
**sidro** *cider*
  **una bottiglia di sidro** *a bottle of cider*
  **un sidro** *a cider*
**sigaretta** (f) *cigarette*

**fumare una sigaretta** *smoke a cigarette*
**sigaretta americana** *cigarette (American type)*
**sigaretta francese** *cigarette (French type)*
**sigarette col filtro** *filter-tipped cigarettes*
**una stecca di sigarette** *a carton of cigarettes (=200)*
**un pacchetto di sigarette** *a packet of cigarettes*
**sigaro** *cigar*
**una scatola di sigari** *a box of cigars*
**un sigaro avana** *a Havana cigar*
**signor / / ** *Mr / /*
**signora / / ** *lady -ies*
  **signora / / ** *Mrs / /*
**signore** *gentleman -men*
**signorina / / ** *Miss / /*
**silenzio** *silence*
  **silenzio, per favore!** *quiet please!*
**silenzioso** *quiet, silent*
**simile** *similar*
**sinagoga** *synagogue*
**sincero** *sincere*
**sinistra** *left (=not right)*
  **a sinistra** *left (direction)*
**sintetico** *synthetic*
**sintomo** *symptom*
**sistema (m) elettrico** *electrical system (car)*
**ski lift (m)** *ski lift*
**slacciare** *unfasten*
**slegare** *untie*
**slittamento** *skid (n)*
**slittare** *skid (vb) (car)*
**smacchiatore (m)** *stain remover*
**smalto per le unghie** *nail varnish*
**smoking (m)** *dinner jacket*
**smorto** *plain (adj) (=not coloured)*
**snack-bar (m)** *snack-bar*
**snorkel (m)** *snorkel (n)*
  **fare lo snorkel** *snorkel (vb)*
  **maschera snorkel** *snorkel mask*
  **tubo snorkel** *snorkel tube*
**sobrio -ri** *sober*

**socio -ci** *partner (business)*
**soddisfacente** *satisfactory*
**soffitto** *ceiling*
**soffrire** *suffer*
  **soffrire di /mal di testa/** *suffer from /headaches/*
**sogliola** *sole (=fish)*
**soldato** *soldier*
**soldi (mpl)** *money*
  **fare soldi** *make money*
**sole (m)** *sun*
  **al sole** *in the sun*
  **prendere il sole** *sunbathe*
**soleggiato** *sunny*
**solido** *solid*
**solitario -ri** *lonely*
**solito** *usual*
  **di solito** *usually*
**solo (adj)** *alone*
**solo (adv)** *only*
**sonaglino** *rattle (baby's rattle)*
**sonnifero** *sleeping pill*
**sonno** *sleep (n)*
  **avere sonno** *be sleepy*
  **ho sonno** *I'm sleepy*
**sopra (adv)** *above (adv)*
  **di sopra** *upstairs*
**sopra** *over (=above)*
**sopra (prep)** *above, over*
  **sopra /la testa/** *above /my head/*
  **volare sopra /le montagne/** *fly over /the mountains/*
**sopracciglio -gli** *eyebrow*
**sopravivere** *survive*
**sordo** *deaf*
**sorella** *sister*
**sorpassare** *overtake*
**sorpresa** *surprise (n)*
**sorpreso** *surprised*
  **sorpreso /del risultato/** *surprised at /the result/*
**sospensione (f)** *suspension (car)*
**sospettare** *suspect (vb)*
**sostanza** *substance*
**sostituire** *replace*
**sotto (adv)** *below (adv)*
**sotto (prep)** *under, below (prep)*

sotto /la sedia/ *below /the chair/*
sottopassaggio -ggi *subway*
sottopiatto *tablemat*
sottoveste (f) *petticoat*
spago -ghi *string*
  un pezzo di spago *a piece of string*
  un rotolo di spago *a ball of string*
spalla *shoulder*
sparare *shoot (vb)*
sparo *shot (n)*
spazio -zi *space (room)*
spazzare *sweep (vb)*
spazzola *brush*
  spazzola per i capelli *hair-brush*
  spazzola per i vestiti *clothes brush*
  spazzola per le scarpe *shoe-brush*
spazzolino
  spazzolino da denti *tooth-brush -es*
  spazzolino per le unghie *nail-brush*
specchio -chi *mirror*
  specchio a mano *hand-mirror*
speciale *special*
spedire *send*
  spedire / / a me *send / / to me*
  spedirlo per posta / / *send it by / / mail*
  spedire /un messaggio/ *send /a message/*
spedire (per nave) *ship (vb)*
spedizione (f) (scientifica) *expedition*
spegnere *switch off, turn off*
spendere *spend (money)*
spento *off (of light etc)*
sperare *hope (vb)*
  spero di no *I hope not*
  spero di sì *I hope so*
spesa *shopping*
  fare la spesa *go shopping*
spese (fpl) postali *postage*
spesso (adv) *often*
spesso (adj) *thick*
spettacolo *performance*
  spettacolo di varietà *variety show*
spezia *spice*
spiaggia -gge *beach -es, shore*
spiccioli (mpl) *small change*
spiegare *explain*

spiegazione (f) *explanation*
spilla *brooch -es*
  spilla d'argento *silver brooch*
spillino *pin*
spina (f) (elettricità) *plug (electric)*
spina dorsale *spine (part of body)*
spinaci (mpl) *spinach (s)*
spingere *push (vb)*
spogliarello *strip show*
spogliatoio *changing room*
sporco *dirty*
sport (m) *sport*
sposa *bride*
sposato *married*
sposo *bridegroom*
spray (m) antighiaccio *deicer*
spray (m) contro le mosche *fly spray*
sprecare *waste (vb)*
spremere *squeeze (vb)*
spugna *sponge (bath s.)*
spuntato *blunt (eg knife)*
spuntino *snack*
sputare *spit (vb)*
squadra *team, side*
squash (m) *squash*
  giocare a squash *play squash*
  una partita a squash *a game of squash*
stadio *stadium*
stagione (f) *season*
stagno *pond*
stalla *stable (for horses)*
stampare *print (vb)*
stampatore (m) *printer*
stanco (m) -chi (mpl) stanca (f) -che (fpl) *tired*
standard *standard (adj)*
stanotte *tonight*
stare (=addirsi) *fit*
  mi sta bene *it's a good fit*
  non mi sta bene *it doesn't fit me*
stare (essere in piedi) *stand (vb)*
stare a / / (=rimanere) *stay at / /*
  da / / a / / *from / / till / /*
  fino a / / *till / /*
  per una notte *for a night*
  per /due/ notti *for /two/ nights*

**per una settimana** *for a week*
**per /due/ settimane** *for /two/ weeks*
**stare con /  /** *go out with /  /*
**starnutire** *sneeze (vb)*
**stato** *state (n)*
  **stato di collasso** *state of shock*
**statua** *statue*
**stazione** (f) *station (=railway s.)*
  **stazione degli autobus** *bus station*
  **stazione dei pullman** *coach station*
  **stazione della metropolitana**
  *underground station*
  **stazione di polizia** *police station*
  **stazione di testa** *railway terminus*
  **stazione ferroviaria** *railway station*
**stecca di /sigarette/** *carton of
/cigarettes/ (=200)*
**stereo** *stereo (n)*
**stereofonico** *stereo (adj)*
  **equipaggiamento stereofonico**
  *stereo equipment*
**sterlina** *pound (money)*
**stesso** *same*
  **lo stesso de /  /** *the same as /  /*
**steward** (m) *steward (plane or boat)*
**stile** (m) *style*
**stilo** *stylus*
  **di ceramica** *ceramic*
  **di diamante** *diamond (adj)*
  **di zaffiro** *sapphire*
**stima** *estimate (n)*
**stingere** *run (vb) (colour)*
  **stinge?** *does it run?*
**stipendio -di** *salary -ies*
**stirare** *iron (vb) (clothing)*
**stitichezza** *constipation*
  **soffrire di stitichezza** *constipated*
**stivali** (mpl) *boots (pl)*
  **stivali di gomma** *rubber boots,
Wellingtons*
  **un paio di stivali** *a pair of boots*
**stoffa** *material (=cloth)*
  **stoffa a quadretti** *checked material*
  **stoffa a tinta unita** *plain material*
  **stoffa leggera** *lightweight material*
  **stoffa pesante** *heavy material*
**stomaco -ci** *stomach*

**ho mal di stomaco** *I've got a stomach
ache*
**ho un disturbo di stomaco** *I've got a
stomach upset*
**stordito** *dizzy*
**storia** *history -ies*
**storta** (f) *sprain (n)*
**storto** *sprained*
**stracciare** *tear (vb)*
**strada** *road, street*
  **strada a doppia corsia** *dual
carriageway*
  **strada principale** *main road*
  **strada secondaria** *side road*
**straniero** (adj) *foreign*
**straniero** (m) **straniera** (f) (n) *foreigner*
**strappo** *tear (n) (= hole in material)*
**stretto** (=non largo) *narrow*
**stretto** (=attillato) *tight*
**strofinaccio -ci** *cloth (dishcloth)*
**strofinare** *rub*
**strumento** *instrument*
  **strumento musicale** *musical
instrument*
**studente** (m) **studentessa** (f) *student*
**studiare** *study*
  **studiare a /  /** *study at /  /*
  **studiare /l'inglese/** *study /English/*
**studio** *study*
**stufa** *heater*
**stufato** (n) *casserole (meal)*
**stufo**
  **essere stufo** *be fed up*
  **sono stufo** *I'm fed up*
**stuoia** *mat*
  **stuoia da bagno** *bath mat*
**stupido** (adj) *stupid*
**stupido** (n) *fool (n)*
**stuzzicadenti** (m) - *toothpick*
**su** (adv) *up*
  **va in su?** *are you going up?*
**su** (prep) *on, over*
  **sul letto** (m) *on the bed*
  **sulla tavola** (f) *on /the table/*
**subito** *immediately*
**succedere** *happen*
**succo** *juice*

**succo di ananas** *pineapple juice*
**succo di arancia** *orange juice*
**succo di limone** *lemon juice*
**succo di pomodoro** *tomato juice*
**succo di pompelmo** *grapefruit juice*
**succoso** *juicy*
**sud** (m) *south*
**sudare** *sweat (vb)*
**sudest** (m) *southeast*
**sudore** (m) *sweat (n)*
**sudovest** (m) *southwest*
**suggerire** *suggest*
**sugo** *gravy*
**suo** (=di lei)
  **il suo** (m) **la sua** (f) **i suoi** (mpl) **le sue**
  (fpl) *her (adj)*
  **il suo passaporto** (m) *her passport*
  **la sua borsa** (f) *her bag*
  **i suoi biglietti** (mpl) *her tickets*
  **le sue chiavi** (fpl) *her keys*
  **è suo** (m) **è sua** (f) *it's hers*
**suo** (=di lui)
  **il suo** (m) **la sua** (f) **i suoi** (mpl) **le sue**
  (fpl) *his*
  **il suo passaporto** (m) *his passport*
  **la sua borsa** (f) *his bag*
  **i suoi biglietti** (mpl) *his tickets*
  **le sue chiavi** (fpl) *his keys*
  **è suo** (m) **è sua** (f) *it's his*
**suo** (forma cortesia)
  **il suo** (m) **la sua** (f) **i suoi** (mpl) **le sue**
  (fpl) *your (polite form, singular)*
  **il suo passaporto** (m) *your passport*
  **la sua borsa** (f) *your bag*
  **i suoi biglietti** (mpl) *your tickets*
  **le sue chiavi** (fpl) *your keys*
  **è suo** (m) **è sua** (f) *it's yours*
**suocera** *mother-in-law/mothers-in-law*
  (pl)
**suocero** *father-in-law/fathers-in-law* (pl)
**suola** *sole (of shoe)*
**suonare** (uno instrumento) *play (vb) (an
instrument)*
**suonare** (di orologio) *strike (vb) (of
clock)*
**suonare il campanello** *ring (vb) at the
door*

**suono** *sound (n)*
**superficie** (f) **-ci** *surface (n)*
**supermercato** *supermarket*
**supplemento** *excess fare*
**supposta** *suppository* **-ies**
**surgelati** *frozen food*
**surriscaldato** *overheated (of engine)*
**sveglia** (orologio) *alarm clock*
**svegliar/mi/** *wake /me/ up*
**sveglio** *awake*
  **è sveglio** *he's awake*
**svendita** *sale*
**svenire** *faint (vb)*
  **mi sento svenire** *I feel faint*
**sviluppare** *develop*
  **sviluppare e stampare** (una pellicola)
  *develop and print (a film)*

# T

**tabacchi** *tobacconist's*
**tabacco** *tobacco*
**tacchino** *turkey*
**tacco** **-chi** *heel*
  **tacchi alti** *high heeled*
  **tacchi bassi** *low heeled*
**tagliare** (a pezzi ineguali) *chop (vb)*
**tagliare** (senso generale) *cut (vb)*
**tagliare** (=disossare) *fillet (vb)*
**tagliare** (i capelli) *trim (vb)*
**taglio** *cut (n)*
  **taglio di capelli** *trim (n)(haircut)*
  **un taglio e asciugare al fon** *a cut
  and blow dry*
**talco** *talcum powder*
**tappetino** *rug*
**tappeto** *carpet*
**tappo** (di sughero) *cork*
**tappo** (altri materiali) *plug (for sink),
stopper*
  **tappi** (mpl) **per gli orecchi** *earplugs
  (pl)*
**tardi** *late*
  **è tardi** *it's late* (=time of day)
  **più tardi** *later* (=at a later time)
**targa** *number plate*
  **numero di targa** *registration number*

**tariffa** (mezzi di trasporto) *fare*
  **tariffa aerea** *air fare*
  **tariffa dell'autobus** *bus fare*
  **tariffa di andata e ritorno** *return fare*
  **tariffa di sola andata** *single fare*
  **tariffa ferroviaria** *train fare*
  **tariffa intera** *full fare*
  **tariffa ridotta** *half fare*
**tariffa** (poste, alberghi) *rate (n)*
  **tariffa giornaliera** *rate per day*
  **tariffa postale** *postal rate*
  **tariffa postale per /l'Italia/** *postal rate for /Italy/*
  **tariffa ridotta** *cheap rate (mail, telephone)*
**tartaruga** *tortoise*
  **di tartaruga** *tortoiseshell (adj)*
**tasca** *pocket*
**tassa** *tax -es*
  **esente da tasse** *tax free*
  **tassa dell'aeroporto** *airport tax*
  **tasso di cambio** *exchange rate*
**tavola** *table*
**taxi** (m) *taxi*
  **in taxi** *by taxi*
  **stazione** (f) **dei taxis** *taxi rank*
**tazza** *cup*
  **una tazza di /  /** *a cup of /  /*
  **tazza /di plastica/** */plastic/ cup*
**tè** (m) *tea*
  **prendere il tè** *have tea*
  **tè cinese** *China tea*
  **tè indiano** *Indian tea*
  **una tazza di tè** *a cup of tea*
  **una teiera di tè** *a pot of tea*
**teatro** *theatre*
  **teatro dell'opera** *opera house*
**teiera** *pot, teapot*
**tela** *canvas (=material)*
  **borsa di tela** *canvas bag*
  **tela per asciugamani** *towelling (material)*
**teleferica -che** *cable car*
**telefonare** *telephone (vb)*
  **telefonare al centralino** *telephone the operator/exchange*
  **telefonare all'ufficio ricevimento**
*telephone Reception*
  **telefonare a questo numero**
*telephone this number*
**telefonata** *telephone call*
  **fare una telefonata** *make a call*
**telefono** *telephone/phone (n)*
  **al telefono** *on the phone*
  **cabina telefonica** *call box -es*
  **elenco telefonico** *telephone directory -ies*
  **telefono esterno** *external phone*
  **interno** *extension*
  **posso usare /il suo telefono/ per favore?** *may I use your phone please?*
**telegramma** (m) **-mi** *telegram*
  **mandare un telegramma** *send a telegram*
  **modulo per telegramma** *telegram form*
**televisione** (f) *television/TV (infml)*
  **alla televisione** *on television/on T.V.*
  **antenna della televisione** *television aerial*
  **televisore** (m) *television set*
  **canale** (m) *television channel*
  **programma televisivo** *television programme*
**televisione** (f) **portatile** *portable television*
**telex** (m) *telex*
  **mandare per télex** *telex (vb)*
**temperatura** *temperature (atmosphere, body)*
**temperino** (coltello tascabile) *penknife -ves*
**tempestoso** *stormy*
**tempio** *temple*
**tempo** (misura) *time*
  **in tempo** *in time*
  **tempo libero** *spare time*
**tempo** (clima) *weather*
  **che tempo fa?** *what's the weather like?*
  **previsioni** (fpl) **del tempo** *weather forecast (s)*
**temporale** (m) *storm*
**tenda** (alla finestra) *curtain*

**tenda** (da campeggio) *tent*
**tenere** *keep*
**tenero** *tender (eg of meat)*
**tennis** (m) *tennis*
  **giocare a tennis** *play tennis*
  **una partita a tennis** *a game of tennis*
**terminale** (m) *terminal*
  **terminale aereo** (m) *air terminal*
  **autobus** (m) **del terminale aereo** *air terminal bus*
**termine** (m) *term (=expression)*
**termometro** *thermometer*
  **termometro clinico** *clinical thermometer*
  **termometro in centigradi** *Centigrade thermometer*
  **termometro in fahrenheit** *Fahrenheit thermometer*
**termos** (m) *vacuum flask*
**terra** (pianeta) *earth (=the earth)*
  **terra** (suolo) *ground (=the ground)*
  **terra** (di coltivare) *land*
**terraglia** *pottery (substance)*
**terrazzo** *terrace*
**terribile** *terrible*
**testa** *head (part of body)*
  **mal** (m) **di testa** *headache*
**testimonio -ni** *witness -es(n)*
**tettarella** *teat*
**tetto** *roof*
**tifoide** (m) *typhoid*
**tifoso** *fan (n) (sports)*
**timido** *shy*
**tingere** *dye (vb)*
  **tingere di /nero/ /questo golf/** *dye /this sweater/ /black/*
**tintinnio** *rattle (noise)*
**tintoria a secco** *dry cleaner's*
**tintura** *tint (n) (=hair t.)*
**tipico** *typical*
**tipo** *kind (n)*
  **un tipo di /birra/** *a kind of /beer/*
**tirare** (=lanciere) *throw (vb)*
  **tirare** (=non spingere) *pull*
**titolo** *title*
**toccare** *touch (vb)*
**togliere** (=dedurre) *deduct*

**togliere /dieci sterline/ dal conto** *deduct /ten pounds/ from the bill*
**togliere** (=levare) *remove, take off*
  **togliere /un cappotto/** *take off /a coat/*
**toilette** (f) *toilet*
**tombola** *bingo*
**tonico -ci** *tonic (water)*
**tonnellata** *ton*
**tonsillite** (f) *tonsillitis*
**topo** *mouse/mice (pl)*
**toppa** *patch (n)*
**torace** (m) *chest (part of body)*
**tornare** *return (=go back)*
  **tornare alle /4.30/** *return at /four-thirty/*
  **tornare a /luglio/** *return in /July/*
  **tornare a /lunedì/** *return on /Monday/*
**torre** (f) *tower*
**torta** *cake*
  **una fetta di torta** *a piece of cake*
**torto** *wrong*
  **avere torto** *be wrong*
  **ho torto** *I'm wrong*
**tosse** (f) *cough (n)*
  **ho la tosse** *I've got a cough*
  **pastiglie** (fpl) **per la tosse** *cough pastilles (pl)*
  **sciroppo per la tosse** *cough mixture*
  **una bottiglia di sciroppo per la tosse** *a bottle of cough mixture*
**tossico** *toxic*
**tossire** *cough (vb)*
**tostare** *toast (vb)*
**totale** (adj) *total (adj)*
**totale** (m) *total (n)*
**tovaglia** *tablecloth*
**tovagliolo** *napkin, serviette*
  **portatovaglioli** *napkin ring*
  **tovagliolo di carta** *paper napkin*
**tra** *among, between*
  **tra /i miei amici/** *among /my friends/* '
  **tra /Londra/ e /Roma** *between /London/ and /Rome*
**traccia -ce** *track (of animal)*
**tradizionale** *traditional*
**tradurre** *translate*

**traduzione** (f) *translation*
**traffico** *traffic*
**traghetto** *ferry -ies*
  **in traghetto** *by ferry*
  **traghetto per le macchine** *car ferry*
**trainare** *tow (vb)*
**tram** (m) *tram*
  **capolinea del tram** *tram terminus*
  **fermata del tram** *tram stop*
  **il tram per / /** *the tram for / /*
  **in tram** *by tram*
**tramonto** *sunset*
**tranquillante** (m) *tranquilliser*
**transatlantico** *liner*
**transistor** (m) *transistor (transistor radio)*
**transito** *transit*
  **in transito** *in transit*
  **viaggiatore** (m&f) **in transito** *transit passenger*
**trappola** *trap (n)*
  **prendere in trappola** *trap (vb)*
  **trappola per topi** *mousetrap*
**trasferire** *transfer (vb)*
  **trasferire il pagamento a destinazione** *reverse the charges*
  **vorrei trasferire il pagamento a destinazione** *I'd like to reverse the charges*
**trasformatore** (m) *transformer*
**trasmessione** (f) *broadcast (n)*
**trasmettere** *broadcast (vb)*
**trasmissione** (t) *transmission*
**trasparente** *transparent*
**trasporto** *transport (n)*
  **trasporto pubblico** *public transport*
**traveller's cheque** (m) *traveller's cheque*
**trementina** *turpentine*
**treno** *train*
  **espresso** *fast train*
  **rapido** *express train*
  **accelerato** *slow train*
  **treno-macchine** (m) *motorail (ie car on a train)*
  **treno per nave** *boat train*
**treppiede** (m) *tripod*

**triangolare** *triangular*
**tribunale** (m) *court (law)*
**trimestre** (m) *term (=period of time)*
**triste** *sad*
**tronco -chi** *trunk (of tree)*
**tropicale** *tropical*
**troppo** (adv) *too (=more than can be endured)*
  **troppo /grande/** *too /big/*
  **troppo** (m) **troppa** (f) **troppi** (mpl)
  **troppe** (fpl) *too much (s) too many (pl)*
**trota** *trout/trout (pl)*
**trottare** *trot (vb)*
**trovare** *find (vb)*
  **trovare /quest'indirizzo/** *find /this address/*
**trucco** *make-up (=face make-up)*
  **trucco per gli occhi** *eye make-up*
**tubo** *tube*
  **un tubo di / /** *a tube of / /*
  **tubo di gomma** *hose (car)*
**tuffarsi** *dive (vb)*
  **andare a tuffarsi** *go diving*
  **tuffarsi dentro / /** *dive into / /*
  **tuffarsi in apnea** *skin-diving*
  **andare a tuffarsi in apnea** *go skin diving*
**tulipano** (m) *tulip*
  **un mazzo di tulipani** *a bunch of tulips*
**turista** (m&f) **-i** (mpl) **-e** (fpl) *tourist*
**turistico**
  **classe** (f) **turistica** *tourist class*
  **ufficio turistico** *tourist office*
**tutto** (adj) *all*
  **tutti /i bambini/** *all /the children/*
  **tutto /il mese/** *the whole /month/*
  **tutto /il tempo/** *all /the time/*
**tutto** (pron) *everything*
**tweed** (m) *tweed*

# U

**ubriaco -chi** *drunk (adj) (=not sober)*
**uccello** *bird*
**uccidere** *kill (vb)*
**udire** *hear*
**ufficiale** *official (adj)*

**ufficio -ci** office
  **ufficio informazioni** information desk
  **ufficio oggetti smarriti** lost property
    office
  **ufficio postale** post office
  **ufficio ricevimento** Reception (eg in a
    hotel)
**uggioso** dull (of the weather)
**uguale** equal
**ulcera** ulcer
**ultimo** last (=final)
**umido** (di oggetto, persona) damp (adj)
**umido** (clima) humid
**umore** (m) mood
  **di buon/cattivo umore** in a
    good/bad mood
**umorismo** humour
  **senso dell'umorismo** sense of
    humour
**ungere** grease (vb)
**unghia** nail (finger/toe)
  **forbicine per le unghie** nail scissors
  **limetta per le unghie** nail file
  **smalto per le unghie** nail varnish
  **spazzolino per le unghie** nailbrush
    -es
**unico** unique
**unito** (=accluso) enclosed
  **qui troverete unito** please find
    enclosed
**università -** university -ies
**uno** (m) **una** (f) (numero) one (adj)
  (number)
**uno,un** (m) **una,un'** (f) a (an)
  **è l'una** it's one o'clock
  **l'uno** (m) **l'una** (f) (sul prezzo) each
    (on price-tag)
**unto** oily
**uomo -mini** man/men (pl)
**uomo d'affari - mini d'affari**
  businessman / businessmen (pl)
**uovo -a** egg
  **uovo alla coque** softboiled egg
  **uovo fritto** fried egg
  **uovo in camicia** poached egg
  **uovo sodo** hardboiled egg
  **uova strapazzate** scrambled eggs

**urgente** urgent
**usare** use (vb)
  **usare /il suo telefono/** use /your
    phone/
**uscire** go out
**uscita** exit
  **uscita di sicurezza** emergency exit
  **uscita di sicurezza** (antincendio) fire
    escape
  **uscita** (all'aeroporto) gate (=airport
    exit)
**utensile** (m) utensil
**utile** useful
**uva** grape
  **un grappolo d'uve** a bunch of grapes
  **uva passa** currant, raisin

# V

**vacanza** (s) holiday
  **in vacanza** on holiday
  **vacanza organizzata** package holiday
**vaccinare** vaccinate
**vaccinazione** (f) vaccination
**vaccino** vaccine
**vaglia** postal order
**vagone** (m) **letto** sleeping car
**vagone** (m) **ristorante** buffet car
**valanga** avalanche
**valere** be worth
  **vale /un milione/ di lire** it's worth /a
    hundred/ F
**valico** mountain pass
**validó** valid
  **/passaporto/ valido** valid /passport/
**valigia** case, suitcase
  **fare la valigia** pack my suitcase
**valle** (f) valley -ies
**valore** (m) value (n)
  **valuta** currency - ies
**valutare** value (vb)
**vaniglia** vanilla
**vantaggio** advantage
**varicella** chicken pox
**varietà -** (= spettacolo) variety show
**varietà -** variety -ies, range (of goods)
**vario -ri** various

**vasellina** *vaseline*
  **un tubo di vasellina** *a tube of vaseline*

**vaso** (=barattolo) *jar*
  **un vaso di /marmellata/** *a jar of /jam/*

**vaso** (da fiori) *vase* (=flower v.)

**vassoio** *tray*

**vecchio -chi** (di persone e cose) *old (of people and things)*

**vecchio -chi** (di cibo) *stale (bread, cheese etc)*

**vedere** *see*
  **vedere /il direttore/** *see /the manager/*
  **vedere /il menù/** *see /the menu/*
  **far vedere** *show (vb)*
  **farme/lo/ vedere** *show /it/ to me*

**vedova** *widow*

**vedovo** *widower*

**vegetariano** *vegetarian*

**veicolo** *vehicle*

**vela** *sail (n)*

**veleggiare** (vb) *sail (vb)*

**veleggiare** (n) *sailing*

**veleno** *poison*

**velenoso** *poisonous*

**velluto** (a corte) *corduroy*

**velluto** (liscio) *velvet*

**veloce** *fast, quick*

**velocemente** *quickly*

**velocità -** *speed*

**vena** *vein*

**vendere** *sell*
  **vendere all'asta** *auction (vb)*

**venduto** *sold*

**venerdì** (m) *Friday*
  **arriverò venerdì** *I'll arrive on Friday*
  **di venerdì** *on Fridays*

**venire** (da) *come (from)*

**ventilatore** (m) *fan, ventilator*

**vento** *wind (n)*

**ventoso** *windy*
  **è ventoso** *it's windy*

**veramente** *really*

**verde** *green*

**verdura** (fs) *vegetables (pl)*

**verdura fresca** *fresh vegetables*
**verdura mista** *mixed vegetables*

**vergognarsi** (di / /) *be a. (of / /)*
  **mi vergogno di /lui/** *I'm ashamed of /him/*

**verità** *- truth*
  **dire la verità** *tell the truth*

**vernice** (f) (colorata) *paint*
  **un barattolo di vernice** *a tin of paint*

**vernice** (f) (trasparente) *varnish -es(n)*

**verniciare** *paint, varnish (vb)*

**vero** (=reale) *real*

**vero** (=non falso) *true*

**versare** *pour*

**vescica -che** *blister*

**vespa** *wasp*
  **puntura di vespa** *wasp sting*

**vestaglia** *dressing gown*

**vestir/si/** *dress /oneself/*

**vestire /il bambino/** *dress /the baby/*

**vestiti** (mpl) *clothes (pl)*
  **spazzola per i vestiti** *clothes brush*

**vestito** (da donna) *dress (n) -es*

**vestito lungo** *evening dress - evening dresses(for women)*

**vestito** (da uomo) *suit (n)*

**vetrerie** *glassware*
  **negozio di vetrerie** *glassware shop*

**vetrina** *shop window*

**vetro** *glass* (=substance)

**via** (=non qui) *away*
  **è via** *he's away*

**via** (attraverso) *via*
  **viaggiare via /Roma/** *travel via /Rome/*
  **via terra** *overland*

**viaggiare** *travel (vb)*
  **a / /** *to / /*
  **a piedi** *on foot*
  **in aereo** *by air*
  **in barca, in autobus** *by boat, by bus*
  **in hovercraft** *by hovercraft*
  **in pullman, in macchina** *by coach, by car*
  **in traghetto** *on the ferry*
  **in treno, in tram, in metropolitana** *by train, by tram, by underground*

**per mare** by sea
**per terra** overland
**viaggiatore** (m) passenger (in train)
  **viaggiatore in transito** transit
  passenger
**viaggio -ggi** (in genere) journey -ies
  **agenzia di viaggio** travel agent's
  **buon viaggio!** have a good trip!
**viaggio -ggi** (per mare) voyage (n)
**viale** (m) (d'accesso) drive (n)
  (=entrance)
**vicino** (=non lontano) near
  **vicino /alla stazione/** near (prep)
  /the station/
**vicino** (molto vicino) next to
  **la casa vicina** the house next door
  **vicino a / /** next to / /
  **vicino /alla stazione/** next /to the
  station/
**vicolo** lane (=small road)
**vigneto** vineyard
**villa** villa (=holiday villa)
**villino** cottage
**vincere** win (vb)
**vino** wine
  **una bottiglia di vino** a bottle of wine
  **una caraffa di vino** a carafe of wine
  **una mezza bottiglia di vino** a half
  bottle of wine
  **un bicchiere di vino** a glass of wine
  **vino bianco** white wine
  **vino dolce** sweet wine
  **vino frizzante** sparkling wine
  **vino rosé** rosé
  **vino rosso** red wine
  **vino secco** dry wine
**violino** violin
**virare** steer (vb) (boat)
**visibilità** visibility
**visita** tour
  **visita guidata** conducted tour
  **fare una visita guidata** go on a
  conducted tour
  **visita medica** medical examination
**visitare** (dal medico) examine
  (medically)
**visitare** (=andare a vedere) visit

**visitare i luoghi interessanti** go
  sightseeing
  **visitare /un museo/** visit /a
  museum/
**visitatore** (m) **visitatrice** (f) visitor
**visone** (m) mink
  **pelliccia di visone** mink coat
**vistare** endorse
  **vistare il mio biglietto per / /**
  endorse my ticket to / /
  **vistare /il mio passaporto/** endorse
  /my passport/
**visto** visa
**vita** life
**vita** (anatomia) waist
  **vita** (=esistenza) life
  **vita notturna** night life
**vite** (f) screw
**vitello** veal
**vivere** live (=be alive)
  **vive** he's alive
**vivo** alive
**vocabolario** dictionary -ies
  **vocabolario inglese/italiano**
  English/Italian dictionary
  **vocabolario italiano/inglese**
  Italian/English dictionary
  **vocabolario tascabile** pocket
  dictionary
**voce** (f) voice
**vodka** vodka
  **una bottiglia di vodka** a bottle of
  vodka
  **una vodka** a vodka
**voga** fashion
  **in voga** popular
**volano** (sport) badminton
  **giocare a volano** play badminton
  **una partita a volano** a game of
  badminton
**volano** (meccanica) flywheel
**volare verso / /** fly to / /
  **andare a volare** go flying
**voler dire** mean (vb) (of a word)
  **che cosa vuol dire?** what does it
  mean?
**volere** want

**volere /comprar/lo** *want to /buy/ it*
**volere /una camera/** *want /a room/*
**vorrebbe /una bibita/?** *would you like /a drink/?*
**volgare** *coarse (of person)*
**volo** (=viaggio in aereo) *flight*
  **volo charter** *charter flight*
  **volo di linea** *scheduled flight*
  **volo in coincidenza** *connecting flight*
  **volo per studenti** *student flight*
**volo** (=il volare) *flying*
**volo a vela** *gliding*
  **fare volo a vela** *go gliding*
**volt** (m) *volt*
  **/cento dieci/ volt** */ a hundred and ten/ volts*
**volta** *time*
  **due volte** *twice*
  **due volte alla settimana** *twice weekly*
  **qualche volta** *sometimes*
  **/sei / volte** */six/ times*
  **una volta** *once* (=one time)
**voltaggio** *voltage*
  **voltaggio alto** *high voltage*
  **voltaggio basso** *low voltage*
**volume** (m) *volume*
**vomitare** *vomit (vb)*
**vomito** *vomit (n)*
**vuotare** *empty (vb)*
**vuoto** (=non pieno) *empty (adj)*
**vuoto** (=cavo) *hollow (adj)*

# W

**watt** (m) *watt*
  **/cento/ watt** */a hundred/ watts*
**western** (m) *Western* (=film)

**whisky** (m) *whisky -ies*
  **una bottiglia di whisky** *a bottle of whisky*
  **un whisky** *a whisky*

# Y

**yogurt** (m) *yoghurt*
  **un vasetto di yogurt** *a carton of yoghurt*
  **yogurt alla frutta** *fruit yoghurt*
  **yogurt semplice** *plain yoghurt*

# Z

**zaino** *rucksack*
**zanzara** *mosquito*
**zanzariera** *mosquito net*
**zattera** *raft*
**zenzero** *ginger (flavour)*
**zerbino** *door mat*
**zero** *zero*
  **sopra zero** *above zero*
  **sotto zero** *below zero*
**zia** *aunt*
**zio** *uncle*
**zoccoli** (mpl) *clogs (pl)*
  **un paio di zoccoli** *a pair of clogs*
**zolletta** *sugar*
  **una zolletta di zucchero** *a lump of sugar*
  **zolletta di zucchero** *sugar lump*
**zuppierina** *bowl*
  *sugar*
**zona** *area (of town)*
**zoo** (m) *zoo*
**zucchero** *sugar*
  **un cucchiaio di zucchero** *a spoonful of sugar*

# Cibo italiano      Italian foods

Here are all the main Italian foods in groups: *antipasti* (hors d'œuvres) *pasta asciutta* (pasta in various forms); rice dishes; soups; fish; meat; poultry and game; vegetables; fruit; sweets; ice creams; cheeses; pizza. At the end of this section there is a selection of regional specialities including some of the principal wines.

Remember:
  I'd like / / please           Vorrei / / per favore
  Have you got / / please?     Ha / / per favore?
At the start of a meal, Italians
  often wish each other:        Buon appetito!
The reply is 'Thank you – the     Grazie, altrettanto
  same to you'

Be careful when ordering coffee:
Un caffè per favore           A black coffee please

| | |
|---|---|
| Un cappuccino per favore | A white coffee please (coffee ready made with whipped milk) |
| Caffè e latte per favore | A pot of coffee (coffee and milk separately) |

## Antipasti/hors d'œuvres

| | |
|---|---|
| antipasto misto | mixture of salami, ham and other salt meats |
| bresaola | dried salt beef |
| carciofi | artichokes (often the hearts served with oil) |
| crostini | fried or baked bread with cheese, anchovies etc. |
| culatello di zibello | specially cured rump of pork |
| fagioli con tonno | Tuscan beans with tunny fish |
| fagiolini | French beans |
| fonduta | melted cheese |
| frittelle | fritters |
| frutti di mare | shellfish |
| mortadella | Bologna sausage |
| olive | olives |
| paté di tonno | tunny fish paté |
| peperoni ripieni | stuffed peppers |
| pomodori | tomatoes |
| prosciutto cotto | cooked ham |
| prosciutto crudo | raw ham or Parma ham (a great delicacy) |

## Pasta asciutta

| | |
|---|---|
| bucatini | spaghetti with a tiny hole down the middle |
| b. ai quattro formaggi | b. with four cheeses (may vary) |

| | |
|---|---|
| b. alla Napoletana | b. with tomatoes, peppers and garlic |
| b. con salsicce | b. with sausage meat |
| b. in salsa verde | b. with spinach |
| cannelloni | rolls of pasta stuffed with meat sauce, served with melted cheese |
| cappelletti (see also tortellini) | 'little hats' of stuffed pasta |
| c. in brodo | c. in clear soup |
| c. asciutti | c. served with sauce and cheese |
| farfalle | pasta cut in butterfly shapes |
| fettucine | pasta cut in 'ribbons' |
| f. con mozzarella | f. with soft Neapolitan cheese |
| f. ai funghi | f. with mushrooms |
| f. con ragù di pollo | f. with chicken sauce |
| gnocchi | little dumplings of flour or potato-flour |
| lasagne al forno | broad strips of pasta with ragoût and béchamel sauce in alternating layers |
| l. verde | green l. (made with spinach) |
| linguine | flattened spaghetti |
| l. ai piselli | l. with peas |
| l. al prosciutto | l. with ham |
| maccheroncini | small macaroni |
| maccheroni | macaroni |
| penne | small tubes of pasta, served with ragoût and béchamel sauce |
| ravioli | pasta squares with meat inside |
| rigatoni | pasta like 'penne' but ribbed |
| spaghetti | spaghetti |

| | |
|---|---|
| s. all'amatriciana | s. with pork, onion and tomato sauce served with cheese made from sheep's milk |
| s. alla carbonara | s. with bacon and egg sauce |
| s. alla marinara | s. with tomatoes and anchovies |
| s. con ragù | s. with meat sauce |
| s. con tonno | s. with tunny fish |
| s. con vongole | s. with mussels |
| tagliatelle | pasta cut in 'ribbons' |
| t. all Bolognese | t. with beef and pork sauce |
| tortellini (see also cappelletti) | stuffed pasta from Bologna |

## Rice dishes/Piatti di riso

| | |
|---|---|
| riso in bianco | boiled rice with Parmesan cheese |
| riso quattro formaggi | boiled rice with four cheeses |
| risotto con pesce | freshwater fish risotto |
| risotto con scampi | scampi risotto |
| risotto frutti di mare | shellfish risotto |

## Soups/Zuppe

| | |
|---|---|
| brodo lungo | thin broth |
| minestra | soup (usually thick) |
| minestrina | thin or clear soup |
| minestrone | thick soup (often with rice or vegetables) |
| zuppa di cozze | mussel soup |
| zuppa di gamberi | prawn soup |
| zuppa di pesce | mixed fish soup (varies in each seaside town) |

## Fish/Pesce

| | |
|---|---|
| acciughe/alici | anchovies |
| anguilla | eel |
| aragosta | lobster |
| baccalà | salt cod |
| calamari/calamaretti | squid |
| cozze | mussels |
| fritto misto | mixed fish fry-up |
| gamberetti | prawns |
| merluzzo | cod |
| palombo | dog-fish |
| polipi | baby octopus |
| sarde | sardines |
| seppie | cuttle fish |
| sgombri | mackerel |
| sogliola | sole |
| tonno | tunny fish |
| triglie | red mullet |

## Meat, poultry and game/Carne, pollame e cacciagione

| | |
|---|---|
| abbacchio | suckling lamb |
| agnello | lamb |
| anitra | duck |
|   a. in agrodolce |   d. in sweet-sour sauce |
| bistecca | steak |
| bollito | mixed boiled meats |
| braciola | cutlet, chop |
| capretto | kid |
| cervella | brains |
| cervo | venison |
| cinghiale | boar |
| coniglio | rabbit |
| costolette/cotolette | cutlets |
| cotechino | spiced sausage |
| cuore | heart |

| | |
|---|---|
| fagiano | pheasant |
| faraona | guinea-fowl |
| fegato | liver |
| fritto misto | mixed fry-up |
| lepre | hare |
| l. in casseruola | stewed h. |
| lesso | boiled meat |
| maiale | pork |
| manzo | beef |
| montone | mutton |
| ossobuco | shin of veal |
| pernice | partridge |
| piccate | escalopes |
| piccioni | pigeons |
| pollo | chicken |
| p. alla cacciatora | c. stew |
| p. al diavolo | grilled c. |
| polpette | meat balls |
| polpettone | meat roll |
| prosciutto | ham |
| rognone | kidney |
| salame | pork sausage (varies in each region) |
| salsicce | sausages |
| saltimbocca | dish of veal, ham, sage and marsala |
| scaloppine | escalopes |
| spezzatino | stew |
| spiedino | meats roasted on a spit |
| stufato | stew |
| tacchino | turkey |
| trippa | tripe |
| uccelli | birds |
| vitello | veal |
| zampone | spiced sausage like 'cotechino', stuffed in pig's trotters |

## Vegetables/Verdure

| | |
|---|---|
| aglio | garlic |
| asparagi | asparagus |
| carciofi | artichokes |
|   c. ripieni |   stuffed a. |
| carote | carrots |
| cavolfiore | cauliflower |
| cavolini di bruxelles | brussels sprouts |
| cavolo | cabbage |
| cipolle | onions |
| fagioli | Tuscan beans |
| fagiolini | French beans |
| funghi | mushrooms |
| insalata | salad |
| mamme romane | large Roman artichokes |
| melanzane | aubergines |
| patate | potatoes |
|   p. al forno |   oven-cooked p. |
|   p. arrosto |   roast p. |
|   p. fritte |   chips |
|   patatine |   crisps |
|   purè di p. |   mashed p. |
| peperoni | peppers |
| peperonata | pepper and tomato stew |
| piselli | peas |
| pomodoro | tomato |
| radicchio | chicory |
| radicchio rosso | crispy dark red lettuce |
| ravanello | radish |
| spinaci | spinach |
| verze | cabbage |
| zucchine | courgettes |

## Fruit/Frutte

| | |
|---|---|
| albicocca | apricot |

| | |
|---|---|
| ananas | pineapple |
| arancia | orange |
| ciliegia | cherry |
| cocomero | water melon |
| fico | fig |
| fragola | strawberry |
| lampone | raspberry |
| limone | lemon |
| mela | apple |
| melone | melon |
| mora | blackberry |
| noce di cocco | coconut |
| pera | pear |
| pesca | peach |
| pompelmo | grapefruit |
| prugna | plum |
| susina | plum |
| uva | grapes |
| u. bianca | white g. |
| u. nera | black g. |

## Sweets/Dolci

| | |
|---|---|
| budino | pudding |
| b. di cioccolata | chocolate p. |
| b. di riso | rice p. |
| creme caramel | caramel |
| crostata di frutta | fruit tart (various fruits) |
| macedonia di frutta | fruit salad |
| torta | cake |
| t. di frutta | fruit c. |
| t. di mandorle | almond c. |

## Ice creams/Gelati

| | |
|---|---|
| gelati | ice creams |
| gelato di banana | banana |

| | |
|---|---|
| di caffè | coffee |
| di cioccolata | chocolate |
| di fragola | strawberry |
| di limone | lemon |
| di malaga | wine-flavoured |
| di noce | walnut |
| di nocciola | hazelnut |
| di torrone | nougat |
| gelato in cono | ice cream in cone |
| gelato in coppa | ice cream in a tub |
| ghiacciolo | iced lolly |
| mattonella | wafer sandwich |
| panna montata | whipped cream |
| pinguino | ice cream on stick (literally 'penguin') |
| semifreddo | not quite iced cream |
| sfusa | mixed flavours |
| sorbetto | sorbet |

## Cheeses/Formaggi

| | |
|---|---|
| asiago | mild mountain cheese from the Veneto |
| bel paese | another mild, soft cheese |
| cacciotto | made of cow's and sheep's milk from the Marches |
| fontina | fat, creamy cheese from Piemonte |
| gorgonzola | the most famous Italian cheese |
| g. dolce | mild g. |
| g. piccante | strong g. |
| grana | another name for Parmesan |
| mascarpone | double cream cheese wrapped in muslin |

| | |
|---|---|
| mozzarella | Neapolitan buffalo's milk cheese used in most pizzas (can also be eaten raw with oil and pepper) |
| parmigiano | Parmesan, often grated for sprinkling on pasta, soup etc. (Can also be eaten by itself) |
| pecorino | sheep's milk cheese, particularly from Sardinia |
| provola | buffalo cheese |
| ricotta | soft sheep's milk cheese |
| stracchino | soft, fatty cheese from Lombardy |
| taleggio | soft, fatty cow's milk cheese |

**Pizza/Pizze**

| | |
|---|---|
| calzone | the dough base is folded over like a pancake and contains ricotta and mozzarella cheeses, ham and tomatoes |
| capricciosa | tomatoes, mozzarella, artichokes, mushrooms, anchovies, olives |
| carciofini | tomatoes, mozzarella, artichokes |
| frutti di mare | seafood |
| funghi | tomatoes, mozzarella and mushrooms |
| margherita | tomatoes and mozzarella (the classic pizza) |
| marinara | tomatoes and anchovies |
| prosciutto | tomatoes, mozzarella and ham |
| provenzale | tomatoes, olives, anchovies and marjoram |

| | |
|---|---|
| quattro stagioni | the base is divided into four areas, one romana, one mushroom, one artichoke, one ham |
| romana | tomatoes, mozzarella and anchovies |
| salsiccia | tomatoes, mozzarella and sausage |

## Regional specialities and wines          Specialità e vini regionali

### Abruzzo

| | |
|---|---|
| Food: arrosto di castrato | roast mutton |
| bigoli alla chitarra | flattened macaroni |
| brodetto di pesce | fish soup |
| Wine: cerasuolo d'Abruzzo | red |
| montepulciano rosso | red |

### Basilicata

| | |
|---|---|
| Food: pesce spada arrosto | roast sword fish |
| pollo con polenta | chicken with maize-flour pudding |
| spaghetti alla ricotta | spaghetti with cottage cheese |
| Wine: malvasia | sweet dessert wine found throughout southern Italy |
| moscato | white, found throughout southern Italy |

### Calabria

| | |
|---|---|
| Food: carciofi in tortiera | artichoke pie |
| lucanica | sausage |
| pecorino | sheep's milk cheese |
| soffrito | onion sauce |
| Wine: ciro | white and red – the most well-known Calabrian wine |

| malvasia | see above |
| moscato | see above |

## Campania

| Food: | agnello e capretto al forno | roast lamb and kid |
| | maccheroni | macaroni |
| | fusilli alla ricotta | type of pasta with cottage cheese |
| | mozzarrella in carrozza | mozzarella cheese and bread fried together |
| Wine: | capri | white |
| | falerno | white and red |
| | lacrima Christi | sweet white |

## Emilia–Romagna

| Food: | cappelletti | 'little hats' of pasta with meat stuffing |
| | culatello | rump of pork |
| | mortadella | Bologna sausage |
| | parmigiano | Parmesan cheese |
| | salame and salted meats of many types | white |
| Wine: | albana | white |
| | lambrusco | red |
| | monterosso | red |

## Friuli–Venezia Giulia

| Food: | cacciagione | game |
| | salsicce o luganeghe con polenta | various types of sausage with maize pudding |
| | prosciutto di San Daniele | San Daniele ham (raw and cured) |
| Wine: | cabernet | red |
| | merlot | red |
| | prosecco di Trieste | white |
| | tocai | white |

## Lazio

Food: abbachio — roast suckling lamb
carciofi alla giudea — large Roman artichokes
gnocchi alla romana — semolina-flour dumplings (In other regions, but not in Lazio, 'gnocchi' are made with potato flour)
porchetta — roast suckling pig
spaghetti all'amatriciana — spaghetti with pork, onion and tomato sauce

Wine: colli Albani — white
est est est — white
frascati — white

## Liguria

Food: antipasto alla Genovese — hors d'œuvres of beans, salami and cheese
focaccia — pizza-tart
fritto misto di pesce — mixed fried fish
lumache — snails

Wine: barbaresco — red
coronata di Genova — white

## Lombardia

Food: cotolette alla Milanese — Milanese veal cutlets
minestrone — thick vegetable soup
panettone — famous Italian cake, eaten particularly at Christmas
ossobuco — shin of veal
zuppa Pavese — broth with egg and fried bread sprinkled with cheese

Wine: barbacarlo — red
sassella — red
grumello — red

## Marche

| Food: | cardi alla parmigiana | thistles cooked with parmesan cheese |
| | minestra di passatelli | soup with egg, breadcrumbs, cheese and nutmeg |
| | olive ripiene | stuffed olives |
| | tartufo nero | black truffle |
| | trippe | tripe |
| Wine: | bianchello di Metauro | white |
| | piceno | white and red |
| | sangiovese | red |
| | verdicchio di Jesi | white |

## Molise

| Food: | agnello e capretto al forno | roast lamb and kid |
| | pesce alla griglia | grilled fish |
| | spaghetti e maccheroni alla chitarra | finely-cut pasta |
| Wine: | cerasuolo | red |
| | montepulciano | red |
| | trebbiano | white |

## Piemonte

| Food: | bollito | boiled meats |
| | cacciagione | game |
| | fonduta con fontina | melted cheese dish |
| | gianduiotti | chocolates |
| | riso con tartufi | rice with truffles |
| Wine: | astispumante | white sparkling |
| | barbera | red |
| | barolo | red |
| | nebbiolo | red |

## Puglia

| Food: | maccheroni alla ruta | macaroni with rue-flavoured sauce |
|---|---|---|
| | minestra di fave | bean soup |
| | orecchiette col ragù d'agnello | pasta with lamb sauce |
| | salame piccante | highly-spiced salami |
| Wine: | aleatico | red |
| | barletta | red |
| | bianco lacorotondo | white |

## Sardegna

| Food: | aragosta | lobster |
|---|---|---|
| | accarraxiau | sucking pig cooked in sheep's stomach |
| | cicioni | dumplings served with sausage, sauce and cheese |
| | culurrones | ravioli |
| | pecorino sardo | sheep's milk cheese |
| Wine: | oliena | red |
| | malvasia | white |
| | vernaccia | white |

## Sicilia

| Food: | cassata | type of ice cream |
|---|---|---|
| | coniglio in agrodolce | rabbit in sweet-sour sauce |
| | pasta | pasta |
| |   p. con zucchine |   p. with courgettes |
| |   p. con sarde |   p. with sardines |
| |   p. con ricotta |   p. with cottage cheese |
| | provola | type of buffalo cheese often roasted |
| | spiedini di fegatelli | chicken livers on the spit |
| Wine: | corvo | white and red |

| | |
|---|---|
| marsala | red |
| Taormina | white and red |
| vini dell'Etna | white and red |

## Toscana

| | | |
|---|---|---|
| Food: | costata Fiorentina | famous Florentine T-bone steak |
| | panforte | sort of gingerbread |
| | risotto alla Fiorentina | risotto |
| | stracotto di bue | beef stew |
| | triglia alla livornese | red mullet |
| Wine: | chianti | red |
| | candia rosé | rosé |
| | vernaccia di San Gimignano | white |
| | vinsanto | white |

## Trentino–Alto Adige

| | | |
|---|---|---|
| Food: | farinata | meal porridge |
| | formaggi di montagna | mountain cheeses |
| | polenta | cooked maize-flour |
| | selvaggina in salmì | game with ragout |
| Wine: | merlot | red |
| | val d'Adige | red |
| | val d'Isarco | red |

## Umbria

| | | |
|---|---|---|
| Food: | pizza di formaggio | cheese pizza |
| | prosciutto di montagna | mountain ham |
| | tartufi neri | black truffles |
| Wine: | Sangiovese | red |
| | nebbiolo | red |
| | Orvieto | white |

## Valle d'Aosta

| Food: | cacciagione | game |
| | fonduta | melted cheese dish |
| | gnocchi | potato-flour dumplings |
| Wine: | bianco di Morgex | white |
| | carema | red |
| | malvasia de Nus | white, rare |
| | torretta rosso | red |

## Veneto

| Food: | anguilla fritta | fried eel |
| | baccalà alla Vicentina | salt cod |
| | fegato alla Veneziana | liver with onions |
| | polenta e osei | cooked maize-flour with small birds eg thrushes |
| | risi e bisi | rice and peas |
| Wine: | Bardolino | red |
| | prosecco | white |
| | recioto | red |
| | Soave | white |
| | Valpolicella | red |

# Segnali italiani     Italian signs

| | |
|---|---|
| ACCESSORI | Accessories |
| ACQUA POTABILE | Drinking water |
| AEREA | Airmail |
| AFFITTASI | To let |
| AGENZIA | Agency |
| AGENZIA DI VIAGGIO | Travel agency |
| ALBERGO | Hotel |
| ALBERGO DIURNO | Public washing facilities |
| ALLACCIARE LE CINTURE DI SICUREZZA | Fasten seat belts |
| ALLOGGIO | Accommodation |
| AL MARE | To the sea |
| ALT | Stop |
| ALTEZZA MASSIMA | Maximum height |
| AMBULANZA | Ambulance |
| AMBULATORIO | Surgery |

| | |
|---|---|
| ANDRÀ INCONTRO A SANZIONI PENALI CHI SARÀ TROVATO IN POSSESSO DI MERCE NON REGOLARMENTE PAGATA | Shoplifters will be prosecuted |
| ANFITEATRO | Amphitheatre |
| A NOLO | For hire |
| ANTICHITÀ | Antiques |
| APERTO | Open |
| ARMADIETTI PER BAGAGLI | Left luggage lockers |
| ARRIVI | Arrivals |
| ASCENSORE | Lift |
| ASSICURATE | Insured (Post Office) |
| ATTENTI AL CANE | Beware of the dog |
| ATTENZIONE | Caution |
| ATTRAVERSARE | Cross now |
| AUTOMATICO | Automatic |
| AUTO NOLEGGIO | Car hire |
| AUTO SERVIZIO | Self-service |
| AUTOSTRADA | Motorway |
| AVANTI | Come in/Cross now |
| AVVISO | Notice |
| | |
| BACINI PORTUALI | Docks |
| BAGAGLIAIO | Left luggage |
| BAGAGLIO | Luggage |
| BAGAGLIO A MANO | Hand luggage |
| BAMBINI | Children |
| BANCA | Bank |
| BARCHE A NOLEGGIO | Boats for hire |
| BENZINA | Petrol/Petrol station |
| BIBITE FREDDE | Cold drinks |
| BIBLIOTECA | Library |
| BIGLIETTERIA | Box office/Booking office |
| BIGLIETTI | Tickets |
| BINARIO | Platform |

| | |
|---|---|
| CALDO (C) | Hot |
| CALZOLAIO | Heel bar/Shoe repairs |
| CAMBI NON SARANNO EFFETTUATI | Goods not exchanged |
| CAMBI NON SARANNO EFFETTUATI SE NON VERRÀ PRESENTATO LO SCONTRINO A COMPROVA DELL'AVVENUTO PAGAMENTO | Goods can only be exchanged on presentation of receipt |
| CAMBIO | Exchange |
| CAMPEGGIO | Camping |
| CAMPO DI GOLF | Golf course |
| CANCELLATO | Cancelled |
| CARABINIERI | Police |
| CARTE E GUIDE | Maps and guides |
| CASSA | Cash desk |
| CASSA CONTINUA | 24 hour safe |
| CENTRO CITTÀ | City centre |
| CHIAMARE | Call (eg bell) |
| CHIESA | Church |
| CHIUDE ALLE ORE 14 | Closes at 2 p.m. |
| CHIUSO | Closed |
| CHIUSO DALLE ORE 12.30 ALLE ORE 15.00 | Closed from 12.30 to 3.00 |
| CHIUSO PER INVENTARIO | Closed for stocktaking |
| CHIUSO PER RESTAURO | Closed for restoration |
| CHIUSO PER RINNOVO DEL LOCALE | Closed for refitting |
| CHIUSO PER SCIOPERO | Closed because of industrial action |
| CINTURE DI SALVATAGGIO | Lifebelts |
| CIRCO | Circus |
| COGNOME | Surname |
| COMPLETO | Full |
| CONTO CORRENTE | Current account |

| | |
|---|---|
| CORRIERA | Coach (sign at coach stops etc) |
| CORSIA | Ward |
| | |
| DEGUSTAZIONE CAFFÈ | Coffee tasting (not free!) |
| DEGUSTAZIONE VINI | Wine tasting (not free!) |
| DENTISTA | Dentist |
| DEPOSITO BAGAGLI | Baggage office |
| DESTINAZIONE | Destination |
| DEVIAZIONE | Diversion |
| DISCHI | Records |
| DISCOTECA | Disco |
| DIVIETO | Prohibited |
| DIVIETO DI AFFISSIONE | Stick no bills |
| DIVIETO DI BALNEAZIONE | No bathing |
| DIVIETO DI SCARICO | No rubbish |
| DIVIETO DI SOSTA | No parking |
| DIVIETO DI TRANSITO | No thoroughfare |
| DIVIETO DI TUFFARSI | No diving |
| DOGANA | Customs |
| DOMENICHE E FESTIVI CHIUSO | Closed on Sundays and holidays |
| DONNE | Women |
| DUE /PANETTONI/ AL PREZZO DI UNO | Two /panettoni/ (type of cake) for the price of one |
| | |
| ECCEZIONALI OCCASIONI | Special bargains |
| ENTRATA | Entrance |
| ENTRATA LIBERA | Admission free |
| ESAURITO | Sold out |
| ESTERO | Abroad (letter box) |
| | |
| FARMACIA | Chemist (look out for a square red cross) |
| FATTO IN ... | Made in ... |
| FERMARE | Shut |
| FERMATA | (Bus) stop |
| FERMO POSTA | Poste restante |

| | |
|---|---|
| FILA | Row |
| FINE | End |
| FIORISTA | Florist |
| FRANCOBOLLI | Stamps |
| FREDDO (F) | Cold |
| FUORI SERVIZIO | Out of order |
| | |
| GABINETTI | Toilets |
| GALLERIA | Tunnel |
| GELATI | Ice creams |
| GIOIELLERIA | Jewellery |
| GITE DI MEZZA GIORNATA | Half-day tours |
| GITE DI UN GIORNO | Day tours |
| GIU | Down |
| GRAN RISPARMIO | Big reductions |
| GRATIS | Free |
| GUARDAROBA | Cloakroom |
| GUIDA | Guide |
| | |
| H (OSPEDALE) | Hospital |
| | |
| IMMIGRAZIONE | Immigration |
| IMMUNIZZAZIONE | Immunisation |
| INDIRIZZO DI UFFICIO | Business address |
| INFORMAZIONI | Information/Enquiries |
| INGRESSO LIBERO | Admission free |
| IN RITARDO | Delayed |
| INTERNAZIONALE | International |
| INTERVALLO | Intermission |
| IN VENDITA QUI | On sale here |
| IVA | VAT |
| | |
| LA PERSONA CIVILE NON | Civilised people don't |
| BESTEMMIA | blaspheme |
| LAVAGGIO AUTO | Car wash |
| LAVANDERIA | Laundry |
| LAVANDERIA AUTOMATICA | Launderette |

| | |
|---|---|
| LETTERE | Letters |
| LETTERE RACCOMANDATE | Registered letters |
| LIBERO | Vacant |
| LIBRERIA | Bookshop |
| | |
| MESSAGGI | Messages |
| METÀ PREZZO | Half-price |
| M (METROPOLITANA) | Underground (Milan and Rome) |
| MONETA | Change |
| MULTA | Fine |
| | |
| NAZIONALE | National |
| NOLEGGIO | Rentals |
| NON CALPESTARE LE AIUOLE | Don't walk on the flowerbeds |
| NON CALPESTARE L'ERBA | Don't walk on the grass |
| NON DISTURBARE | Do not disturb |
| NON GETTARE BOTTIGLIE | Don't throw bottles |
| NON PARLARE CON L'AUTISTA | Do not speak to the driver |
| | |
| OCCASIONI | Bargains |
| OCCUPATO | Engaged |
| OFFERTA SPECIALE | Special offer |
| OLIO | Oil |
| ORARIO | Timetable/Office hours/Opening hours |
| ORARIO DI PARTENZA | Departure times |
| ORARIO D'UFFICIO DAL LUNEDÌ AL VENERDÌ 8.30–18.30 | Office hours Monday to Friday 8.30–6.30 |
| ORARIO SS MESSE FESTIVE 7 8.30 10 11.30 17 | Mass times on Sundays and feast days 7, 8.30, 10, 11.30 and 5 o'clock |
| OSPEDALE | Hospital |
| OSTELLO DELLA GIOVENTÙ | Youth hostel |
| OTTICO | Optician |

| | |
|---|---|
| PACCHI RACCOMANDATI | Registered parcels |
| PARCHEGGIO (ESAURITO) | Parking/Car park (full) |
| PARRUCCHIERE | Hairdressing salon |
| PARTENZE | Departures |
| PASSAGGERI IN TRANSITO | Transit passengers |
| PASSAGGIO CARRABILE | Entrance in constant use |
| PASSAGGIO A LIVELLO | Level crossing |
| PASSAPORTI | Passports |
| PEDAGGIO | Toll |
| PENSIONE | Guest house |
| PERICOLO | Danger |
| PER LA CITTÀ | For the city (letter box) |
| PERMANENTE CONTINUA | No parking |
| PER TUTTE LE ALTRE DESTINAZIONE | All other destinations (letter box) |
| PISCINA | Swimming pool |
| PIZZERIA AL TAGLIO | Pizza sold by the slice |
| PORTATA MASSIMA | Maximum load (lift) |
| POSTA TELEGRAFO | Post and Telegraph Office |
| POSTE | Letter box |
| POSTO | Seat |
| PRENOTATO | Reserved |
| PRENOTAZIONI | Advance booking |
| PREZZI | Charges/prices |
| PREZZO MINIMO | Minimum charge |
| PRIMA CLASSE | First class |
| PRIVATO | Private |
| PROFUMERIA | Perfumery |
| PULITURA A SECCO | Dry cleaning |
| PULLMAN | Coach |
| REGALI | Gifts |
| REPARTO | Department (shop) |
| RESA VUOTI | Return empties |
| RIBASSATO | Reduction (price) |
| RICAMBI | Spare parts (car) |

| | |
|---|---|
| RICEVIMENTO | Reception |
| RIMBORSI NON SARANNO EFFETTUATI | No refunds given |
| RIMBORSI NON SARANNO EFFETTUATI SE NON VERRA PRESENTATO LO SCONTRINO A COMPROVA DELL'AVVENUTO PAGAMENTO | Refunds only given on presentation of receipt |
| RIPARAZIONE | Repairs |
| RISTORANTE | Restaurant |
| RIVISTE | Magazines |
| SALA DI ATTESA | Waiting room |
| SALA DI PARTENZA | Departure lounge |
| SALDI | Sale |
| SALDI DI FINE STAGIONE | End of season sale |
| SALOTTINI PROVA | Fitting rooms |
| SALOTTO | Lounge |
| SCALA MOBILE | Escalator |
| SCONTO 15% | 15% discount |
| SCUOLA | School |
| SECONDA CLASSE | Second class |
| SENSO UNICO | One way |
| SERVIZIO (NON) COMPRESO | Service (not) included |
| SERVIZIO GRATIS | Free service |
| SERVIZIO IN CAMERA | Room service |
| SIGNORE | Ladies |
| SIGNORI | Gentlemen |
| SOLO RESIDENTI | Residents only |
| SOTTOPASSAGGIO | Subway |
| S.p.A. (SOCIETÀ PER AZIONI) | Limited company |
| SPESE | Charges/prices |
| SPETTACOLO | Performance |
| SPINGERE | Push |
| SPOGLIATOIO | Changing room |

| | |
|---|---|
| SPUNTINI | Snacks |
| STANZE DA AFFITTARE | Rooms to let |
| STAZIONE | Station |
| SU | Up |
| SULLE SCALE MOBILI TENETE BAMBINI IN BRACCIO, STACCATE GLI OMBRELLI DAI GRADINI, NON PORTARE CANI. GRAZIE. | On the escalators carry children, lift umbrellas clear, don't take dogs. Thank you. |
| SUPPLEMENTI | Extras/excess fares |
| T (TABACCAIO) | Tobacconist |
| TASSO DI CAMBIO | Rates of exchange |
| TASSA PER ECCESSO DI PESO | Excess baggage charge |
| TEATRO | Theatre |
| TELEGRAMMI | Telegrams |
| TELEVISIONE | Television |
| TERMINALE | Terminal |
| TIRARE | Pull |
| TOTOCALCIO | Football pools |
| TRAGHETTO | Ferry |
| UFFICIO CORRISPONDENZE E PACCHI | Post and parcels office |
| UFFICIO DI OGGETTI SMARRITI | Lost property office |
| ULTIMO TRENO | Last train |
| USCITA | Exit |
| USCITA DI SICUREZZA | Emergency exit |
| VELENO | Poison |
| VERIFICATE CHE L'IMPORTO DELLO SCONTRINO CORRISPONDA A QUANTO DA VOI PAGATO | Check your receipt |
| VIAGGI IN PULLMAN GUIDATI | Conducted coach tours |

| | |
|---|---|
| VIETATO | Prohibited. |
| VIETATO AL MINORI DI 14 ANNI | No children under 14 |
| VIETATO AI NON ADDETTI AL LAVORO | No entry to those not employed on the site |
| VIETATO ENTRARE | No entry |
| VIETATO FUMARE | No smoking |
| VIETATO INTRODURRE BICICLETTE E CANI | No bicycles or dogs |
| VOLO | Flight |
| VUOTO | Empty |

# Chiave per l'autista

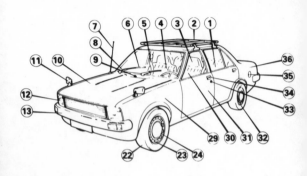

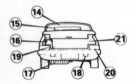

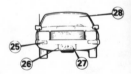

| |  |  |
|---|---|---|
| 1 | sedile posteriore | back seat |
| 2 | portapacchi | roof rack |
| 3 | poggiatesta | headrest |
| 4 | sedile anteriore destro | passenger seat |
| 5 | cintura di sicurezza | seat belt |
| 6 | spazzola tergicristallo | windscreen wiper blade |
| 7 | antenna | aerial |
| 8 | braccio tergicristallo | windscreen wiper arm |
| 9 | lavacristallo | windscreen washer |
| 10 | cofano | bonnet |
| 11 | specchietto retrovisore esterno | exterior mirror |
| 12 | proiettore | headlight |
| 13 | paraurti | bumper |
| 14 | lunotto posteriore | rear window |
| 15 | riscaldamento lunotto posteriore | rear window heater |
| 16 | ruota di scorta | spare wheel |
| 17 | serbatoio | fuel tank |
| 18 | segnale luminoso di pericolo | hazard warning light |
| 19 | fanalino dei freni | brake light |
| 20 | fanale posteriore | rear light |
| 21 | baule | boot |
| 22 | gomma | tyre |
| 23 | ruota anteriore | front wheel |
| 24 | coppa | hubcap |
| 25 | fanale laterale | sidelight |
| 26 | targa | number plate |
| 27 | numero di targa | registration number |
| 28 | parabrezza | windscreen |
| 29 | parafango anteriore | front wing |
| 30 | sedile di guida | driver's seat |
| 31 | porta | door |
| 32 | ruota posteriore | rear wheel |
| 33 | serratura | lock |
| 34 | maniglia | door handle |
| 35 | tappo della benzina | petrol filler cap |
| 36 | parafango posteriore | rear wing |

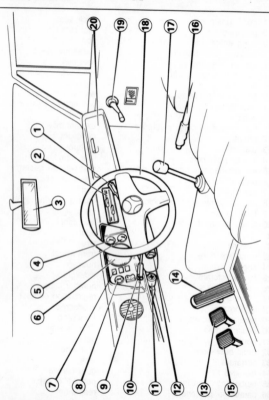

| | |
|---|---|
| 1 commutatore luci | dipswitch |
| 2 impianto di riscaldamento | heater |
| 3 specchio retrovisore | interior mirror |
| 4 termometro acqua | water temperature gauge |
| 5 amperometro | ammeter |
| 6 contachilometri | speedometer |
| 7 spia pressione olio | oil pressure warning light |
| 8 indicatore livello carburante | fuel gauge |
| 9 tromba | horn |
| 10 indicatore di direzione | direction indicator |
| 11 valvola dell'aria | choke |
| 12 interruttore accensione | ignition switch |
| 13 pedale freni | brake pedal |
| 14 pedale acceleratore | accelerator |
| 15 pedale frizione | clutch pedal |
| 16 freno a mano | handbrake |
| 17 leva cambio | gear lever |
| 18 volante | steering wheel |
| 19 maniglia alzacristallo | window winder |
| 20 cassetto ripostiglio | glove compartment |

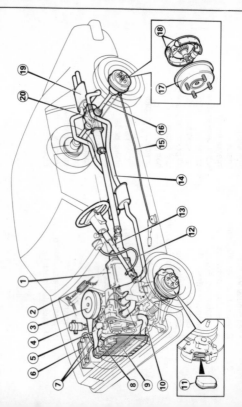

| | | |
|---|---|---|
| 1 | scatola cambio | gearbox |
| 2 | scatola porta fusibili | fuse box |
| 3 | filtro dell'aria | air filter |
| 4 | accensione | ignition coil |
| 5 | tubo radiatore superiore | radiator hose (top) |
| 6 | batteria | battery |
| 7 | conduttori | leads (battery) |
| 8 | tappo | filler cap (radiator) |
| 9 | radiatore | radiator |
| 10 | tubo radiatore inferiore | radiator hose (bottom) |
| 11 | pastiglia (del freno) | disc brake pad |
| 12 | cavetto per contachilometri | speedometer cable |
| 13 | albero volante | steering column |
| 14 | tubo scarico | exhaust pipe |
| 15 | cavetto freno a mano | handbrake cable |
| 16 | asse posteriore | rear axle |
| 17 | tamburo di freno | brake drum |
| 18 | ceppo del freno | brake shoe |
| 19 | silenziatore | silencer |
| 20 | differenziale | differential |

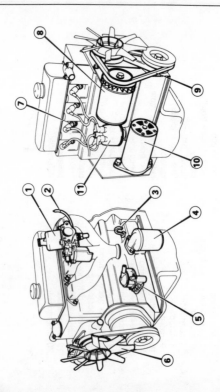

| | | |
|---|---|---|
| 1 | carburatore | carburettor |
| 2 | cavo per traino | cable |
| 3 | asticella per controllo livello olio | oil dipstick |
| 4 | filtro olio | oil filter |
| 5 | pompa carburante | fuel pump |
| 6 | ventilatore | fan |
| 7 | candela | sparking plug |
| 8 | dinamo | alternator |
| 9 | cinghia per ventilatore | fan belt |
| 10 | motorino di avviamento | starter motor |
| 11 | distributore | distributor |

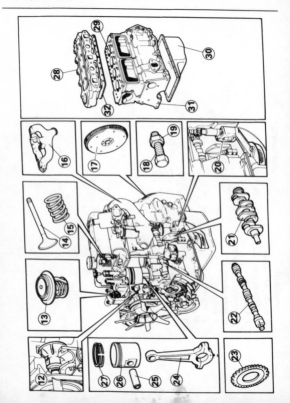

| | | |
|---|---|---|
| 12 | pompa acqua | water pump |
| 13 | termostato | thermostat |
| 14 | valvola | valve |
| 15 | molla | spring |
| 16 | collettore d'ammissione e scarico | manifold, inlet and exhaust |
| 17 | volano | fly wheel |
| 18 | bullone | bolt |
| 19 | dado | nut |
| 20 | pompa olio | oil pump |
| 21 | albero motore | crankshaft |
| 22 | albero a camme | camshaft |
| 23 | ruota dentata | sprocket |
| 24 | biella | connecting rod |
| 25 | spinotto | gudgeon pin |
| 26 | pistone | piston |
| 27 | anelli del pistone | piston rings |
| 28 | testa del cilindro | cylinder head |
| 29 | cilindro | cylinder |
| 30 | coppa olio | oil sump |
| 31 | monoblocco | cylinder block |
| 32 | guarnizione | gasket |

# Numeri, giorni e mesi

## Numeri

| | | | |
|---|---|---|---|
| 0 | oh | 54 | fifty-four |
| 1 | one | 65 | sixty-five |
| 2 | two | 76 | seventy-six |
| 3 | three | 87 | eighty-seven |
| 4 | four | 98 | ninety-eight |
| 5 | five | 100 | a hundred |
| 6 | six | 101 | a hundred and one |
| 7 | seven | 211 | two hundred and eleven |
| 8 | eight | 322 | three hundred and twenty-two |
| 9 | nine | 433 | four hundred and thirty-three |
| 10 | ten | 544 | five hundred and forty-four |
| 11 | eleven | 655 | six hundred and fifty-five |
| 12 | twelve | 766 | seven hundred and sixty-six |
| 13 | thirteen | 877 | eight hundred and seventy-seven |
| 14 | fourteen | | |
| 15 | fifteen | 988 | nine hundred and eighty-eight |
| 16 | sixteen | 1000 | a thousand |
| 17 | seventeen | 1001 | a thousand and one |
| 18 | eighteen | 2112 | two thousand one hundred and twelve |
| 19 | nineteen | | |
| 20 | twenty | 3223 | three thousand two hundred and twenty-three |
| 21 | twenty-one | | |
| 32 | thirty-two | 4334 | four thousand three hundred and thirty-four |
| 43 | forty-three | | |
| | | 10,000 | ten thousand |

0,1 = 0.1 nought point one
nei numeri telefonici ecc. si usa '0'(pronunciato 'oh') oppure 'zero'. Si usa 'nought' soltanto nei decimali in matematica.

## I giorni della settimana

| | |
|---|---|
| Lunedì | Monday |
| Martedì | Tuesday |
| Mercoledì | Wednesday |
| Giovedì | Thursday |
| Venerdì | Friday |
| Sabato | Saturday |
| Domenica | Sunday |

## I mesi dell' anno

| | |
|---|---|
| Gennaio | January |
| Febbraio | February |
| Marzo | March |
| Aprile | April |
| Maggio | May |
| Giugno | June |
| Luglio | July |
| Agosto | August |
| Settembre | September |
| Ottobre | October |
| Novembre | November |
| Dicembre | December |

# Equivalenti

## Denaro inglese

Pounds = £    Pence = p    £1 = 100p
£2.72 two pounds seventy-two p.

**Monete** (Coins)
½p a half penny (a half p.)
1p a penny (one p.)
2p two pence (two p.)
5p five pence (five p.)
10p ten pence (ten p.)
20p twenty pence (twenty p.)
50p fifty pence (fifty p.)
£1 a pound, one pound

**Banconote** (Notes)
£1 a pound, one pound
£5 five pounds
£10 ten pounds
£20 twenty pounds
£50 fifty pounds

Alla banca possono chiedervi come volete il denaro:

Come lo vuole?
in biglietti da /uno/
in biglietti da /cinque/
in biglietti da /dieci/
in biglietti da /venti/

How would you like it?
in /ones/
in /fives/
in /tens/
in /twenties/

## Distanze

1,6 chilometri = 1 miglio . . . . . . . . . 1 mile = 1.6 kilometres

| Miglia | 10 | 20 | 30 | 40 | 50 | 60 | 70 | 80 | 90 | 100 | Miles |
|--------|----|----|----|----|----|----|----|----|----|-----|-------|
| Chilometri | 16 | 32 | 48 | 64 | 80 | 96 | 112 | 128 | 144 | 160 | Kilometres |

## Lunghezze e misure

Alcuni equivalenti:

| **Metrico** | **Inglese** |
|---|---|
| 2.5 centimetres (centimetri) | = 1 inch (pollice) |
| 15 centimetres | = 6 inches |
| 30 centimetres | = 1 foot (piede) = 12 inches |
| 60 centimetres | = 2 feet (piedi) = 24 inches |
| 91 centimetres | = 1 yard (iarda) = 3 feet/36 inches |
| 1 metre (metro) | = 1 yard 3 inches |

## Misure di abbigliamento (compresi petto e fianchi)

| Italia | GB | USA | cm | Pollice |
|---|---|---|---|---|
| 36 | 8 | 6 | 76/81 | 30/32 |
| 38 | 10 | 8 | 81/86 | 32/34 |
| 40 | 12 | 10 | 86/91 | 34/36 |
| 42 | 14 | 12 | 91/97 | 36/38 |
| 44 | 16 | 14 | 97/102 | 38/40 |
| 46 | 18 | 16 | 102/107 | 40/42 |
| 48 | 20 | 18 | 107/112 | 42/44 |
| 50 | 22 | 20 | 112/117 | 44/46 |
| 52 | 24 | 22 | 117/122 | 46/48 |
| 54 | 26 | 24 | 122/127 | 48/50 |

## Misure della cintura

| (cm) Italia | 56 | 61 | 66 | 71 | 76 | 81 | 86 | 91 | 97 | 102 | 107 | 112 | 117 | 122 | 127 |
|---|---|---|---|---|---|---|---|---|---|---|---|---|---|---|---|
| (pollice) GB/USA | 22 | 24 | 26 | 28 | 30 | 32 | 34 | 36 | 38 | 40 | 42 | 44 | 46 | 48 | 50 |

## Misure del collo

| (cm) Italia | 36 | 37 | 38 | 39 | 40 | 41 | 42 | 43 |
|---|---|---|---|---|---|---|---|---|
| (pollice) GB/USA | 14 | $14\frac{1}{2}$ | 15 | $15\frac{1}{2}$ | 16 | $16\frac{1}{2}$ | 17 | $17\frac{1}{2}$ |

## Misure di scarpe

| Italia | 36 | 37 | 38 | 39 | 40 | 41 | 42 | 43 | 44 | 45 |
|--------|----|----|----|----|----|----|----|----|----|----|
| GB | 3 $3\frac{1}{2}$ 4 | $4\frac{1}{2}$ 5 | $5\frac{1}{2}$ 6 | $6\frac{1}{2}$ 7 | $7\frac{1}{2}$ 8 | $8\frac{1}{2}$ 9 | 10 | 11 | 12 | |
| USA | $4\frac{1}{2}$ 5 | $5\frac{1}{2}$ 6 | $6\frac{1}{2}$ 7 | $7\frac{1}{2}$ 8 | $8\frac{1}{2}$ 9 | $9\frac{1}{2}$ 10 | $10\frac{1}{2}$ $11\frac{1}{2}$ | $12\frac{1}{2}$ $13\frac{1}{2}$ | | |

## Misure dei cappelli

| Italia | 54 | 55 | 56 | 57 | 58 | 59 | 60 | 61 | 62 |
|--------|----|----|----|----|----|----|----|----|----|
| GB | $6\frac{5}{8}$ | $6\frac{5}{8}$ | $6\frac{7}{8}$ | 7 | $7\frac{1}{8}$ | $7\frac{1}{4}$ | $7\frac{3}{8}$ | $7\frac{1}{2}$ | $7\frac{5}{8}$ |
| USA | $6\frac{3}{4}$ | $6\frac{7}{8}$ | 7 | $7\frac{1}{8}$ | $7\frac{1}{4}$ | $7\frac{3}{8}$ | $7\frac{1}{2}$ | $7\frac{5}{8}$ | $7\frac{3}{4}$ |

Le misure dei guanti sono uguali in tutti i paesi.

# Pesi

Alcuni equivalenti:

*ounces* (oz) (once) e *pounds* (lbs) (libbre):
*16 ounces* (16 ozs) = 1 *pound* (1 lb)
*grams* (g) (grammi) e *kilograms* (kgs) (chilogrammi):
1000 *grams* (1000 g) = 1 *kilogram* (1 kilo/kg)

| | |
|--|--|
| 25 grams (g) | = 1 ounce (oz) |
| 100/125 grams | = 4 ounces (ozs) ($\frac{1}{4}$ of a pound) |
| 225 grams | = 8 ounces ($\frac{1}{2}$ a pound) |
| 450 grams | = 1 pound (16 ozs) |
| 500 grams ($\frac{1}{2}$ kilogram) | = 1 pound 2 ounces |
| 1 kilogram (1 kilo) | = 2 pounds 4 ounces |
| 6 kilograms | = 1 stone (14 pounds) |

## Peso del corpo

Il peso del corpo in Gran Bretagna si misura di solito in *'stones'* (1 *stone* = 14 *pounds*) (= 6,3 kg), negli Stati Uniti si misura in *'pounds'*

Alcuni equivalenti:

| Chilogrammi | Libbre | Stones |
|-------------|--------|--------|
| 12½ | 28 | 2 |
| 19 | 42 | 3 |
| 25 | 56 | 4 |
| 32 | 70 | 5 |
| 38 | 84 | 6 |
| 45 | 98 | 7 |
| 51 | 112 | 8 |
| 57½ | 126 | 9 |
| 63 | 140 | 10 |
| 70 | 154 | 11 |
| 76 | 168 | 12 |
| 83 | 182 | 13 |
| 90 | 196 | 14 |

## Misure dei liquidi

In Gran Bretagna e negli Stati Uniti i liquidi si misurano di solito in *'pints'*, *'quarts'* e *'gallons'*. Però le misure americane sono leggermente più piccole di quelle britanniche. *'Pints'* (GB) e *'quarts'* (USA) vengono usati per quantità piccole, spesso in bottiglie (*a pint/ quart of milk*); *'gallons'* vengono usati per grandi quantità: es. la benzina.

Alcuni equivalenti:

1 pint = 0,57 litres (litri)
1 quart = 2 pints = 1.14 litres
1 gallon = 4 quarts = 4.55 litres

| **Litri** | | **Misure GB** |
|---|---|---|
| 0,5 | = | 1 pint (20 fluid ounces) (fl. ozs.) |
| 1 | = | 1.7 pints |
| 5 | = | 1.1 gallons |
| 10 | = | 2.2 gallons |
| 15 | = | 3.3 gallons |
| 20 | = | 4.4 gallons |
| 25 | = | 5.5 gallons |
| 30 | = | 6.6 gallons |
| 35 | = | 7.7 gallons |
| 40 | = | 8.8 gallons |
| 45 | = | 9.9 gallons |

## Temperatura

| | **Caelsius** (C) | **Fahrenheit** (F) |
|---|---|---|
| Punto di ebollizione | 100° | 212° |
| | 40° | 104° |
| Temperatura del corpo | 36.9° | 98.4° |
| | 30° | 86° |
| | 20° | 68° |
| | 15° | 59° |
| | 10° | 50° |
| Punto di congelamento | 0° | 32° |
| | − 5° | 23° |
| | − 18° | 0° |

Trasformate i gradi Fahrenheit in centigradi sottraendo 32 e moltiplicando per 5/9. Trasformate i gradi centigradi in Fahrenheit moltiplicando per 9/5 e aggiungendo 32.

Temperatura: si può dire '75 degrees' (75 gradi) oppure '75 degrees Fahrenheit/Centigrade' (75 gradi Fahrenheit/centigradi). Il termine 'Centigrade' è usato più comunemente di 'Celsius' (Caelsius).

## Pressione delle gomme

| kg/cm² | = lb/sq. in. | kg/cm² | = lb/sq. in. | kg/cm² | = lb/sq. in. |
|--------|--------------|--------|--------------|--------|--------------|
| 1.40 | = 20 | 1.68 | = 24 | 2.10 | = 30 |
| 1.47 | = 21 | 1.82 | = 26 | 2.39 | = 34 |
| 1.54 | = 22 | 1.96 | = 28 | 2.81 | = 40 |

# Paesi, unità monetarie, nazionalità e lingue

| Paese, zona o continente | | Unità monetaria | Nazionalità | Lingua (–e) principale (–i) |
|---|---|---|---|---|
| Africa | Africa | — | African | — |
| Albania | Albania | Lek | Albanian | Albanian |
| Algeria | Algeria | Dinar | Algerian | Arabic/French |
| Arabia Saudita | Saudi Arabia | Riyal | Saudi Arabian | Arabic |
| Argentina | Argentina | Peso | Argentinian | Spanish |
| Asia | Asia | — | Asian | — |
| Australia | Australia | Dollar | Australian | English |
| Austria | Austria | Schilling | Austrian | German |
| Bahrain | Bahrain | Dinar | Bahraini | Arabic |
| Belgio | Belgium | Franc | Belgian | Flemish/French |
| Birmania | Burma | Kyat | Burmese | Burmese |
| Bolivia | Bolivia | Peso | Bolivian | Spanish |
| Brasile | Brazil | Cruzeiro | Brazilian | Portuguese |
| Bulgaria | Bulgaria | Lev | Bulgarian | Bulgarian |
| Canadà | Canada | Dollar | Canadian | English/French |
| Cecoslovacchia | Czechoslovakia | Koruna | Czechoslovakian | Czech/Slovak |
| Cile | Chile | Peso | Chilian | Spanish |
| Cina | China | Yuan | Chinese | Chinese |

| | | | |
|---|---|---|---|
| Cipro | Pound | Cypriot | Greek/Turkish |
| Columbia | Peso | Colombian | Spanish |
| Costarica | Colon | Costa Rican | Spanish |
| Cuba | Peso | Cuban | Spanish |
| Danimarca | Krone | Danish | Danish |
| Ecuador | Sucre | Ecuadorean | Spanish |
| Egitto | Pound | Egyptian | Arabic |
| Etiopia | Dollar | Ethiopian | Amharic |
| Europa | — | European | — |
| Finlandia | Markka | Finnish | Finnish |
| Francia | Franc | French | French |
| Galles | Pound | Welsh | English/Welsh |
| Gana | New Cedi | Ghanean | English/Akan |
| Germania | | | |
| G. Occidentale | Deutsch-mark | German | German |
| G. Orientale | Mark | German | German |
| Giamaica | Dollar | Jamaican | English |
| Giappone | Yen | Japanese | Japanese |
| Giordania | Dinar | Jordanian | Arabic |
| Grecia | Drachma | Greek | Greek |
| Guatemala | Quetzal | Guatemalan | Spanish |
| Guiana | Dollar | Guyanese | English |
| Hong Kong | Dollar | from Hong Kong | Chinese/English |
| India | Rupee | Indian | Hindi/English |
| Indonesia | Rupiah | Indonesian | Bahasa Indonesian |

| Paese, zona o continente | | Unità monetaria | Nazionalità | Lingua (–e) principale (–i) |
|---|---|---|---|---|
| Inghilterra | England | Pound | English | English |
| Irak | Iraq | Dinar | Iraqi | Arabic |
| Iran | Iran | Rial | Iranian | Farsi |
| Irlanda del sud (Repubblica Irlandese) | Eire | Punt | Irish | English/Gaelic |
| Islanda | Iceland | Krona | Icelandic | Icelandic |
| Israele | Israel | Pound | Israeli | Hebrew |
| Italia | Italy | Lira | Italian | Italian |
| Iugoslavia | Yugoslavia | Dinar | Yugoslavian | Serbo-Croat |
| Kenia | Kenya | Shilling | Kenyan | Swahili |
| Kuwait | Kuwait | Dinar | Kuwaiti | Arabic |
| Libano | Lebanon | Pound | Lebanese | Arabic |
| Libia | Libya | Dinar | Libyan | Arabic |
| Lussemburgo | Luxemburg | Franc | a Luxemburger | French/German |
| Malesia | Malaysia | Dollar | Malaysian | Malay/Chinese |
| Malta | Malta | Pound | Maltese | Maltese/English |
| Marocco | Morocco | Dirham | Moroccan | Arabic/French |
| Messico | Mexico | Peso | Mexican | Spanish |
| Nicaragua | Nicaragua | Cordoba | Nicaraguan | Spanish |
| Nigeria | Nigeria | Naira | Nigerian | Hausa/Ibo/Yoruba/English |
| Norvegia | Norway | Krone | Norwegian | Norwegian |
| Nuova Zelanda | New Zealand | Dollar | New Zealand | English |

| | | | | |
|---|---|---|---|---|
| Olanda | Holland | Guilder | Dutch | Dutch |
| Pakistan | Pakistan | Rupee | Pakistani | Urdu |
| Paraguai | Paraguay | Guarani | Paraguayan | Spanish |
| Perù | Peru | Sol | Peruvian | Spanish |
| Polonia | Poland | Zloty | Polish | Polish |
| Portogallo | Portugal | Escudo | Portuguese | Portuguese |
| Regno Unito (Inghilterra, Galles, Irlanda del nord, Isole Normanne, Scozia) | United Kingdom (UK) (England, Wales, Northern Ireland, Channel Islands, Scotland) | Pound Sterling | British | English |
| Romania | Romania | Leu | Romanian | Romanian |
| Scozia | Scotland | Pound | Scottish | English/Gaelic |
| Singapore | Singapore | Dollar | Singaporean | Malay/Chinese/English/Tamil |
| Siria | Syria | Pound | Syrian | Arabic |
| Spagna | Spain | Peseta | Spanish | Spanish |
| Stati Uniti d'America (USA) | United States of America (USA) | Dollar | American | English |
| Sud Africa | South Africa | Rand | South African | Afrikaans/English |
| Sudan | Sudan | Pound | Sudanese | Arabic |
| Svezia | Sweden | Krona | Swedish | Swedish |

| Paese, zona o continente | | Unità monetaria | Nazionalità | Lingua (-e) principale (-i) |
|---|---|---|---|---|
| Svizzera | Switzerland | Franc | Swiss | French/German/Italian/Romansh |
| Tailandia | Thailand | Baht | Thai | Thai |
| Tanzania | Tanzania | Shilling | Tanzanian | Swahili |
| Tunisia | Tunisia | Dinar | Tunisian | Arabic |
| Turchia | Turkey | Lira | Turkish | Turkish |
| Ungheria | Hungary | Forint | Hungarian | Hungarian |
| Unione delle Repubbliche Socialiste Sovietiche (URSS)/Russia | Union of Soviet Socialist Republics (USSR)/Russia | Rouble | Russian | Russian |
| Uruguay | Uruguay | Peso | Uruguayan | Spanish |
| Venezuela | Venezuela | Bolivar | Venezuelan | Spanish |
| Vietnam | Vietnam | Dong | Vietnamese | Vietnamese |
| Zaire | Zaire | Zaire | Zairean | French/Lingala |
| Zimbabwe | Zimbabwe | Dollar | Zimbabwean | English/Shona/Ndebele |

# Suggerimenti per il viaggiatore

### Indirizzi utili

*A Londra – London Tourist Board*, di fronte al binario 15, Victoria Station (730 0791 – multi-lingue) 9–18 tutti i giorni.
*British Tourist Authority*, 64 James's Street, SW1 (499 9325) 9–18 da lunedì a venerdì, 10–13 sabato
*London Transport*, St James's Park ed altre stazioni principali della metropolitana (222 1234 – servizio continuo giorno e notte) 8–18 tutti i giorni. Piante gratuite degli autobus e della metropolitana.
Nelle altre città seguite l'indicazione : informazioni.

### Come comportarsi

Mr/Mrs/Miss sono usati soltanto davanti al cognome o al nome e cognome. Per attrarre l'attenzione cercate di farvi notare in silenzio, e se non ci riuscite dite 'Excuse me'.
Mettevi scrupolosamente in coda per prendere autobus, biglietti o davanti a sportelli vari.
Non chiedete sconti.
Quando accettate ospitalità, è gentile portare o mandare fiori, cioccolatini ecc.

### Alloggio

A Londra rivolgetevi al London Tourist Board o alla British Tourist Authority.
Potete alloggiare presso:
Grandi alberghi internazionali
Alberghi non troppo grandi e meno costosi
Rooms (camere)/Bed and Breakfast (letto e colazione). Cercate presso case private l'indicazione Vacancy/B&B (Bed and Breakfast). Sono più economiche degli alberghi e il prezzo include la colazione inglese. Ostelli/alloggi per studenti. Rivolgetevi al 'Budget Accommodation' (London Tourist Board, Victoria Station).
Consultate anche la pubblicazione 'Time Out'.

**1** ✈ **Glasgow–Abbotsinch** Autobús cada 20 min. (06.50h–22.40h), al centro (20 min.; 15km).

**2** ✈ **Manchester–Ringway** Autobús cada 30 min. (06.30h–22.45h) a Chorlton Street/Victoria Station (40 min.; 18km).

**3** ✈ **Birmingham** Autobús 58 cada 20 min. a High Street (10km.) Autobús especial al centro cada hora.

**4** ✈ **Londres–Heathrow** (O. de la ciudad) Metro línea Piccadilly, cada 5 min. hasta el centro de Londres (45 min.; 24km. Autobús cada 15 min. (06–14.30h) a Buckingham Palace Road, cada 20 min. (15h.–21h.) (45 min.)

**5** ✈ **Luton** Autobús cada 13 min. a Bute Street.

**6** ✈ **Stansted** Tren cada 35 min. (días laborables), cada 2 horas (fines de semana) a Bishops Stortford (tren de conexión con Liverpool Street, Londres).

**7** ✈ **Londres–Gatwick** (S. de la ciudad), tren cada 15 min. (06h–24h) a la Estación Victoria (Londres) (cada hora de 24h–06h) (40 min.; 45km). Servicio de Autobuses a los aeropuertos de Heathrow y Luton cada hora.

**8** ✈ **Dublín** Autobús a Store Street (20 min.), 11km.